GENDER, RACE
& CANADIAN LAW

GENDER, RACE
& CANADIAN LAW

A CUSTOM TEXTBOOK FROM
FERNWOOD PUBLISHING

Edited by
Wayne Antony, Gillian Balfour, C. Lesley Biggs,
Carolyn Brooks, Lynn Caldwell, Elizabeth Comack,
Pamela J. Downe, Susan Gingell, Margot A. Hurlbert,
Carrianne Leung, Darryl Leroux,
Les Samuelson and Bernard Schissel

Compiled for Julie E. Dowsett
Department of Social Science and School of Gender,
Sexuality and Women's Studies, York University

FERNWOOD PUBLISHING
HALIFAX & WINNIPEG

Editing: Mark Ambrose Harris
Cover design: John van der Woude
Printed and bound in Canada

Published by Fernwood Publishing
32 Oceanvista Lane, Black Point, Nova Scotia, B0J 1B0
and 748 Broadway Avenue, Winnipeg, Manitoba, R3G 0X3

www.fernwoodpublishing.ca

Fernwood Publishing Company Limited gratefully acknowledges the financial support of the Government of Canada through the Canada Book Fund, the Manitoba Department of Culture, Heritage and Tourism under the Manitoba Publishers Marketing Assistance Program and the Province of Manitoba, through the Book Publishing Tax Credit, for our publishing program. We are pleased to work in partnership with the Province of Nova Scotia to develop and promote our creative industries for the benefit of all Nova Scotians. We acknowledge the support of the Canada Council for the Arts, which last year invested $153 million to bring the arts to Canadians throughout the country.

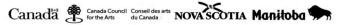

Library and Archives Canada Cataloguing in Publication

Gender, race & Canadian law : a custom textbook from
Fernwood / edited by Wayne Antony [and 12 others] ; compiled
for Julie E. Dowsett, Department of Social Science and School
of Gender, Sexuality and Women's Studies, York University.

Includes bibliographical references.
ISBN 978-1-55266-918-1 (paperback)

1. Sociological jurisprudence--Canada. 2. Feminist jurisprudence--
Canada. 3. Women--Legal status, laws, etc.--Canada. 4. Sex discrimination--
Law and legislation--Canada. 5. Race discrimination--Law and legislation--
Canada. 6. Minorities--Legal status, laws, etc.--Canada. 7. Canada--Race
relations. I. Antony, Wayne Andrew, 1950-, editor II. Dowsett, Julie E.,
compiler III. Title: Gender, race and Canadian law.

KE427 G36 2016   349.7101   C2016-905003-3
KF4483 C5 G36 2016

CONTENTS

VIOLENCE / 365

ABOUT THE BOOKS

C. Lesley Biggs, Pamela Downe and Susan Gingell (eds.), 2011, *Gendered Intersections: An Introduction to Women's and Gender Studies*, 2nd edition. Fernwood Publishing.

Mélissa Blais, 2014, *"I Hate Feminists!" December 6, 1989 and Its Aftermath.* Fernwood Publishing.

Carolyn Brooks and Bernard Schissel (eds.), 2015, *Marginality and Condemnation: A Critical Introduction to Criminology*, 3rd edition. Fernwood Publishing.

Elizabeth Comack, 2012, *Racialized Policing: Aboriginal People's Encounters with the Police.* Fernwood Publishing.

Elizabeth Comack (ed.), 2014, *Locating Law: Race/Class/Gender Connections*, 3rd edition. Fernwood Publishing.

Elizabeth Comack and Gillian Balfour, 2004, *The Power to Criminalize: Violence, Inequality and the Law.* Fernwood Publishing.

Lynn Caldwell, Darryl Leroux and Carrianne Leung (eds.), 2013, *Critical Inquiries: A Reader in Studies of Canada.* Fernwood Publishing.

Margot Hurlbert (ed.), 2011, *Pursuing Justice: An Introduction to Justice Studies.* Fernwood Publishing.

Peter Knegt, 2011, *About Canada: Queer Rights.* Fernwood Publishing.

Les Samuelson and Wayne Antony (eds.), 2012, *Power and Resistance: Critical Thinking About Canadian Social Issues*, 5th edition. Fernwood Publishing.

ABOUT THE AUTHORS

Constance Backhouse is a professor in the Faculty of Law at the University of Ottawa. Her most recent publications include *Petticoats & Prejudice: Women and Law in Nineteenth-Century Canada* 2nd ed. (2015), *Carnal Crimes: Sexual Assault Law in Canada, 1900–1975* (2008) and *The Heiress versus the Establishment: Mrs. Campbell's Campaign for Legal Justice* (co-authored with Nancy L. Backhouse, 2004).

Gillian Balfour is an associate professor in the Department of Sociology at Trent University. Her publications include two editions of *Criminalizing Women* (co-edited with Elizabeth Comack, 2006, 2014) and *The Power to Criminalize: Violence, Inequality and the Law* (co-authored with Elizabeth Comack, 2004).

Mélissa Blais is a feminist activist, and a lecturer in feminist studies and a PhD student in sociology at Université du Québec à Montréal.

Karen Busby is a professor in the Faculty of Law and the director of the Centre for Human Rights Research at the University of Manitoba. She has worked on cases and law reform projects with Women's Legal Action Fund, Egale Canada and other equality rights organizations.

Wendy Chan is a professor in the Department of Sociology and Anthropology at Simon Fraser University. She is the author of five books including *Racialization, Crime and Criminal Justice in Canada* (co-authored with Dorothy Chunn, 2014), *Criminalizing Race, Criminalizing Poverty* (co-authored with Kiran Mirchandani, 2007), and *Crimes of Colour* (co-edited with Kiran Mirchandani, 2001).

Sandra Ka Hon Chu is Director of Research and Advocacy with the Canadian HIV/AIDS Legal Network where she works on HIV-related human rights issues concerning prisons, harm reduction, sex work, women and immigration. In 2009, she co-edited *The Men who Killed Me,* which features testimonials of seventeen survivors of sexual violence during the 1994 Rwandan genocide.

Elizabeth Comack is a professor in the Department of Sociology at the University of Manitoba. Her recent publications include *Criminalizing Women, 2nd edition* (co-edited with Gillian Balfour, 2014), *Locating Law: Race/Class/Gender Connections, 3rd edition* (2014), *"Indians Wear Red" Colonialism, Resistance and Aboriginal Street Gangs* (co-authored with Larry Morrissette, Lawrence Deane and Jim Silver, 2013), *Racialized Policing: Aboriginal People's Encounters with the Police* (2012), *Out There/ In Here: Masculinity, Violence and Prisoning* (2008), and *The Power to Criminalize: Violence, Inequality and the Law* (co-authored with Gillian Balfour, 2004).

Raewyn Connell is professor emerita at the University of Sydney, and a Life Member of the National Tertiary Education Union. She is one of the pioneers of research on masculinities. Her books include *Gender* (3rd edition, 2015), *Southern Theory* (2007) and *Masculinities* (2nd edition, 2005).

Pamela Downe is an associate professor in the Department of Anthropology at the University of Saskatchewan. She has written widely in medical anthropology and feminism. Her publications include two editions of *Gendered Intersections, 2nd edition* (co-edited with C. Lesley Biggs and Susan Gingell, 2005, 2011).

Deborah H. Drake is senior lecturer in Criminology in the Faculty of Social Sciences at The Open University. She is author of *Prisons, Punishment and the Pursuit of Security* (2012) and co-editor of *Crime and Justice: Local and Global* (with J. Muncie and L. Westmarland, 2009) and co-editor of *The Palgrave Handbook of Prison Ethnography* (with R. Earle and J. Sloan, 2015).

Rod Earle is a senior lecturer in Youth Justice in the Faculty of Health and Social Care at The Open University. He has written and published mainly about men in prison, race and ethnicity, masculinity and gender. He helped to establish British Convict Criminology, a group mainly composed of, and that supports, ex-prisoners working as criminologists. His latest book is *Convict Criminology — Inside and Out* (2016).

Eve Haque is an associate professor in the Department of Languages, Literatures and Linguistics at York University. She is the author of *Multiculturalism within a Bilingual Framework: Language, Race and Belonging in Canada* (2012).

Joanna Harris is an associate with Thomas Rogers, specializing in family and children's law, matrimonial litigation, civil litigation and class action suits (including residential school claims). She served as Judicial Clerk for the Superior Court of Justice in 2006–2007.

Margot A. Hurlbert is an associate professor at the University of Regina, cross-appointed in the departments of Justice Studies and Sociology. Her research and writing interests are in justice for marginalized people, climate change and environmental justice. Her publications include *School Law and the Charter of Rights and Freedoms, 2nd edition* (1992) and *Pursuing Justice: An Introduction to the Study of Justice* (2010).

Lisa Marie Jakubowski is an associate professor in the School of Leadership and Social Change at Brescia University College. Her publications include two books, *Immigration and the Legalization of Racism* (1997) and *Teaching Controversy* (with Livy Visano, 2002), as well as several articles and book chapters. Lisa's recent research focuses on service-learning, specifically, the transformative potential of high impact community experiences.

Peter Knegt is a writer, filmmaker and activist and currently works as a producer at CBC Arts. He has written widely on popular culture and LGBTQ issues in *Indiewire, Film Quarterly, Variety, Xtra!* and *The Toronto Star,* among many others. He also serves on the board of the University of Toronto's Sexual Diversity Studies program.

Ruth M. Mann is an associate professor in the Department of Sociology, Anthropology and Criminology at the University of Windsor. She is author of *Who Owns Domestic Abuse?* (2000) and numerous articles on the politics and practice of domestic violence and youth justice policy making and intervention.

Peggy McIntosh is a senior research scientist at the Wellesley College Center for Research on Women is also the founder and now Senior Associate of the National SEED Project on Inclusive Curriculum (Seeking Educational Equity & Diversity). She is widely known for her groundbreaking article, "White Privilege and Male Privilege: A Personal Account of Coming to See Correspondences through Work in Women's Studies" (1988).

Marilou McPhedran was the principal at the University of Winnipeg Global College before becoming director of its Institute of International Women's Rights. She founded the International Women's Rights Project (University of Victoria), is a founding mother of the Women's Legal Education and Action Fund and was Chief Commissioner of the Saskatchewan Human Rights Commission.

Martin Rochlin (1928–2003) was the first openly gay clinical psychologist in Los Angeles. He was a pioneer in the field of gay-affirmative psychotherapy through his clinical practice, mentorship of students, contributions through programs of the American Psychological Association, conferences and public appearances.

INTRODUCING CANADIAN LAW AND THE "OFFICIAL VERSION OF LAW"

Chapter 1

LAW AND JUSTICE

Margot A. Hurlbert

From: *Pursuing Justice: An Introduction to Justice Studies*, pp. 215–243 (reprinted with permission).

It is important to understand that law is a social system, like any other (for example, our system of reproduction, part of which is the family, or our system of education, part of which are schools). One way societies institutionalize particular views of justice is through their legal system. The critical analysis of the institution of law allows its weaknesses, inconsistencies and inequities to be revealed, which is an important first step in not taking the justice of the legal system for granted and in advocating for social justice change.

Legal justice, or the justice that emerges from the legal system and the workings of its component parts (such as courts and written laws), is regarded by some as the ultimate expression of justice. An issue such as whether an Aboriginal person can hunt is thought dependent on various licensing acts and land ownership issues; an issue such as whether a credit company can charge 30 percent interest for cashing a paycheque is dependent on whether the law allows such a high interest rate. If it does, then according to this approach to justice, receiving $69 for a $100 paycheque is unjust while receiving $70 is just.

Wading through licensing regulations, ownership issues and credit legislation are all tasks of accessing the law. Law schools in North America study the law in this manner, as internal to itself, a rational, orderly system much like an exact science, where specific legal questions always have specific legal answers generated within the legal system. This is a "jurisprudence" approach to the study of law. Most people think of the law in this jurisprudential way, as an institution which dispenses justice in an unbiased manner, without favour or ill will. The definition of the law and legal rules begins with the state and proceeds on the assumptions that legal decision-making is rational and that legal processes are legitimate and essential to social order (Milovanovic 1988). The law is presented as a formal and coherent body of rules, doctrines and principles concerned with interpretation of acts, case readings and legal doctrines. The law constitutes itself through textual manifestations of legal decisions, judgments and opinions (Banakar and Travers 2005: 22). This is often described as the "official version of the law" (Naffine 1990: 12), and this approach informs formal justice, the first theme of justice of this book. Formal justice is partly composed of the coherent body of rules embodied in jurisprudence law.

Legal "justice" is much a broader concept than this starting point for formal justice and treating equals equally. Justice is much more than solving a problematic situation or conflict between people by applying the set of rules encompassed in the law. Justice is also constituted by considerations of substantive justice (treating unequals unequally) and ethical practice (the second and third themes of this book). In order to expand the study of law and justice, first we must recognize that the normativity, moral and philosophical perspectives reflected in the law are debatable and debated; next we must undertake a critical analysis of the law's influence on relations between people, especially in light of unequal power and social structures in society. In the example of the Aboriginal hunter, a narrow review of provincial licensing acts disregards promises of hunting rights made in the late nineteenth century through treaties, the fact that an Aboriginal hunting right pre-existed colonization and a history of oppression and colonization of Aboriginal people. These justice arguments are expanding the law to recognize Aboriginal rights previously unrecognized by the courts, and they illustrate the importance of an expanded study of legal justice from the traditional jurisprudence approach taught at law schools. Through this process, substantive justice is discovered; unequal or different situations can be treated differently. However, more than this is also needed. To truly begin to treat unequals unequally or achieve substantive justice, sometimes we need to go outside of our formal structure of legal justice. A structure of legal justice constructed by different people, such as Aboriginal people, is needed. Consider the following perspective.

Because Canadian law is taught, practised and dispensed based on the jurisprudence approach, only a limited amount of societal change can occur within the confines of the Canadian legal system. Recognizing and empowering Aboriginal people and their customs often occurs outside the legal system. Aboriginal legal scholars document their experience of attending law school and their shock at learning concepts of "property" law. An example is the state owning all land because the land was legally vacant upon discovery by Europeans, or the "doctrine of discovery" (Martin 2002: 229). Obviously Aboriginal people occupied the land at this time. Through acquiring jurisprudence legal knowledge, these scholars challenge traditional legal assumptions (Mi'kmaq people had elaborate systems of government such that the land was "occupied," not vacant) and enable the governance of Aboriginal people in Aboriginal courts. Martin writes that victories for the Mi'kmaq have been rare or marginal at best in "newcomers' courts" and that the Mi'kmaq are resisting the legal and social structures forced upon them when the first newcomers came, challenging the economic and political powers that usurped their jurisdiction and its laws of "property." By asserting Aboriginal jurisdiction (now incrementally recognized in areas such as fishing rights and child welfare), the Mi'kmaq are building a nation-to-nation relationship with Canada (Martin 2002: 244). In this way, Mi'kmaq law exists and is practised in a sphere on its own, outside of Canadian jurisprudence law.

A solid foundation in understanding legal justice includes an appreciation of formal legal justice, including how the law is created and how it is applied. It is important to also understand the components of the legal justice system, including the court system and the difference between civil and criminal matters. Understanding substantive justice is facilitated by using different theoretical perspectives to analyze the law as a social system; this chapter reviews the approaches of structural functionalism, symbolic interactionism, conflict theory, post-structuralism and feminism. These non-jurisprudential perspectives expose differing power relations that produce and reproduce within the structure of the law. Such perspectives inform an ethical practice to start reforming the law to attain justice for the neediest in society.

THE LAW AS A SOCIAL SYSTEM

The law is a social structure that represents the society within which it is situated. The law creates, produces, reflects and informs interactions and relations between people. This is a critical insight for those studying justice and has been a historical focus of study by scholars like Max Weber, Emile Durkheim and Karl Marx. This insight assists in explaining why laws differ between countries and different historical periods (a focus of Emile Durkheim). The fact that divorce can now be accessed after a couple lives separately for one year (without regard to fault for marriage breakdown), and that this type of divorce was not available fifty years ago, reflects something about change in Canadian society and relations between couples.

Weber, a lawyer by training, focused on how the law affected relations between people. Weber was concerned with interactions of people and the meaning people ascribed to these interactions. He outlined the characteristics of a formal rational legal system within the basis of a modern political authority as part of a more general theory of sociology. In theorizing about order and conduct in society, Weber (1922: 319) analyzed, contrasted and distinguished "custom" (a practice valid because of practical convenience), "convention" (a practice valid through external guarantee) and "law" (a practice externally guaranteed through a specialized staff expressly in charge of compliance). These concepts form a continuum of not mutually exclusive categories, the boundaries of which are fluid and often imperceptible. A custom might be the first person walking through a door holding it open for another; a convention is having only one intimate partner at a time (the breach of which is met with disapproval but no legal sanction); and a law, not speeding or committing murder. Weber distinguished between substantive rationalization, which is based on certain values and conceptions of justice, and formal rationalization, which rests on general rules and procedures. Maintaining one monogamous intimate relationship at a time would qualify as substantive rationalization. People often regard their intimate partner's infidelity as unjust. This action would only qualify as formal rationalization if one were legally married (and breach of this rule entitled one to divorce). This distinction similarly holds between substantive and procedural justice. Formal rationalization reflects the conception of formal or procedural justice and is enshrined in law; substantive rationalization relates to substantive justice or treating people and groups of people differently to achieve justice. This justice is not always reflected in law but sometimes is.

Durkheim (1893) conceived of the law as the most important observable manifestation of the collective consciousness and its transformation. As such it was a visible symbol of social solidarity, and he used it as a methodology to study society. Although parallels can be seen to Weber's work, Durkheim concentrated on laws and behaviours of groups, as opposed to a more micro approach on how individuals interpreted specific actions. There are parallels between Durkheim's work and later analysis using a structural functionalist lens. Expanding on some of Durkheim's principles, Sorokin (1957) distinguished between official law (obligatory law norms protected and enforced by authoritative power of government) and unofficial law (or law norms not politically overseen but restricted to other groups). A similar conception was made earlier by Ehrlich (1913), who referred to the "living law" as the whole of law dominating social life (even though it may not have been posited in legal propositions and juristic law). Living law could be observed in various aspects of everyday life, whether legally recognized as such or not.

Although Marx (Marx and Engels 1848: 475) did not write specifically on the topic of legal justice, his ideas on the law within his perspective of historical materialism have been influential. Marx asserted that the economic conditions of society (the base of society) determine what type of state will develop. In a capitalist society, the state operates on behalf of the capitalist class (the bourgeoisie) to secure their economic rights and privileges and to moderate class conflict. For Marx, the state was part of what he called the superstructure of society. He similarly viewed the law and legal system as an instrument of control serving bourgeois interests. Rather than endorsing the principle of the rule of law (which holds that it is just for the law to be applied equally and fairly to all), Marx maintained that capitalist law actually enhances the conditions of inequality that exist in capitalist society. The legal system in capitalism contributes to, as well as legitimates, the inequalities that exist as a result of capitalist economic conditions. Individualized rights of freedom benefit those who own while disfavouring those who are without property. In the final analysis and at a fundamental level, the law will protect the economic interests of capitalists and the well off. Formal equality (granted in law by treating various parties who are in contract with one another or with the state as equal) contributes to developing and sustaining the economic inequalities that exist among legal subjects. Although formal legal equality is not a complete sham, it is more easily accessed by those with economic means. As such, the law takes the form of a bourgeois ideology. Its ultimate triumph is that the ideology of capitalist law becomes widely accepted, even among those members of society who are economically disadvantaged and subject to inequalities (Marx 1842). Marx laid the foundation for analyzing the law and inequality based on power imbalances in society, discussed below.

The study of law as a social system is a topic too vast to cover here. However, with some basic legal justice information, including the court structure, the distinction between civil and criminal matters, and the sources of law, we can begin such an analysis.

STRUCTURE OF THE COURT SYSTEM

If people are unable to resolve their conflicts, the ultimate forum of resolution is a court of law. At first the variety and diversity of courts may appear complex. Yet, there are really just three important court characteristics: the government creating it (provincial/territorial or federal), its place in the hierarchy of courts (whether it is a court of first instance or an appeal court) and what types of matters it can deal with (for example, criminal matters, family divorce matters or human rights complaints).

The Court System of Canada

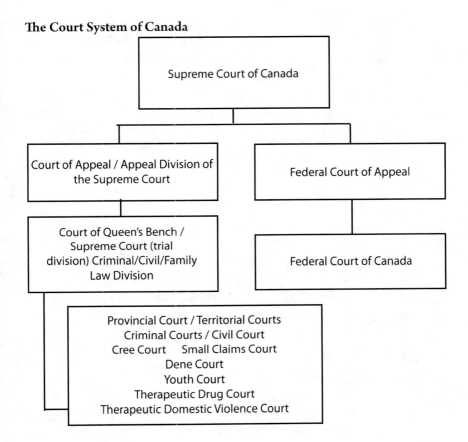

Provincial/Territorial Courts

There is considerable diversity in the ten provincial and three territorial court systems. Generally, however, there are two types of courts, those dealing with criminal matters and those dealing with all other matters (termed "civil," which is explained in more detail later). (In Nunavut, the Nunavut Court of Justice deals with both civil and criminal matters.) The names given in each province differ. For example, the civil court is the Court of Queen's Bench in Saskatchewan, Alberta, Manitoba and New Brunswick and is almost identical to the Supreme Court (trial division) in Ontario, the Northwest Territories and Yukon and the Cour Supérieur in Québec. These are the courts where trials take place in most of the matters which are not criminal and also the more serious criminal matters not dealt with by the lower criminal courts, such as murder. When a party to one of these trials believes the judge hearing the matter made an error, an appeal may be made to an appeal court. This court is called the Court of Appeal in Alberta, British Columbia, Manitoba, New Brunswick, Ontario, Québec and Saskatchewan, and the Appeal (or Appellate) Division of the Supreme Court in other provinces. Most criminal trials occur in criminal courts, termed provincial and territorial courts (although in some provinces, for example, Alberta, New Brunswick and Saskatchewan, these have been amalgamated with the superior courts).

In some instances, such as in Ontario and Saskatchewan, divisions or branches known as family courts and juvenile courts have been created to handle specific kinds of cases. Saskatchewan even has specialized courts such as criminal courts which operate in the Cree or Dene language, and many provinces have therapeutic courts for drug offenders and courts which deal exclusively with domestic violence.

Federal Courts

The only federally constituted courts in Canada are the Federal Court of Canada, the Federal Court of Appeal and the Supreme Court of Canada. The Federal Court of Canada hears and decides legal disputes arising in the federal domain, including claims against the Government of Canada and citizenship, taxation, immigration, copyright and patent issues. Appeals from this court are taken to the Federal Court of Appeal. The Supreme Court of Canada hears appeals from provincial appeal courts and from the Federal Court of Appeal and is the final judicial authority on the entire body of Canadian law, including the civil law of Québec. It is presided over by nine judges, appointed by the federal government.

Quasi-Judicial Tribunals

The federal and provincial governments also create quasi-judicial tribunals to handle specialized cases such as trade union matters and complaints arising from human rights abuses, occupational health and safety and workers' compensation. Although the details of structure and function vary from province to province, these bodies are limited to the authority invested in them by statute and do not have all of the power that a court of law would have; thus they are "quasi" or "partly" judicial. Decisions and awards by quasi-judicial bodies are in all cases subject to some review by courts of law. These bodies, which often take the form of administrative tribunals, are usually characterized by:

- a concern with some form of specialization of subject matter, for example, human rights, collective bargaining or contract terminations;
- judicial procedures in establishing facts, calling witnesses and arriving at conclusions; and
- the authority to decide the dispute.

In a strictly jurisprudence approach to the study of law, the rules regarding court hierarchy are essential. The Supreme Court of Canada is the highest court in the land, and its judgments are binding on all other courts. Similarly, within a province or territory, quasi-judicial tribunals must follow decisions of courts of law, and all courts follow decisions of courts of appeal. A broader study of justice recognizes this normative ordering of hierarchical decision-making but does not take it for granted. Rather, an alternative approach identifies and studies the inconsistencies, resistance and restructuring occurring between the lived experience of the people participating in the various places where disputes are resolved and the way in which those unofficial forums of dispute resolution and courts visualize or construct those lives and relationships. Some scholars have termed this broader approach to studying the social system of law "legal pluralism" (Merry 1988, 2008), and it has been used to analyze systems of legal ordering in relation to tuna courts in Tokyo (Feldman 2006) and business instruments (letters of credit, export credit insurance, etc.) in the United States (Levit 2005). Other possible new areas of study might be the lived experience of people participating in the therapeutic drug or domestic violence courts, both relatively recent creations in the legal system.

The origin of legal pluralism is in the study of colonial societies (Merry 1988: 874). In the imperial/colonial context, many scholars reject the law-centredness of traditional studies of jurisprudence law and argue that not all law takes place in courts. Researchers document the symbols of law operating in unofficial forums of dispute resolution incorporating the law and legal traditions of the colonized. As an example, Pospisil (1979) studied the people of New Guinea and wrote a classic text on Indigenous law.

CRIMINAL LAW AND CIVIL LAW

Courts are divided between those that deal with criminal cases and those that deal with all other matters, called civil cases. The legal system makes a sharp distinction between criminal and civil matters. A jurisprudence approach to the determination of what is "criminal" is based on Constitutional law. The federal government has the official legal authority to decide what is or is not criminal, pursuant to section 91(27) of the *British North America Act, 1867* or Canada's Constitution. Most of our criminal law is embodied in the *Criminal Code*. One Canadian authority states: "Criminal law can be defined in many ways but it is essentially a prohibition coupled with a penalty" (Beckton 1982: 2). MacKay (1984: 204) states: "Criminal matters involve disputes between individuals and the state." The gist of these definitions is that society, through government, determines what is harmful or undesirable and uses the sanctions of fines and/or imprisonment to enforce its view. In terms of the legal system, criminal misbehaviour is behaviour that is deemed in law to be the most harmful to individuals and society. Thus, the state actually defines these behaviours as transgressions against the state itself.

In studying justice, however, an additional concern is analyzing what particular actions by which particular actors are designated by society as "criminal" or "not criminal." Or as civil rather than criminal. Why is loitering in a public place a crime? What is the socio-economic status of people who are charged with this offence? Why is it a crime to carry a concealed weapon in Canada but not the United States? A broader study of justice concerns itself with exploring these questions and how dominant, powerful groups and interests determine what activities and actions are illegal. Consider the following examples of what our society deems criminal and not criminal.

Like any aspect of the law, determining what is or is not a crime is an exercise in social construction. The delineation of something as "criminal" is based on social norms and power and effected by a combination of social, actors including judges and legislatures (see the Sources of Law section below). Thinking critically about what constitutes a "crime" requires careful consideration of what harms are done and what is morally reprehensible. Most would agree that acts of violence and

---

Corporate "Death"

Individuals comprise the overwhelming majority of cases proceeding through the criminal justice system. Occasionally an individual is charged for a crime committed in the course of their employment or business, such as fraud in a business transaction or criminal breach of trust as a result of wrongfully taking money. Examples include better-known cases such as Martha Stewart and Sir Conrad Black. Corporations, although regarded as "individuals" according to the law, are rarely, if ever, charged for crimes. Realistically, given that a corporation's main and primary goal is the accumulation of profit, and not a moral existence, this warrants further exploration. Here are a few specific cases:

Asbestos: The health dangers of asbestos have been known since 1900 (exposure is linked with potentially fatal illness, scarring the lungs, stifling breath and impeding the flow of oxygen to the blood) and have been documented in medical journals as far back as 1935 as linked to cancer (Snider 2006: 187). Yet, with full knowledge of these risks, companies continue to mine asbestos, largely in Québec, exposing their workers and customers to health risks. Is the killing of people through exposure to asbestos any different from killing someone during a robbery?

Bhopal, India, and Union Carbide: In 1984 a gas leaked from storage at the plant and killed over two thousand people and maimed over half a million more. The company, Union Carbide, cut costs, first by choosing this location where safety standards were lower than those of the United States. Then the company violated safety regulations, failed to train employees, failed to respond to warning signs and tried to deny culpability (Rajan 2001: 381).

In neither of these cases were there criminal charges. Why do we as a society not think of these actions by these corporations as "criminal"?

killing cannot be condoned and are correctly labelled (and codified) as "crime." However, consider harm in our society a bit more expansively. How many people are harmed by cigarette smoking, workplace accidents or stress, faulty products and unsafe medication? If our definition of crime is harmful behaviour or acts that cause harm to people, why are these harms not considered crimes?

Using a conflict theoretical perspective, one would argue that our law turns a blind eye to these behaviours because they relate to powerful entities in our society, large corporations. Although we like to think that everyone is treated equally before the law, the reality is that powerful groups and interests — individuals and corporations — escape the full force of the law. In this way, the law perpetuates the power structures in our society and makes it appear natural that our criminal justice system only deals with individuals killing individuals.

In a criminal case the Crown prosecutor must prove the guilt of the accused person beyond a reasonable doubt. This is not easy to define. However, reference is usually made to moral or honest certainty that a person is guilty. The usual caveat is that moral certainty does not mean absolute certainty. For instance, accused are often convicted on the basis of circumstantial or "surrounding" evidence. This means there was no evidence directly proving that they did the crime (such as a witness who saw them commit the specific offence) but rather there was evidence that they were in the vicinity or had the opportunity and motive to commit the offence. If the judge or jury is convinced based on this evidence and believe there is no reasonable doubt as to the accused's guilt, they may convict. This occurred in the case of David Milgaard. Without any direct evidence linking him to the murder of Gail Miller, he was convicted and served twenty-three years in prison. He merely had previous interaction with the police for minor offences, a bad reputation and had been in the vicinity at the time of the murder. In the summer of 1997, DNA evidence provided positive proof of his innocence (Anderson and Anderson 1998: 62).

Civil law and civil cases are defined as misbehaviour that is not criminal. These cases are diverse and range from family matters, such as divorce and child custody, to disputes about trademarks, wills or wrongful dismissals from jobs. In a civil case, there is no "accused," but rather a plaintiff, or complainant, and a defendant. In these cases, the state acts to facilitate resolving a conflict between parties. The state establishes civil courts for the resolution of these disputes (courts of Queen's Bench or superior courts) and often imposes mandatory mediation at the outset in an attempt to streamline the settlement of the dispute.

In a civil case, the plaintiff need not prove beyond a reasonable doubt that the defendant is guilty (the standard of a criminal case). Instead, a lesser burden of proof is required, based on the balance of probabilities; that is, the court must answer the question of whether the allegations made by the plaintiff are probably true. An example of a civil case is a court action against a doctor for negligently performing a medical procedure. If it can be proven with greater than 50 percent probability that the doctor did not meet an acceptable standard for a medical doctor, then the doctor will be found liable. The jurisprudence approach to law assumes that both parties are more or less of equal strength. As a result there is thought to be less need to protect the litigants, and rules concerning admissibility of evidence may not be as strict as in criminal cases. The reality is, though, that many people do not have the resources to protect themselves through civil law, which can be exceedingly expensive. Injured patients, for example, almost always have less money, less stamina and access to fewer resources (such as expert medical witnesses) than doctors, who are covered by medical insurance companies and assisted by medical colleges and associations. More generally, corporations are protected more by civil law than individual citizens. Many can and do break the (civil) law, but the individuals they injure are constrained from acting by the cost of civil litigation.

Making matters worse, legitimate political activities by social activists challenging unjust actions of corporations and governments have been the subject of lawsuits by corporations and governments in an attempt to prevent opposition. These lawsuits are termed "strategic litigation against public participation,"

O.J. Simpson

Consider the case of Nicole Brown and O.J. Simpson. Nicole Brown suffered violence and abuse at the hands of her ex-husband during her marriage and after her separation and divorce. O.J. Simpson was accused of murdering Nicole Brown and her friend, Ron Goldman. The criminal court found O.J. Simpson not guilty. However, the civil action by Nicole Brown's and Ron Goldman's families for wrongful death was successful. O.J. Simpson was ordered to pay damages of $33.5 million (O.J. Simpson 2008).

Why would the criminal courts find O.J. Simpson not guilty of murder, while in the civil court he was found guilty of wrongful death? The reason for this has to do with the burden of proof. In the criminal trial, the prosecution had to prove that O.J. Simpson committed the murder beyond a reasonable doubt. In the civil trial, the standard of proof was only on the balance of probabilities — that is, it was easier to prove that O.J. Simpson probably killed Brown and Goldman than it was to prove that beyond a reasonable doubt.

Now consider this case in the context of social justice, not as just a jurisprudence matter. Nicole Brown was a battered spouse. As a spouse, the legal system failed to protect her from her battering husband; as a divorcee, the family law system failed to protect her and her friend from her murdering ex-husband; as a family, the law failed to provide her children and parents with justice in finding anyone guilty of her and her friend's murder. Consider whether this case illustrates the failure of our laws to regulate behaviour (for example, domestic abuse leading to murder) or whether the law and the entire legal system protect men over women. In this particular case the interests were those of a popular sports star.

or SLAPPs. SLAPPs are civil lawsuits alleging that the activities of protesters and members of social movements have somehow caused the private corporation or government official some damage or injury. SLAPPs divert attention and resources away from the "real" public issue and potentially cost the defendants many dollars in legal fees (Sheldrick 2004: 49). Examples of SLAPPs include lawsuits for civil damages for loss of reputation or court orders to prevent further communications that private corporations or government officials have alleged are "defamatory." One such lawsuit resulted when protesters handed out pamphlets titled, "What's Wrong With McDonald's? — Everything they don't want you to know" outside of McDonald's restaurants (Sheldrick 2004: 50).

Even though criminal law and civil law are distinctly different from each other, an act by an individual may constitute at the same time both a crime and a civil wrong, or "tort" in legal terms. For example, a person committing assault against another might be charged with a crime under the *Criminal Code* and might also be sued by the victim in civil court for compensation. The concerns, proceedings and results would be very different in each case.

In a criminal case, the concern relates to the accused's duty to the public to obey the law and keep peace and order in society; in a civil case the concern relates to the duty of the offender not to cause injury to another individual and to pay damages when found guilty of such action. In criminal proceedings, the focus is on the behaviour of the accused, and a conviction may be decided even when no injury was caused to the victim. In a civil case, the focus of the proceedings is on both the offender and the victim and, for example, whether injury resulted to the victim, whether there was contributory cause on the part of the victim and the extent of both. These considerations are all very important in determining whether the plaintiff (victim) is allowed to succeed or whether the defendant (offender) has a right to dismissal of the lawsuit.

CRIME AND INTENT

In general every crime has a physical element (*actus reus*, that is, guilty or wrongful act) and a mental element (*mens rea*, that is, guilty mind). If either element is missing, then no crime is committed. The *actus reus* of a crime relates to the conduct of an accused, the consequences of that conduct and the surrounding circumstances of the conduct. In *mens rea*, the focus is on such considerations as whether the accused had the mental intent to commit the crime, that is, whether the accused foresaw the consequences of the wrongful act, was aware of the contingent circumstances and intended to cause the consequences. For example, if a person hits another without that other person's consent, they will be guilty of assault only if they intended or meant to hit the other person. If the act of hitting was an accident, no intent, *mens rea*, would exist and no criminal assault would have been committed.

In addition to intention and knowledge, a third type of *mens rea* relates to reck-lessness. The Supreme Court of Canada has held that a person is reckless when that person foresees the possibility of a harmful consequence and then takes the unreasonable risk that harm will not result. Stated another way, a person must be aware of the danger involved and if that person does not have awareness or foresight regarding consequences, then that person is not reckless. In addition, if the risk is reasonable to take or justifiable, the person will not be held to be reckless (*Creighton v. R.* 1993). Hence, there is a great deal of difference between a responsible doctor who operates on a patient who, consequently, dies and an irresponsible hunter who target shoots in a public park and, consequently, kills a child at play.

The intent for recklessness and the *mens rea* previously described are called subjective *mens rea* in that it is the accused's state of mind that is important. It is for the trier of facts (judge or jury) to determine what was in the mind of the accused at the relevant time. This is contrasted with an objective intent, which is a determination of what a reasonable person in the accused's situation would have or might have believed. The jurisprudence approach to law and those practising it resolutely assert that judges and juries are capable of hearing evidence and deter-mining what the accused did or did not believe (Roach 2009: 154). Approaching law in a critical manner and analyzing it as a social structure makes one question this (Norrie 1998: 717). How is a judge capable of determining exactly what was in an accused's mind at the time of the offence? Would a judge not always be "objectively" judging the accused or applying an "outside" standard, a standard of conduct influenced by the background and biases of the judge?

THE SOURCES OF LAW

The major sources of Canadian law include the Constitution, regular statutory law (including regulations and policy) and common law. The people who actually create the law within these sources are the Canadian Parliament, the provincial legislatures and the courts. Parliament and the provincial legislatures make the law by passing statutes; courts make law through judicial decision (what we term "common law"). A jurisprudence approach simply takes these sources of law for granted — that they represent the consensus of society on what should be deemed misbehaviour and the degree of that misbehaviour. However, the discussion of how law is created in the study of justice requires deeper consideration. The law is developed within a society; thus, all aspects of society, particularly its social structure will come into play. Hence, the law must be the product of the power structure of society and develops through struggle, activism and social change. Different kinds of law may not necessarily represent actual differences in harm to individuals and society.

Constitutional Law

A country's Constitution defines the powers and limits of power that can be exercised by different levels and branches of government. It is the foundation of a country's political and legal system. It is contained in statute, so it is part statutory law, but it is not "regular" statutory law because of its importance and the difficulty entailed in amending the Constitutional statutory documents.

After the occupation of the land of Aboriginal people by French and British colonists, Canada became a country, a nation-state, by an act of the Parliament of Great Britain. It is noteworthy that there was no consent or participation in this by Aboriginal people. On April 17, 1982, the Constitution of Canada was patriated (or brought home from Britain). A number of important statutes, for example, the *Constitution Act, 1867* (formerly called the *British North America Act, 1867*), continue to form an important part of our Constitution. These documents (which include some thirty acts and orders) declare the Constitution of Canada to be the supreme law of Canada. They also affirm Canada's dual legal system, with provinces having jurisdiction in relation to some matters, such as property and civil rights, and the federal government over other matters, such as peace, order and good government and the criminal law. The Constitution also affirms Aboriginal rights, such as those related to the historical occupancy and use of the land by Aboriginal peoples, treaty rights and agreements between federal/provincial/territorial governments and Aboriginal groups in relation to self-government.

The *Constitution Act, 1867*, which established Canada as a federal state, continues to include in its preamble a statement that Canada is to have a Constitution similar in principle to that of the United Kingdom. This one single phrase covers a vital part of Canada's Constitution. Consequently, British Constitutional principles have been read into the *Constitution Act, 1982* as required, and Canada is full heir to British common-law principles, conventions and prerogatives. For example, Canadian laws, both civil and criminal (outside of Québec), fall within the traditions of British jurisprudence; the pre-eminence of statute law over common law, or legislative supremacy, was to apply in Canada as it did in Britain; and there was no need for the *Constitution Act, 1982* to mention how our prime minister, cabinet, political parties or civil service would function. An important point to be emphasized in this context is that the *British North American Act, 1867* is not dead but still very much alive as the new (in-name-only) *Constitution Act, 1982*. Canada's Constitution, therefore, continues to be partially written and partially unwritten.

In a Western democracy such as Canada, the Constitution is the final or ultimate source of law. It provides a legal framework for legislative enactments and judicial decisions at all levels of jurisdiction. Unlike regular statutory law, the written Constitution can only be amended in accordance with a formula agreed to by the federal and provincial governments.

In addition to a new *Canadian Charter of Rights and Freedoms*, the *Constitution Act, 1982* added other new provisions to our Constitution, including an affirmation of existing rights of Aboriginal peoples, the principle of equalization and the strengthening of provincial powers over resources. The addition of the *Canadian Charter of Rights and Freedoms* was important for it gave certain rights Constitutional status, protecting them from amendment and infringement by governments. The enactment of the *Canadian Charter of Rights and Freedoms* as part of Canada's written Constitution (Sections 1–34 of the *Constitution Act, 1982*) emphasizes society's increasing attention to diverse values, interpersonal tensions and fundamental rights and freedoms for all Canadians. The Charter protects fundamental freedoms (religion, expression, association), democratic rights (voting), mobility rights (entering, remaining or leaving the country), legal rights (life, liberty, security of a person, right to a lawyer), equality rights, language rights (English and French), minority language educational rights and Aboriginal rights. Significantly, the *Canadian Charter of Rights and Freedoms* does not include economic rights.

Statute Law

"Statute law," or written or enacted law, did not exist in British jurisprudence prior to the thirteenth century. Only with the granting of the *Magna Carta Charter* and the abolition of serfdom did statute law begin to constitute an important part of English law. In the Canadian context, statute or statutory law refers to legislative enactment, for example, the passing of an act which makes legal provision for something to be done or not to be done. Statute laws may be enacted by a government to cover circumstances not covered in existing law, to change existing law or to make existing laws more certain and ascertainable. Statutes achieve the goals of making the law accessible and written. However, the challenge is that it is very difficult to write laws which cover every circumstance and situation. As a result, judges must interpret and apply the law to various eventualities. These decisions form the basis of the common law.

Common Law

Canada, with the exception of Québec, is a "common law" state. British common law began to evolve soon after the Norman conquest of 1066, and an early Norman monarch, King Henry II, who reigned during the twelfth century, is regarded as its founder. King Henry sent judges throughout the realm to service the king's courts. The judges would travel through the country holding court in the larger villages and trading centres. The route was known as a "circuit." The appointed judges worked together, compared cases and made group decisions, thereby establishing a consistent law in the interests of the king. This coincided with the development of a penal code and prosecution of "criminal" matters on behalf of the king or state. These circuit judges began a process for the development and evolvement of one law for all of England, that is, common to all, and hence, called the common law. British common law has continued to evolve over the centuries and was brought to Canada and the United States by colonists. Hence, the common-law system is shared by a number of countries, including Australia and New Zealand. Although the basic laws of these countries have similarities, many differences have evolved.

The common law is much more than an accumulation of judicial decisions over time, usually referred to as "case law." The common law is also referred to as "unwritten law," which is a misnomer because judicial decisions and precedents are systematically recorded and organized. Case law is only unwritten in the sense that it is not enacted by the legislature. However, in a technical sense, the written record — the case law — is not the law; it is only evidence of how the law applies in a specific case. In another case circumstances may be different, and a different result may occur in the application of the law. It is this feature that makes the common law dynamic and elastic, rather than rigid and unadaptable to changing times and conditions. In this manner a certain amount of substantive justice is meted out in the case law as unequal cases or those of differing circumstances are handled differently.

Where Does the Law Come From?

This trilogy of sources of law is where law is derived. A jurisprudence perspective assumes that these three sources create a logical body of rules independent of surrounding social institutions. In philosophy, there are at least three ideas about where the law comes from. These ideas have some similarities to the three sources of law just discussed. Legal positivism views the law as being created and written by governments (this is similar to the source of statute law); legal interpretation holds that the law is interpreted by judges (this is similar to the source of common law); and finally, natural law holds that the law is true for all societies or countries and has universal, unchanging and everlasting application.

In past times (such as those of Aristotle and Aquinas), some believed in the idea of "natural law." Natural law is that arising in nature or that which naturally is or ought to be. The intersection between law and morals can be described as "natural law." The Roman lawyer Cicero, drawing on Stoic philosophy, identified the following three components of natural law:

(1) true law is right reason in agreement with nature, universal application, unchanging and everlasting;

(2) it is a sin to alter or repeal or abolish natural law;

(3) God is the author and enforcing Judge of natural law. (Wacks 2006: 3)

Over time the idea of natural law has waxed and waned and been embellished. Most recently, resurgence has occurred with the United Nations' *Universal Declaration of Human Rights* and the *Canadian Charter of Rights and Freedoms*. As we learned in our introduction to international law, in order to enforce international law on a country whose government is not complying, it is necessary to regard this law as inherent and binding on everyone in this world, regardless whether the country's particular government has passed laws contradictory to this law. An example is Hitler passing the Nuremberg laws to deny Jewish people rights. This denial of rights and the apathy of people to it resulted in the eventual genocide of Jewish people by Nazi Germany in World War II. International rules and laws, which are based on "natural law" (as well as various international treaties) making genocide a criminal act, overrode the laws passed by Hitler in Germany. This example is illustrative of the tension existing between the three sources of law for philosophers, common law, statute law and natural law, which are still debated by philosophy and legal scholars today (Roach 2001).

A Canadian example of the tension of these ideas of the sources of law can be seen in the famous case of *R. v. Morgentaler* (1988) (the case which legalized abortion). The *Criminal Code* clearly made it a criminal offence to terminate a pregnancy unless the procedural requirements of the section (which required the approval of a committee at a hospital) were followed. This section was challenged on the basis of section 7 of the *Canadian Charter of Rights and Freedoms*. It was argued that this provision of the *Criminal Code* denied women their right to life, liberty and security of the person, as the decision about whether she could have an abortion was placed with a committee and therefore inconsistent with her rights.

The Supreme Court of Canada had the task of reconciling these two laws: the Charter right to security and the *Criminal Code* restriction of abortion. When judges perform tasks such as the reconciliation of legal principles which results in a statute law being rendered ineffective, this is often termed as "judicial activism." The actual dispute in the Morgentaler case was over having to obtain approval of a committee for an abortion instead of a woman being empowered to make her own decisions. The latter principle and the unequal access to abortion across Canada for women resulted in the abolishment of the sections of the *Criminal Code* requiring committee approval. The Supreme Court of Canada did invite Parliament to amend the *Criminal Code* and introduce a crime of having an abortion which would meet Charter standards. This has not been done. As with many justice issues, this legal decision had strong support from women's organizations, yet strong opposition from groups supporting the right to life of the unborn. The court's exercise of its power of legal interpretation doesn't preclude the government's ability to pass law and thereby exercise its power of legal positivism.

Socio-legal scholars approach the issue of where laws come from, or their source, differently. American legal scholar Holmes rejected this jurisprudence approach (which he termed "legal formalism") and the proposition that judges merely find the law in legal codes, which they apply in specific cases. He recognized that judges contribute to formulating law by selecting the relevant principles and precedents of law to take into account when deciding the outcomes of cases. As a result, the judges' normative conceptions — their values, beliefs and experience — influence the law. Pound (1942, 1959) regarded the law as a form of social control and an institution which could be adapted to respond to changing societal conditions.

Another view of the sources of law can be found in the political economy and philosophy of Marx. Unlike Pound, Marx did not view the law as an institution which could be changed in order to change society. For Marx, the economic relations of society, which created and perpetuated the unequal power relations in society, required transformation. Once economic change occurred, the law or the juridical superstructure would be changed. Yet, Marx saw the state and thus the laws that it created as serving the long-term interests of the capitalist class. In the end, for Marx, theory and praxis (practice) have to come together in order to explain as well as change the world (Marx 1869). More recent conflict theorists expand this thinking to recognize that the law is a reflection of the social arrangements of power in which some groups are marginalized based on social factors and locations determined by such things as age, sex and racialization. These marginalized groups are much more likely to find themselves acting outside the law and/or being labelled as outside of the law and as "criminals." Abolishing inequalities of wealth and poverty and these social factors affecting life chances must occur if the root causes of crime are to be addressed; for these theorists, crime is that behaviour that is seen as problematic within the social power arrangements of the time (Taylor, Walton and Young 1988: 282).

In summary, the law comes from the legislatures and Parliament, which write and pass laws (the view of the legal positivist). The law is also made by judges as they perform their task of deciding cases, just as we saw with the Morgentaler case. Natural law reflects the idea that some laws arise and exist in a universal unchanging manner based on everlasting morals. No one position is correct or incorrect. In a jurisprudence approach, law comes from all three sources.

PERSPECTIVES ON LAW AND SOCIETY

In the social study of the law many perspectives can be utilized. The various socio-political approaches to the structure and nature of the legal system more or less emphasize or reject a jurisprudence approach. As well, each perspective tends to lean towards either formal or substantive justice, yet all try to explain why our legal system takes the shape it does and whether or not that system is just.

Structural Functionalism

A structural functionalist perspective of the law uses a society-as-organism meta-phor to illustrate the law. Key social institutions are needed for society to operate effectively, and the law (statutes, the court system, etc.) is one such institution. The law resolves the myriad of social conflicts. All societies are a combination of func-tions and dysfunctions. For instance, a family is a social institution, and there are dysfunctional family relationships and also functional ones. Generally over time, dysfunctions are alleviated, and institutions like the family or the law tend toward equilibrium. The law is thought to remedy dysfunction and bring any conflicts which are dysfunctional to society into alignment with societal consensus. The law does not function so much to impose one group's will on others but is seen to control, reconcile and mediate the diverse and conflicting interests of individuals and groups within society in order to maintain harmony and social integration (Vago 1994: 18). Both Pound and Durkheim, discussed earlier, are structural functionalists because of their grand macro theories of law as an institution and its place in society.

One particular legal systems theorist, Luhmann (1993), envisioned the law as a closed system (meaning a system without external influences). Luhmann endorsed the view that the practice of law and dispensation of justice through the law was completely self-referential, based on statutes, legal decisions and reasoning, such that there were no outside influences. Even new scientific methods of evidence such as DNA testing didn't exist within the law until a judge determined that the methods were credible and applicable in a particular case. Luhmann's conclusions are based on the specialized actors and institutions of the law and utilize a similar logic to the jurisprudence view of law.

There are many problems with the structural functionalist perspective of the law. First, social values are rarely uniform. Interpersonal conflict is generally rooted in differing values, priorities and interests. This view also fails to explain social inequality in our society. By assuming a relatively uniform standard of values and interests, it fails to take into account the plight of those who are poor, marginalized and discriminated against. Not only can it not take into account social inequality, as it has no contribution to analyzing power dynamics in society, but it also can-not explain social change. The use of this perspective often only "reifies" (ratifies and reproduces) current laws and practices (that is, functionalists take the "official version of law" — that law is just and unbiased — for granted) or calls for harsher laws to bring dysfunctional behaviour into alignment. As well, the structural func-tionalist perspective assumes that all people can access the legal system to partake in its justice; the reality is that access to expensive lawyers and courts is really only available to the wealthy. However, the structural functionalist perspective does emphasize mediation and reconciliation, often used in labour-management disputes and negotiations, and other court processes, a significant component of many Western democratic societies. This perspective emphasizes a formal justice perspective and is akin to a jurisprudence approach to studying law.

Symbolic Interactionism

Expanding on Durkheim's ideas on the law as a manifestation of collective consciousness and Ehrlich's ideas, discussed earlier in the chapter, Cotterrell (1996: 29) regards the law as a social structure, both shaping and being shaped by the society in which it operates. Seen this way, the law is more than a set of codified legal rules but rather a "living law," or a set of rules actually followed by individuals in social life. Stated another way, there is what is termed an "official version of the law," but within society another structure, often called the "living law," is not only greatly influenced by the law but also informs such official endeavours as law reform. An example can be found in the highly technical area of water rights. The determination of water right priorities can be made with a technical, legalistic review of interests, dates of licences, types of use, etc. However, a study of actual behaviour in times of water conflict (or disagreement over who has priority to water during times of shortage when all people can't receive their water share) found that rules as to water priorities were largely ignored (Hurlbert 2009). This research included interviews with people affected by the water shortage and ascertained the "living law," or norms and behaviours, which resolved the conflict. Community practices of sharing and maximization of benefits were found to predominate. This study shows that the official version of the law may be very different from the living law.

Although symbolic interactionism illustrates discrepancies between law in practice and its official version, it fails to analyze power differentials or provide any praxis to remedy the unequal power relations. In the water research study, an affected First Nation was omitted from the dialogue respecting water (Hurlbert 2009a: 238). In fact, from a jurisprudence, or "official version of law" viewpoint, Aboriginal water rights have not been recognized (Laidlaw 2010: 2; *Tsuu T'ina First Nation* v. *Alberta*), and as such the Crown or federal government "owns" all of the water (Hurlbert 2009b: 47) and continues to marginalize and silence Aboriginal people. Exploring the living experience of law, or the reality of social practices of water sharing, and comparing this with the official version of the law only highlights the marginalized space of Aboriginal people. Power imbalance is more aptly addressed through the conflict perspective.

Conflict

In the 1960s and 1970s, building on Marxian ideas and concepts, the analysis of social control and criminal law as important aspects of criminalization emerged. Instrumental Marxists see capitalists as having direct access to those who pass

---

The Law and Wealthy People

Elected officials often meet with constituents, interest groups and the public to discuss issues that the government is or should be considering and debating, including various laws. Instrumental and structural Marxists see this process as resulting in the powerful more often than not having their interests taken into account, often to the detriment of the rest of society. Consider the following examples:

In the modern banking system, there have always been laws preventing banks from using their depositors' money to engage in high-risk financial speculation. But, in the two most recent depressions, those laws were changed. In 1910, representatives of the two most powerful banks in the United States met with the president and convinced him to go against the recommendations of his solicitor general and allow laws facilitating the speculation of banks in stock trading. These banks effectively controlled portfolios worth, in today's dollars, $850 billion. These banks then became involved in increasingly risky stock market speculation which only a couple years earlier would have been illegal. As those risky stocks began to crumble in 1929, so did the banks which had been speculating with depositors' money, resulting in the Great Depression. The CEO of one of the banks continued to earn his salary of five million per annum through 1930–1932 (McQuaig and Brooks 2010).

Again in the late 1990s, banks and financial institutions flagrantly violated these same laws prohibiting their involvement in risky speculation in stocks and other sorts of financial investments and instruments, such as subprime mortgages and credit default swaps. Regulators not only failed to take any action, but in 1999, through the early part of the 2000s, after much vigorous lobbying by banks and financial corporations, governments around the world (but especially in the U.S.) repealed many of those financial regulations (this is known as deregulation — one of the outcomes of neo-conservative strategy). This eventually resulted in the subprime mortgage recession of 2008, with massive layoffs and the loss for many Americans of their homes. Many of the main lobbyists for these changes to the laws on banking were the same financial institutions that required and received the lion's share of the massive $1 trillion bailout in the U.S. Orchestrators such as John Paulson took advantage of this and emerged making $3.7 billion. The deregulation that financiers like Paulson pushed so hard for legalized financial activities which only a few years earlier would have been illegal. (McQuaig and Brooks 2010)

---

statute laws in the legislatures and Parliament because of connections among the elite. Structural Marxists see this influence as resulting because of the predominance of the economy (with the capitalists and the state actors all pursuing the advancement of the economy and maximization of profits as goals). The result of these pressures is that most often laws are passed which benefit the upper classes. Hunt (1981), for one, developed a comprehensive Marxist perspective of the law by questioning the extent to which major justice or legal ideals have not been realized in capitalist societies. Although our society espouses the idea that any person through enough hard work and determination can succeed, the reality is that the very poor people in society have limited opportunity to change their life circumstances (see Gerlach and Hurlbert 2011). Hunt studied the contribution of the law as a social system, generally regarded as fair and equal, to this oppression. The starting point of Marxist analysis is not the immediate form of the law — the statutes, common law, system of courts, rules of trials and so on — which is fair on its face. Rather, the law is conceptualized in the context of a class-divided and unequal society and is viewed as reproducing the stratification of society, involving a continuous process whereby the oppressive structures of society are shaped and reshaped. These law-inequality processes occur within specific socio-historical circumstances. The law functions as a means of domination, perpetuating the hegemony of societal structures among the social institutions and practices involved in the legal system (Hunt 1993). In simple terms, from this perspective, both what comes to be defined in law as criminal and how the criminal system operates, in the end, protect the interests of the economically dominant groups/classes. Recall the discussion above asking why behaviours of corporations that cause death are treated not as criminal but rather as violating less important regulatory laws. In a conflict analysis approach, the law/legal system in an unjust and unequal society cannot by definition be just, even if it appears to be.

Post-Structuralism

A newer perspective on the law that has emerged from the conflict tradition (more precisely from a sympathetic critique of the conflict tradition) and is based largely on the insights of Michel Foucault is post-structuralism, which sees the law is a site through which social power operates (Comack and Balfour 2004). This theoretical perspective sheds light on the perpetuation of inequality in our society. Post-structuralists view the jurisprudence approach to the law as a reproduction of dominant thinking about the social world and a perpetuation of idealized liberalism, with its preoccupation with rights of the individual. They see judges as preserving social inequality in their decision-making, rationalized by references to precedent case law (the common law) — which simply refers to an already flawed system of "justice." The prolonged preoccupation with individual rights, which is the focus of jurisprudence, fails to show how individuals are a product of both the socio-economic forces and the legal authority that put them before the law to begin with (MacDonald 2002: 31).

A post-structural perspective focuses on the way power operates through the language of the law and its practices. It compares and contrasts legal discourses (court transcripts, statutes, written court decisions, that is, internally constructed by the law) with social discourses (or institutional practices external to the law). This analysis shows that peoples' lived experience of discrimination, violence and injustice is often covered over by legal discourse. The key aspect of this analysis is that law is shown to be part of the social process through which inequality is perpetuated. Stated another way, the ways that laws are made and enforced, in the long run, protects the interests of powerful groups in society.

As an example, Razack (2002) analyzed the language or discourse in the 1995 trial of the men who murdered Pamela George, a Saulteaux (Ojibway) Nation woman. The victim is referred to as the "hooker" or prostitute, and other than for a few moments when one witness remembered her as a nice person and the mother of two children who did crafts and could cook, Pamela George never left the racially bounded space of prostitution and degeneracy when referred to during the trial. In contrast, the accused, Steven Kummerfield and Alex Ternowetsky, two White, athletic college boys, never left the place of White respectability, being referred to instead as "boys who did pretty darn stupid things" (Razack 2002: 148). The ultimate expression of Kummerfield's place of privilege is his reply to the Crown prosecutor when asked why he left town after his actions: "I really didn't want to be arrested or anything like that just because there are so many opportunities I had to be successful" (Razack 2002: 149). No regret was expressed for the loss of life and murder of Pamela George. Ultimately Kummerfield and Ternowetsky were sentenced to six and a half years in prison with credit for the twenty months served awaiting trial.

Similarly, Smart (1989) used the process of a rape trial to illustrate how people's experiences are translated within the legal process to become "legal relevance." Rape from the victim's standpoint is a terrifying ordeal and an experience of humiliation, degradation and violation. When testifying during the trial, the woman's experience is sifted through by the prosecutor and defence counsel to ascertain legally relevant "facts" for the determination of the guilt of the accused. Issues such as whether the woman was previously of chaste character and whether she consented by her actions (such as the manner of her dress) become the battleground of the lawyers, with the woman and her body the stuff of evidence and the purpose of the trial the ultimate disqualification of women's experiences (Smart 1989: 33). This post-structuralist approach to analyzing justice targets the law's power to define and disqualify; such an analysis uses the discourses of the law to deconstruct it. Exposing how the law operates within relationships of power and powerlessness can facilitate the emergence of a law reform strategy to assist the marginalized (Smart 1989: 164).

Smart's and Razack's work illustrates the context within which law operates in cases involving oppressed and marginalized people. Through studies such as these, sites of oppression can be identified. In this way, the dominant discourse of the official version of the law and the law's impartiality, neutrality and objectivity can be challenged and possibilities for substantive justice illuminated. Once law's mechanisms of power are revealed, then targeted actions to advance an ethical practice of "leximin" can occur.

Feminism

The feminist perspective of the law has existed since the nineteenth century. Like the conflict and post-structural perspectives, it challenges the jurisprudence perspective that law is inherently just and impartial (Boyd and Sheehy 1989: 255). In analyzing the law's role in perpetuating inequality in society, Naffine (1990: 12) argues that what she calls "the official version of the law" is not coherent, logical, internally consistent and rational. In fact, Naffine notes that the law reflects the "priorities of the dominant patriarchal social order" (Naffine 1990: 13). Laws, to put it bluntly, have been largely written by men, for men.

Although advances have been made in recent decades, especially with the advent of the right to equality guaranteed by section 15 of the *Charter of Rights and Freedoms*, some feminists argue that many gains have been illusory. For instance, MacKinnon (1987: 1) notes a string of defeats and declines for women, including lack of effective sex-equality provisions for pay, opposition to the right to safe abortion and a movement towards sharing custody of children after separation, all which leave the ideal of women's equality before the law far from realized.

Schneider (2000: 228) explores the law and domestic violence over the last several decades, concluding that the assertion of domestic violence claims has advanced a "political conversation" and succeeded in making what used to be private, public. However, the fundamental vision of equality generated by the feminist-led movement against domestic violence has been subverted (Schneider 2000: 229). Women who come forward with their experiences are seen as "unreasonable" and "difficult," and there is a tendency to view them as "sick" (pathologize them, for example, by asking why they didn't leave their abusive partners). Although intimate violence has been recognized as a public harm, the recognition is almost always couched in the discourse of individual problems, not a systemic or social one. Various kinds of quick-fix explanations and solutions in the end deny the link to gender; for example, violence against women is most often referred to as family violence, obscuring that "family" violence is mostly men abusing their female partners. As a result, "the thirty-year history of feminist lawmaking on battering reveals both the affirmative vision of equality, liberty, and freedom that has shaped legal strategy and decision-making, and the inevitable limitations of legal reform that does not take gender into account" (Schneider 2000: 232).

NEO-LIBERALISM AND NEW PERSPECTIVES ON LEGAL JUSTICE

The jurisprudence approach to studying the law has parallels with neo-liberalism, an ideology and political strategy emphasizing the life choices of individuals and de-emphasizing social problems (see Hurlbert and Mulvale 2011). The jurisprudence approach emphasizes the application of the rational, rule-based legal system to individual cases, accentuating the life choices which have brought an individual in contact with the legal system. The social structures which contributed to the person's legal problems have very little if any relevance when analyzing their situation.

In the jurisprudence context of analyzing individual legal problems, the emphasis is on the individual and their choices in relation to their legal problems. This is consistent with the neo-conservative political strategy, which emphasize individual choice and controlling crime through harsh penalties and longer jail terms. This political strategy does not result in a reduction of government services (one of the features of neo-liberalism) but rather an increase in court and jail services. The complex relationship between neo-liberalism, emerging in the late twentieth century, and the associated political strategy of neo-conservatism has had a significant effect on the criminal justice system. Neo-conservatism calls for disciplining those who (as the middle classes see it) threaten to get out of control — the poor and people of colour (Garland 2001: 99–100) —and increasingly locking them up in jail. This strategy was espoused by Prime Minister Harper with his political agenda of getting tough on crime, imposing increasingly harsher penalties and keeping more people in jail.

The reduced ideological focus on the contribution of social problems to individuals' trouble with the law thus reduces emphasis on dealing with crime through social programs that alleviate poverty, meet the needs of troubled youths or provide early childhood special education. Government services in these areas are cut back; prison infrastructure and the criminal justice system are enlarged (Lynch and Groves 1989).

Expanding the focus of legal justice to include an analysis of the social problems associated with legal problems increases the ambit of the study of legal justice to include social justice and substantive justice. The problematic of a justice issue comes to light when the law is approached through different theoretical frameworks, including structural functionalism, symbolic interactionism and conflict theory. Individuals are viewed not just as rational actors making individual choices but as agents living and functioning in a social system, affected by the institution or social system of law, which informs and contributes to their life chances. Seeing individuals as living within a certain social context illuminates important differences in these individuals' lives and how they should be treated differently (unequals treated unequally). Viewing legal justice in this expanded way, which includes an analysis of substantive justice in addition to the procedural and formal rules enshrined in the system of law, increases the chances that reform of the law and policy will achieve justice.

Adding the dimension of power relations to the analysis of the law through a conflict, post-structural or feminist perspective and dissecting the language of the law or legal discourse furthers the problematic of a justice issue. This process of examining and analyzing legal discourse from a place of otherness or marginalization makes visible the structure of the law, which is generally described as the official version of the law and is thought to epitomize "justness" because of its perceived impartiality, neutrality and objectivity. However, through the methodology of discourse analysis, using the written text of the law and court trials, various structures of power, including ethnocentrism, patriarchy and classism, are revealed.

Such methods of analysis are important in the pursuit of justice as these structures and practices of power are usually not maliciously motivated through prejudice, false beliefs and bad attitudes, but they are institutional or societal and embedded and naturalized, so that they are often taken for granted and not questioned. These structures of power are often the least visible in day-to-day life but have a powerful effect on individuals. By revealing these dominant, or hegemonic, forms of oppression, an ethical practice at both the individual and institutional levels can be envisioned.

The result of this theoretical approach to analyzing the law is ultimately to explore how multicultural global postcolonial institutions, cultures and practices create opportunities to raise new questions, engage new dialogues and foster new discussions. In this way, through the process of raising awareness, an ethical practice of leximin emerges as does an emancipatory social project promoting positive social structural change to decentre mainstream, White, middles-class, patriarchal, dominant discourse and empower marginalized "other" discourse.

References

Anderson, B., and D. Anderson. 1998. *Manufacturing Guilt: Wrongful Convictions in Canada.* Halifax, NS: Fernwood.

Banakar, R., and M. Travers. 2005. *Theory and Method in Socio-Legal Research.* Oxford: Hart.

Beckton, C.F. 1982. *The Labour and the Media.* Toronto, ON: Carswell.

Boyd, S., and E. Sheehy. 1989. "Overview: Feminism and the Law in Canada." In T. Caputo, M. Kennedy, C. Reasons and A. Brannigan (eds.), *Law and Society: A Critical Perspective* (pp. 255–70). Toronto, ON: Harcourt Brace Jovanovich.

Comack, E., and G. Balfour. 2004. *The Power to Criminalize: Violence, Inequality and the Law.* Halifax, NS: Fernwood Publishing.

Cotterrell, R. 1964 [1893]. *The Division of Labour in Society.* New York: Free Press.

_____. 1996. *Law's Community: Legal Theory in Sociological Perspective.* Oxford: Clarendon Press.

Ehrlich, E. 1962 [1913]. *Fundamental Principles of the Sociology of Law*. New York: Russell & Russell.

Feldman, E.A. 2006. "The Tuna Court: Law and Norms in the World's Premier Fish Market." *California Law Review* 94: 313.

Garland, D. 2001. *The Culture of Control: Crime and Social Order in Contemporary Society*. Oxford: Oxford University Press.

Gerlach, L., and M. Hurlbert. 2011. "Social Justice, Stratification and Oppression." In M.A. Hurlbert (ed.), *Pursuing Justice: An Introduction to Justice Studies*. Halifax and Winnipeg: Fernwood Publishing.

Hunt, A.J. 1981. "Marxism and the Analysis of Law." In A. Podgorecki and C.J. Whelan (eds.), *Sociological Approaches to Law* (pp. 91–109). New York: St Martin's Press.

____. 1993. *Explorations in Law and Society: Toward a Constitutive Theory of Law*. New York: Routledge.

Hurlbert, M.A. 2009. "An Analysis of Trends Related to the Adaptation of Water Law to the Challenge of Climate Change: Experience from Canada." *International Journal of Climate Change Strategies and Management* 1, 3: 230–40.

____. 2009a. "The Adaptation of Water Law to Climate Change." *International Journal of Climate Change Strategies and Management* 1, 3: 230–40.

____. 2009b. "Comparative Water Governance in the four Western Provinces." *Prairie Forum* (special edition on climate change) 34, 1: 45–77.

____. 2011. "Theorizing Justice." In M.A. Hurlbert (ed.), *Pursuing Justice: An Introduction to Justice Studies*. Halifax and Winnipeg: Fernwood Publishing.

Laidlaw, D.K. 2010. "Water Rights and Water Stewardship: What About Aboriginal People?" *Canadian Institute of Resources Law* 107.

Levit, J. K. 2005. "A Bottom-Up Approach to International Lawmaking: The Tale of Three Trade Finance Instruments." *Yale Journal of International Law* 30: 125.

Luhmann, N. 2004 [1993]. *Law as a Social System*. Oxford: Oxford University Press.

Lynch, M.J., and B.W. Groves. 1989. *A Primer in Radical Criminology*. Albany, NY: Harrow and Heston.

MacDonald, G.M. 2002. *Social Context & Social Location in the Sociology of Law*. Peterborough, ON: Broadview Press.

MacKay, A.W. 1984. *Education law in Canada*. Toronto, ON: Emond-Montgomery.

MacKinnon, C. 1987. *Feminism Unmodified: Discourses on Life and Law*. Cambridge: Harvard University Press.

Martin, M. 2002. "The Crown Owns All the Land?" In G.M. MacDonald, *Social Context & Social Location in the Sociology Of Law* (pp. 229–246). Peterborough, ON: Broadview Press.

Marx, K. 1842. "Debates on the Law on Thefts of Wood." Supplement to the *Rheinische Zeitung*, October–November. <marxists.org/archive/marx/works/download/ Marx_Rheinishe_Zeitung.pdf>.

____. 1869. "Report of the General Council on the Right of Inheritance." Written on behalf of the International Workingmen's Association. <marxists.org/archive/marx/iwma/ documents/1869/inheritance-report.htm>.

Marx, K., and F. Engels. 1848. *The Communist Manifesto*. New York: Washington Square Press.

McQuaig, L., and N. Brooks. 2010. *The Trouble with Billionaires: Why Too Much Money at the Top Is Bad for Everyone*. Toronto: Penguin Canada.

Merry, S.E. 1988. "Legal Pluralism." *Law & Society Review* 22: 869–895.

____. 2008. "International Law and Sociologic Scholarship: Toward a Spatial Global Legal Pluralism." Special issue: Law and society reconsidered. *Studies in Law, Politics, and Society* 41: 149–168.

Milovanovic, D. 1988. *A Primer in the Sociology of Law*. New York: Harrow & Heston.

Naffine, N. 1990. *Law and the Sexes: Explorations in Feminist Jurisprudence*. Sydney, Australia: Allen & Unwin.

Norrie, A. 1998. "The Limits of Justice: Finding Fault in the Criminal Law." In M.S. Archer (ed.), *Critical Realism, Essential Readings* (pp 702–722). New York: Routledge.

Pospisil, L. 1979. "Legally Induced Culture Change in New Guinea." In R. Pound (1942), *Social Control through Law* (pp. 127–144). New Haven, CT: Yale University Press.

Pound, R. 1942. *Social Control through Law*. New Haven, CT: Yale University Press.

____. 1959. *Jurisprudence* (Vols. 1–5). St. Paul, MN: West.

Rajan, S.R. 2001. "Towards a Metaphysics of Environmental Violence: The Case of the Bhopal Gas Disaster." In N.L. Peluso and M. Watts (eds.), *Violent Environments* (pp. 380–398). Ithaca, NY: Cornell University Press.

Razack, S. 2002. "Gendered Racial Violence and Spatialized Justice: The Murder of Pamela George." In S. Razack (ed.), *Race Space and the Law: Unmapping a White Settler Society*. Toronto, ON: Between the Lines.

Roach, K. 2009. *Criminal Law*. Toronto, ON: Irwin Law.

Schneider, E.M. 2000. *Battered Women and Feminist Lawmaking*. London: Yale University Press.

Sheldrick, B. 2004. *Perils and Possibilities: Social Activism and the Law*. Winnipeg: Fernwood Publishing.

Smart, C. 1989. *Feminism and the Power of Law*. London: Routledge.

Snider, L. 2006. "Relocating Law: Making Corporate Crime Disappear." In E. Comack (ed.), *Locating Law: Race, Class, Gender, Sexuality Connections* (second ed.). Black Point, NS: Fernwood Publishing.

Sorokin, P. 1957. *Social and Cultural Dynamics: A Study of Change in Major Systems of Art, Truth, Ethics, Law, and Social Relationships* (revised and abr. ed.). New Brunswick, NJ: Transaction.

Taylor, I.R., P. Walton and J. Young. 1988. *The New Criminology: For a Social Theory of Deviance (International Library of Sociology)*. London: Routledge.

Vago, S. 1994. *Law and Society* (fourth ed.). Upper Saddle River, NJ: Prentice Hall.

Wacks, R. 2006. *Philosophy of Law: A Very Short Introduction*. Oxford: Oxford University Press.

Weber, M. 1978 [1922]. *Economy and Society: An Outline of Interpretive Sociology* (G. Roth and C. Wittich, eds.). Berkeley, CA: University of California Press.

Legislation

British North America Act, 1867, 30-31 Vict., c. 3 (U.K.).

Canadian Charter of Rights and Freedoms, Part 1 of the *Constitution Act, 1982*, being Schedule

B to the *Canada Act 1982*, (U.K.), 1982, c. 11.

Constitution Act, 1867, (U.K.), 30 & 31 Victoria, c. 3.

Constitution Act, 1982, being Schedule B to the *Canada Act 1982* (U.K.), 1982, c. 11.

Criminal Code, R.S.C. 1985, c. C-46.

Universal Declaration of Human Rights, G.A. Res 217A (III), U.N. Doc. A/810 (Dec. 10, 1948 [UDHR].

Legal Cases

Creighton v. R. [1993] 3 S.C.R. 3.

R. v. Morgentaler [1988] 1 S.C.R. 30.

Tsuu T'ina Nation v. Alberta (Environment), 2008, ABQB 547.

Chapter 2

THEORIZING LAW

Elizabeth Comack and Gillian Balfour

From: *The Power to Criminalize: Violence, Inequality and the Law*, pp. 20–49 (reprinted with permission).

For some time now the tension between the two key readings of law — as a fair and impartial arbiter of social conflicts or as a site in society for the reproduction of gender, race and class inequalities — has occupied the attention of criminologists and socio-legal scholars. Borrowing from the work of a number of radical, feminist, critical-race and post-structuralist theorists who have offered various ways of sorting out this tension, and by considering the role of lawyers in the criminalization process, we intend to elaborate on how and where inequality intersects with the law's claims to fairness, justice and equality.

To carry out that task, we require a theory capable of linking micro-processes of human agency (what lawyers do in the course of their work) with broader social-structural conditions (inequalities of gender, race and class). One theorist who has developed these linkages in his work is James Messerschmidt. In his book *Crime as Structured Action*, Messerschmidt (1997: 3) adopts Anthony Giddens's concept of "structured action" to theorize what people in specific social settings "do to construct social relations and social structures, and how these social structures constrain and channel behavior in specific ways." A key problem Messerschmidt addresses is the need to understand the interconnections between gender, race and class and how they figure in the nexus of individual agency and social structure.

Messerschmidt notes that gender, race and class are neither static "things" nor finished products. The character and meaning of gender, race and class categories are given concrete expression by the specific social situations and historical contexts in which they are located. For example, gender, race and class look very different when acted out in corporate boardrooms by privileged white men than they do in encounters between young Aboriginal men on the street. In this sense, gender, race and class are simultaneously "accomplished" as people construct their own identities and attribute identities to others in different situations and contexts. Given numerous ways of constructing masculinity and femininity, it makes sense to speak of masculinities and femininities. Similarly, there is a variety of ways of constructing race and class (Aboriginal identities, middle-class identities and so on).

The practices by which gender, race and class are "made" do not occur in a vacuum; they are influenced by social-structural constraints. Social structures are "regular and patterned forms of interaction over time that constrain and channel behavior in specific ways" (Messerschmidt 1997: 5). In this sense, social structures are not simply "out there." They are enacted in everyday interactions by knowledgeable human agents: "people who know what they are doing and how to do it" (Messerschmidt 1997: 5). One such structure is the division of labour, which refers to "the definition of work (legitimate and illegitimate, paid and unpaid) and how work is allocated" (Messerschmidt 1997: 6). Relations of power are imbedded in and reinforced by divisions of labour based on gender, race and class. According to Messerschmidt, "Social practices of who does what for whom and the way the results of that labor are appropriated and by whom, operate to construct relations of power and inequality" (Messerschmidt 1997: 7). But while power emanates from material and institutional locations (such as the workplace or the courtroom), it is also realized at the interpersonal level: "The capacity to exercise power is, for the most part, a reflection of one's position in social relationships" (Messerschmidt 1997: 9).

In Messerschmidt's theorizing, then, structure and action are inseparable. "Social structures are realized only through social action and social action requires structure as its condition" (Messerschmidt 1997: 113). His book's main concern is to locate crime within the context of "doing" gender, race and class, and he uses four case studies — the lynching of Black men in the American South in the late nineteenth century, the life of Malcolm X, violence among working-class girls in gangs and the decision to launch the space shuttle *Challenger* in 1986 — to explore how and in what respects gender, race and class are constituted in certain settings at certain times, and how each construct relates to various types of crime. For our purposes, Messerschmidt's theorizing offers a way of situating the role of lawyers within the process of criminalization. More specifically, we view criminalization as one site of structured action in which lawyers participate in the "making" of gender, race and class under the social-structural constraints that prevail at given historical points in time.

Still, to further situate lawyering as structured action, we need to develop a number of other dimensions in our theorizing. The first dimension is the structure or form of law, which is embodied in what Ngaire Naffine (1990) refers to as the "Official Version of Law." Elements of due process and professional codes of conduct that prescribe the role of lawyers in the adversarial system promote the appearance of legal practice as a series of procedural requirements and technical exercises that both constrain Crown attorneys and defence lawyers and enable them to carry out their roles. The second dimension is the discursive nature of legal practice. In their case-building strategies, lawyers draw upon and work within particular discourses (such as those relating to masculinity, femininity, "Indianness" and dangerousness) to constitute legal subjects in gendered, racialized and class-based ways. The third dimension is the socio-political context in which these discursive claims are made and from which they gain their salience. In particular we look at how neo-liberalism and neo-conservatism have altered the practice of law in recent times.

All of these dimensions come together to inform the agency of lawyers. Indeed, lawyering is one site of structured action in which structure, discourse and socio-political context assemble in the "making" of gender, race and class inequalities.

THE FORM OF LAW: THE OFFICIAL VERSION OF LAW

> The official version of law — what the legal world would have us believe about itself — is that it is an impartial, neutral and objective system for resolving social conflict. (Naffine 1990: 24)

As Naffine suggests, impartiality, neutrality and objectivity are the cornerstones of the modern legal system. They are symbolically represented in the image of the blindfolded maiden who holds the scales used to dispense justice — an icon found in most courtrooms across the country. This image speaks volumes about the messages that law endeavours to convey about itself. A maiden is a virginal young (white?) woman — presumably untouched, untainted or uncorrupted. That she is blindfolded suggests she is not swayed or influenced by the characteristics of those who stand before her; she sees no class, race or gender distinctions. In words often used, she dispenses "blind justice." The scales she is holding connote the measured and precise nature of the decisions produced. But the Official Version of Law is reflected in elements other than the symbol of the blindfolded maiden. In both its form and method, law asserts its claim to be impartial, neutral and objective.

Perhaps the most central doctrine on which law is founded is that of the rule of law, which encompasses two broad claims. First, everyone, even the sovereign or ruler, is subject to the law, because the law is something separate and distinct from the interests of particular groups or classes. "Equality of all before the law" speaks to a claim central to Western liberal democracy — that all persons accused of a crime are entitled to a full and complete answer to a charge before a judge or trier of fact. Second, the law treats everyone the same, as "legal equals" (Hunt 1976). The main intent of this particular legal form is to ensure that the civil liberties of citizens are protected against the arbitrary exercise of power by the state. Thus, the law is held to be dispassionate, predictable, objective, impartial and — above all — *just* in its search for the truth.

From this legal form flows a set of procedural requirements, known as due process, that are designed to ensure that prosecution of a criminal matter takes place in accordance with lawful procedures and fairness before an independent and impartial tribunal. Due process or procedural fairness is at once a "moral imperative of a democracy" and a "managerial concept of crime control" (Lacey and Wells 1998). In other words, although due process is held to be the means by which the rule of law is administered, it also connotes a bureaucracy in which officers of the court execute their professional duties. The administration of justice involves legally trained experts (Crown prosecutors, defence counsel and trial judges) whose power to criminalize (or not) is legitimated by the state. Within this adversarial system, each of the legal actors performs a specific role.

The Role of the Crown Attorney

In Canada, both the police and Crown attorneys can lay charges. The usual practice, however, is for the police to lay charges and then pass the file over to the Crown attorney's office for prosecution. The office of the Crown attorney may decide not to prosecute the charges laid by the police. In that case, Crown attorneys can substitute other charges or decide to stay the proceedings. Where doubt exists that a conviction would result, it is the responsibility of the Crown attorney to advise the police to continue their investigation.

Under the requirements of due process, it is the responsibility of the Crown in a criminal case to meet the burden of proof and establish the guilt of the accused "beyond a reasonable doubt." The Crown must establish the criminal liability of the accused in terms of action (*actus reus*) and intent (*mens rea*). All actions of the accused are assessed in terms of voluntariness: did the accused voluntarily and intentionally commit the act or fail to act? The intentionality of the accused's actions is assessed in accordance with an objective standard: would a "reasonable person" perceive the accused as intentionally committing a criminal act or failing to act? The Crown is required to prove that the accused's intent was not diminished by forces such as mental disorder, extreme intoxication, provocation or duress. As well, the Crown's case must be supported by sufficient factual and persuasive evidence. Due process requires that evidence be assessed in terms of its rational connection to the offence. In 1955 Justice Ivan Rand summarized the role of the Crown in a criminal prosecution:

> It cannot be over-emphasized that the purpose of a criminal prosecution is not to obtain a conviction; it is to lay before the jury what the Crown considers to be credible evidence relevant to what is alleged to be a crime. Counsel have a duty to see that all available legal proof of the facts is presented; it should be done firmly and to its legitimate strength, but it must also be done fairly. The role of prosecutor excludes any notion of winning or losing; his function is a matter of public duty than which in civil life there can be none charged with greater personal responsibility. (*Boucher* v. *The Queen*, [1955] S.C.R. 16 at 23–25, cited in Hamilton and Sinclair 1991: 65)

The decision of the Crown to prosecute is informed by two fundamental principles. Is there enough evidence to justify the continuation of the proceedings? If there is, does the public interest require a prosecution to be pursued? Crown counsel is expected to continually re-evaluate the decision to prosecute throughout the entire trial process, as "not all offences must be prosecuted as the resources available for prosecution are not limitless, and should not be used to pursue inappropriate cases" (Pomerant and Gilmour 1997: 3). As well, the Crown is obligated to disclose to the accused the evidence that the Crown intends to rely on at trial, as well as any evidence that may assist the accused.

The Role of Defence Counsel

Under the Code of Professional Conduct of the Canadian Bar Association adopted by the law societies, the primary concern of all lawyers is the protection of the public interest. The role of defence lawyers is to ensure that individuals are not convicted improperly and that the principles of fundamental justice enshrined in the *Charter of Rights and Freedoms* are not overlooked. In fulfilling this role, defence lawyers must only take on cases for which they feel they are able to provide proper attention and solid, independent advice. Defence lawyers must also inform their clients of any available options, such as the possibility of conviction for a lesser offence or an acquittal for the main offence. It is also the responsibility of defence lawyers to advise a client of any possibility that the Crown will permit the accused to plead guilty to a lesser charge, which means that going to trial could be avoided. After examining all the facts of a case, defence lawyers are entitled to put forward any and all possible defences at trial.

One of the central tasks of the defence is to ensure that the Crown proves its case against the accused "beyond a reasonable doubt" and that the accused's rights are not violated during the investigation and prosecution of the offence. Defence counsel is not required to prove or disprove any fact (except in rare situations). Reasonable doubt can be raised, for instance, by challenging the credibility or reliability of witnesses (Knoll 1994). Because the zealous representation of the accused is seen as a necessary means of protecting his or her rights to a full and complete defence, defence lawyers are expected to vigorously cross-examine Crown witnesses to establish the truthfulness of their testimony. Indeed, to *not* probe the credibility and character of a witness is considered unethical professional conduct on the part of the defence. As Justices A.C. Hamilton and C.M. Sinclair (1991: 58) note: "The role of the defence counsel is not always understood by the public. What may at times appear to be the protection of criminals by lawyers may only incidentally be that. A lawyer is cloaked with certain privileges which he or she must exercise on behalf of clients."

Defence lawyers can also raise reasonable doubt by introducing a legally recognized defence of the accused's actions. Given that criminal responsibility is premised on the Crown establishing that the defendant acted voluntarily and possessed *mens rea,* individuals whose criminal acts are not of free will or whose actions are justified because of extraordinary circumstances can be deemed to be either less responsible or not responsible for their behaviour. In the case of criminal homicide, for example, the law recognizes a number of legal justifications or excuses that either mitigate or absolve the accused's criminal liability — self-defence and intoxication are two of them. While self-defence justifies the actions of the accused, the defence of intoxication excuses the accused.

Self-defence, as a justification rather than an excuse of the accused's actions, focuses on the context of the event rather than the accused's "human infirmity" or emotional state. Historically the premise of the self-defence argument has been that the court considers the reasonableness of the accused's use of violence against an unprovoked attack, like that encountered in a barroom brawl between two strangers. This use of force is justifiable and hence lawful if the force was no more than what was necessary for the purpose of self-defence. In the event of a lethal assault (homicide), an accused can also claim self-defence if the defence can show "appreciable evidence of sufficient and probative value" to establish the deceased's previous acts of violence against the accused or a third person (Knoll 1994: 121).

The legal doctrine of self-defence differentiates between an unprovoked assault upon the accused and the intent — or lack of intention — to cause death or considerable harm (Verdun-Jones 2002). Section 34.1 of the *Criminal Code* states:

> Everyone who is unlawfully assaulted without having provoked the assault is justified in repelling force by force if the force he uses is not intended

to cause death or grievous bodily harm and is no more than is necessary to enable him to defend himself.

Whereas section 34.2 states:

Everyone who is unlawfully assaulted and who causes death or grievous bodily harm in repelling the assault is justified if:

(a) he causes it under reasonable apprehension of death or grievous bodily harm from the violence with which the assault was originally made or with which the assailant pursues his purposes, and

(b) he believes, on reasonable grounds, that he cannot otherwise preserve himself from death or grievous bodily harm.

Section 34.2 applies even if the accused was the initial aggressor of the series of events that led to the use of extreme force in self-defence. As well, section 34.2 does not require that the degree of force used by the accused be proportionate to that inflicted by the deceased or complainant. Rather, the court must decide if the accused believed on reasonable and probable grounds that he or she could not otherwise protect him/herself.

Prior to 1996 in Canada, the *Criminal Code* made no formal mention of the defence of intoxication. Canadian courts followed the decisions made by the English judiciary in treating intoxication as a partial defence; it could operate to reduce the severity of the charge (Verdun-Jones 2002). As well, the defence of intoxication could only be raised in crimes of *specific intent* (such as murder, robbery, and break and enter), but not for crimes of *general intent* (such as manslaughter, aggravated assault or sexual assault).[1] Unlike the general rule by which the burden of proof rests with the Crown to prove its case against the accused, a defence that cites intoxication carries the burden of proving its case based on the balance of probabilities and with the support of expert testimony. For example, when an accused is charged with murder (a specific intent offence), defence counsel can raise the issue of intoxication to get the charge reduced to manslaughter; the argument can be supported through the testimony of an expert witness as to the impact of extreme levels of drugs and/or alcohol upon a person. The trial judge must instruct the jury (if present) to consider the impact of intoxication as an inhibitor of a person's normal conduct.

In 1994 the Supreme Court of Canada (in *R. v. Daviault*) altered the traditional approach to intoxication by ruling that a defendant charged with a general intent offence (such as sexual assault) might use the defence of intoxication where extreme drunkenness had resulted in a "state akin to automatism or insanity." In response to the *Daviault* case, Parliament passed legislation dealing with intoxication as a defence to a criminal charge. Added to the *Criminal Code* in 1996, section 33.1

places limits on the use of intoxication for general intent offences. Specifically the law does not accept intoxication as a defence to any general intent offence that "includes as an element an assault or any other interference or threat of interference with the bodily integrity of another person." Intoxication, then, can be used as a defence in crimes of specific intent where it prevents the accused from forming the requisite intent (for example, intent to kill). It can also be used in crimes of general intent where the offence does not involve an element of assault or any other interference (or threat of interference) with the bodily integrity of another person (it can be used, for example, in cases involving damage to property) and where the intoxication is so extreme as to produce a state akin to automatism or insanity (Verdun-Jones 2002).

The Role of the Judge

In law's Official Version, the role of the judge is to discern the "legally relevant facts" of the case — to find the "truth" about the matter brought before the court. In the process:

> Members of the Bench ... do not invoke their own personal beliefs of the rights or wrongs of an individual or a case. Nor do they operate with any particular set of social or cultural values. Instead, they are obliged to treat all who come before them in an unbiased fashion, fairly and dispassionately. To quote from the English judicial oath, the obligation on the judicial officer is to "do right to all manner of people ... without fear or favour, affection or ill will." (Naffine 1990: 24–25)

That judges are impartial in their deliberations is reflected in the doctrine of the separation of powers; that is, the legislature (which makes the laws) is separated from the judiciary (which administers the laws). This doctrine suggests that law is an autonomous, internally consistent system, divorced from the more political processes of the state. Further assisting the impartiality and fairness of the proceedings is the doctrine of *stare decisis* or "to stand by decided matters," according to which judges are bound to follow precedent. Developed under the common-law tradition of case law, precedent implies that "like cases are to be treated alike." In making their decisions judges are to rely on previous cases, and lower courts must follow the decisions reached by higher courts. These principles are said to promote and ensure that law is predictable, consistent and certain.

Under the Official Version of Law, then, specific doctrines prescribe the roles of the Crown, defence counsel and judges, which are subject to different codes of professional conduct. The backdrop to these role performances is the criminal trial itself, which brings together the procedural requirements of due process, the rights of the accused and the professional obligations of Crown attorneys and defence lawyers. Within the court structure, more serious criminal matters — such as crimes that cause serious harm — are most often heard before a superior court of criminal jurisdiction (variously called the Court of Queen's Bench, Supreme Court, Superior Court or Divisional Court). Most cases appearing before a superior court have a preliminary hearing (except when a trial proceeds by direct indictment) and a pre-trial conference prior to the criminal trial proper. Across these two stages, Crown attorneys and defence lawyers will regularly become engaged in sentence resolution negotiations or plea bargaining.

The Preliminary Hearing

The contrasting roles of Crown attorneys and defence lawyers are clearly marked at the preliminary hearing of a criminal trial. The purpose of the preliminary hearing is for a judge to determine whether sufficient evidence exists to warrant committing the accused to trial. The judge does not rule on guilt, but must decide if the Crown, on the face of it, has evidence on each of the specific elements of the crime that could prove guilt (Cunningham and Griffiths 1997: 182). Strategically, the preliminary hearing is where the Crown's theory of the case and evidence is revealed to defence counsel. The defence can vigorously cross-examine the statements of complainants and witnesses to challenge the credibility of the Crown's case against the accused. Discredited testimony from witnesses and complainants can be used to raise reasonable doubt as to the Crown's case.

The Pre-trial Conference

In addition to the preliminary hearing, where a trier of fact determines the weight of the Crown's case against the accused, proceedings can also include a pre-trial conference. At a pre-trial conference the defence counsel, the Crown and a trial judge meet to "promote a fair and expeditious hearing" (Abell and Sheehy 1998:118). These conferences are mandatory when an accused elects a jury trial.[2] Conference judges can advise lawyers as to the strength of their case and suggest a possible pre-trial resolution or plea bargain. The pre-trial conference can often serve as an opportunity for the accused to obtain discovery of the Crown's case or to discuss the possibility of making an agreement to plead guilty in return for some concession from the Crown (Griffiths and Verdun-Jones 1994).

Plea Bargaining

Plea bargaining between the Crown and the defence counsel is intended to "lead to a narrowing of the issues at trial which may avoid unnecessary litigation altogether, and forms an important and necessary part of the criminal justice system" (Pomerant and Gilmour 1997: 27).[3] Securing the guilty plea of an accused person in exchange for a more lenient sentence is not a formalized process bound by statutory provisions. Rather, it is a practice that includes a broad range of outcomes that can involve informal negotiation between the accused and the Crown "at the eleventh hour on the courtroom steps" (Cunningham and Griffiths 1997: 182).

Plea negotiations take many forms, including charge bargaining (a reduction of the charge to a lesser or included offence), sentence bargaining (a promise by the Crown to make a particular recommendation in relation to sentencing or a promise not to appeal a sentence imposed at trial) and fact bargaining (a promise by the Crown not to mention a circumstance of the offence that the judge may interpret as an aggravating factor) (Griffiths and Verdun-Jones 1994). Although plea negotiations encompass a wide range of stages in the trial process, the Crown and the defence counsel have clearly defined roles throughout.

Codes of professional conduct[4] typically mandate that a plea bargain must satisfy a number of principles, including: the defence lawyer foresees that the accused will not be acquitted of the charge; the accused must fully admit the factual and mental elements; the accused has been fully advised by the defence as to the implications and consequences of a guilty plea, and the sentence is at the discretion of the judge; and the accused instructs his or her defence lawyer in writing of his or her agreement to the terms of the plea negotiation. The plea negotiation entered into by the accused and the Crown must not compromise the public interest. Throughout the negotiation process, the defence plays a key role in advising the accused, although entering into a plea bargain is ultimately the client's decision. The role of the defence counsel is ostensibly not to function as a double agent trying to facilitate assembly-line justice. Rather, it is to support the client's freedom to choose by providing sound legal advice (Proulx and Layton 2001).

The Criminal Trial

The matter proceeds to the trial proper if the Crown has presented a prima facie case[5] against the accused at the preliminary hearing, if a plea bargain cannot be reached between the Crown and the accused or if the accused pleads not guilty. In law's Official Version, the aim of a criminal trial is to preserve societal standards of conduct laid down in legislation and precedent. The criminal trial engages several legal actors within a series of rationalized and highly formalized events that have an array of possible outcomes for the accused. Once again, the roles of defence counsel and the Crown are prescribed according to different codes of professional conduct. The backdrop to these role performances is the criminal trial itself, with its established procedural requirements, emphasis on the rights of the accused, and professional obligations.

In most cases the accused can elect a trial by a provincial court judge, trial by a superior court judge sitting alone, or trial by a superior court judge and a jury.[6] Once the trial has begun, the Crown calls witnesses — including the complainant(s) — to testify and present evidence in support of its position, which is that the accused is guilty. The Crown must adduce evidence covering all the major elements of the offence (*mens rea* and *actus reus*). After the Crown has presented its case to the court, the defence cross-examines the witnesses and complainant(s) to challenge the admissibility of the Crown's evidence and to put forward "any claim which, if accepted, would lead to an acquittal" (MacIntosh 1995: 327). The accused is not required to testify on his or her behalf, but if he or she decides to do so, the Crown is then free to enter in as evidence the accused's criminal record. If the accused does not testify, the judge (and jury, if present) is not apprised of the accused's prior convictions (until sentencing). The outcome of the case is decided by the trial judge, who rules on whether the Crown has proven all elements of the offence or if the defence has offered a credible claim that acquits the accused of the charge(s), finds the accused not guilty, or excuses or justifies the actions of the accused.

Under this rights-based adversarial system, it is the interests of the accused — not the state — that are ostensibly paramount. Specifically, the adversarial process is premised on the presupposition that the accused is entitled to have access to the resources of the court to prepare a full and complete defence to be heard before a neutral trier of fact who establishes the veracity of the Crown's case against the accused (Proloux and Layton 2001). In this way, the adversarial process is held to be non-partisan.

Yet this adversarial system may not be all that it seems. As Naffine (1990: 44) describes it, "The road to legal truth runs through a highly artificial form of conflict." She maintains that the legal process is actually a carefully controlled and contrived contest between two parties who each present a version of events relating to the criminal charge. The rules of evidence and procedure ensure that each case is presented in a highly stylized manner and that only parts of each story are deemed to be legally admissible. It is, therefore, not the "total truth" that law seeks — but a more circumscribed "legal truth" of the matter. Although the traditional conception of legal decision-making is that there is a legal truth "out there," waiting to be discovered, "the reality is that each case before the court is susceptible to many readings" (Naffine 1990: 46; see also McBarnet 1981).

According to the Official Version of Law, the criminalization process unfolds in a context of impartiality, neutrality and objectivity. Nevertheless, the idea that criminal cases are susceptible to many readings opens up the possibility that there is more going on within criminalization than "what the legal world would have us believe about itself" (Naffine 1990: 24). The power of law is not limited to principles of fundamental justice. Law deals not only in formal rules and procedures, but also in *ideology* and *discourse*. In these terms, law is not simply a formalized structure through which criminal cases are processed, but a contested terrain on which various discourses operate to produce and reproduce certain claims to "truth." And it is here where we can begin to locate law's role in the making of gender, race and class inequalities.

LAW AS A DISCURSIVE PRACTICE

Theorists who adhere to the reading of law as a discursive practice invariably express their indebtedness to the work of Michel Foucault (1977, 1979 and 1984), and especially his analysis of the relation between power and knowledge. Foucault rejected the notion of power as a "thing" or commodity that can be owned. Instead, he concentrated on the mechanisms of power that came with the development of what he called the "disciplinary society," characterized by the growth of new knowledges (such as medicine and criminology) that led to new modes of surveillance and regulation of the population. For Foucault, knowledge is not objective, but political; the production of knowledge has to do with power. A reciprocal relation exists between the two: power is productive of knowledge, and knowledge is productive of power. Furthermore, "it is in discourse that power and knowledge are joined together" (Foucault 1979: 100).

Bodies of knowledge such as medicine, science, law, psychology and sociology are *discourses*, historically specific systems of meaning or ways of making sense of the world. These discourses are shaped by social practices and in turn shape social relationships and institutions. Because they join together power and knowledge, certain discourses — and their corresponding discursive practices or ways of acting — come to dominate society at particular points in history. Foucault was therefore interested in "discovering how certain discourses claim to speak the truth and thus can exercise power in a society that values this notion of truth" (Smart 1989: 9).

Socio-legal theorists have adopted Foucault's ideas as a means of understanding the power of law in society. Carol Smart (1989), for one, suggests that law is a form of knowledge, and therefore a form of power. That power derives, in part, from law's ability to impose its definition of events onto everyday life. It does this not simply through rendering judgments, but by disqualifying other accounts. For instance, within the courtroom, Smart (1989: 11) argues:

> Non-legal knowledge is ... suspect and/or secondary. Everyday experiences are of little interest in terms of their meaning for individuals. Rather these experiences must be translated into another form in order to become "legal" issues and before they can be processed through the legal system ... So the legal process translates everyday experience into legal relevances, it excludes a great deal that might be relevant to the parties, and it makes its judgement on the scripted or tailored account.

The process of the rape trial illustrates how legal practice translates people's experiences into "legal relevances." From a woman's standpoint, rape is, more often than not, an experience of humiliation, degradation and violation — a terrifying ordeal. The rape trial, however, involves sifting through that experience to extract those "facts" of the case that law views as being relevant to the determination of the guilt or innocence of the accused. For instance, did the woman complainant consent? As a key witness for the Crown, is her testimony credible? Is there physical evidence to support or corroborate her claim that it was rape? As one woman who experienced a rape trial notes, complainants are expected to speak in a legal language that is precise and exact, with times and dates attached:

> I was never allowed to describe the crime in my own words but was required to respond to a template designed to protect the rights of the rapist. I will never forget the final question put to me in defence of the man who had raped me. I was asked, as were the other four women [whom he had raped], whether my rape had been violent. Despite the knife, the threats against my life, the forced entry, the ghoul's mask and the binding of my eyes, he asked if my rape had been violent. Despite the police manhunt, the public outcry, the rapist's criminal history of violence, the packed courtroom, and the media scrutiny, the rapist's lawyer asked if my rape had been violent. Despite everything we know about the violent nature of rape, he asked if my rape had been violent. When I did not answer, could not answer, the judge instructed me that because I had not been cut or stabbed with the rapist's knife, because he hadn't beaten or mutilated or (most decisive of all) killed me, I must answer that my rape had not been violent.
>
> And my testimony was over. (Doe 2003: 72)

As a claim to power, law sets itself above other knowledges (such as psychology or common sense) and professes to have a method — the adversarial system — to establish the "truth" of events. In this sense, the practice of law is akin to a game constituted by certain rules (such as due process) and involving certain key players (lawyers, judges, complainants, the accused) (Chunn and Lacombe 2000: 15). Lawyers play the game using moves such as persuasion and negotiation, and they appeal to certain authoritative discourses to achieve their immediate aims. In these terms, the practice of law is more than just professional codes of conduct and prescribed roles of legal actors. Law is also a series of *strategies* that constitute both the identities of legal subjects and their social relations with each other.

In her later work, Carol Smart turned her attention to the questions of how gender works in law and how law works to produce gender. She suggests that law is a "gendering strategy" — one of society's discourses that is "productive not only of gender difference, but quite specific forms of polarized difference" (Smart 1992: 34). Law, she says, "brings into being not only gendered subject positions" but also "subjectivities or identities to which the individual becomes tied or associated" (Smart 1992: 34). These gendering strategies vary according to history and culture, and they can be strategies without authors "in as much as we should not imagine that strategy here implies a plan, masterminded in advance by extra-cultural (Cartesian) actors" (Smart 1992: 35).

For Smart (1995: 218), law is "a mechanism for *fixing* gender differences and constructing femininity and masculinity in oppositional modes." Her main interest is with the "Woman" of legal discourse. Law is a means by which "Woman" (in contradistinction to "Man") and "types of Woman" (the female criminal, the prostitute, the unmarried mother) are brought into being. These constructions work symbiotically, as a double strategy:

> Woman has always been *both* kind and killing, active and aggressive, virtuous and evil, cherishable and abominable, not *either* virtuous or evil. Woman therefore represents a dualism, as well as being one side of a prior binary distinction. Thus in legal discourse the prostitute is constructed as the bad woman, but at the same time she epitomizes Woman in contradistinction to Man because she is what any woman could be and because she represents a deviousness and a licentiousness arising from her (supposedly naturally given) bodily form, while man remains innocuous. (Smart 1992: 36)

While Smart elaborates on the significance of law as a gendering strategy for women, law also genders men's lives. The work of Robert Connell (1987, 1995 and 2000), for instance, has been instrumental in bringing the issue of masculinity to bear on criminological research and theorizing. Drawing from Gramsci's notion of hegemony — the "systems of domination which are formed through power struggles and become sedimented over time" (Howarth 2000: 84) — Connell theorizes that a certain culturally idealized form of masculinity becomes hegemonic in society. Emerging from socially organized power relations between men and women and among men, "hegemonic masculinity" is constructed in relation to women (what Connell calls "emphasized femininity") as well as various "subordinated" or "oppositional" masculinities (such as male homosexuality). In contemporary Western industrialized societies, hegemonic masculinity is characterized by "whiteness (race), work in the paid labor market (gender division of labor), the subordination of girls and women (gender relations of power), professional-managerial (class), and heterosexism (sexuality)" (Messerschmidt 1997: 10). As a culturally dominant discourse, hegemonic masculinity has a bearing on how men are constructed within law. As Smart (1992: 32–33) observes, "Law does not serve the interests of *men* as a homogeneous category any more than it serves the interests of *women* as a category." It follows, then, that law will make sense of men accused of criminal acts according to prevailing hegemonic scripts of masculinity. These scripts will also be informed by presuppositions of race, class and sexuality.

Working with Smart's typology of law as a gendering strategy, Kathleen Daly (1994: 460) suggests that we investigate law as a racializing strategy — that is, "how race and ethnicity are brought forth as racialized subject positions by criminal law and justice system practices." The term "racialization" is used to refer to the process by which discourses can become permeated with racial dimensions (Henry and Taylor 2002: 11). In adopting this view, we need not assume that justice system practices invariably exploit minority groups and serve the majority group. Rather, racializing discourses can be "everywhere apparent and move in cross-cutting ways" (Daly 1994: 460). For instance, because race is "not simply attached to people's bodies as a natural or stable characteristic" (Daly 1994: 461), racist imageries (relating to dangerousness, culpability and/or victimhood) can inform legal actors' constructions of crime.

The 1971 police investigation of the murder of Helen Betty Osborne reveals how racialization can profoundly influence the response of the criminal justice system to violent crime. Helen Betty Osborne, a young Aboriginal college student, lived in The Pas, a predominantly white town in Northern Manitoba. One night while walking home, she was forced into a car by four young white men who were "cruising" for an Indian girl. She was driven to an isolated spot outside of town, and there brutally beaten and stabbed to death with a screwdriver. The police investigation that followed the discovery of her body focused almost exclusively on Helen's Aboriginal friends. Police questioned Aboriginal youth in the community without the consent of parents, brought numerous people to the morgue to view Helen's battered body and widely distributed photos of her for the purposes of identification. Although the police were made aware of the suspicious activities of four white men following Helen's murder, the officers failed to follow up on that information. Instead they arrested, stripped-searched and detained two Aboriginal youth for questioning. In the words of the commissioners of the Aboriginal Justice Inquiry:

> It is clear that Helen Betty Osborne would not have been killed if she had not been Aboriginal. The four men who took her to her death from the streets of The Pas that night had gone looking for an Aboriginal girl with whom to "party." They found Betty Osborne. When she refused to party she was driven out of town and murdered. Those who abducted her showed a total lack of regard for her person or her rights as an individual. Those who stood by while the physical assault took place, while sexual advances were made and while she was being beaten to death showed their own racism, sexism and indifference. Those who knew the story and remained silent must share their guilt. (Hamilton and Sinclair 1991: 98)

Marlee Kline (1994) is another writer who locates law as one of the discourses in which racism is constructed, reproduced and reinforced in society. In her analysis of the "colour of law" with respect to First Nations people, Kline introduces us to an understanding of how judges and lawyers, as social actors, bring with them into the court racist ideologies that are rooted in the wider society. In these terms, racism flows from the ideological form of law rather than the isolated acts of individuals:

> Judges, like other members of dominant society, operate within discursive fields in which racist ideology helps constitute what is and is not to be taken for granted as "just the way things are." The appearance of racist ideological representations within judicial discourse may be more of a reflection of the power and pervasiveness of such dominant ideology in the wider society and the particular susceptibility of legal discourse to it, than individual racial prejudice on the part of judges. (Kline 1994: 452)

According to Kline, ideological representations of Aboriginal peoples developed out of the material relations of colonialism and continue to be constructed, reproduced and reinforced in a wide variety of discursive contexts, including what she refers to as the "abstracted and indeterminate form of law" (Kline 1994: 452). Inquiring as to how judges are allowed to import ideological frameworks into law, Kline suggests that it is the appearance of the neutrality of law (promoted by law's Official Version) that obscures law's power to naturalize and legitimize racist ideologies.

Sherene Razack (1998) further refines our discussion of law-as-racialized. She suggests that violence and drunkenness have come to be viewed as naturally occurring and inevitable features of places inhabited by Aboriginal peoples. According to Razack (2000: 117), violence is "an event that is routine when the bodies in question are Aboriginal." While violence has come to be associated with racialized spaces of the inner city — especially in the Prairie provinces, where inner-city neighbourhoods are heavily populated by Aboriginal peoples — violence in white middle-class neighbourhoods is constituted as different from "other" (Indian) spaces (Razack 1998, 2000 and 2002).

Razack's analysis reveals how "legal and social constructs naturalize spatial relations of domination, highlighting in the process white respectability and Aboriginal criminality." Writing of the murder of Pamela George, a young Aboriginal woman who worked as a prostitute in Regina, Razack (2000: 6) argues that "because Pamela George was considered to belong to a space in which violence routinely occurs, and to have a body that is routinely violated, whereas her killers were presumed to be far removed from this zone, the enormity of what was done to her remained largely unacknowledged in the law." For instance, Razack (2000:

114) notes how lawyers described the site of the murder as "a romantic place where couples are often necking or petting in vehicles." She also acknowledges the historical and contemporary racial and spatial parallels between the murders of Helen Betty Osborne and Pamela George. In both the Osborne and George cases, "White men forcibly and fatally removed Aboriginal bodies from the city space, a literal cleansing of the white zone" (Razack 2000: 115). In the words of Justices A.C. Hamilton and C.M. Sinclair (1991: 96):

> To the people of The Pas, Osborne was not the girl next door; she was Aboriginal in a white town. Even though she had lived in The Pas for two years by the time she was murdered, she was a stranger to the community, a person almost without identity. She was unknown to those who heard the rumours. Because of the racial separation of The Pas, those who cared about Betty Osborne, her Aboriginal friends, were not privy to the rumours about those who took her life.

Throughout the trial, Pamela George was referred to as the "hooker" or the "Indian," whereas the accused men — two white, middle-class university students — were characterized by their lawyers as "boys who did pretty darn stupid things" (Razack 2000: 117). Razack (2000: 17) maintains that these strategies constitute the identities of Pamela George and the men as well as the place where the death occurred in such a way that "no one could be really held accountable for her death, at least not to the extent that there would have been accountability had she been of [white] spaces within the domain of justice."

The Pamela George case is significant because it highlights not only the role of race and gender in law, but also the role of class. The two male accused who were convicted of manslaughter in George's death were clearly privileged by their class position. They used their parents' credit cards to obtain cash to pay George for oral sex and later to purchase plane tickets to travel to Banff, where they hid from police.

Most writers who consider law as a discursive practice have not focused much attention on how law places value on a particular set of class relations. In large part, this is due to their adherence to a post-structuralist theoretical orientation. Post-structuralists — such as Foucault and Smart — are sceptical of theorizing premised on "totalizing structures" such as capitalism, imperialism or patriarchy. These vocabularies or concepts, they argue, are too cumbersome to capture the fragmented nature of social life; they also assume a reality that exists outside of or apart from individuals. Instead, post-structuralists place their emphasis on "agency and the habitat in which agency operates" (Smart 1995: 211). In response to this charge, we maintain that there are good reasons for retaining the notion that social structures exist, not the least of which is that systems like capitalism *are* "totalizing structures" (Fudge and Glasbeek 1992); they condition and contour the economic, social and political lives of the individuals who move within them (Comack 1999a: 66). In this regard, one of the advantages of adopting Messerschmidt's notion of "structured action" is that it acknowledges how social structures (like capitalism) are enacted in everyday interactions and in specific locations. And one of those locations is law.

Much goes missing, then, if gender and race are separated out from class. We need to be mindful of how class privilege and economic marginalization enter into legal practice. Nevertheless, given the ways in which gender, race and class so often intersect, clear lines of distinction are difficult to draw. Daly (1994: 451), for instance, notes how "whiteness" has both race and class dimensions:

> It includes notions of what constitutes appropriate dress, demeanor, ways of speaking, and child-rearing practices; it means believing that existing rules and authorities are legitimate and fair; and it implies trust that schooling is related to paid employment and that decisions in schools and work sites are based on meritocratic principles of ability and discipline.

To the extent that the practices of criminal law and the justice system embrace such constructions, they will be "color-coded and class-compounded" (Daly 1994: 451).

By attending to the ways in which law operates as a discursive practice, we can begin to see how gender, race and class inequalities enter into the picture. While principles of fundamental justice and professional codes of conduct may constrain and enable the discretion of legal actors, lawyering also involves a series of strategies that constitute the identities of legal subjects, social relations and social spaces in gendered, racialized and class-based terms. Why is the rule of law susceptible to these strategies? How is it that certain truth claims come to have salience in the case-building strategies of lawyers? To address such questions we need to broaden our focus to include the wider socio-political context in which the criminalization process occurs.

THE SOCIO-POLITICAL CONTEXT

Neo-Liberalism and Neo-Conservatism
The socio-political context can be defined as the institutions, practices and discourses that legitimate modes of domination and control (Kellner 1989). In his own work, Messerschmidt (1997) explored slavery in the American South as a socio-political context that made the lynching of Black men possible by legitimating claims of white supremacy. In today's context we should assess how neo-liberalism and neo-conservatism can alter the practice of law.

Over the past three decades, the increasingly international or global nature of production and exchange has led to significant transformations within particular nation-states, including Canada. Corporate restructuring and downsizing — designed to keep up with these new forms of global production relations and financial systems — have led to heightened levels of inequality and immiseration. According to a United Nations report, "Worldwide, the top 20 percent of the world's population increased their share of total global wealth from 70 percent in 1960 to 85 percent in 1991, and the share 'enjoyed' by the poorest 20 percent actually *declined* from 1960 to 1991, falling from 2.3 percent to 1.4 percent" (quoted in Snider 1999: 184). Of the one hundred largest economies in the world, fifty-one are now corporations. Walmart, the number-twelve corporation, is bigger than 161 countries (*Canadian Forum* 1997: 48). Conditions in Canada are equally distorted. A Statistics Canada survey of assets, debts and wealth documented how millions of families and individuals were living on the brink of financial disaster at the same time as a small proportion of people were managing to accumulate huge slices of the wealth pie.

> All in all, Canadians had total personal wealth of more than $2.4 trillion in 1999, or an average of $199,664 for each family unit. The actual distribution of wealth, however, was anything but equitable. The wealthiest 10% of family units in Canada held 53% of the personal wealth, and the top 50% controlled an almost unbelievable 94.4% of the wealth. That left only 5.6% to be shared among the bottom 50%. (Kerstetter 2002: 1)

These economic transformations have occurred in tandem with a new political ethos: *neo-liberalism*. Premised on the values of individualism, freedom of choice, market security and minimal state involvement in the economy, neo-liberalism marks a dramatic shift in emphasis from collective or social values towards notions of family and individual responsibility. In their adherence to these neo-liberal ideals, governments have noticeably retreated from any professed commitment to social welfare. Instead of formulating policies and targeting spending on programs that would meet the social needs of the members of society (education, health care, pensions, social assistance), governments now focus on enhancing economic efficiency and international competitiveness. With the "privatization" of responsibility, individuals and families are left to look after themselves.

The impact of this shift is profound. As Janine Brodie (1999:44) notes, "This 'rebirth' of the individual marks the systematic erasure of structural factors in the formation of social policy. The poor become responsible for their own plight while the state becomes preoccupied with using its power to enforce the individualization of social costs." Joblessness becomes an individual rather than a social problem;

the poor are stigmatized and made personally to blame for their own situation. According to Brodie, "Welfare dependency, similar to drug addiction, is a mark of individual weakness, irresponsibility and immaturity and, most of all, is avoidable." But it is not just the poor who feel the impact of these transformations. As Jock Young (1999: 8) notes, "The resulting effect of lean production and re-engineering is to remove a sizeable proportion of middle income jobs and to engender a feeling of precariousness in those previously secure." With the disappearance of secure, well-paying jobs and the stable communities that went with them comes increased anxiety and social unease.

While some writers have conceptualized neo-liberalism as a policy agenda adopted by nation-states that are ushering in new political regimes to match corporate globalization, others define neo-liberalism as "both a political discourse about the nature of rule and a set of practices that facilitate the governing of individuals from a distance" (Larner 2000: 6). Drawing on post-structuralist theories of "governmentality," these writers make a distinction between "government" and "governance." According to this view, while neo-liberalism may mean less government, it does not mean less governance. According to Wendy Larner (2000: 12), "It involves forms of governance that encourage both institutions and individuals to conform to the norms of the market." People are thereby encouraged to see themselves as "individualized and active subjects responsible for enhancing their own well-being" (Larner 2000: 13).

How have these developments altered criminal justice policies and practices? Criminologists have noted the extraordinary expansion — especially since the early 1990s — in the scope and scale of penalization. One of the clearest indicators is the expansion of prison populations in most Western societies. In the United States, for example, the populations of state and federal prisons increased fivefold between 1970 and 1996, from less than 200,000 inmates to 1,182,000. In 1995 the United States spent some $55.1 billion on new prison construction (Taylor 1999: 186). In Canada the number of offenders in provincial institutions rose by 25 percent between 1986 and 1996, while federal inmates increased by an even more substantial 34 percent (Statistics Canada 1997). In 1999 more than twice as many offenders were admitted to prison than were placed under supervision in the community (Statistics Canada 2000a). Accompanying this expansion in the use of prison has been a radical change in the discourses used to legitimate it.

Prior to the 1970s in North America and Western Europe, crime control strategies were rooted in the welfare state, or what David Garland (2001) calls the "penal welfare model": crime prevention through social engineering and rehabilitation. However, rising crime rates and a growing economic recession in the 1980s gave way to a crime control strategy that rejected liberal claims that poverty and racism caused crime. Rehabilitation, resocialization and "correction" were replaced with a concern for the policing and minimization of risk that offenders pose to the wider community.

"Risk management" is a neo-liberal strategy that relies on actuarial techniques of quantifying and assessing the risk that offenders pose; it is concerned not with changing offenders so much as with identifying and managing a person at risk of re-offending, while minimizing the potential risk to the community (Hannah-Moffat 2002). As such, offenders are depicted as "culpable, undeserving and somewhat dangerous individuals who must be carefully controlled for the protection of the public and the prevention of future offending. Rather than clients in need of support, they are seen as risks that must be managed" (Garland 2001: 175). Under this "responsibilization" model of crime control, then, criminals are made responsible for the choices they make. Those deemed to be unable or unwilling to manage their own risk or to exercise self-discipline are "the excluded." According to Nikolas Rose (2000: 331), the excluded are those individuals who inhabit "marginalized spaces," "savage spaces" and "anti-communities" because of an adjudged lack of competence or capacity for responsible, ethical self-discipline. Criminalization is intended to "transform and to reconstruct self-reliance in the excluded" (Rose 2000: 335).

Neo-liberalism is not the only ideology that informs criminal justice system policies and practices. As Kelly Hannah-Moffat (2000: 512) notes, neo-liberal strategies of government develop alongside and operate in conjunction with other forms of political rationalities. Indeed, as "vampire capitalism" replaces welfare capitalism (Chunn 1999: 256), increasing numbers of people are left to fend for themselves without the benefit of a social safety net. According to John Pratt (1999: 149),

The subjection of economies to market forces and the cutting back of welfare programmes of assistance has led to the re-creation of risk which welfarism had alleviated — poverty, unemployment and the formation of a new indigent class of vagrants, beggars, homeless, the mentally ill with criminal tendencies who now find themselves left to roam the streets.

Added to this, the precariousness of middle-income families engenders a social anxiety that easily translates into fear of crime — and of "the excluded" — leading to calls for more law and order. Such calls for law and order solutions to crime are also aligned with demands by feminists and women's advocates, who see the criminalization of domestic violence as necessary for the safety of women and children (Schechter 1982; Martin 1983; Stanko 1985; MacLeod 1987; Walker 1990). *Neo-conservative* crime control policies — like zero-tolerance for domestic violence, "supermax" prisons (complete with special handling units for dangerous offenders), parole-release restrictions, community notification laws and boot camps for young offenders — have become the order of the day.

Under the sway of neo-conservatism, police resources and practices have been strengthened and important aspects of the trial process have been altered to ensure the success of prosecutions. For example, since 1990 most provinces in Canada have implemented zero-tolerance policies on domestic violence. The programs include mandatory charging directives to police and vigorous prosecution policies. Laureen Snider (1998) points out that zero-tolerance has led to an overrepresentation of working-class men (and women) within the "net" of the criminal justice system, especially because these people often lack the resources necessary to acquire adequate legal counsel. Snider argues that these types of criminal justice policies are a form of "compulsory criminalization" in that they target groups — such as inner-city Aboriginal people — who are incapable of resisting the power of the state.

Neo-liberalism and neo-conservatism are not incompatible discourses. To the extent that neo-liberalism marks a retreat from social welfare and publicly funded commitments to equity and social justice, it advances in tandem with neo-conservatism's more hierarchical, patriarchal, authoritarian and inequitable vision of society (Knuttila and Kubik 2000: 151). What is more, the widening inequities of the neo-liberal market economy engender not only relative deprivation amongst the poor (which gives rise to crime), but also an anxiety amongst those better off — an anxiety that breeds intolerance and greater punitiveness towards the lawbreaker (Young 1999: 8). Given their concern for tradition, order, hierarchy and authority, conservatives place emphasis on family values and the need to restore individual responsibility. This focus on family and the individual meshes well with neo-liberalism's privatization of responsibility; it is not the state — but individuals and families — who are to be held accountable. While neo-liberals advocate deregulation and market freedom, conservatives call for a more orderly, disciplined and tightly controlled society. Nevertheless, the need for more social control is not a generalized one, but instead is a much more focused and specific demand, targeted on particular groups and behaviours. As Garland (2001: 99–100) notes, "The new conservatism proclaimed a moral message exhorting everyone to return to the values of family, work, abstinence, and self-control, but in practice its real moral disciplines fastened onto the behaviour of unemployed workers, welfare mothers, immigrants, offenders, and drug users."

The new global economy has thus given rise to a particular ideology — neo-liberalism — that appears to be anti-state in its rhetoric, yet relies on an expanding criminal justice system premised on risk management and "responsibilization." In harmony with neo-conservative calls to "get tough on crime," neo-liberalism rationalizes and legitimates the dismantling of the welfare state and the retrenchment of penalization. This socio-political context forms the backdrop in which lawyering takes place.

THE AGENCY OF LAWYERS

> Lawyers know they create law and are organized to police effectively the discursive mode of this creativity ... the unanimity achieved by this policing enables them to see the law "itself" as unchanging, while in all its particulars it is infinitely malleable ... Those wishing to understand lawyers should read what they say about themselves, no matter how pompous, tedious or self-adulatory the text may be. Lawyers are not wrong about themselves. The problem is rather that they do not understand the implications of their being so right. (Cain 1994: 20)

While Maureen Cain describes how instrumental lawyers are in the legal process, the role of lawyers in criminal litigation has actually received little attention in recent critical socio-legal theory.[7] Most of the focus has been on law as an "ideological terrain" or "discursive field," and within this context solicitor-client interactions are located as one of the more mundane aspects of law. But rather than being a merely mundane aspect of law, lawyers, we maintain, are powerful social actors in the administration of criminal justice. In his theory of crime as "structured action," Messerschmidt (1997: 5) notes that structures are enacted in everyday interactions by "people who know what they are doing and how to do it." In this respect, lawyering is one form of structured action in which lawyers exercise considerable agency.

Within their prescribed roles, Crown attorneys and defence counsel are empowered by the very form of law to legitimate normative definitions of gender, race and class. For instance, the form of law is premised upon the so-called "objective standard of reasonableness." This standard is used in criminal cases to judge whether a "reasonable" person would perceive an accused as intentionally committing a criminal act or failing to act, and the Crown is obliged to prove its case against an accused "beyond a reasonable doubt." Yet such criteria may not be as objective as they appear. As Sue Lees (1994: 125) notes, "An invitation to lawyers and judges to interpret what is reasonable is an invitation to them to fall back on their common sense, their culture, their class, race and gender-based stereotypes."

To suggest that lawyers exercise agency in their work also runs counter to professional codes of conduct that stipulate a lawyer's duty and obligation to his or her client. In theory, as Naffine (1990: 125) puts it, "The lawyer is the servant to the client, he is there to interpret the law and represent the client's interests, to act according to the client's view of the matter, not his own." But as she goes on to note, this service model of the lawyer-client relationship does not accord with legal practice. Rather, the evidence suggests that in the criminal jurisdiction many lawyers regard their clients — "who are, in the main, socially disadvantaged" — as being "incapable of making decisions and so proceed to take control of the case." Naffine

(1990: 126) also finds evidence "that lawyers do not always present themselves in court in a neutral fashion, as the client's representative, but seek to establish a social distance between themselves and the individuals who hire their services."

Indeed, in his classic study of the court process, Abraham Blumberg (1967) found that the practice of law was a "confidence game" in which defence attorneys acted as "double agents," pressuring their clients to reach a plea bargain in the interest of maintaining the efficiency of court procedures. According to Blumberg, defence lawyers identify not with their clients but with other members of the court. In particular, a working relationship emerges over time between Crown attorneys and defence counsel that "overshadows the relationship between clients and their lawyers." Blumberg argued that rather than participating in an adversarial system, the defence and prosecution become co-opted by the organizational goals of the criminal justice system; they come to rely upon one another's co-operation "for their continued professional existence and so the bargaining between them tends to be reasonable rather than fierce" (Blumberg 1967: 219).

A Canadian study by Richard Ericson and Patricia Baranek (1982) reinforced Blumberg's earlier findings. They found that court actors have a vested interest in maintaining mutually beneficial relationships amongst themselves, rather than in acquiring a satisfactory outcome for the accused. The common opinion of the lawyers they interviewed was that the lawyer should make the main decisions affecting the case, because the accused did not appreciate the processes of law.

Lawyering involves agency in an even larger sense as well. Crown attorneys and defence lawyers take turns presenting their competing accounts before the presiding judge, using techniques of persuasion and negotiation in the process of arriving at the "legal truth" of the matter. Cain (1994: 33) describes lawyers as "symbol traders"; they are imaginative traders in words. In a similar vein, Anita Kalunta-Crumpton (1998: 568–569) describes lawyering as a "claims-making activity" whereby lawyers "negotiate knowledge through language in the bid to persuade." The legally relevant facts of a case form an important part of this claims-making process. Nevertheless, these are not facts that simply "speak for themselves." They require a *translation* or *deciphering*. In the process, judgments are made on the legal subjects, in terms not only of what they have done, but also of who they are and the social settings or spaces in which they move.

David Sudnow's (1968) work is instructive here (see also Worrall 1990). Sudnow uses the concept of "normal crime" to examine the criminalization process. He argues that over time prosecutors and defence lawyers develop proverbial characterizations of offences that encompass features beyond the statutory conception of an offence. These features include the typical manner in which offences are committed, the social characteristics of the persons who regularly commit them, the settings in which they occur and the type of victim often involved. In the course of their work, lawyers come to learn how to speak knowledgeably about different types of offenders and "to attribute to them personal biographies, modes of usual criminal activity, criminal histories, psychological characteristics, and social backgrounds" (Sudnow 1968: 162).

Sudnow's work carries a number of implications. The first is that — to the extent that Crown attorneys and defence lawyers come to agree on what is "normal" in their processing of criminal cases — they draw on similar stocks of knowledge for their case-building strategies. These shared understandings derive from their own specific visions or angles on the world, as well as from discourses that resonate within the wider society. Second, similar to Blumberg's (1967) analysis, the working relationship between the legal actors would appear to be not so much adversarial but more like a cartel. In this respect, Crown attorneys and defence lawyers will come to know and anticipate each other's moves as they go about the business of developing their case-building strategies. A third implication has to do with *who* lawyers are most likely to encounter in their routine work on cases. Rather than corporate embezzlers or environmental polluters, criminal lawyers are most likely to meet up with individuals whose lives are characterized by poverty, addiction and violence. The features and settings in which these individuals move will therefore come to form the conceptions of "normal crime" under which lawyers operate.

Finally, to the extent that criminal cases will be subject to a process of "normalization," when criminal cases reach the court both the illegal action and the person who commits that action are measured in relation to categories that are "already known and recognized" (Worrall 1990: 21). "Troubles are created," Sudnow (1968: 164) writes, "when offenses whose features are not readily known occur, and whose typicality is not easily constructed." Cases that do not conform to the constructions of "normal crime" will therefore require special explanation. If, for example, "normal violent crime" is premised on constructions of aggression as male activity, then what happens when the defendant is female? In these situations we might expect agency to be most evident as lawyers endeavour to constitute the identities of defendants who breach the known categories.

Sudnow's work centred on how guilty pleas are arrived at before cases go to trial. Lawyers, however, also have considerable agency during the course of a trial. Mike McConville and his colleagues explain the influence of lawyers at trial:

> It lies in their capacity to question witnesses, how hard they push certain points, their use of irony or ridicule and a whole range of rhetorical devices; the quality and thoroughness of their preparation; the astuteness of the way in which they use their knowledge not only of the law, but of jury reactions, those of a particular judge. In these ways, these agents materially affect the outcome of the cases in which they are involved and

in ways which do not relate directly to substantive rules or principles of criminal law. (McConville et al. quoted in Lacey and Wells 1998: 76)

As McConville and his colleagues point out, the role expectations of lawyers enable them to choose or exploit particular strategies to influence the trial process. Yet, to be effective, the strategies of lawyers must also resonate with the wider socio-political context in which law rests — and today's socio-political conditions enable lawyers to normalize crime-producing conditions of inner-city communities and obscure the deepening of social inequality brought on by neo-liberal economic and social policies. Law is indeed a contested terrain on which various discourses operate to produce and reproduce certain claims to "truth." As Cain (1994: 20) points out, "In all its particulars [law] is infinitely malleable."

THEORIZING LAW

To unravel two apparently conflicting readings of law — as a fair and impartial arbiter versus a site for the reproduction of gender, race and class inequalities — we have laid out a theoretical synthesis that endeavours to capture the micro- and macro-processes that inform the practice of law. Messerschmidt's (1997) theory of structured action provides us with an analytical framework for situating gender, race and class within the nexus of individual agency and social structure. Specifically, we theorize criminalization as one site of structured action in which lawyers participate in the "making" of gender, race and class inequalities. Still, to locate lawyering as structured action requires going beyond Messerschmidt's work to identify how principles of fundamental justice sit uneasily with the gendering, racializing and class-based practices in which lawyers engage, and to consider how these practices are altered by the wider socio-political context in which they unfold.

Our main interest is to understand how law works to reproduce gender, race and class inequalities in the criminalization of interpersonal violence. To guide this analysis, we need to ask:

- How do gendered, racialized and class-based presuppositions influence the strategies that lawyers use in violent crime cases?
- How is violence normalized? How and where is it made atypical?
- Is the practice of law in violent crime cases structured by neo-liberal and neo-conservative values? What influence do socio-political conditions have on efforts to address violence in society?
- How do lawyers assert their agency under the procedural constraints of due process?

Notes

1. Specific intent offences are those offences where the accused focuses on producing a particular outcome, therefore highlighting a greater element of criminal intent, whereas general intent offences are those acts that do not produce a specific consequence, as the mental element is minimal (Abell and Sheehy 1998; Verdun-Jones 2002).
2. Pre-trial conferences are becoming commonplace in non-jury cases as they present an opportunity to resolve any potential problems and prevent excessive pre-trial motions, as well as for a trial judge to assess the strategies of the Crown and defence (Cunningham and Griffiths 1997).
3. A study of criminal prosecutions in Britain reveals that plea bargains account for the outcome of over 80 percent of criminal matters (Ashworth 1995). In Canada, going to trial is the exception rather than the rule. Some 62 percent of all cases result in a finding of guilt; but 90 percent of those accused persons plead guilty as part of a plea bargain with the Crown (Statistics Canada 1999: 75).
4. See, for example, Canadian Bar Association's Code of Professional Conduct (cited in Boyd 1998: 174–77); Law Society of Manitoba, 1992.
5. Prima facie means "on the face of it." In other words, there is enough evidence to substantiate a strong likelihood of conviction at trial.
6. The *Charter of Rights and Freedoms* guarantees the right to a jury trial if the alleged offence carries a maximum sentence of more than five years' imprisonment (Cunningham and Griffiths 1997: 183).
7. Not everyone would agree with this statement. Robert Granfield (1996), for instance, begins his review essay on three books concerning the legal profession (none of which deal with criminal litigation) with the comment that "empirical investigation of lawyers has occupied a prominent site of inquiry within socio-legal studies." Nevertheless, the themes that Granfield indicates to be salient are "the relationship between the legal profession, capitalism and the state; the embeddedness of hierarchy across the distinct hemispheres of the legal profession; and the dark history of inequality within the legal profession that excluded the working class, ethnic minorities, and women from the practice of law." As we noted in the Introduction, the methodological difficulties encountered in researching the practice of law in criminal cases might account for some of this inattention.

References

Abell, Jennie, and E. Sheehy. 1998. *Criminal Law & Procedure: Cases, Context, Critique,* second edition. Toronto: Captus Press.

Blumberg, Abraham S. 1967. "The Practice of Law as a Confidence Game." *Law and Society Review* 1 (June).

Boyd, Neil. 1998. *Canadian Law: An Introduction,* second edition. Toronto: Harcourt Brace.

Brodie, Janine. 1999. "The Politics of Social Policy in the 21st Century." In D. Broad and W. Antony (eds.), *Citizens or Consumers?* Halifax: Fernwood Publishing.

Cain, Maureen. 1994. "Symbol Traders." In M. Cain and C. Harrington (eds.), *Lawyers in a Postmodern World.* New York: New York University Press.

Canadian Forum. 1997. "Index on Global Corporate Power." January/February: 48.

Chunn, Dorothy. 1999. "Feminism, Law and 'the Family': Assessing the Reform Legacy." In E. Comack (ed.), *Locating Law: Race/Class/Gender Connections*. Halifax, NS: Fernwood Publishing.

Chunn, Dorothy, and Dany Lacombe (eds.). 2000. *Law as a Gendering Practice*. Don Mills, Ontario: Oxford University Press.

Comack, Elizabeth. 1999a. "Theoretical Excursions." In E. Comack (ed.), *Locating Law: Race/Class/Gender Connections*. Halifax: Fernwood Publishing.

Connell, R.W. 1987. *Gender and Power: Society, the Person, and Sexual Politics*. Stanford, CA: Stanford University Press.

____. 1995. *Masculinities*. Cambridge: Polity.

____. 2000. *The Men and the Boys*. Berkeley: University of California Press.

Cunningham, Alison Hatch, and Curt T. Griffiths. 1997. *Canadian Criminal Justice: A Primer*. Toronto: Harcourt Brace.

Daly, Kathleen. 1994. "Criminal Law and Justice System Practices as Racist, White and Racialized." *Washington and Lee Law Review* 51, 2: 431–464.

Doe, Jane. 2003. *The Story of Jane Doe: A Book about Rape*. Toronto: Random House.

Ericson, Richard, and Patricia Baranek. 1982. *The Ordering of Justice*. Toronto: University of Toronto Press.

Foucault, Michel. 1977. *Discipline and Punish*. New York: Vintage Books.

____. 1979. *History of Sexuality: An Introduction*. Vol. 1. London: Penguin.

____. 1984. *The Foucault Reader*. Edited by Paul Rabinow. New York: Pantheon Books.

Fudge, Judy, and Harry Glasbeek. 1992. "The Politics of Rights: A Politics with Little Class." *Socio-Legal Studies* 1, 1: 45–70.

Garland, David. 2001. *Culture of Control*. New York: Oxford University Press.

Granfield, Robert. 1996. "Lawyers and Power: Reproduction and Resistance in the Legal Profession." *Law and Society Review* 30, 1.

Griffiths, Curt T., and Simon Verdun-Jones. 1994. *Canadian Criminal Justice*, second edition. Toronto: Harcourt Brace.

Hamilton, A.C., and C.M. Sinclair. 1991. *Report of the Aboriginal Justice Inquiry of Manitoba*. 2 vols. Winnipeg: Queen's Printer.

Hannah-Moffat, Kelly. 2000. "Prisons That Empower: Neo-liberal Governance in Canadian Women's Prisons." *The British Journal of Criminology* 40: 510–551.

____. 2002. "Governing through Need: The Hybridization of Risk and Need in Penality." Paper presented to the annual meetings of the British Society of Criminology, Keele University, England.

Henry, Frances, and Carol Taylor. 2002. *Discourses of Domination: Racial Bias in the Canadian English-Language Press*. Toronto: University of Toronto Press.

Howarth, David. 2000. *Discourse*. Buckingham: Open University Press.

Hunt, Allan. 1976. "Law, State and Class Struggle." *Marxism Today* 20: 178–187.

Kalunta-Crumpton, Anita. 1998. "The Prosecution and Defence of Black Defendants in Drug Trials." *British Journal of Criminology* 38, 4: 561–590.

Kellner, Douglas. 1989. *Critical Theory, Marxism and Modernity*. Baltimore: Johns Hopkins University Press.

Kerstetter, Steve. 2002. "Top 50% of Canadians Hold 94.4% of Wealth, Bottom Half 5.6%." *The CCPA Monitor* 9, 6: 1 and 7.

Kline, Marlee. 1994. "The Colour of Law: Ideological Representations of First Nations in Legal Discourse." *Social and Legal Studies* 3: 451–476.

Knoll, Patrick. 1994. *Criminal Law Defenses,* second edition. Scarborough, ON: Carswell.

Knuttila, Murray, and Wendy Kubik. 2000. *State Theories: Classical, Global and Feminist Perspectives,* third edition. Halifax: Fernwood Publishing.

Lacey, Nicola, and Celia Wells. 1998. *Reconstructing Criminal Law: Critical Perspectives on Crime and the Criminal Process,* second edition. London: Butterworths.

Larner, Wendy. 2000. "Neo-liberalism: Policy, Ideology, Governmentality." *Studies in Political Economy* 63 (Autumn): 5–25.

Law Society of Manitoba. 1992. *Special Committee on Disciplinary Procedures.* Winnipeg, Manitoba.

Lees, Sue. 1994. "Lawyers' Work as Constitutive of Gender Relations." In M. Cain and C. Harrington (eds.), *Lawyers in a Postmodern World.* New York: New York University Press.

MacIntosh, D.A. 1995. *Fundamentals of the Criminal Justice System,* second edition. Toronto: Carswell.

MacLeod, Linda. 1987. *Battered But Not Beaten: Preventing Wife Battering in Canada.* Ottawa: Canadian Advisory Council on the Status of Women.

Martin, Sheilah L. 1993. "Proving Gender Bias in the Law and the Legal System." In J. Brockman and D. Chunn (eds.), *Investigating Gender Bias: Law, Courts and the Legal Profession.* Toronto: Thompson Educational Publishing.

McBarnet, Doreen. 1981. *Conviction: Law, the State and the Construction of Justice.* London: Macmillan.

Messerschmidt, James. 1997. *Crime as Structured Action: Gender, Race, Class, and Crime in the Making.* Thousand Oaks, CA: Sage.

Naffine, Ngaire. 1990. *The Law and the Sexes: Explorations in Feminist Jurisprudence.* Sydney: Allen and Unwin.

Pomerant, David, and Glen Gimour. 1997. *A Survey of the Preliminary Inquiry in Canada.* Ottawa: Department of Justice.

Pratt, John. 1999. "Governmentality, Neo-Liberalism and Dangerousness." In R. Smandych (ed.). *Governable Places: Readings on Governmentality and Crime Control.* Brookfield U.S.A.: Aldershot.

Proloux, Michel, and David Layton. 2001. *Ethics and Canadian Criminal Law.* Toronto: Irwin Law.

Razack, Sherene. 1998. *Looking White People in the Eye: Gender, Race, and Culture in Courtrooms and Classrooms.* Toronto: Oxford University Press.

____. 2000. "Gendered Racial Violence and Spatialized Justice: The Murder of Pamela George." *Canadian Journal of Law and Society* 15, 2: 91–130.

____. 2002. *Race, Space and the Law: Unmapping a White Settler Society.* Toronto: Between the Lines.

Rose, Nikolas. 2000. "Government and Control." *British Journal of Criminology* 40: 321–339.

Schechter, Susan. 1982. *Women and Male Violence: The Visions and Struggles of the Battered Woman's Movement.* Boston: South End Press.

Smart. Carol. 1989. *Feminism and the Power of Law.* London: Routledge.

____. 1992. "The Woman of Legal Discourse." *Social and Legal Studies* 1: 29–44

____. 1995. *Law, Crime and Sexuality.* New York: Routledge.

Snider, Laureen. 1998. "Towards Safer Societies." *The British Journal of Criminology* 38, 1 (Winter): 1–38.

_____. 1999. "Relocating Law: Making Corporate Crime Disappear." In E. Comack (ed.), *Locating Law: Race/Class/Gender Connections.* Halifax: Fernwood Publishing.

Stanko, E. 1985. *Intimate Intrusions: Women's Experience of Male Violence.* London: Routledge and Keagan Paul.

Statistics Canada. 1997. *Juristat* 17, 9. Ottawa: Canadian Centre for Justice Statistics.

_____. 1999. *Crime Statistics in Canada.* 19. 9. Ottawa: Canadian Centre for Justice Statistics.

_____. 2000. *Adult Correctional Services in Canada.* 21. 5. Ottawa: Canadian Centre for Justice Statistics.

Sudnow, David. 1968. "Normal Crimes: Sociological Aspects of the Penal Code." In E. Rubington and M. Weinberg (eds.), *Deviance: The Interactionist Perspective.* London: Macmillan.

Taylor, Ian. 1999. *Crime in Context: A Critical Criminology of Market Societies.* Cambridge: Polity Press.

Verdun-Jones, Simon. 2002. *Criminal Law in Canada: Cases, Questions and the Code,* third edition. Toronto: Harcourt Brace.

Walker, Gillian A. 1990. *Family Violence and the Women's Movement: The Conceptual Politics of Struggle.* Toronto: University of Toronto Press.

Worrall, Anne. 1990. *Offending Women: Female Lawbreakers and the Criminal Justice System.* New York: Routledge and Kegan Paul.

Young, Jock. 1999. *The Exclusive Society.* London: Sage Publications.

Case Law

R. v. Daviault. 1994. 158 Supreme Court Reports 63.

RACE AND PRIVILEGE

Chapter 3

UNDERSTANDING RACE AND RACIALIZATION

Elizabeth Comack

From: *Racialized Policing: Aboriginal People's Encounters with the Police*, pp. 18–19 (reprinted with permission).

UNDERSTANDING RACE AND RACIALIZATION

The notion of race is not as straightforward as it might first seem. Its meaning has changed over time. When the term first appeared in the English language in the early sixteenth century, it was used primarily to distinguish between differ-ent nation-states, such as England and France. In the English case, for instance, Anglo-Saxons were described as a "race" of people (Miles 1989: 31; Banton 1987). With the growth of scientific inquiry in the nineteenth century, race came to be understood as a means of demarcating different groups on the basis of their phenotypic characteristics (especially their skin colour). Science was used to demonstrate "not only the number and characteristics of each 'race,' but also a hierarchical relationship between them" (Miles 1989: 32). These biologically based categorizations soon extended to include a range of intellectual, physical and social capabilities of each group (such as intelligence, industriousness and criminality). As one example, social Darwinism, in conjunction with its claims of an evolutionary process of "survival of the fittest," conceived of original races as pure and biologically determined. These supposed innate or essential "differences" between groups of people provided the basis for establishing a hierarchy of races, each having a variable capacity for "civilization" (Miles 1993: 2). Typically, white Europeans were positioned at the top of this racial hierarchy, thereby providing a justification for their supposed racial superiority and the corresponding racial inequality experienced by other racialized groups.

This view of race as a biological category or an ascribed characteristic on which difference is based informed the emerging social science disciplines, including criminology. Nineteenth-century criminologists Cesare Lombroso and William Ferrero, for instance, adopted social Darwinism to argue that criminals were primitive, "atavistic" throwbacks to an earlier stage of evolution. Atavism was associated with moral inferiority; atavists were "innately driven to act as a normal ape or savage would but such behaviour is deemed criminal in our civilized society" (Gould 1981, cited in Linden 2000: 187). In Lombroso and Ferrero's view, Black people constituted an "inferior race." Because they supposedly had not advanced as far along the evolutionary continuum, Black people were considered to be more prone to the "savagery" represented by criminal activity.

During the first half of the twentieth century, advances in scientific knowledge demonstrated conclusively that the world's population could not legitimately be categorized into distinct, biologically based racial groups (Miles 1989; Miles and Torres 2007). Nonetheless, the idea of race continued to hold strong purchase in public discourse. The term became part of common-sense understandings, as both a way of demarcating groups of people on the basis of features such as skin colour, culture, religion and language, and a way of indicating corresponding ways of acting on these distinctions.

Several writers argue that because the concept of race has been so soundly disproven to be a distinct, biologically based entity — that is, that there are no "races" per se — then our focus should be on the meanings that are attached to it. In other words, race is not a biological category but a *social construction*. Viewing race as socially constructed — in effect, as a discourse or way of making sense — draws attention to its variable social meanings and to the social relations reproduced in the process. As Robert Miles (2000: 137) notes, race is "an idea created by human beings in certain historical and material conditions and is used to represent the world in certain ways." The idea of "race," then, is one of the ways (gender is another) in which individuals are differentiated from each other.

In Miles's (1989: 75) terms, differentiating between people on the basis of race is to engage in a process of *racialization*: "those instances where social relations between people have been structured by the signification of human biological characteristics in such a way as to define and construct differentiated social collectivities." Racialization, therefore, involves the production of difference; it is the process of constructing racial categories, identities and meanings. With its root in a verb as opposed to a noun, racialization has the advantage of shifting the focus from the people being racialized to those *doing* the racializing. As George Dei (2009: 237) explains, "The process of racializing is thus external and strategic, and it is not the responsibility of the person who is targeted." Emphasis is on the doing or making of difference rather than the categories of difference in and of themselves. Attending to this process of racializing leads to yet another set of questions. Why do particular meanings of race become socially significant, and what are the historical and contextual processes and practices through which individuals, groups and nations become racially differentiated?

Engaging in racialization, recognizing difference between people, does not in and of itself constitute a problem. Difference can be acknowledged and celebrated without imposing hierarchy. Rather, it is the attachment of negative meanings to this difference that is problematic. In these terms, the idea of race becomes *ideological* when it is used as a rationalization for the dominance of one racial group over another (Miles 2000: 137); in other words, when it is used to promote racism.

Racism and Othering

Miles (1989) defines *racism* as "ideas that delineate group boundaries by reference to race or to real or alleged biological characteristics, and which attribute groups so racialized with other negatively evaluated characteristics." But more than this, racism is a social practice connected to *power*; it is the use of racial categories to define an Other. The idea of race, in this sense, is an effect of power. This effect is evidenced when the process of racialization becomes a "representational process of defining an Other" (Miles 1989: 75).

It is when racialization involves "Othering," then, that racism occurs. At its core, this process of Othering entails establishing a binary between Us and Them. As Stuart Hall (1997: 258) elaborates, the practice "facilitates the 'binding' or bonding together of all of Us who are 'normal' into one 'imagined community'; and it sends into symbolic exile all of Them — 'the Others' — who are in some way different — 'beyond the pale.'" Othering, therefore, is the exercise of a particular form of power by those who are racially privileged. Allan Johnson (2005: 103) explains "privilege" as a position that

> grants the cultural authority to make judgments about others and to have those judgments stick. It allows people to define reality and to have prevailing definitions of reality fit their experience. Privilege means being able to decide who gets taken seriously, who receives attention, who is accountable to whom and for what.

Drawing attention to racial privilege — to the ability to make judgments about Others "stick" — showcases how those on the privileged side of the "Us versus

Them" dualism are able to avoid such markings. In other words, in societies in which white people are the dominant group, whiteness goes unmarked. Whiteness becomes the unacknowledged norm or standard by which all Others are measured. As Richard Dyer notes:

> Research ... repeatedly shows that in Western representation whites are overwhelmingly and disproportionately predominant, have the central and elaborated roles, and above all are placed as the norm, the ordinary, the standard. Whites are everywhere in representation. Yet precisely because of this and their placing as norm they seem not to be represented to themselves as whites but as people who are variously gendered, classed, sexualized and abled. At the level of racial representation, in other words, *whites are not of a certain race, they're just the human race.* (Dyer 1997: 3; emphasis added)

According to this viewpoint, racism comes to be understood as a particular discourse or ideology that offers an explanation of how the world works. Racism organizes, preserves and perpetuates the power structures of a society (Henry et al. 2009); it rationalizes, legitimizes and sustains patterns of inequality (Barrett 1987: 7). Hall explains that racist ideas are

> not a set of false pleas which swim around in the head. They're not a set of mistaken perceptions. They have their basis in real material conditions of existence. They arise because of concrete problems of different classes and groups in society. Racism represents the attempt ideologically to construct those conditions, contradictions, and problems in such a way that they can be dealt with and deflected in the same moment. (Hall 1978: 35)

Racism, therefore, involves more than just holding particular negative beliefs or attitudes about certain groups in society or acting towards individuals on the basis of racial stereotypes. Racism has a systemic basis. Racist discourse not only has its basis in material conditions but is also supported by — and reinforces — institutional and social practices in society that privilege certain racialized groups over the Others.

Racism does not exist in isolation from other social relations; specifically, those based on gender and class. In combination, race, gender and class provide the basis for our location in society; they are also factors that mediate our experiences. Speaking about the connections between race and gender, for instance, Patricia Monture-Angus (1995: 177–78) comments:

> It is very difficult for me to separate what happens to me because of my

gender and what happens to me because of my race and culture. My world is not experienced in a linear and compartmentalized way. I experience the world simultaneously as Mohawk and as woman ... To artificially separate my gender from my race and culture forces me to deny the way I experience the world.

Rather than as compartmentalized or additive factors, then, race, gender and class need to be understood as interlocking features of our social existence; they operate in relation to each other and inform people's perceptions, interactions and experiences.

References

Banton, M. 1987. "The Classification of Races in Europe and North America: 1700–1850." *International Social Science Journal* 39, 1.

Barrett. S.R. 1987. *Is God a Racist? The Right Wing in Canada.* Toronto: University of Toronto Press.

Dei, G. 2009. "Speaking Race: Silence, Salience, and the Politics of Anti-Racist Scholarship." In M. Wallis and A. Fleras (eds.), *The Politics of Race in Canada.* Toronto: Oxford University Press.

Dyer, R. 1997. *White.* London: Routledge.

Hall, S. 1978. "Racism and Reaction." In *Five Views of Multi-Racial Britain.* London: Commission for Racial Equality.

____. 1997. "The Spectacle of the 'Other.'" In S. Hall (ed.), *Representation: Cultural Representations and Signifying Practices.* Milton Keynes: Open University.

Henry, F., C. Tator, W. Mattis, and T. Rees. 2009. "The Ideology of Racism." In M. Wallis and A. Feras (eds.), *The Politics of Race in Canada.* Toronto: Oxford University Press.

Johnson, A. 2005. "Privilege as Paradox." In P. Rothenberg (ed.), *White Privilege: Essential Readings on the Other Side of Racism.* New York: Worth Publishers.

Linden, R. 2000. *Criminology: A Canadian Perspective,* fourth edition. Toronto: Harcourt Brace.

Miles, R. 1989. *Racism.* Milton Keynes: Open University Press.

____. 1993. *Racism after 'Race Relations.'* London: Routledge.

____. 2000. "Apropos the Idea of 'Race'... Again." In L. Black and J. Solomos (eds.), *Theories of Race and Racism.* London: Routledge.

Miles, R., and R. Torres. 2007. "Does 'Race' Matter? Transatlantic Perspectives on Racism after 'Race Relations.'" In T. Das Gupta, C.E. James, R. Maaka, G-E. Galabuzi, and C. Andersen (eds.), *Race and Racialization: Essential Readings.* Toronto: Canadian Scholars Press.

Monture-Angus, P. 1995. *Thunder in My Soul: A Mohawk Woman Speaks.* Halifax: Fernwood Publishing.

____. 2000. "Gendered Racialized Violence and Spatialized Justice: The Murder of Pamela George." *Canadian Journal of Law and Society* 15, 2.

Chapter 4

CRIMINALIZING RACE

Wendy Chan

From: *Marginality and Condemnation: A Critical Introduction to Criminology*, third edition, pp. 247–267 (reprinted with permission).

Recent efforts to monitor racial bias in the "carding" practices of the Toronto police force highlight the troubled history that racialized communities have with criminal justice institutions (Rankin and Winsa 2013). Carding, or street checks, is a police practice that involves stopping, questioning and documenting people in mostly non-criminal encounters. A study by the *Toronto Star* paper found that Black people in Toronto were more likely than white people to be carded in 2013, even though the overall number of people carded had dropped from previous years (Rankin and Winsa 2013). Critics contend that this is evidence of systemic discrimination. In response, the Toronto police force claims they are working hard to eliminate racial bias from police practices.

The above example highlights how the issue of race and criminal justice in Canada is a complex one, shaped to a large extent by historical policies and practices. In the present day, the issue of race and criminal justice simmers in the background, punctuated at times by well-publicized events such as the mistreatment of undocumented migrants to Canada or the tensions between Aboriginal communities and the state. Unlike the United States, Canada has not seen the same level of antagonism between racialized communities and the criminal justice system. However, this is not to say that the issue of racism and criminal justice in

Canada is unproblematic. Perceptions and allegations of discriminatory treatment of racialized groups have been and continues to be commonplace, with problems of racial profiling, over-incarceration and inadequate responses to victimization, to name a few, receiving ongoing attention by policy-makers and critical scholars.

This chapter unpacks the complex relationship between race and criminal justice in Canada. My starting point is the recognition that race and racism in Canada are still very relevant. Contrary to claims that we now live in a post-racial society, there remains unresolved tensions between racialized minorities and the state. Within the criminal justice system, racialized Canadians, particularly Black and Aboriginal Canadians, continue to experience higher levels of criminalization and incarceration. Stereotypes about who is more likely to commit crimes or engage in deviant behavior (e.g., "driving while Black," "shopping while Black," "flying while brown") remain strong reference points in shaping public perceptions about crime, dangerousness, fear and safety. Mainstream media have reinforced specific messages about race and criminality, making it easier to justify the punitive treatment of racialized minorities. Furthermore, there is a deep reluctance to acknowledge that these problems are structurally rooted, rather than the work of a "few bad apples" in the justice system. The legacy of colonization and racial discrimination in Canada has shaped contemporary processes of criminal justice, with racial injustices reflecting the differential power relations between white and non-white groups over time. Thus, the unequal treatment of racialized minorities in the criminal justice system is not accidental. It is the result of both conscious and unconscious practices, individual choice, institutional dynamics and systemic practices. As Omi and Winant (1994) observe, the state is inherently racial in that it does not stand above racial conflicts, but is thoroughly immersed in racial contests. Racial injustices in the criminal justice system are a reflection of the wider society. Therefore, recognizing how racial discrimination is structurally embedded in the justice system is the first step towards eradicating the harms and injustices that stand in the way of social and political equality for racialized minorities in Canada.

This chapter is organized around three key sections. In the first section, I examine contemporary debates on race and crime in Canada and the different intellectual approaches that have shaped the research in this area. For example, the positivist tradition, which uses the concept of race as a socio-demographic variable to describe victims and offenders in empirical research, has played a significant role in developing ideas about crime and criminals. I examine the limitations of this approach as well as the problems of conducting research on race and crime in Canada when there is limited access to statistical data on the racial and/or ethnic background of victims and offenders. I explore the problems associated with conceptualizing race as a fixed identity, and I situate the impact of these problems in the context of the criminal justice system. For example, the tendency to view some racial groups as more prone to criminal behaviour than others is one consequence to emerge from "race thinking." Critical approaches to race and crime emerged as a counter to the positivist tradition. I highlight the key issues critical criminologists have focused on in striving for racial equality and anti-racist practices in the criminal justice system. This section ends with a brief discussion of why many critical scholars have turned to the concept of racialization to frame discussions about racism and criminal justice in Canada.

Section two critically examines racialized constructions of crime in Canada. Drawing on a range of different examples, I demonstrate how the practice, discourse and policies of criminal justice have been shaped by racial stereotypes and myths or misperceptions about racialized groups. As many critical criminologists have pointed out, definitions of crime and criminal behaviour focus on street crimes or property crimes rather than corporate or white-collar crimes. Typically, racialized minorities are overrepresented in so-called street crimes. This creates the perception that danger or threat is strongly associated with racialized individuals and groups. Increased police attention and harsher sentences are then justified in the name of crime control.

The final section of this chapter explores the other side of this dynamic — the ways in which processes of criminalization target racialized individuals and groups. While some scholars have highlighted how crime is racialized in Canada, other scholars add that racialized groups are also more likely to have their acts and behaviours labelled as deviant and/or criminal. As such, they are at greater risk of being policed, investigated and prosecuted. Practices of racial profiling, over-policing and increased detention have resulted in the disproportionate representation of Aboriginal people, racialized Canadians and non-citizens, migrants and refugees in the criminal justice system. The effects of criminalization on racialized people has been devastating — they are widely demonized as the cause of chaos and disorder, and they have been denied basic human rights. Paying attention to patterns of criminalization will expose how racism is embedded in criminal justice practices, how it influences decision-making and reinforces stereotypes about racialized minorities.

Throughout this chapter, race is understood to be a socially constructed category where meanings are not fixed, but contested and transformed through political struggle. The concept of race has always been problematic, and many scholars use the term in inverted commas to highlight the complex, political and contested nature of is usage (Mason 2000). Some scholars have argued for the use of ethnicity instead. I believe that the term is still analytically relevant. When used as an analytical term rather than a descriptive one, it highlights the power relationships that have shaped contemporary social relations in Canada, even while still recognizing its problematic status.

Race also intersects with other social characteristics, such as gender, class and sexual orientation, to produce racialized positions. Where possible, I use an intersectional approach to raise awareness of the complexity in the lives of racialized minorities. For example, many Aboriginal women who have been battered choose not to call authorities for help because they do not want to further criminalize male Aboriginal members of their community. Their responses differ from many battered non-Aboriginal women due to the convergence of factors such as gender, race and social class. By taking a wider lens to the study of race and crime, I hope to capture the nuances of these convergences in influencing crime and victimization as well as criminal justice policy and practice.

THE CONSTRUCTION OF THE RACE-CRIME PROBLEM IN CANADA

Mainstream criminological research on race and crime conceptualizes race as a socio-demographic variable. Much of this research is positivist in orientation, with a focus on highlighting the crime patterns of different racial and ethnic groups and comparing them to other social groups to locate causative factors. One of the central claims of mainstream criminologists is that criminals are different from non-criminals and that it is these differences, "criminogenic properties," that compels them into crime. These differences can include having different biological or genetic features such as low IQ or testosterone levels, or they may be different social conditions such as poverty, education and age. Once these differences are identified, and an individual has gone through intervention, treatment and reform, that person can be steered away from deviant and criminal behavior. This body of scholarship typically relies on official statistics to provide victim and offender profiles or to establish the crime rates and incarceration rates of a particular racial group (Trevethan and Rastin 2004). In Canada, the most discussed racialized group in the criminal justice system is Aboriginal people (Wood and Griffiths 1996). This is likely attributed to their history of being overrepresented in the criminal justice system. Other racialized groups, such as Black Canadians and immigrants, have received sporadic attention from Canadian criminologists (Roberts and Doob 1997; Gordon and Nelson 1996).

There are many limitations to treating race as an independent variable in criminological research. While positivist criminology offers a detailed picture of who is involved in the criminal justice system, there are also fears that the research creates false pathologies that may be used to naturalize and reify racialized people as inherently criminal (Phillips and Bowling 2003). For example, official crime statistics have been heavily criticized for its overrepresentation of marginalized and vulnerable social groups. Furthermore, the racial categories found in official statistics are often adopted at face value, raising further questions about the role of these statistics in perpetuating racial inequalities. Seeing some racialized groups as more criminogenic than others not only reinforces negative racial stereotypes, but also leads to racialized groups being blamed for high levels of crime and delinquency. Methodologically, race scholars have pointed out how the classification of different racial groups is inconsistently defined (Mann 1993), and they question whether or not humankind can be divided according to skin colour. As geneticist James King (1981) explains, formulating a typology of races is an arbitrary exercise because there is no objective (biological) criteria for dividing humans in this way. Thus, attempts to develop a racial classification scheme cannot be easily divorced from the assumptions about human origins and group inferiority and superiority that inform these classification systems.

Efforts to move beyond crude and essentialist categorizations of racialized minorities have been taken up by critical criminologists who have adopted a different approach. Contrary to the positivist tradition, these criminologists regard race as the product of social interactions and argue that racial categories are not fixed and immutable, but fluid and subject to change. That is, race is a social idea where racial categories and meanings are constructed by the dominant group in society as one way to mark difference. Racial differences are used to justify discriminatory treatment and the differential allocation of rights and resources. Much of the work of critical criminologists centres on examining whether or not the treatment of offenders and victims by the criminal justice system is racially biased and highlighting differential trial outcomes and overrepresentation or underrepresentation in the prisons, for example. Comack's (2012) study of policing of Aboriginal communities is exemplary. She highlights how the relationship between Aboriginal people and the justice system is shaped by colonization, decades of mistreatment and inequality. As a result, Aboriginal people do not trust the police and are reluctant to cooperate with the justice system, while police officers have been accused of over-criminalizing Aboriginal people. For critical scholars, then, racial prejudice and discrimination are key factors in explaining the differential criminal justice treatment and outcomes of non-white offenders and victims. Tanovich (2008: 656) questions whether or not fundamental justice is possible for Aboriginal and racialized communities given the limited impact of reforms on racial injustice in Canada.

Whether consciously or unconsciously, criminological research has reproduced racial hierarchies, but it has also been the site of resistance. For example, although historically there were criminal anthropologists such as Lombroso arguing that criminals were evolutionary throwbacks and the "white races [were] the triumph of the human species" (quoted in Miller 1996: 185), others such as Bonger were challenging the fascist movement and the superiority of Nordic peoples (Hawkins

1995: 23). Today, similar tensions within the study of race and crime persist, albeit in a more nuanced form. Positivist criminologists continue to analyze crime using official statistics and racial classification schemes, but they are cautious about claiming that racialized groups are more criminogenic as they recognize that unequal treatment affects the overrepresentation of racialized groups in the justice system. Critiques of biological determinism by critical criminologists also persist, with the added recognition that racial categories are unstable and that crime and definitions of crime are subject to change. Indeed, as they have pointed out, the socially constructed nature of both race and crime tells us more about systems of control and regulation and how the criminal justice system is used by the powerful to dominate and subordinate the powerless than it does about racial groups.

It is within this context of criminological scholarship that an ongoing debate has been taking place in Canada over whether or not the government should even be collecting data on race and crime. The Canadian government has never systematically collected race-based data in the criminal justice system, and as a result, it has been more difficult to provide a detailed portrait of the relationship between race and crime in Canada. While there is a wealth of information in the U.K. and the U.S. on this topic, there is much less research available in Canada. The only data that is routinely collected in this area are federal imprisonment rates for Aboriginal people. During the 1990s, Canadian criminologists were engaged in a lively debate over whether or not statistics on race and crime should be collected. Scholars such as Thomas Gabor (1994) argued that restricting access to this information is both "alarmist" and "paternalistic" and that the public should not be denied access to information about their security and safety (Gabor 1994: 154). Furthermore, race-based crime statistics can be used to challenge racial inequality by invalidating biological explanations of crime, by identifying areas of criminal justice practices that are in need of reform and by identifying problems that disproportionately impact minority communities (Wortley 1999). Scholars who support the continued ban on collecting raced-based crime statistics state that racism in the justice system can be studied without the need for race-based crime statistics (Johnston 1994). They express a number of concerns, such as fears that the police would not be able to collect reliable and accurate data, that the accuracy of race-based crime statistics would be hampered by the changing definitions of race and crime, that the public will misinterpret the data and that racism and discrimination against minority groups will increase as a result of this data (Johnston 1994; Roberts 1994). Instead of an all-or-nothing approach, Wortley (1999) suggests several compromises such as restricting who would have access to the data and the type of analysis that would be permitted with the data.

Successive governments in Canada have not indicated any interest in changing the status quo. What has changed since the 1990s is that many minority groups are now calling for the collection of race-based crime statistics in order to redress racial discrimination in the justice system (Owusu-Bempah and Millar 2010) because they recognize that the lack of race-based crime data is a double-edged sword: while not collecting data may prevent further racism and discrimination from taking place, the absence of race-based data also makes understanding racial discrimination and mistreatment by criminal justice officials much more difficult. More recently, Paul Millar and Akwasi Owusu-Bempah (2011) have made a spirited call for change, arguing that race-based crime data is necessary to conduct quantitative anti-racism research. They attempt to put more pressure on policy-makers to revisit the ban on data collection by claiming that criminal justice institutions in Canada are deliberately suppressing race-based crime data and that this is an attempt to avoid accountability and to "whitewash" the criminal justice system. Indeed, in this post-September 11 context, where racism has reached new heights in many minority communities due to fears around national security, previous concerns that race-based crime data would exacerbate or act as a justification for discriminatory behavior appear moot. Racial profiling, for example, is now routinely practised by law enforcement agents, and many minority communities have suffered grave injustices (e.g., Arab and Muslim communities) without the ability to counter official claims and negative public perceptions due to the lack of data available.

Despite the absence of race-based crime statistics in Canada, criminologists have produced a small, but rich, body of qualitative scholarship examining topics such as racial profiling (Satzewich and Shaffir 2009), the criminal justice treatment of racialized Canadians (Anand 2000) and perceptions of crime and justice by minority communities (Oriola and Adeyanju 2011). Intellectual interest in this area of study remains strong, particularly by critical scholars carrying out research examining the treatment of racial minorities as an index of social control and how the criminal justice system is used to perpetuate racial inequality (Gordon 2006; Nelson 2011).

Yet critical researchers are increasingly wary of using the concepts "race" and "crime," with some scholars opting instead for terms like racialization and criminalization. As mentioned earlier, one significant consequence of this way of thinking has been the tendency to view entire communities as predisposed for criminal behavior by virtue of their racial identity. Furthermore, others suggest that race as an analytical concept in criminal justice is too limiting. Walsh and Yun (2011) argue that it would be more fruitful to consider race as both a biological reality *and* a social construction. Although there is no scientific basis to the category of race, the concept of race still exists and continues to be used in official and unofficial discourse. They state that "we cannot change the underlying reality, but we can certainly change our beliefs about the representation of that reality" (Walsh and Yun 2011: 1281).

An emphasis on racialization draws attention to the process in which racial understandings are formed and re-formed in the creation of racialized positions, thus recognizing that social understandings and the implications and consequences of race change over time. For example, southern and eastern Europeans have been deracialized and assigned to the broad category of white. As Satzewich observes, "Many European groups that are now routinely thought of as white were far from being considered white as little as two or three generations ago ... Groups from the southern and eastern periphery of Europe were particularly prone to racialized othering" (2000: 277). Yet Omi and Winant (1994) are careful to point out that the creation and characterization of racial categories is a variable process that has played out differently for different groups. For example, Aboriginal people in Canada were subjected to harsh assimilation policies, and Asian and Black people were excluded from Canada; more recently, Arab and Muslim Canadians are labelled as terrorists. Different processes of racialization have resulted in a racial hierarchy that sees whites on top and minorities, particularly Aboriginal and African/Black Canadians, at the bottom (Omi and Winant 1994). In the context of criminal justice, decades of disproportionate representation of Aboriginal people in Canadian prisons is evidence that a certain type of "race thinking" makes this phenomenon possible. The state's capacity to wield such power over a certain segment of society demonstrates its ability to reproduce racial hierarchies and maintain racial hegemony. Thus, even if race has no essence, racism persists, and mapping out the complex manifestations of racism in the criminal justice system by highlighting the power differentials implicated in the practice of racism is a central feature of racialization.

Within Canadian society, racism is often either denied through claims that we live in a multicultural society and race no longer matters, or it is held to be an individual problem, rather than a structural or systemic issue. Where racial inequality occurs, it is often regarded as a problem "of the people who fail to take responsibility for their own lives" (Brown et al. 2005: vii) rather than an institutional problem. This view can be found across many social institutions in Canada, from police chiefs denying that racial profiling occurs (Satzewich and Shaffir 2009), to politicians labelling asylum seekers coming to Canada as illegitimate or illegal (Levine-Rasky 2012), to the mainstream media virtually ignoring the topic of racism altogether (Décoste 2013a). Yet, when you commit a crime, as Rachel Décoste (2013b) notes, your race matters. Compare the treatment of Rob Ford, ex-mayor of Toronto, or Mike Duffy, a Conservative senator, two public figures caught in crime-related scandals, to the treatment of racialized offenders, whom the previous minister of citizenship and immigration, Jason Kenny, would like to "deport without delay" from Canada (Décoste 2013b). In contrast, there has not been any discussion of a similarly punitive treatment for Rob Ford or Mike Duffy. For many race scholars in Canada, this double standard comes as no surprise. The multicultural discourse in

Canada celebrates a tolerance of Aboriginal and racialized minorities while ignoring acts of colonial violence, genocide, residential schools and racist immigration policies. Respect for racial differences are based on white decisions and their definition of what are *allowable* differences (O'Connell 2010: 540). While ethnic food and cultural celebrations are welcomed, social and economic demands are not. As Bannerji (1997: 35) states, "Multiculturalism is itself a vehicle for racialization. It establishes Anglo-Canadian culture as the ethnic core culture while 'tolerating' and hierarchically arranging others around it as 'multiculture.'" Dua, Razack and Warner (2005) add that national mythologies operate to sustain Canada's vision of itself as a white nation, even though many urban centres like Vancouver and Toronto are increasingly moving towards a majority-minority population.

Problems of racial discrimination in Canada are more subtle today compared to historical practices, but they have not disappeared. The everyday racism found in body language or tone of voice is one that many racialized Canadians experience. As one Ontario community organizer noted, "Racism is prevalent, persisting and perpetually growing [in Canada]" (Douglas and Rosella 2013). In the criminal justice system, racial discrimination takes on many forms — from not being able to access services and programs, to harsher sentences and deaths in police custody. The paucity of research in Canada has allowed culturally produced images of crime and criminals, by mainstream media in particular, to reinforce racial stereotypes and myths about crime and victimization. Like many Western states, criminal justice in Canada is heavily racialized.

RACIALIZED CONSTRUCTIONS OF CRIME IN CANADA

In Ontario, allegations and counter-allegations of a race problem in the justice system led to a public inquiry into the issue of systemic racism in the criminal justice system in the mid-1990s. The Commission's key findings were that Black males in Ontario were significantly more likely to be stopped by the police, to receive harsher treatment by judges, to be refused bail or release before trial and to be given a prison sentence than whites or other racialized minorities (Commission on Systemic Racism in the Ontario Criminal Justice System 1995). Other studies show that close to one-quarter of those incarcerated in Canada are Aboriginal, even though Aboriginal people make up only 4 percent of the population. Black and Aboriginal inmates are dramatically overrepresented in Canada's maximum security federal penitentiaries and segregation placements — they are also more likely to have force used on them, to incur a disproportionate number of disciplinary charges, to be released later in their sentences and to have less access to day or full parole (Correctional Investigator of Canada 2013).

Despite these findings, the problem of crime has been, and continues to be, framed primarily as a problem of deviant, minority communities. Whether it is the suggestion that these groups are "innately criminal" or that they possess deviant cultural values, public anxieties about crime and chaos fuel the ongoing hostility about their presence and alleged criminal tendencies. Crime is racialized when individual behaviours are attached to the traits of a wider racial community or group such that "whole categories of phenotypically similar individuals are rendered pre-criminal and morally suspect" (Covington 1995: 547). In Canada, the pool of people that comprise the "dangerous classes" has been, and continues to be, drawn largely from racial and ethnic communities, thereby allowing for their over-policing and subsequent disproportionate representation in the criminal justice system (Roach 1996).

Monaghan documents how Aboriginal leaders at the end of the nineteenth century were subjected to a campaign of surveillance and labelled as "good" or "bad" characters, depending on their willingness to assimilate and promote the colonialist project of expansionism (2013: 499). Fears of Indigenous danger and backwardness led to Aboriginal activities being problematized as suspect and dangerous and to the construction of Aboriginal leaders as abnormal and deviant because they threatened the advancement of settler colonialism with their demands for rights and dignity (Monaghan 2013). Similarly, Mosher's (1996) historical study of Black offenders in Ontario at the turn of the twentieth century found that they were more likely to be imprisoned for public order offences such as prostitution or vagrancy and to receive harsher sentences than white offenders. D'Arcy's (2007) study shows that, in Toronto, the "Jamaican criminal" has become a taken-for-granted category of pathology who embodies a threat to public safety and from whom "we" need to be protected, a perception that has remained unchanged for decades (D'Arcy 2007).

Law and order campaigns targeting behaviours linked to racialized communities magnify the perception that crime is implicitly associated with these communities. The war on drugs in Canada is an example. Gordon (2006: 74) argues that it is typically working-class people and immigrants of colour who are the main targets in the "drug war" even though they are mostly small-time dealers and people in possession of cannabis. Furthermore, under the pretext of drug criminalization, the police have been able to intervene more broadly in these minority communities to maintain social order. Similarly, Silverstein's (2005) study of parole hearings found that the racial identity of inmates was a factor in the decision-making process. Parole board members set out conditions using different standards depending on the inmate's racial background. Aboriginal inmates were required to have more community involvement in their rehabilitation compared to other inmates, while Hispanic and Asian inmates were required to demonstrate higher levels of shame for their crimes. These expectations, done in the name of protecting society, were often based on racial and ethnic stereotyping, and they raise many questions about fairness and due process in parole hearings (Silverstein 2005).

When crime rates rose during the 1990s in Canada, the government at the time implemented many tough-on-crime policies such as mandatory minimum sentences, longer maximum sentences, restricted access to parole and easier transfers for youths committing serious offences to adult courts. Public fear of crime and violence, and a perceived decline in public safety, created escalating anxiety amongst Canadians. These harsher policies and practices were not unusual, as the United States and the U.K. had enacted similar crime policies during this period. A number of high-profile cases also led the public to believe that the crime problem was caused by racialized offenders. For example, the 1994 Just Desserts case in Toronto, where Georgina Leimonis was shot and killed in the Just Desserts café by two men of Jamaican heritage, led to a moral panic where the public believed that there was a Jamaican crime wave in Toronto (D'Arcy 2007). Minority communities fought back against these claims, pointing out how only two years earlier, two police officers in the Toronto region were acquitted of killing Michael Wade Lawson, a 17-year-old Black youth, and Raymond Lawrence, a 22-year-old Jamaican immigrant. Nonetheless, the report by the Commission on Systemic Racism in the Ontario Criminal Justice System (1995) found that in the minds of criminal justice managers, planners and workers, crime is strongly associated with particular racialized groups. Thus, the explosion of "get tough" measures aimed at assuaging public fears about crime had an implicit racial subtext.

Several decades later, the march towards increased punitiveness continues, despite falling crime rates and overcrowded prisons. In the fall of 2013, Stephen Harper's Conservative Government passed crime legislation that included the controversial provision of mandatory minimum sentences. Many critics argue that a tough-on-crime agenda is no longer appropriate, while one United Nations group has criticized the legislation for being "excessively punitive" on youth and expressed concern about the fact that Aboriginal and Black children are already dramatically overrepresented in the criminal justice system (*Toronto Star* August 19, 2013; Canadian Press 2012). Critics add that successive studies have demonstrated that incarceration is ineffective and unsustainable and that draconian policies have had little influence on curbing undesirable behaviours (*Toronto Star* August 19, 2013).

Further criticism from Howard Sapers, the Correctional Investigator of Canada, highlights the depth of the problem. In his annual report, he notes that federal correctional centres are currently overcrowded, dangerous and violent, all factors that could potentially result in riots (Correctional Investigator of Canada 2013). Sapers observes that "the growth in the custody population appears to be policy, not crime driven" (Correctional Investigator of Canada 2013). In other words, the drive towards punitive criminal justice treatment is not undertaken due to problems with high crime rates. Rather, it is a symbolic gesture by politicians seeking to demonstrate their ability to govern, and this relies on using racialized minorities as scapegoats. These "reforms" find their support in public opinion rather than criminal justice experts and professionals, and these reforms give priority to the interests of victims and victims' families (Garland 2000).

It has been suggested by scholars that current crime policies are a symbol for other social anxieties such as high unemployment and increasing poverty (Wacquant 2001). The "Blackening" of the carceral system is part of a larger risk management project to surveil and neutralize populations that are superfluous to the global economy and deemed a threat to social stability (Wacquant 2001).

This phenomenon is not only racialized, but it is also deeply gendered. For example, in Canada, the number of Black inmates, the majority of whom are men, has increased 75 percent in the last ten years (Correctional Investigator of Canada 2013), highlighting how these individuals have become collateral damage in the current neo-liberal economic regime, where secure, full-time work is no longer the norm. While women are being funnelled into part-time, precarious employment, unemployed, racialized men are increasingly being managed by the penal system (Wacquant 2001). Government efforts to rehabilitate or retrain citizens have been displaced by strategies aimed at simply neutralizing and managing these populations. Thus, those who are unable to find a place for themselves in the labour market are penalized and criminalized, and this is more likely in racialized communities where there are higher levels of economic deprivation and poverty.

RACIAL PROFILING

The use of race as a proxy for dangerousness is best exemplified by the practice of racial profiling. Targeting individuals for law enforcement based on the colour of their skin demonstrates how race informs the contemporary understanding of who or what poses a risk to society. In Canada, the debate on racial profiling has mostly focused on whether or not police forces actual practice racial profiling. A series of articles on racial profiling in the *Toronto Star* in 2002 highlighted the use of racial profiling, such as stop and searches, by the Toronto police force, sparking an intense public debate. In a follow-up report, the African Canadian Community Coalition on Racial Profiling found that there is widespread evidence that racial profiling exists in the Greater Toronto Area, with Black people being the primary targets of police stop and searches (Brown 2004). There have been many subsequent reports confirming the use of racial profiling in other provinces.

Racial profiling in Canada is a controversial practice, and police forces have routinely denied that they racially profile, despite many complaints by racialized Canadians (Smith 2006). However, after September 11, racial profiling became more widely accepted as a necessary tool for combatting terrorism and maintaining national security. Bahdi (2003: 295) states that in the context of the war against terrorism, racial profiling debates focused on whether Canadian society can morally, legally or politically condone the practice. Arab and Muslim communities became key targets of law enforcement. Arabs and Muslims found themselves subjected to multiple layers of screening at Canada's borders, with pre-entry assessments, fingerprinting and interviews with security or border officials becoming a common routine for many who wished to travel. Stories of people being denied access onto a plane, removed from planes for praying, denied visas to other countries or questioned extensively about their Canadian identity played out in a context where public sympathy was in short supply and recourse to fair treatment was not a priority.

Several high-profile cases of Arab and Muslim people being mistreated demonstrates how different life is for them compared to other Canadians. Maher Arar, a dual Canadian and Syrian citizen, was detained at JFK airport in New York while en route home to Ottawa from a vacation. Arar was (falsely) accused by U.S. officials of being linked to al-Qaeda and was deported to Syria, where he was imprisoned for ten months, during which time he was beaten, tortured and forced to make a false confession (maherarar.net). A Commission of Inquiry into Arar's case found that he was cleared of all terrorism allegations. In a similar case, Abousfian Abdelrazik, a Black, Muslim Canadian citizen, was accused of being a supporter of al-Qaeda and a terrorist during a trip he took to Sudan to visit his sick mother in 2003 (Brown 2008). He was jailed and tortured for nine months but never charged. Abdelrazik was arrested again in November 2005 and released in July 2006 (Brown 2008). The Sudanese government formally exonerated Abdelrazik in 2005, finding that there was no evidence of any links to al-Qaeda or terrorism (Koring 2011).

The consequences, both intended and unintended, suffered by Maher Arar and Abousfian Abdelrazik, and the many other racialized minorities in Canada, suggests that their suffering is not inconsequential. The lives of these two men have been shattered by Canada's national security agenda, which allows the terrorist label to be applied to citizens as easily as it is applied to non-citizens. Bahdi (2003) argues that while some people may argue that the harms endured are justified as the price to pay for fighting terrorism, the consequences, when viewed from a community perspective of systematic exclusion and marginalization, are not insignificant. Acts of discrimination fuel the belief that members of Muslim and Arab communities are dangerous internal foreigners despite their citizenship status (Dhamoon and Abu-Laban 2009). As Bahdi (2003: 317) states, "Those who turn to racial profiling as an anecdote for uncertainty will find neither solutions nor comfort. Racial profiling will produce only illusions of security while heightening the disempowerment and sense of vulnerability of racialized groups in Canada."

The association in the minds of many people between crime and racialized groups stems from crime legislation and from the activities of law enforcement agencies. It is also reinforced by the disproportionate media coverage of racialized individuals involved in crime. Numerous studies have found that racialized minorities are underrepresented in positive roles and overrepresented in negative portrayals that link them to social disorder and criminal behavior (Larsen 2006). Furthermore, recurring images in the mainstream media of racialized people generally having undesirable, dangerous or inferior traits or behaviours reinforces biases about the guilt or innocence the defendant (Entman and Gross 2008). Thus, when news stories focus on violent crimes, racialized people are more likely to appear as the perpetrators rather than the victims (Entman and Gross 2008). When racialized people are criminally victimized, their experiences are either minimized or ignored altogether. For example, media coverage of the missing/murdered Aboriginal women in Canada highlights the value judgments made by media institutions in which white women are positively portrayed as legitimate, innocent and worthy victims — "the girl next door" — while Aboriginal women victims are largely ignored and rendered invisible (Jiwani and Young 2006). Amnesty International notes that this hierarchy of worthiness creates an underclass of victims that could increase the victimization of Aboriginal women since the message to the rest of society is that these women don't matter (Amnesty International 2009). Media stereotyping of racial groups exacerbates the mentality that Canadian society is composed of "us" and "them," making it much more difficult for racialized and marginalized groups and individuals to be heard and treated with dignity and respect.

Thinking about how crime is racialized allows us to interrogate the policies and practices in the criminal justice system that continue to subjugate racialized people by labelling and treating them as deviant and dangerous. Historically, the criminal justice system has been, and continues to be, a key institution used to control racialized populations. As the discussion in this section illustrates, racialized groups have been the targets of moral panics and continue to be stereotyped as the criminal other. As Angela Davis remarks, "The figure of the 'criminal' — the racialized figure of the criminal — has come to represent the most menacing enemy of 'American society'" (1998: 270). The legacy of institutional and systemic racism has brutalized many communities, leaving them socially excluded, economically impoverished and politically disenfranchised. The politicization of crime in Canada, evident in the most recent crime legislation by the Conservative Government, will do little to mend the problems of racial inequality in the justice system.

CRIMINALIZING RACIALIZED BODIES

Racialized communities are the target of law enforcement practices due in large part to how we define what is a crime and who are the criminals in our midst. However, these communities have also been constructed and identified by the state as problematic and in need of greater surveillance and control. The racialization of crime works in tandem with the criminalization of race, which refers to the ways that racialized groups and individuals are labelled and targeted by the state as undesirable, leading to their subsequent criminalization, illegalization, marginalization and exclusion. In this final section, I examine how different racial groups have been the objects of increased criminalization and how various state agencies have relied increasingly on criminal justice strategies to manage a broad range of social issues such as immigration and welfare services. As Simon (2007: 8) observes, we govern through crime when we see crime as "the problem through which we seek to know and act on the conduct of others." Crime provides the metaphors and narratives for those seeking to make claims on those who are being governed in a non-criminal context such as immigration, schools or the welfare system. Governments are then able to deploy the use of criminal law and its associated technologies and mentalities as crime becomes the dominant rationale for governance. Simon (2007) states that "governing through crime" is now the default response by many governments to social, political and economic problems, and this wider use of crime control strategies in non-criminal contexts has expanded the net of control and punishment in racialized communities.

Immigrants and Refugees as "Criminals"

Within the last decade, migrants and asylum seekers have increasingly become the objects of intense policing. As migration becomes synonymous with risk, many developed nations have securitized their borders as a strategy for managing contemporary anxieties and fears arising from the effects of globalization. A key strategy adopted by Canada and other Western states for preventing unwanted migrants and immigrants from entering their respective countries is to criminalize their activities. The increasing criminalization of immigration taking place across many Western nations is the result of immigration and criminal justice practices merging and unifying to fend off the "criminal alien" (Kanstroom 2005). Aas (2007) notes that the image of the "deviant immigrant" is not new and has been a recurring theme in social research. Foreigners were often depicted as possessing powerful criminal tendencies, and their appearance as a threat typically occurs in concert with global and national migratory movements (Aas 2007).

Current images of the "deviant immigrant" are a prominent feature in Canadian political and media discourse. For example, Jason Kenney, the previous minister for immigration, repeatedly referred to asylum seekers as "bogus" or "queue jumpers," suggesting that their need for state protection is not legitimate, particularly those who come from countries he claimed were "safe" (Levine-Rasky 2012). The mainstream media also routinely depicts refugees as the cause of chaos and disorder, suggesting that their troubled backgrounds and cultural differences make them unsuitable for Canada (Bradimore and Bauder 2011). The treatment of 492 Sri Lankan asylum seekers who came by cargo ship to the west coast of Canada in the summer of 2010 illustrates this process. They were portrayed and treated as deviant and criminal rather than given compassion and protection. All of the asylum seekers were detained for several months, including women and children, with most of them eventually being deported from Canada. The representation of the Sri Lankan asylum seekers as posing a very real threat, as being "different from us," underscores how poverty and racial difference, disguised as dangerousness, is mobilized to justify the violation of their human rights. The government's response in light of this event was to introduce legislation, the *Protecting Canada's Immigration System Act*, which would impose mandatory detention for those the government deems to be "irregular arrivals," by which they are primarily referring to large numbers of boat migrants. Not only would these migrants be automatically detained for up to one year, they would also have reduced access to health care and delayed access to permanent residency, family reunification and travel documents even if they were found to be "genuine" refugees (Alboim and Cohl 2012).

Immigrants who are not highly skilled and economically independent do not fit the government's image of immigrants who are worthy and desirable. Instead, these "undesirable" immigrants and migrants have been constructed as deviant for causing social problems or needing state protection. For example, the passage of a recent parliamentary bill (C-43 — *Faster Removal of Foreign Criminals Act*) seeking to expedite the process of removing "foreign criminals" has been criticized for suggesting that Canada is "overrun with foreign terrorists, escaped convicts, war criminals and the like" (*Huffington Post* 2012). Non-citizens who have been convicted of a crime and sentenced to six months imprisonment or more will be deported without access to the appeals process. Critics have described this bill as an American-style, "one strike and you're out" policy (Godfrey 2012). One major criticism of this policy is the removal of long-time permanent residents who have lived in Canada since childhood but never applied for citizenship. Lorne Waldman (2013) contends that this law has nothing to do with "foreign criminals" — it is about stripping appeal rights from permanent residents.

Immigration enforcement has been given higher priority over issues such as refugee protection or humanitarian cases. Within the *Immigration and Refugee Protection Act* is a long list of preventative and deterrent measures that have been added or bolstered to control non-citizens and police the external borders. Expanded visa regimes (travellers who come from countries that require a visa to enter Canada), increased fines and penalties for airlines transporting foreign nationals without proper documentation, increased use of immigration detention and greater denial of access to appeals demonstrates how "undesirable" immigrants have been rebranded as security and criminality risks. Their treatment by the state reinforces and reproduces the boundaries between citizen and non-citizen, between those who belong to the nation and those who do not, and, in the process, it offers us a very particular vision of national identity. Racial politics are deeply embedded in immigration policies, making it possible to routinely deny basic rights to racialized groups defined as outsiders.

As a result of growing suspicion and resentment towards immigrants and refugees, public support for all these harsh measures has been high. This is not a new phenomenon, as there have always been groups of immigrant and refugees that have been the targets of intolerance and hate. However, as more people migrate around the world due to wars, environmental disasters or economic turmoil, rather than providing support for migrants, Western governments have bolstered their exclusionary policies in order to demonstrate that they are in control of their borders. The current Canadian government has incorporated many criminal law practices into immigration proceedings without providing procedural protections to immigrants and refugees. Immigrants and refugees who arrive in Canada without proper documentation, who seek asylum or who arrive through irregular channels such as using the help of smugglers to escape have all been rebranded as criminals. One of the harshest criticisms levelled at the Canadian government is the use of prisons to detain immigrants, a practice that has been widely condemned by national and international organizations, since many immigrants are detained for non-criminal offences and the mixing of non-criminals with criminals is seen as highly undesirable.

The criminalization of immigrants and refugees illustrates how the mythical figure of the "deviant immigrant" has come to embody the dangers, insecurities and perceived risks of a rapidly changing global environment (Melossi 2003). The connection between migration and crime has been reinforced by the construction and treatment of foreignness as a criminal threat, and it has paved the way for punitive and restrictive policies. Furthermore, when these policies and practices are based on the racially motivated stereotype of migrants as the cause of crime and disorder, it is much more difficult to challenge their legitimacy. As Bosworth (2011) observes, foreign offenders often have limited numbers of supporters, therefore governments seldom experience any qualms about disrupting social relationships or violating human rights.

Policing Non-white People

However, it is not just immigrants and refugees who are subjected to intrusive levels of surveillance and policing. Aboriginal communities have been particularly impacted by intensive policing practices and mistreatment. Black people in the Greater Toronto Area, for example, are grossly overrepresented in use of force statistics, especially in police shooting incidents (Wortley 2006). Not surprisingly, various studies conducted on minority views of the police have found that visible minorities have less confidence in the police (Cao 2011) and that Canadian-born minorities perceive the justice system to be more biased than people of colour born outside of Canada (Wortley and Owusu-Bempah 2009).

A number of high-profile incidents involving Aboriginal men point to the tense relationship between these communities and the criminal justice system. In 1998, Frank Paul was picked up by the police in Vancouver's downtown eastside for being drunk in a public place, placed in lockup, released, then taken into custody again where the sergeant in charge refused to accept him a second time. At the time of his second arrest, he could barely walk. Frank Paul was then left in an alleyway, where he was found dead of hypothermia a few hours later (Razack 2012: 909). Six Aboriginal men in Saskatchewan have also died as a result of mistreatment by the police. These men froze to death when they were given a "starlight tour" — the police picked up the intoxicated Aboriginal men, drove them to a remote area of town and then dropped them off, leaving them to find their way home (Comack 2012). In most cases of starlight tours, the men are only lightly dressed and not prepared for the cold weather. While Aboriginal leaders argued that the treatment of these men demonstrates the pervasive racism in the Saskatoon Police Service, the police force and its supporters denied any wrongdoing and claimed that the stories were myths (Comack 2012). Eventually, an inquiry was conducted into the death of one of the men, Neil Stonechild, with the conclusion that the police did not adequately investigate the case for fear that one of their own officers may have been involved his death (Cheema 2009: 91). A public inquiry was also held to investigate Paul's death, and although the report acknowledged how racism and colonialism contributed to Frank Paul's demise, in the end, no one was found criminally responsible for his death (Davies 2011). Finally, there is also the well-known case of Donald Marshall, a Mi'kmaq man from Halifax who was wrongly convicted of killing Sandy Seale in the 1970s. He spent eleven years in prison until he was finally released and an inquiry was held to investigate his wrongful conviction. The Commissioners for the Inquiry concluded that the criminal justice system had failed Donald Marshall (Hickman 1989). Not only did the courts accept perjured evidence, but also the Crown, the judge and even the defence lawyer for Marshall had made many errors in his case (Hickman 1989). It was only by coincidence that his innocence was finally established (Hickman 1989: 5).

While many of these well-known cases involved racialized men, racialized women's experiences of the criminal justice have not been significantly more positive. For example, their experiences of criminal victimization has often been minimized or dismissed by the justice system. It is not uncommon for police officers to view violence within racialized communities as normal or reasonable, and, therefore, when racialized women are victimized, they are often left with few options for seeking protection (Adelman et al. 2003). Furthermore, Aboriginal women's sexual victimization is often not believed in court trials and the harms they suffer are trivialized (Dylan, Regehr and Alaggia 2008). Racialized and indigenous women typically do not fit the role of the "ideal" or "authentic" victim of sexual assault because racial stereotypes depict them as more blameworthy and less deserving of protection (Randall 2010). Women in general are reluctant to report crimes of sexual assault or domestic violence, but racialized women, despite higher rates of victimization, are even less likely to seek legal redress through the justice system for fears of not being believed or being revictimized by the system (Regehr et al. 2008).

Race and Poverty

Poor people, particularly poor, racialized women, are typically portrayed as individuals with moral or psychological deficiencies (Fraser and Gordon 1994). Despite years of significant cutbacks in state support, the assumption held by many is that poor people deserve their life situations because they fail to rise up to the challenges of the labour market. Constructions of their poverty emphasize their pathological lifestyles, such as the belief that women of colour are hypersexed and promiscuous and that they have children to obtain more welfare money (Abramovitz 2006). Many people thus assume that poor people, especially poor, racialized individuals, are receiving state support illegitimately and believe that punitive action is needed to control this population. Municipalities across Canada have passed bylaws and legislation criminalizing the activities of poor people. Panhandling, squeegeeing, sleeping in public and loitering are activities that have been reconstituted as disorderly and result in criminal sanctions (Hermer and Mosher 2002). Welfare policies have also been recrafted with the presumption that recipients are "guilty until proven innocent," that their conduct needs to be carefully supervised and remedied by restrictive and coercive measures and that deterrence and stigma are necessary to modify behavior (Wacquant 2009: 79). This approach rejects racism and sexism, believing that anyone who really wants to work hard will succeed (Davis 2007). The convergence of penal and welfare practices illustrates how harsher treatment will be the default response to managing the problems of poverty.

MARGINALIZED AND CONDEMNED

The criminalization and marginalization of racialized communities has been made possible by depicting people of colour as less deserving of state protection or support and more likely to be in need of surveillance and control. For example, in 2005, concerns about gun violence by young Black men in Toronto led to explanations that the problem was one of family dysfunction, where many Black youths were growing up in households without a father figure (Lawson 2012). Media discourse at the time repeatedly highlighted how Black single mothers were failing to raise their children properly and how these Black youths were now becoming a dangerous class. Rarely was there acknowledgement of the structural barriers such as inadequate education or employment discrimination that shape and limit the possibilities of parenting in Black families. Even less talked about are the ways in which criminal justice practices, such as over-policing and racial profiling, destabilize Black families, which is seen most clearly in the high rates of incarceration for Black males and the high rates of Black, single-female parented families (Lawson 2012: 815–16) As a result, even as crime rates decline in the twenty-first century, the disproportionate representation of people of colour throughout Canada's justice system remains. Racialized patterns of crime and punishment are taking place in a context where public discourse about crime excludes and/or dismisses the problems of race and racism and, therefore, excludes any need to acknowledge or address issues of racial discrimination in the justice system. Yet, racism continues to shape the social and economic outcomes for many people, and while many social institutions may eschew racialized language in their policies, practices and discourse, the prevalence of racism's institutional entrenchment — most evident in the criminal justice system — is clear.

There is a deep reluctance in the justice system and, arguably, in Canadian society to address issues of racial discrimination and engage in meaningful discussions about the treatment of racialized Canadians. Even as criminal justice practices are now extending into other social institutions such as immigration and welfare services as a way to manage potential threats and security issues, and even though the co-optation of criminal justice policies and practices has a disproportionate effect on racialized communities, there is a "socially recurrent blindness to racism" present (Hesse 2011). Racism is no longer seen as a social problem, and discussions about race in the public sphere are taboo. As a result, practices of race privilege, racial discrimination and racial profiling are now denied public representation. There is a tendency to avoid any acknowledgement of racialization and state-racial arrangements, yet, under the threat of terror or crime, the state simultaneously enforces racial oppression through increased surveillance and policing. As the examples throughout this chapter highlight, there are many state policies and practices that disproportionately disadvantage racial groups but have been legitimated as necessary in order to protect Canadians. The discourse of risk and safety allows the state to police racialized people and communities, overriding equality laws. Thus, commitments to address racial inequalities and to uphold the values of equality, due process and justice dissolve.

References

Aas, F. 2007. *Globalization and Crime*. London: Sage Publications.

Abramovitz, M. 2006. "Welfare Reform in the United States: Gender, Race and Class Matter." *Critical Social Policy* 26, 2: 336–264.

Adelman, M., E. Erez and N. Shalhoub-Kevorkian. 2003. "Policing Violence Against Minority Women in Multicultural Societies: 'Community' and the Politics of Exclusion." *Police and Society* 7: 105–33.

Alboim, N., and K. Cohl. 2012. *Shaping the Future: Canada's Rapidly Changing Immigration Policies*. Toronto: Maytree Foundation.

Amnesty International. 2009. *No More Stolen Sisters*. London: Amnesty International Publications.

Anand, S. 2000. "The Sentencing of Aboriginal Offenders, Continued Confusion and Persisting Problems: A Comment on the Decision in *R. v. Gladue*." *Canadian Journal of Criminology* 42: 412–420.

Bahdi, R. 2003. "No Exit: Racial Profiling and Canada's War Against Terrorism." *Osgoode Hall Law Journal* 41, 2&3: 293–317.

Bannerji, H. 1997 "Geography Lessons: On Being an Inside/Outsider to the Canadian Nation." In L. Roman and L. Eyre (eds.), *Dangerous Territories: Struggles for Differences and Equality*. New York: Routledge.

Bosworth, M. 2011. "Deportation, Detention and Foreign-National Prisoners in England and Wales." *Citizenship Studies* 15, 5: 583–595.

Bradimore, A., and H. Bauder. 2011. *Mystery Ships and Risky Boat People: Tamil Refugee Migration in the Newsprint Media*. Metropolis BC, Working Paper Series 11-02.

Brown, J. 2008. "Ottawa Refuses to Help Canadian in Sudan: Lawyer." *Toronto Star*, April 28.

Brown, M. 2004. *In Their Own Voices: African Canadians in the Greater Toronto Area Share Their Experiences of Police Profiling*. Toronto: African Canadian Community Coalition on Racial Profiling.

Brown, M.K., M. Carnoy, E. Currie, T. Duster, D. Oppenheimer, M. Schultz and D. Wellman. 2005. *White-Washing Race: The Myth of a Color-Blind Society*. Berkeley: University of California Press.

Canadian Press. 2012. "Canada's Tough-on-Crime Agenda 'Excessively Punitive.'" *Canadian Press*, October 9.

Cao, L. 2011. "Visible Minorities and Confidence in the Police." *Canadian Journal of Criminology & Criminal Justice* 53, 1: 1–26.

Cheema, M. 2009. "Missing Subjects: Aboriginal Deaths in Custody, Data Problems, and Racialized Policing." *Appeal* 14: 84–100.

Comack, E. 2012. *Racialized Policing: Aboriginal People's Encounters with the Police*. Black Point, NS: Fernwood Publishing.

Commission on Systemic Racism in the Ontario Criminal Justice System. 1995. *Final Report*. Toronto: Queens Printer.

Correctional Investigator of Canada. 2013. *Annual Report of the Office of the Correctional Investigator 2012–2013*. Ottawa: The Correctional Investigator of Canada.

Covington, J. 1995. "Racial Classification in Criminology: The Reproduction of Racialized Crime." *Sociological Forum* 10, 4: 547–568.

D'Arcy, S. 2007. "The 'Jamaican Criminal' in Toronto, 1994: A Critical Ontology." *Canadian Journal of Communications* 32: 241–259.

Davies, W.H. 2011. *Inquiry into the Death of Frank Paul. Final Report: Alone and Cold*. Victoria, BC: Ministry of the Attorney General, Criminal Justice Branch.

Davis, A. 1998. "Race and Criminalization: Black Americans and the Punishment Industry." In W. Lubiano (ed.), *The House That Race Built*. New York: Vintage Books.

Davis, D. 2007. "Narrating the Mute: Racializing and Racism in a Neoliberal Moment." *Souls* 9, 4: 346–460.

Décoste, R. 2013a. "Don't Ask, Don't Tell: Canada's Approach to Racism." *Huffington Post*, November 18.

____. 2013b. "When You Commit a Crime, Your Race Matters." *Huffington Post*, May 27.

Dhamoon, R., and Y. Abu-Laban. 2009. "Dangerous (Internal) Foreigners and Nation-Building: The Case of Canada." *International Political Science Review* 30, 2: 163–183.

Douglas, P., and L. Rosella. 2013. "Racism Is Prevalent, Persisting and Perpetually Growing, Experts Warn." *Mississauga.com*, November 25.

Dua, E., N. Razack and J. Warner. 2005. "Race, Racism, and Empire: Reflections on Canada." *Social Justice* 32, 4: 1–10.

Dylan, A., C. Regehr and R. Alaggia. 2008. "And Justice for All? Aboriginal Victims of Sexual Violence." *Violence Against Women* 14: 678–696.

Entman, R., and K. Gross. 2008. "Race to Judgment: Stereotyping Media and Criminal Defendants." *Law and Contemporary Problems* 71: 93–133.

Fraser, N., and L. Gordon. 1994. "A Genealogy of 'Dependency': Tracing a Keyword of the U.S. Welfare State." *Signs* 19, 2: 309–336.

Gabor, T. 1994. "The Suppression of Crime Statistics on Race and Ethnicity: The Price of Political Correctness." *Canadian Journal of Criminology* 36: 153–163.

Garland, D. 2000. "The Culture of High Crime Societies." *British Journal of Criminology* 40: 347–375.

Godfrey, T. 2012. "Proposed Deportation Law Under Fire." *Toronto Sun*, October 1.

Gordon, R., and J. Nelson. 1996. "Crime, Ethnicity and Immigration." In R. Silverman, J. Teevan and V. Sacco (eds.), *Crime in Canadian Society*, fifth edition. Toronto: Harcourt Brace.

Gordon, T. 2006. "Neoliberalism, Racism and the War on Drugs in Canada." *Social Justice* 33, 1: 59–78.

Hawkins, D. 1995. *Ethnicity, Race and Crime*. Albany: State University of New York Press.

Hermer, J., and J. Mosher. 2002. *Disorderly People: Law and the Politics of Exclusion in Ontario*. Halifax: Fernwood Publishing.

Hesse, B. 2011. "Self-Fulfilling Prophecy: The Postracial Horizon." *The South Atlantic Quarterly* 110, 1: 155–178.

Hickman, T.A. 1989. *Royal Commission on the Donald Marshall, Jr., Prosecution: Digest of*

Findings and Recommendations. Halifax, N.S.

Huffington Post. 2012. "Canada: A Nation of Foreign Terrorists According to Bill C-43." October 23. <http://www.huffingtonpost.ca/irwin-cotler/billc-43_b_2005209.html> accessed November 5, 2012.

Jiwani, Y., and M.L. Young. 2006. "Missing and Murdered Women: Reproducing Marginality in News Discourse." *Canadian Journal of Communication* 31, 4: 895–917.

Johnston, J.P. 1994. "Academic Approaches to Race-Crime Statistics Do Not Justify Their Collection." *Canadian Journal of Criminology* 36: 166–174.

Kanstroom, D. 2005. "Immigration Law as Social Control." In C. Mele and T. Miller (eds.), *Civil Penalties, Social Consequences.* New York: Routledge.

King, J. 1981. *The Biology of Race.* Berkeley: University of California Press.

Koring, P. 2011. "Canadian Abousfian Abdelrazik Taken off United Nations Terror List." *Globe and Mail,* November 30. <http://www.theglobeandmail.com/news/world/canadian-abousfian-abdelrazik-taken-off-united-nations-terror-list/article4179856/> accessed November 13, 2012.

Larsen, S. 2006. *Media & Minorities: The Politics of Race in News and Entertainment.* Lanham, MD: Rowman and Littlefield.

Lawson, E. 2012. "Single Mothers, Absentee Fathers, and Fun Violence in Toronto: A Contextual Interpretation." *Women's Studies* 41: 805–828.

Levine-Rasky, C. 2012. "Who Are You Calling Bogus? Saying No to Roma Refugees." *Canadian Dimension,* September 25. <http://canadiandimension.com/articles/4959/> accessed November 11, 2012.

Mann, C. 1993. *Unequal Justice: A Question of Color.* Bloomington: Indiana University Press.

Mason, D. 2000. *Race and Ethnicity in Modern Britain.* Oxford: Oxford University Press.

Melossi, D. 2003. "'In a Peaceful Life': Migration and the Crime of Modernity in Europe/Italy." *Punishment and Society* 5, 4: 371–397.

Miller, J. 1996. *Search and Destroy: African-American Males in the Criminal Justice System.* Cambridge: Cambridge University Press.

Monaghan, J. 2013. "Settler Governmentality and Racializing Surveillance in Canada's North-West." *Canadian Journal of Sociology* 38, 4: 487–508.

Mosher, C. 1996. "Minorities and Misdemeanours: The Treatment of Black Public Order Offenders in Ontario's Criminal Justice System, 1892–1930." *Canadian Journal of Criminology* 38: 413–438.

Nelson, J. 2011. "'Partners or Thieves': Racialized Knowledge and the Regulation of Africville." *Journal of Canadian Studies* 45, 1: 121–142.

O'Connell, A. 2010. "An Exploration of Redneck Whiteness in Multicultural Canada." *Social Politics* 17, 4: 536–563.

Omi, M., and H. Winant. 1994. *Racial Formation in the United States From the 1960s to the 1990s.* Second edition. New York: Routledge.

Oriola, T., and C. Adeyanju. 2011. "Perceptions of the Canadian Criminal Justice System Among Nigerians: Evidence from a local Church in Winnipeg, Manitoba." *International Journal of Human Sciences* 8, 1: 635: 56.

Owusu-Bempah, A., and P. Millar. 2010. "Revisiting the Collection of Justice Statistics by Race in Canada." *Canadian Journal of Law and Society* 24, 1: 97–104.

____. 2011. "Whitewashing Criminal Justice in Canada: Preventing Research through Data

Suppression." *Canadian Journal of Law and Society* 26, 3: 653–661.

Phillips, C., and B. Bowling. 2003. "Racism, Ethnicity and Criminology: Developing Minority Perspectives." *British Journal of Criminology* 43: 269–290.

Randall, M. 2010. "Sexual Assault Law, Credibility, and 'Ideal Victims': Consent, Resistance, And Victim Blaming." *Canadian Journal of Women and the Law* 22: 397–433.

Rankin, J., and P. Winsa. 2013. "Toronto Police Propose Purging Carding Information from Database." *Toronto Star*, October 4.

Razack, S. 2012. "Memorializing Colonial Power: The Death of Frank Paul." *Law & Social Inquiry* 37, 4: 908–932.

Regehr, C., R. Alaggia, L. Lambert and M. Saini. 2008. "Victims of Sexual Violence in the Canadian Criminal Courts." *Victims & Offenders* 3, 1: 99–113.

Roach, K. 1996. "Systemic Racism and Criminal Justice Policy." *Windsor Yearbook of Access to Justice* 15: 236–249.

Roberts, J. 1994. "Crime and Race Statistics: Toward a Canadian Solution." *Canadian Journal of Criminology* 36: 175–185.

Roberts, J., and A. Doob. 1997. "Race, Ethnicity and Criminal Justice in Canada." *Crime and Justice* 21: 469–522.

Satzewich, V. 2000. "Whiteness Limited: Racialization and the Social Construction of 'Peripheral Europeans'." *Social History* 66: 271–290.

Satzewich, V., and W. Shaffir. 2009. "Racism versus Professionalism: Claims and Counter-Claims about Racial Profiling." *Canadian Journal of Criminal and Criminal Justice* 51, 2: 199–226.

Silverstein, M. 2005. "What's Race Got to Do with Justice: Responsibilization Strategies at Parole Hearings." *British Journal of Criminology* 45: 340–354.

Simon, J. 2007. *Governing Through Crime*. New York: Oxford University Press.

Smith, C. 2006. "Racial Profiling in Canada, the United States, and the United Kingdom." In F. Henry and C. Tator (eds.), *Racial Profiling in Canada*. Toronto: University of Toronto Press.

Tanovich, D. 2008. "The Charter of Whiteness: Twenty-Five Years of Maintaining Racial Injustice in the Canadian Criminal Justice System." *Supreme Court Law Review* 40: 655–686.

Toronto Star. 2013. "Editorial: Harper Government's Tough-On-Crime Laws Are Outdated." August 19. <thestar.com/opinion/editorials/2013/08/19/harper_governments_ toughoncrime_laws_are_outdated_editorial.html>.

Trevethan, S., and C. Rastin. 2004. *A Profile of Visible Minority Offenders in the Federal Canadian Correctional System*. Ottawa: Correctional Service of Canada.

Wacquant, L. 2001. "Deadly Symbiosis: When Ghetto and Prison Meet and Mesh." *Punishment and Society* 3, 1: 95–134.

____. 2009. *Punishing the Poor: The Neoliberal Government of Social Insecurity*. Durham: Duke University Press.

Waldman, L. 2013. "Faster Deportations Come at the Cost of Compassion and Fairness." *Globe and Mail*, May 14.

Walsh, A., and I. Yun. 2011. "Race and Criminology in the Age of Genomic Science." *Social Science Quarterly* 92, 5: 1279–1296.

Wood, D., and C. Griffths. 1996. "Patterns of Aboriginal Crime." In R. Silverman, J. Teevan and V. Sacco (eds.), *Crime in Canadian Society,* fifth edition. Toronto: Harcourt Brace.

Wortley, S. 1999. "A Northern Taboo: Research on Race, Crime and Criminal Justice in Canada." *Canadian Journal of Criminology* 41: 261–274.

____. 2006. *Police Use of Force in Ontario: An Examination of Data from the Special Investigations Unit. Final Report.* Toronto, ON.

Wortley, S., and A. Owusu-Bempah. 2009. "Unequal Before the Law: Immigrant and Racial Minority Perceptions of the Canadian Criminal Justice System." *Journal of International Migration and Integration* 10, 4: 447–473.

Chapter 5

WHITE PRIVILEGE

Unpacking the Invisible Knapsack

Peggy McIntosh

From: *Gendered Intersections: An Introduction to Women's and Gender Studies,* *2nd edition*, pp. 108–111. Originally published as: Peggy McIntosh, 1989, "White Privilege: Unpacking the Invisible Knapsack," *Peace and Freedom Magazine* (July/August): Women's International League for Peace and Freedom. Copyright fees are donated to National Seed Project on Inclusive Curriculum (Seeking Educational Equity and Diversity) (reprinted with permission).

Through work to bring materials from Women's Studies into the rest of the curriculum, I have often noticed men's unwillingness to grant that they are overprivileged, even though they may grant that women are disadvantaged. They may say they will work to improve women's status, in the society, the university, or the curriculum, but they can't or won't support the idea of lessening men's. Denials which amount to taboos surround the subject of advantages which men gain from women's disadvantages. These denials protect male privilege from being fully acknowledged, lessened or ended.

Thinking through unacknowledged male privilege as a phenomenon, I realized that since hierarchies in our society are interlocking, there was most likely a phenomenon of white privilege which was similarly denied and protected. As a white person, I realized I had been taught about racism as something which puts others at a disadvantage, but had been taught not to see one of its corollary aspects, white privilege, which puts me at an advantage.

I think whites are carefully taught not to recognize white privilege, as males are taught not to recognize male privilege. So I have begun in an untutored way to ask what it is like to have white privilege. I have come to see white privilege as an invisible package of unearned assets which I can count on cashing in each day, but about which I was "meant" to remain oblivious. White privilege is like an invisible weightless knapsack of special provisions, maps, passports, codebooks, visas, clothes, tools and blank checks.

Describing white privilege makes one newly accountable. As we in Women's Studies work to reveal male privilege and ask men to give up some of their power, so one who writes about having white privilege must ask, "Having described it, what will I do to lessen or end it?"

After I realized the extent to which men work from a base of unacknowledged privilege, I understood that much of their oppressiveness was unconscious. Then I remembered the frequent charges from women of color that white women whom they encounter are oppressive. I began to understand why we are justly seen as oppressive, even when we don't see ourselves that way. I began to count the ways in which I enjoy unearned skin privilege and have been conditioned into oblivion about its existence.

My schooling gave me no training in seeing myself as an oppressor, as an unfairly advantaged person, or as a participant in a damaged culture. I was taught to see myself as an individual whose moral state depended on her individual moral will. My schooling followed the pattern my colleague Elizabeth Minnich has pointed out: whites are taught to think of their lives as morally neutral, normative and average, and also ideal, so that when we work to benefit others, this is seen as work which will allow "them" to be more like "us."

I decided to try to work on myself at least by identifying some of the daily effects of white privilege in my life. I have chosen those conditions which I think in my case *attach somewhat more to skin-colour privilege* than to class, religion, ethnic status or geographical location, though of course all these other factors are intricately intertwined. As far as I can see, my African American co-workers, friends and acquaintances, with whom I come into daily or frequent contact in this particular time, place, and line of work, cannot count on most of these conditions.

1. I can if I wish arrange to be in the company of people of my race most of the time.

2. If I should need to move, I can be pretty sure of renting or purchasing housing in an area which I can afford and in which I would want to live.

3. I can be pretty sure that my neighbors in such a location will be neutral or pleasant to me.

4. I can go shopping alone most of the time, pretty well assured that I will not be followed or harassed.

5. I can turn on the television or open to the front page of the paper and see people of my race widely represented.

6. When I am told about our national heritage or about "civilization," I am shown that people of my color made it what it is.

7. I can be sure that my children will be given curricular materials that testify to the existence of their race.

8. If I want to, I can be pretty sure of finding a publisher for this piece on white privilege.

9. I can go into a music shop and count on finding the music of my race represented, into a supermarket and find the staple foods which fit with my cultural traditions, into a hairdresser's shop and find someone who can cut my hair.

10. Whether I use cheques, credit cards or cash, I can count on my skin color not to work against the appearance of financial reliability.

11. I can arrange to protect my children most of the time from people who might not like them.

12. I can swear, or dress in second-hand clothes, or not answer letters, without having people attribute these choices to bad morals, the poverty, or the illiteracy of my race.

13. I can speak in public to a powerful male group without putting my race on trial.

14. I can do well in a challenging situation without being called a credit to my race.

15. I am never asked to speak for all the people of my racial group.

16. I can remain oblivious of the language and customs of persons of colour who constitute the world's majority without feeling in my culture any penalty for such oblivion.

17. I can criticize our government and talk about how much I fear its policies and behaviour without being seen as a cultural outsider.

18. I can be pretty sure that if I ask to talk to "the person in charge," I will be facing a person of my race.

19. If a traffic cop pulls me over or if the IRS (Internal Revenue Service) audits my tax return, I can be sure I haven't been singled out because of my race.

20. I can easily buy posters, postcards, picture books, greeting cards, dolls,

toys, and children's magazines featuring people of my race.

21. I can go home from most meetings of organizations I belong to feeling somewhat tied in, rather than isolated, out-of-place, outnumbered, unheard, held at a distance or feared.

22. I can take a job with an affirmative action employer without having coworkers on the job suspect that I got it because of my race.

23. I can choose public accommodation without fearing that people of my race cannot get in or will be mistreated in the places I have chosen.

24. I can be sure that if I need legal or medical help, my race will not work against me.

25. If my day, week, or year is going badly, I need not ask of each negative episode or situation whether it has racial overtones.

26. I can choose blemish cover or bandages in "flesh" color and have them more or less match my skin.

I repeatedly forgot each of the realizations on this list until I wrote it down. For me white privilege has turned out to be an elusive and fugitive subject. The pressure to avoid it is great, for in facing it I must give up the myth of meritocracy. If these things are true, this is not such a free country; one's life is not what one makes it; many doors open for certain people through no virtues of their own.

In unpacking this invisible knapsack of white privilege, I have listed conditions of daily experience which I once took for granted. Nor did I think of any of these perquisites as bad for the holder. I now think that we need a more finely differentiated taxonomy of privilege, for some of these varieties are only what one would want for everyone in a just society, and others give license to be ignorant, oblivious, arrogant and destructive.

I see a pattern running through the matrix of white privilege, a pattern of assumptions which were passed on to me as a white person. There was one main piece of cultural turf; it was my own turf, and I was among those who could control the turf. *My skin color was an asset for any move I was educated to want to make.* I could think of myself as belonging in major ways, and of making social systems work for me. I could freely disparage, fear, neglect or be oblivious to anything outside of the dominant cultural forms. Being of the main culture, I could also criticize it fairly freely.

In proportion as my racial group was being made confident, comfortable and oblivious, other groups were likely being made unconfident, uncomfortable and alienated. Whiteness protected me from many kinds of hostility, distress and violence, which I was being subtly trained to visit in turn upon people of color.

For this reason, the word "privilege" now seems to me misleading. We usually think of privilege as being a favoured state, whether earned or conferred by birth or luck. Yet some of the conditions I have described here work to systematically overempower certain groups. Such privilege simply *confers dominance* because of one's race or sex.

I want, then, to distinguish between earned strength and unearned power conferred systematically. Power from unearned privilege can look like strength when it is in fact permission to escape or to dominate. But not all of the privileges on my list are inevitably damaging. Some privileges, like the expectation that neighbors will be decent to you, or that your race will not count against you in court, should be the norm in a just society. Others, like the privilege to ignore less powerful people, distort the humanity of the holders as well as the ignored groups.

We might at least start by distinguishing between positive advantages which we can work to spread, and negative types of advantages which, unless rejected, will always reinforce our present hierarchies. For example, the feeling that one belongs within the human circle, as Native Americans say, should not be seen as privilege for a few. Ideally it is an *unearned entitlement*. At present, since only a few have it, it is an *unearned advantage* for them. This paper results from a process of coming to see that some of the power which I originally saw as attendant on being a human being in the U.S. consisted in *unearned advantage* and *conferred dominance*.

I have met very few men who are truly distressed about systemic, unearned male advantage and conferred dominance. And so one question for me and others like me is whether we will be like them, or whether we will get truly distressed, even outraged, about unearned race advantage and conferred dominance and, if so, what we will do to lessen them. In any case, we need to do more work in identifying how they actually affect our daily lives. Many, perhaps most, of our white students in the U.S. think that racism doesn't affect them because they are not people of colour; they do not see "whiteness" as a racial identity. In addition, since race and sex are not the only advantaging systems at work, we need similarly to examine the daily experience of having age advantage, or ethnic advantage, or physical ability, or advantage related to nationality, religion or sexual orientation.

Difficulties and dangers surrounding the task of finding parallels are many. Since racism, sexism and heterosexism are not the same, the advantaging associated with them should not be seen as the same. In addition, it is hard to disentangle aspects of unearned advantage which rest more on social class, economic class, race, religion, sex and ethnic identity than on other factors. Still, all of the oppressions are interlocking, as the Combahee River Collective Statement of 1977 continues to remind us eloquently.

One factor seems clear about all of the interlocking oppressions. They take *both active forms* which we can see *and embedded forms* which, as a member of the dominant group, one is taught not to see. In my class and place, I did not see myself as a racist because I was taught to recognize racism only in individual acts of meanness by members of my group, never in invisible systems conferring unsought racial dominance on my group from birth.

Disapproving of the systems won't be enough to change them. I was taught to think that racism could end if white individuals changed their attitudes. [But] a "white" skin in the United States opens many doors for whites whether or not we approve of the way dominance has been conferred on us. Individual acts can palliate, but cannot end, these problems.

To redesign social systems we need first to acknowledge their colossal unseen dimensions. The silences and denials surrounding privilege are the key political tool here. They keep the thinking about equality or equity incomplete, protecting unearned advantage and conferred dominance by making these taboo subjects. Most talk by whites about equal opportunity seems to me now to be about equal opportunity to try and get into a position of dominance while denying that *systems* of dominance exist.

It seems to me that obliviousness about white advantage, like obliviousness about male advantage, is kept strongly inculcated in the United States so as to maintain the myth of meritocracy, the myth that democratic choice is equally available to all. Keeping most people unaware that freedom of confident action is there for just a small number of people props up those in power, and serves to keep power in the hands of the same groups that have most of it already.

Though systemic change takes many decades, there are pressing questions for me and, I imagine, for some others like me if we raise our daily consciousness on the perquisites of being light-skinned. What will we do with such knowledge? As we know from watching men, it is an open question whether we will choose to use unearned advantage to weaken hidden systems of advantage, and whether we will use any of our arbitrarily awarded power to try to reconstruct power systems on a broader base.

Reference
Combahee River Collective. 1977. "The Combahee River Collective Statement." <circuitous. org/scraps/combahee.html>.

HETERONORMATIVITY

Chapter 6

THE HETEROSEXUAL QUESTIONNAIRE

Martin Rochlin

From: *Gendered Intersections: An Introduction to Women's and Gender Studies,* second edition, pp. 183–184

Martin Rochlin (1928–2003) was the first openly gay clinical psychologist in Los Angeles. For his obituary, see Stephen F. Morin and Douglas Kimmel, 2004, "Martin Rochlin" in *American Psychologist* 59, 9. The "Heterosexual Questionnaire," first published in 1972, is widely available on the Internet. See, for example, <masculineheart.blogspot.com/2010/01/martin-rochlin-phd-heterosexual.html>.

This questionnaire is for self-avowed heterosexuals only. If you are not openly heterosexual, pass it on to a friend who is. Please try to answer the questions as candidly as possible. Your responses will be held in strict confidence and your anonymity fully protected.

1. What do you think caused your heterosexuality?
2. When and how did you first decide you were a heterosexual?
3. Is it possible your heterosexuality is just a phase you may grow out of?
4. Could it be that your heterosexuality stems from a neurotic fear of others of the same sex?

5. If you've never slept with a person of the same sex, how can you be sure you wouldn't prefer that?

6. To whom have you disclosed your heterosexual tendencies? How did they react?

7. Why do heterosexuals feel compelled to seduce others into their lifestyle?

8. Why do you insist on flaunting your heterosexuality? Can't you just be what you are and keep it quiet?

9. Would you want your children to be heterosexual, knowing the problems they'd face?

10. A disproportionate majority of child molesters are heterosexual men. Do you consider it safe to expose children to heterosexual male teachers, pediatricians, priests or scoutmasters?

11. With all the societal support for marriage, the divorce rate is spiraling. Why are there so few stable relationships among heterosexuals?

12. Why do heterosexuals place so much emphasis on sex?

13. Considering the menace of overpopulation, how could the human race survive if everyone were heterosexual?

14. Could you trust a heterosexual therapist to be objective? Don't you fear s/he might be inclined to influence you in the direction of her/his own leanings?

15. Heterosexuals are notorious for assigning themselves and one another rigid, stereotyped sex roles. Why must you cling to such unhealthy role-playing?

16. With the sexually segregated living conditions of military life, isn't heterosexuality incompatible with military service?

17. How can you enjoy an emotionally fulfilling experience with a person of the other sex when there are such vast differences between you? How can a man know what pleases a woman sexually or vice-versa?

18. Shouldn't you ask your far-out straight cohorts, like skinheads and born-agains, to keep quiet? Wouldn't that improve your image?

19. Why are heterosexuals so promiscuous?

20. Why do you attribute heterosexuality to so many famous lesbian and gay people? Is it to justify your own heterosexuality?

21. How can you hope to actualize your God-given homosexual potential if you limit yourself to exclusive, compulsive heterosexuality?

22. There seem to be very few happy heterosexuals. Techniques have been developed that might enable you to change if you really want to. After all, you never deliberately chose to be a heterosexual, did you? Have you considered aversion therapy or Heterosexuals Anonymous?

Chapter 7

LEGAL REFORM

Peter Knegt

From: *About Canada: Queer Rights*, pp. 31–52 (slightly revised and reprinted with permission).

There is absolutely no doubt that the relationship between Canadian law and the queer community has seen drastic and far-reaching improvements since official organizing first began. Just over forty years ago, homosexuality was illegal and could result in jail time and being labelled "a dangerous sexual offender." Today, queer Canadians enjoy some of the most progressive legislation in the world.

This happened largely through three stages of law reform. The first, decriminalization, saw activists in the late 1960s fight to have laws inspired by a moral conservative strategy of sexual regulation that prohibited the simple act of two same-sex persons having consensual sex overturned. The second stage, equality, involved having human rights protection enacted to prevent discrimination on the grounds of sexual orientation, particularly in areas such as employment and housing. This long battle culminated in a series of huge legal victories in the 1980s and 1990s, the most substantial of which was the reading of "sexual orientation" into section 15 of the *Canadian Charter of Rights of Freedoms*. From this, the cases flowed into the third stage, relationship recognition, which saw laws giving equal treatment to same-sex relationships.

There are a few very important things to note when considering Canada's relatively newfound status as an international queer rights leader. First, attributing these strides forward to lawmakers or judges is inappropriate. Particularly in the 1970s and 1980s, these battles were largely won because activists fought long and hard for them. Second and most importantly, the battle is not over. Same-sex marriage is not the final frontier of the queer rights movement. There remain the questions of whether same-sex marriage is a progressive idea in the first place and, if it is, of who exactly benefits from it. It wasn't even an issue for most of the pioneers of the Canadian movement, while some issues they did very much believe in — like sexual censorship and the decriminalization of many consensual sex acts — remain unresolved. There are still several fires burning, and this book will explore them, but first let us turn to the many remarkable fires that were put out, and exactly how that occurred.

DECRIMINALIZATION

Modelled after the British equivalent, the Consolidated Statutes of Canada was created in 1859, and included "buggery" (a British term for "sodomy") as an offence punishable by death. In 1892, it was reclassified as an "offence against morality," which more broadly targeted all male homosexual activity. Notably, the laws contained no reference to lesbians until the 1950s. In *Coming Out: Homosexual Politics in Britain from the Nineteenth Century to the Present,* Jeffrey Weeks explains that this omission reflected the belief that "lesbian sexuality was either non-existent or should not be encouraged by being mentioned" (Weeks 1977: 106–107). Changes to the code took place in 1948, and then again in 1961. These changes would brand gay men first as "criminal sexual psychopaths" and then as "dangerous sexual offenders," both charges that carried indeterminate prison sentences (Warner 2002: 19). This meant that only a celibate homosexual could be assured of not going to prison, potentially for life.

In the 1960s, political and social consensus began building around decriminalization though overall social attitudes towards homosexuals remained intensely negative. This, like early Canadian law, was partially influenced by the British. In 1957, the British government released the Wolfenden Report (U.K. 1957), which argued against criminalizing homosexual sex acts, unless they occurred in public or involved youth. The report led to the 1967 decriminalization of homosexual acts between consenting adults in Britain. Two years later, Canada followed suit with the help of its first gay community organizations. Vancouver's Association for Social Knowledge (ASK) suggested a Wolfenden Report–type *Criminal Code* reform in a paper to the Criminal Law Subsection of the British Columbia Division of the Canadian Bar Association.

The country's first gay groups — referred to as homophile organizations — very much relied on support from some liberal psychiatrists and politicians, the courts and even religious organizations. In October 1964, Professor William Nicholls, an Anglican priest who was head of religious studies at the University of British Columbia, stated that criminal law "should be changed to permit homosexual acts in private between consenting adults, and that the church should encourage stable unions between homosexuals" (McLeod 1996: 13). These sorts of statements went a long way, largely because they were made by heterosexuals.

An important figure in this first phase of legal reform was Everett George Klippert, a mechanic in the Northwest Territories who was first investigated by police in connection with an arson committed in 1965. He had no connection to the fire, but during the investigation, Klippert voluntarily admitted to having

---

"We Demand" was a brief presented to the federal government in August 1971. Written and researched by Toronto Gay Action, it was supported by gay organizations across Canada. On August 28, 1971, over 200 people rallied on Parliament Hill in support of the brief. The action was the first of its kind in Canada. Here were the demands:

1. The removal of the nebulous terms "gross indecency" and "indecent act" from the *Criminal Code* and their replacement by a specific listing of offences, and the equalization of penalties for all remaining homosexual and heterosexual acts; and defining "in private" in the *Criminal Code* to mean a "condition of privacy."
2. Removal of "gross indecency" and "buggery" as grounds for indictment as a "dangerous sexual offender" and for vagrancy.
3. A uniform age of consent for all female and male homosexual and heterosexual acts.
4. The *Immigration Act* be amended so as to omit all references to homosexuals and "homosexualism."
5. The right of equal employment and promotion at all government levels for homosexuals.
6. The *Divorce Act* be amended so as to omit sodomy and homosexual acts as grounds for divorce; moreover, in divorce cases homosexuality per se should not preclude the equal right of child custody.
7. The right of homosexuals to serve in the Armed Forces and, therefore, the removal of provisions for convicting service personnel of conduct and/or acts legal under the *Criminal Code*; further, the rescinding of policy statements reflecting on the homosexual.
8. To know if it is a policy of the Royal Canadian Mounted Police to identify homosexuals within any area of government service and then question them concerning their sexuality and the sexuality of others; and if this is the policy we demand its immediate cessation and the destruction of all records obtained.
9. All legal rights for homosexuals which currently exist for heterosexuals.
10. All public officials and law enforcement agents to employ the full force of their office to bring about changes in the negative attitudes and de facto expressions of discrimination and prejudice against homosexuals.

For the complete document, see "We Demand: The August 28th Gay Day Committee," *The Body Politic*, November/December 1971.

consensual sex with other men. As a result, he was arrested and sentenced to three years in prison. When a court-ordered psychiatrist assessed Klippert as "incurably homosexual," he was sentenced to indefinite imprisonment as a "dangerous sexual offender" (Warner 2002: 46). His appeal to the Court of Appeal for the Northwest Territories was rejected.

On November 7, 1967, Klippert's case finally reached the Supreme Court of Canada, and in a highly controversial move, it was dismissed in a 3–2 decision. The next day, New Democratic Party leader Tommy Douglas raised Klippert's name in the House of Commons, stating that homosexuality should not be considered a criminal issue. For once, even the mainstream media, which had gone into a frenzy over the decision, largely agreed. Six weeks later, Pierre Trudeau (then justice minister of Canada, he would become prime minister the following April) introduced Bill C-150 into the House of Commons, and famously proclaimed, "the state has no place in the bedrooms of nation." One part of the bill would decriminalize homosexual acts between two consenting adults if they were twenty-one years of age or older. Representatives of the "homophile" community weren't entirely impressed. At the fourth annual North American Conference of Homophile Organizations (NACHO) in August 1968, they adopted a resolution harshly criticizing the age of consent limitations in Bill C-150.

When Bill C-150 was finally discussed in the House of Commons in the spring of 1969, Justice Minister John Turner declared that it was not intended to condone, endorse or encourage homosexuality and that it "doesn't even legalize this kind of conduct" (McLeod 1996: 41–42). Instead, "it lifted the taint or stigma of the law" from these sexual acts. Despite numerous complaints from the more conservative political parties that the bill was "bringing the morals and values of skid row into the salons and drawing rooms of the nation," the bill passed by a vote of 149 to 55, and came into effect on August 26, 1969. Despite this, Klippert would remain in prison until July 21, 1971 (Kinsman 1996: 159).

While these events set the stage for the emergence of lesbian and gay liberation groups and their quest for equality, Bill C-150 itself was not as extensive a victory as it may appear. For one, the record of the debate of the bill in the House of Commons was described by George Smith as perhaps "the most heterosexist document in Canadian government history" (Smith 1982). Moreover, it led to a limited form of decriminalization that did not actually legalize homosexuality itself and allowed for the continued regulation of queer sex. A Canadian coalition of gay and lesbian liberation groups was quick to point out this aspect in the 1971 public statement "We Demand":

> In 1969, the *Criminal Code* was amended so as to make certain sexual acts between consenting adults, in private, legal. This was widely

misunderstood as "legalizing" homosexuality and thus putting homosexuals on an equal basis with other Canadians. In fact, this amendment
was merely a recognition of the non-enforceable nature of the *Criminal
Code* as it existed. Consequently, its effects have done little to alleviate
the oppression of homosexual men and women in Canada. In our daily
lives we are still confronted with discrimination, police harassment,
exploitation and pressures to conform, which deny our sexuality. (*Body
Politic* 1971)

EQUALITY

The early 1970s saw the momentous surge in lesbian and gay organizing that led
to the eventual passing of human rights laws. As noted with reference to specific
communities in the previous chapter, activist organizations working within the
ideology of lesbian and gay liberation emerged all over the country between 1970
and 1975. Driven by a newly adopted militancy in stark contrast to the tactics of
homophile organizing, these groups made a lasting mark on the history of queer
Canadians. Their goals and battles were certainly not limited to achieving human
rights legislation, but these groups would bring the human rights of queer people
from non-existent to what they are today. Tactics included sending letters and
briefs to legislatures and politicians, meeting with representatives of human rights
commissions, and protesting a variety of events. Examples of each are endless.

The first public action that centred on gay rights reform occurred in June 1972,
when twenty-five members of Toronto groups CHAT and TGA joined in protest in
front of the Ontario Legislature about the omission of a sexual orientation clause
from Bill 199, an amendment to the *Ontario Human Rights Code* then being considered by the Legislature. Later that year, Vancouver's GATE sent a letter to B.C.
Minister of Labour William King asking for amendments to the *British Columbia
Human Rights Act* to outlaw discrimination based on sexual orientation. King's
response was that he "found it rather difficult to conceive of a situation where a
homosexual would be discriminated against unless his tendencies were of public
knowledge" (*Body Politic* 1973a).

Throughout the 1970s, essentially every gay group across the country began
compiling briefs on cases where homosexuals had been discriminated against and
submitting them to their respective provincial human rights commissions. The first
sign of potential success came in 1973, when the Saskatchewan Human Rights
Commission responded to Saskatoon activists' demands by recommending the
expansion of anti-discrimination legislation and equal opportunity programs in
the province, including the outlawing of discrimination based on sexual orientation. This was the first time that a human rights commission in Canada had called

for the inclusion of sexual orientation in human rights legislation, though the call was not successful.

The first actual victories were municipal. On October 10, 1973, after significant lobbying from GATE, Toronto City Council became the first legislative body in Canada to prohibit discrimination based on sexual orientation. The resolution passed by a vote of 15–1. The *Body Politic* called it "our first win" (*Body Politic* 1973b). Ottawa would follow suit in April 1976, followed by Windsor in March 1977. But it would not be until late 1977 that any major change would happen on a provincial or federal level, and this particular change was an isolated and unexpected one. In December 1977, a "quiet late night session" of the Québec National Assembly amended the *Québec Charter of Human Rights* to include sexual orientation, making Québec the first province — and first political jurisdiction larger than a city or county in the entire world — to provide legal protection for homosexuals. Tom Warner suggests in *Never Going Back* that the decision was in part the result of the angry community response to the Truxx bathhouse raids earlier that year, which "caused unwelcome publicity for a government wanting to project a progressive image" (Warner 2002: 148–149) Shortly after the raids, activists demanded that the Québec Human Rights Commission recommend a sexual orientation amendment in their charter. They did, and the government passed it very quickly and very quietly within a matter of days.

Sadly, this precedent did not spill over into the remaining provinces, where activist groups had to continue the fight for human rights legislation. The battle in Ontario was particularly intense as activists fought against an extraordinarily homophobic Progressive Conservative government well into the 1980s. Even with the seemingly left-wing New Democratic Party in power — albeit a minority government struggling to maintain public support — Manitoba's government failed to include sexual orientation in an amendment in 1984, despite it being recommended by the Manitoba Human Rights Commission and over sixty organizations, including the Manitoba Teacher's Society (Moreau 1984). Similar situations occurred across the country, and the next provincial amendment did not occur again until 1986 in Ontario.

Although most of the legal victories would eventually occur in the 1980s and 1990s, one of the biggest battles for equality was won outside the courtroom in the decade before. In 1979, activist Michael Lynch wrote the *Body Politic* article "The End of the Human Rights Decade," which proudly declared:

> There is now a gay community that sees itself, and is seen by others, as a political "minority." Gay life has been brought to public consciousness; the facts of oppression, real and undeniable, have been made known. The strategy built to achieve human rights legislation may have failed in that

one aim, but it has been wildly successful in fulfilling the other, subsidiary goals which may finally prove more valuable than a few changes in
law (Riordan 1979).

In the years following Lynch's declaration, inarguably the greatest legislative
advancement in the history of queer Canada was slowly beginning to take shape.
In 1982 the *Canadian Charter of Rights and Freedoms* came into effect under Pierre
Trudeau's Liberal government. Section 15 of the *Charter*, enacted three years
later, assured equality and non-discrimination. While section 15 did not explicitly
include sexual orientation as a "prohibited ground of discrimination," it was written in an open-ended matter, so that courts could potentially interpret additional
grounds for discrimination. For the first time, there was a significant sense that
queer people could actually obtain legal protection of their rights. While the lesbian and gay liberationists of the 1970s generally *expected* their court cases to fail,
but pursued them anyway to raise public consciousness and mobilize community,
suddenly the equation was fundamentally altered.

From 1985 onwards, courts began to apply the equality guarantees of the *Charter*
to queer-related cases and profound changes began to take place in legal reform.
It did not happen immediately, and at first queer activists were uncertain just how
much the *Charter* would help their cause. But two cases in particular gave considerable clarity to that question: *Egan and Nesbit v. Canada* and *Vriend v. Alberta.*

**Amendments to Human Rights Legislation to Include Sexual Orientation,
by Jurisdiction**

Jurisdiction	Year
Québec	1977
Ontario	1986
Yukon	1987
Manitoba	1987
Nova Scotia	1991
New Brunswick	1992
British Columbia	1992
Saskatchewan	1993
Canada	1995
Prince Edward Island	1998
Alberta	1998
Nunavut	1999
NWT	2002

The former case concerned the application of James Egan (the same man noted as "Canada's first gay activist") for spousal benefits for his partner Jack Nesbit under Old Age Security. The case went to the Supreme Court, where four out of five judges decided that no discrimination occurred in the denial of the pension benefit. However, the judges also decided at the same time that "sexual orientation" should indeed be read into section 15 of the Charter (Smith 1999: 91-91). Though it was a contradictory and unenthusiastic decision — pension benefits apparently were a reasonable limit of discrimination based on sexual orientation — it set a monumental precedent that would effectively prohibit discrimination by employers, landlords, service providers and governments.

The growing jurisprudence that the Charter brought forth also led to the amendment of the *Canadian Human Rights Act*, via Bill C-41 in June 1995, as well as provincial human rights laws. Some provinces were more cooperative than others, with Ontario the first province to pass such legislation (in 1986) since Québec nearly a decade earlier, and Manitoba and the Yukon (despite the latter having no organized queer groups at the time) doing so a year later. For a timeline of each provincial amendment, see Table 1, though Alberta's situation warrants some extended discussion.

The aforementioned court battle, *Vriend v. Alberta,* was the catalyst for Alberta's amendment, which saw the Supreme Court of Canada forcing the province to include "sexual orientation" in its human rights legislation. This came after three decades of the intensely conservative Alberta government repeatedly refusing to do so, despite the efforts of local queer activists. As late as 1989, an Alberta cabinet minister declared in a speech that he could not support such an amendment because it would allow "homosexuals to teach in schools" (Interview, Michael Phair 2010). Oddly enough, one of said homosexual teachers would force the Alberta government into compliance with the Charter. In 1991, Delwin Vriend was fired from his employment at King's College, a Christian school in Edmonton. When offered the job in 1987, he disclosed his sexual orientation and was told it would

---

Section 15 of the *Canadian Charter of Rights and Freedoms*

15. (1) Every individual is equal before and under the law and has the right to the equal protection and equal benefit of the law without discrimination and, in particular, without discrimination based on race, national or ethnic origin, colour, religion, sex, age or mental or physical disability.

(2) Subsection (1) does not preclude any law, program or activity that has as its object the amelioration of conditions of disadvantaged individuals or groups including those that are disadvantaged because of race, national or ethnic origin, colour, religion, sex, age or mental or physical disability.

not be a problem. But when Vriend started being more public about his sexuality, the college fired him because "homosexual practice goes against the Bible" (Warner 2002: 209). Vriend filed a complaint with the Alberta Human Rights Commission, which was refused. This led him to file a lawsuit arguing that Alberta's *Individual Rights Protection Act* (IRPA) did not adhere to Canada's Charter. After years of legal setbacks that featured some exceptional homophobia on behalf of Alberta's judiciary, the case made its way to the Supreme Court of Canada. On April 2, 1998, the Court unanimously agreed that IRPA's omission of sexual orientation denied rights guaranteed by the Charter.

The decision resulted in homophobic hysteria by Albertan conservatives, with openly gay Edmonton city councillor Michael Phair even receiving death threats (Interview, Michael Phair 2010). Premier Ralph Klein — who has been one of the great villains in the narrative of official Canadian homophobia — attempted to use a constitutional provision to circumvent the court's ruling. Clearly many Albertans agreed with him, as dozens of letters to both the *Calgary Herald* and the *Edmonton Journal* equating homosexuality to sin, bestiality and pedophilia showed (Filax 2006: 160). But in the end, the amendment went through, completing human rights protection across all provinces.

RELATIONSHIP RECOGNITION

As lesbian and gay liberationists gained ground in terms of civil rights through the Charter, the movement became more identified with reform, and less with liberationist ideology. The cause was also being fought more and more in the courtrooms, and not on the streets where a sense of community could be negotiated. The politics of these legal cases became more defined by the individuals and their lawyers, whereas legal decisions before this usually occurred in the context of social struggles and organizing. Essentially, rights were no longer a means to an end, as the liberationists had sought, but an end in themselves. This came out of a more assimilationist agenda to bring queers into mainstream society. The great example of this is same-sex marriage, which was never really on the agenda of lesbian and gay liberation. In fact, most queer liberationists dreamed of the day that marriage would be abolished altogether. "We took a constructionist view of homosexuality," Gerald Hannon, a liberation activist and one of the founders of the *Body Politic* said, "and thought that all people should be free of repressive social institutions like marriage that bring with it traditional gender and sex roles. The government should be out of the marriage business period. We shouldn't be trying to get in" (Interview, Gerald Hannon 2010).

But we did get in, and did so at an accelerated speed relative to other stages in queer law reform. As David Rayside notes, the Canadian story regarding queer rights began like that of the United States. But in the 1990s, it "picked up enough speed that we can refer to 'take-off.' We see this in a few other countries, mostly in Northern Europe, but nowhere as clearly as the Canadian case" (Rayside 2008: 4). How did this "take-off" take place? Initially, there was some liberationist involvement in the fight for relationship recognition, though this was more dominant in the earlier stages of the campaign. The Coalition for Lesbian and Gay Rights Ontario (CLGRO) — one of the few surviving gay and lesbian liberation organizations in the country — had a huge role in fighting for relationship recognition through the province's rocky road to Bill 167 in the early 1990s (though their involvement divided members unsure if it adhered to the liberationist agenda)(Warner 2002: 218–35). Bill 167 would not have granted legal recognition to same-sex marriages, but would have amended "spouse" and "marital status" to include lesbians and gays in 56 provincial laws. The CLGRO had taken advantage of a rare and relatively progressive NDP provincial government in Ontario at the time, putting significant pressure on the party to address their concerns.

But when the bill was drawn up, even members of the NDP caucus shied away from supporting it, fearing backlash in the upcoming provincial election or perhaps just showing their true homophobic colours. One NDP backbencher declared he would not support Bill 167 because "every time you walk down the street people would say 'there goes that guy who supports the queer people.'"(Walker 1994). Due to a lack of consensus among the NDP caucus, resounding and aggressive disapproval from the provincial Progressive Conservative party (which would overwhelmingly take power in the province the following spring), and, as Gary Kinsman argues, not enough mobilization on behalf of queer activists, the bill finally failed in June 1994 (Kinsman 1996: 313–317 and Warner 2002: 232–234). The night after it was defeated, eight thousand people took to the streets in protest (it was the first public protest surrounding the bill, which was a little too late), and it proved "an important setback for lesbian and gay organizing" in that it put similar provincial and federal legislative initiatives on the backburner (Kinsman 1996: 313).

It would not be until the 1999 case *M. v. H.* that the Supreme Court of Canada would once again help push things forward. The case involved a lesbian couple that split up after years of living together, one of whom sought support payments that the other had refused. The landmark decision ruled that the definition of spouse as a "man and woman" under Ontario's *Family Law Act* was unconstitutional based on the Charter, and gave the Ontario government six months to bring their law into line. They did so via Bill 5, which created a new category, "same sex partner," through which said partners would receive the same legal rights and responsibilities as common law heterosexual couples. In doing so, the government — led by Progressive Conservative Premier Mike Harris — also made clear it was being forced to pass the bill, notable in the bill's ridiculous name: *An Act to Amend Certain Statutes as a Result of the Supreme Court Decision in M. v. H.* (Warner 2002: 239).

In February 2000, the federal government responded to *M. v. H.* with Bill C-23, which guaranteed a host of rights and benefits for same-sex partners, including child-care tax benefits, pension benefits for widowed spouses, tax breaks on retirement savings plans, even conjugal prison visits. It passed by a vote of 174–172, though activists were not impressed either by the fact that it did not include overdue amendments in the *Immigration Act,* or that the bill had been altered to appease opposition by leaving the definition of marriage as "the union of a man and a woman to the exclusion of all others."

But it would not be long before that would change, even if many governments begrudgingly accepted the mixed advances allowed so far. The fact that there was a real possibility that same-sex marriage could be legalized mobilized people who hadn't been part of queer activism thus far. Predominantly white, middle- and upper-class gays and lesbians who saw an economic advantage in the legal recognition of same-sex relationships donated money to the queer movement like never before. Their voice was heard through groups like Egale, which differed from liberationist groups in their main strategy of lobbying MPs and government. At the peak of the same-sex marriage debate, Egale and its spinoff, Canadians for Equal Marriage, raised nearly $1 million to intervene in court challenges and lobby Parliament. This helped move things along very quickly. In 2002, the Law Commission of Canada, Parliament's advisors, told Canada's justice minister that same-sex marriage should indeed be legalized, and that Bill C-23 was discriminatory. Shortly thereafter, the Canadian Human Rights Commission suggested the same. One by one, courts of appeal in various provinces deemed the ban on same-sex marriage unconstitutional, effectively legalizing it: Ontario on June 10, 2003; British Columbia on July 8, 2003; and Québec on March 19, 2004.

As one might expect, there was considerable opposition from conservative groups and politicians. In September 2003, future prime minister and then Canadian Alliance Leader Stephen Harper accused the federal government of "stacking Canada's courts with liberal-minded judges over the years in a covert effort to legislate same-sex marriage" (Globe and Mail 2003). "They wanted to introduce this 'same-sex marriage' through back channels," Harper told reporters.

> They didn't want to come to Parliament. They didn't want to go to the Canadian people and be honest that this is what they wanted. They had the courts do it for them, put the judges in they wanted, then they failed to appeal, failed to fight the case in the court. (quoted in Globe and Mail 2003)

Harper went so far as to introduce a motion in September 2003 that called on Parliament to preserve the definition of marriage as, once again, "the union of a man and a woman to the exclusion of all others."

But the motion narrowly failed by a vote of 137–132, a ratio that seemed to reflect the Canadian public. An SES Research poll in September 2003 showed that 47 percent of Canadians supported same-sex marriage, while 44 percent opposed it. Notably, support was highest in Québec and British Columbia at 53 percent, and lowest in Alberta at just 28 percent (SES Research Poll 2003). This was a large increase from just six years earlier, when 63 percent of Canadians opposed it.

By the end of 2004, every province but New Brunswick, Prince Edward Island and Alberta had legalized gay marriage. At this point, Prime Minister Paul Martin announced in Parliament that Bill C-38 would be introduced to expand marriage rights to same-sex couples. Much debate and acrimony divided Parliament, with many Liberals and all Conservatives against the idea. But on June 28, 2005, the bill passed its final reading with a vote of 158–133. Less than a month later, it received royal assent, making Canada the fourth country in the world to legalize same-sex marriage (after the Netherlands, Belgium and Spain). Expectedly, Alberta — which had not legalized it independently at that time — tried to fight the decision, with Premier Ralph Klein even suggesting the Alberta government would stop solemnizing marriages altogether. But Alberta was forced to obey the legislation and — "much to our chagrin" as Klein publicly stated — the Alberta government began allowing same-sex marriages (*Xtra!* 2005).

There is no denying the monumental dramatics of this narrative, or that this kind of formal recognition is productive in a certain sense. Many queer Canadians clearly have embraced the decision (see Table 2), and despite the ideology of lesbian and gay liberationists, even they could understand why same-sex marriage had its importance. "Either you're equal or you're not," one said in an interview, "and when you are that means something" (Interview, Ed Jackson 2010).

But there remains the justified liberationist notion that same-sex marriage should not be viewed as some sort of legal end game in the fight for queer rights. Even beyond the argument that marriage is an oppressive and state-sanctioned institution that should have never been a goal in the first place, there is the simpler question of whom exactly marriage serves. Like heterosexuals, not every queer person *wants* to get married, nor do they always end up in relationships that warrant marriages even if they wanted them to. It brings up the issue of the law's privileging of conjugal relationships. An imperative study written by Brenda Cossman for the Law Commission of Canada argues that governments need to pursue a "more comprehensive and principled approach" to the legal recognition and support of the "full range of close personal relationships among adults," not

Same-Sex Marriage 2006/2011

Jurisdiction	Date of legalization	Number of same-sex marriages 2006	Number of same-sex couples 2006*	Number of same-sex marriages 2011	Number of same-sex couples 2011*
Ontario	June 10, 2003	3,765	17,510	8,375	23,380
Québec	March 19, 2004	1,260	13,685	3,655	18,430
British Columbia	July 8, 2003	1,370	7,035	3,445	10,000
Alberta	July 20, 2005	510	3,055	3,325	6,360
Nova Scotia	September 24, 2004	140	1,255	605	1,835
Manitoba	September 16, 2004	100	935	515	1,465
Saskatchewan	November 5, 2004	100	565	425	1,000
New Brunswick	June 23, 2005	125	770	385	1,215
Newfoundland and Labrador	December 21, 2004	50	310	160	520
Prince Edward Island	July 20, 2005	15	140	65	190
Northwest Territories	July 20, 2005	15	40	35	80
Yukon	July 14, 2004	10	30	30	75
Nunavut	July 20, 2005	10	15	15	20
Canada	July 20, 2005	7,465	45,345	21,015	64,575

*Refers to same-sex couples that completed census
Source: Statistics Canada, 2006, 2011.

just those who cohabitate under romantic circumstances (Law Commission of Canada 2001).

Essentially, same-sex marriage only serves people who are in a position to take advantage of such expanded recognition. It also maintains the idea of heterosexual marriage as a "norm" to which queer people should aspire. And as we will see, it leaves many other important issues out in the cold.

SEX AND CENSORSHIP

While the remaining chapters in this book will take on some of the most outstanding examples of other issues facing today's queer people, notably education and health, a few issues remain that fall in the realm of law and public policy.

Sex and censorship comprise an enormous and complex set of issues in the Canadian queer narrative that warrant substantially more discussion. There are numerous works noted at the end of this book that provide much more extensive analysis. But for the purposes of understanding the legal issues that don't quite fit into the "three stages" of this chapter, we will briefly delve into them (Cossman 1996).

Issues surrounding sex and censorship have always been contentious, even within the queer community. Though liberationists put them at the forefront of their movement, more conservative activists have been uneasy taking up many of these issues, especially where the sexuality of youth is involved. In 1972, the *Body Politic* published an article, "Of Men and Boys," by Gerald Hannon, that discussed the sexual relationship between older and younger men. When Toronto-area newspapers caused an uproar about the article, suggesting it "counselled the seduction of young boys," the local lesbian and gay organization CHAT publicly dissociated itself from the article (McLeod 1996: 103–104).

As one may imagine, mainstream Canadian society has been even more inhospitable to these sorts of issues. When a similarly themed article entitled "Men Loving Men Loving Boys," also written by Hannon, was published in the *Body Politic* five years later, the newspapers again took notice with very critical editorials. Except this time the furor in the papers led to a police raid on the *Body Politic* offices. The raid resulted in a six-year legal battle that saw two provincial court trials, three other separate court actions, six appeals, two trips to the Supreme Court of Canada and over $100,000 in legal fees. The charge against Hannon and fellow *Body Politic* writers Ed Jackson and Ken Popert were for "using the mails to transmit immoral or indecent material" (*Body Politic* 1978).

It is important to note that the charges against the *Body Politic* came in the midst of a trial surrounding the rape and murder in Toronto of twelve-year-old shoeshine boy Emanuel Jacques by a group of men. The murder had brought forth a hysterically homophobic climate that classified gay men as predators of children, and the *Body Politic* article became a target. While in the end Hannon, Jackson and Popert were acquitted, the emotional and financial costs of the ordeal were devastating. It also made clear that if there was one thing mainstream society was uncomfortable with regarding queer people, it was their relationship with children.

Many similar, though often less dramatic, acts of censorship have occurred, and much energy in the lesbian and gay liberation movement has been directed toward them and other issues surrounding sex. The abolition of age-of-consent laws, removal of pornography legislation, state-sanctioned obscenity determinations and "bawdyhouse" laws (used in both bathhouse and bar raids targeting homosexual people) are examples. The divisiveness surrounding these issues varied (the former two were far more controversial within the queer community than the latter two), but they were all issues that received a lot of attention. But when the mid-1980s brought forth a drastic shift in advocacy, new groups showed little interest in taking these issues on. Though there are countless examples of how more controversial topics were sidestepped by the focus on rights recognition and, more dominantly, same-sex marriage, the case of Little Sister's Book and Art Emporium is by far the most epic, and truly one of the most important legal battles regarding freedom of expression — queer or otherwise — in Canadian history.

A lesbian and gay bookstore in Vancouver, Little Sister's, like its Toronto counterpart Glad Day Bookshop, was a huge target of Canada Customs during an intensified period of harassment in the late 1980s and early 1990s (though this kind of censorship was present beforehand). Changes to censorship laws had been required following a 1985 Federal Court of Appeal decision that freedom of expression rights guaranteed by the Charter did not fall in line with provisions permitting the seizure of "immoral or indecent" materials. The response to this was Memorandum D-9-11, which had been introduced by the Conservative Mulroney government and changed very little. It still allowed for the seizure or banning of any material "containing depictions or descriptions of anal penetration, including depictions or descriptions involving implements of all kinds," and worse, gave Customs officials "the authority to use their own personal judgment as to what qualified as obscene" (Orr 1986).

By 1990, nearly 75 percent of all books and magazines being shipped to queer-related bookstores were being seized (Warner 2002: 275). At this point, Little Sister's was already in the midst of their battle with Canada Customs. By December 1996, Customs had seized more than 600 books and magazines from the store, and were not showing any signs of stopping. So the Vancouver community rallied to help the store hire a lawyer and fund the extraordinarily costly process — which several times nearly put the store out of business — of a Charter challenge against Canada Customs.

The trial was continuously delayed, did not begin until late 1994, and provided a book's worth of fascinating material (and a movie's worth, as exemplified by Aerlyn Weissman's must-see 2002 documentary *Little Sister's vs. Big Brother*). For example, testimony by a Crown witness who had done a study of the effects on Customs officers of reviewing pornography found that 20 percent of the officers were themselves homophobic while over 70 percent "appeared to find homosexual acts repulsive" (Weissman 2002).

The trial ended with a mixed result in January 1996, when the B.C. Supreme Court ruled that Canada Customs had applied the law in a discriminatory man-ner against Little Sister's. However, they felt that the *administration* of the law was flawed, but not the law itself. Little Sister's appealed, and eventually met the Supreme Court of Canada in December 2000 where, once again, there was a disappointing decision. All nine judges believed Little Sister's had been targeted and harassed by Customs, but they did not find the existing definitions of obscenity threatening to freedom of expression.

Within a year of the Supreme Court ruling, Customs once again seized books from Little Sister's. They appealed again and another battle with Customs (now called the Canadian Border Services Agency) began. Except this time, Little Sister's couldn't raise the money necessary to go through with a trial, despite nearly $1 million being donated to the concurrent fight for same-sex marriage (Gallant 2009). So where does that leave the issues? Largely unresolved. Even though Memorandum D-9-11 has been revised as recently as 2008, it still does suggest that most sexually explicit material involving adults is constitutionally protected expression. As recently as 2009, three gay-themed films were held at the border en route to Ottawa's lesbian and gay film festival (McCann 2009).

Beyond that issue, section 197 of the Canadian *Criminal Code* still defines a "common bawdyhouse" as a public place "for the purposes of prostitution and the practices of acts of indecency." As we saw in the previous chapter, arrests made under the "common bawdyhouse" law in raids on bathhouses and bars have been a huge catalyst for queer activism over the years. They have occurred as recently as 1999 and 2000 (in Toronto), 2002 (in Calgary), 2003 (in Montreal) and 2004 (in Hamilton). That said, while Parliament has not shown any indication they will change the law, two 2005 companion cases — R. v. Labaye and R. v. Kouri — concerning two heterosexual "swingers" clubs in Montreal set a precedent. The decisions upheld consensual group sex and swinging activities in a club and alleged that "bawdyhouses" were consistent with personal autonomy and liberty (Warner 2010: 99–100). However, the implications regarding queer sex have yet to be tested. The ruling does not preclude the bawdyhouse legislation being used against queer sex (although such convictions are likely to be much more difficult), and the use of liquor laws to police sexual behaviour in bathhouses remains a considerable threat.

Age-of-consent laws also remain problematic. Forty years ago, just after Bill C-150 half-heartedly decriminalized *some* forms of homosexual activity, we learned that early queer activists marched in Ottawa with ten demands. Nine of these have now been met, but one remains — "A uniform age of consent for all female and male homosexual and heterosexual acts." The age of consent in Canada is sixteen (raised from fourteen in 2008, much to the chagrin of many queer activists). However, the *Criminal Code of Canada* still states under section 159 that anal intercourse is illegal if either partner is under the age of *eighteen*, unless those partners are married. It is also still illegal to have anal sex when there are more than two parties involved (of any age), and if the anal intercourse takes place anywhere but in private, which is punishable with a $10,000 fine or six months in prison (Interview, Brenda Cossman 2010). Though courts in Ontario (1995), Québec (1998) and, surprisingly, Alberta

(2002) have independently declared section 159 unconstitutional, the fact that it remains is a symbol of the official homophobia that lingers in Canada. It also potentially has an impact on youth sexuality and safer sex education and on the criminalization of young people for engaging in consensual sex. While same-sex marriage — in all its heteronormativity — may be legally available, same-sex *sex* is still clearly a point of discomfort. This is a major contradiction.

References

Body Politic. 1971. "We Demand: The August 28th Gay Day Committee." November/ December.

____. 1973a. "Labour Minister Responds." February.

____. 1973b. "City Bars Job Discrimination." November.

____. 1978. "TBP Raided and Charged." February.

Cossman, Brenda. 1996. *Bad Attitude/s on Trial: Pornography, Feminism, and the Butler Decision.* Toronto: University of Toronto Press.

Filax, Gloria. 2006. *Queer Youth in the Province of the "Severely Normal."* Vancouver: UBC Press.

Gallant, Paul. 2009. "The Honeymoon's Over: What's Next for the Gay Rights Movement?" *This Magazine,* September/October.

Globe and Mail. 2003. "Harper vs. the Globe and Mail." September 6.

Hannon, Gerald. 1972. "Of Men and Boys." *Body Politic.*

____. 1977. "Men Loving Men Loving Boys." *Body Politic* 39.

Kinsman, Gary. 1996. *The Regulation of Desire: Homo and Hetero Sexualities.* Montreal: Black Rose Books.

Law Commission of Canada. 2001. *Beyond Conjugality: Recognizing and Supporting Close Personal Adult Relationships.* Ottawa: Law Commission of Canada.

McCann, Marcus. 2009. "PG-rated gay film seized en route to Ottawa film fest," *Xtra!,* November 21.

McLeod, Donald. 1996. *Lesbian and Gay Liberation in Canada.* Toronto: ECW Press.

Moreau, John. 1984. "Gay Rights Back on Manitoba's Agenda," *Body Politic,* July–August.

Orr, Alan. 1986. "Sex Is Okay — If It's Not Gay," *Body Politic,* September. Toronto.

Rayside, David. 2008. *Queer Inclusions, Continental Divisions.* Toronto: University of Toronto Press.

Riordan, Michael. 1979. "The End of the Human Rights Decade." *Body Politic,* July.

SES Research Poll. 8 September 2003. <http://www.sesresearch.com/news/press_releases/ PR September 7 2003.pdf>.

Smith, George. 1982. "In Defence of Privacy: Or, Bluntly Put, No More Shit." *Action!* Publication of the Right to Privacy Committee, 3, 1. Toronto.

Smith, Miriam. 1999. *Lesbian and Gay Rights in Canada: Social Movements and Equality- Seeking, 1971–1995.* Toronto: University of Toronto Press.

Statistics Canada. 2006. *Census of Population.* Catalogue no. 97-553-XCB2006024. Ottawa: Statistics Canada.

____. 2011. *Census of Population.* Catalogue no. 98-312-XCB2011046. Ottawa: Statistics Canada.

U.K., Departmental Committee on Homosexual Offences and Prostitution. 1957. "Report of the Departmental Committee on Homosexual Offences and Prostitution." (Wolfenden Report.) London: Queen's Printer.

Walker, William. 1994. "Same-Sex Rights Bill Will Go to Free Vote," *Toronto Star*, May 11.

Warner, Tom. 2002. *Never Going Back: A History of Queer Activism in Canada*. Toronto: University of Toronto Press.

____. 2010. *Losing Control: Canada's Social Conservatives in the Age of Rights*. Toronto: Between the Lines.

Weeks, Jeffrey. 1977. *Coming Out: Homosexual Politics in Britain from the Nineteenth Century to the Present*. London; Quartet Books.

Weissman, Aerlyn. 2002. *Little Sister's vs. Big Brother*. Documentary, National Film Board of Canada.

Xtra! 2005. "Alberta gives in to same-sex marriage." July 21.

Legislation

The Criminal Law Amendment Act. 1968-69. (S.C. 1968-69, c. 38). (Bill C-150).

Constitution Act, 1982. (80) Part I, *Canadian Charter Of Rights And Freedoms*.

Legal Cases

Egan and Nesbit v. Canada. 1995. 2 SCR 513.

M. v. H. 1999. 2 S.C.R. 3.

R. v. Labaye. 2005. 3 S.C.R. 728, 2005 SCC 80.

R. v. Kouri. 2005. SCC 81 (CanLII).

Vriend v. Alberta. 1998. 1 S.C.R. 493.

MONTREAL MASSACRE

Chapter 8

"I HATE FEMINISTS!"

Introduction

Mélissa Blais

From: *"I Hate Feminists," December 6, 1989 and its Aftermath*, pp. 14–15 (reprinted with permission).

On December 6, 1989, at around 5:00 p.m., as the women engineers-to-be at the École Polytechnique were studying or writing their end-of-term examinations, Marc Lépine, a twenty-five-year-old man dressed in army fatigues, went up to the second floor of the school and entered a classroom occupied by about sixty students, female and male (Gracia 1990; Pelchat and Boileau 1989). He separated the class into two groups and told the men to leave. When he was alone with the women students, he proclaimed: "I hate feminists!" One of the students, Nathalie Provost, replied that they were not feminists (*Le Devoir* 1989). He fired. It was 5:10 p.m., and a call immediately went out to emergency services (Lapointe 1990: 3). Marc Lépine left the classroom and fired at several other women as he moved to the third floor (Pelchat and Boileau 1989). The police arrived on the scene between 5:23 and 5:34 p.m., but stayed outside the building. In a classroom on the third floor, Lépine fired on more women students, and then took his own life with a final bullet at 5:29 p.m. The police entered the building at 5:37 p.m. (*La Presse* 1989; Lapointe 1990: 20), and began evacuating the injured around

6:05 p.m. Marc Lépine left fourteen women dead and fourteen people wounded (Lapointe 1990: 6).[1]

The killer was not known to the police. The newspapers revealed his identity the day after the shootings. The daily newspaper *La Presse* described his father's Algerian origin and gave his birth name, Gamil Gharbi (Gagnon and Laroche 1989).[2] It was then that we learned that he was out to get feminists. The Montreal police department had given the media a summary of his motives as expressed in the suicide note found on his body; with the note was a list of women and men he had been planning to murder, women who were pioneers in their fields (including the first woman firefighter and the first woman police officer), well-known feminists, and members of a pro-feminist group, the Collectif masculin contre le sexisme (Men's collective against sexism).[3] However, the public would not have access to the contents of the letter until November 24, 1990, when a contributor to *La Presse*, Francine Pelletier, received a copy of it, sent anonymously. In the letter, Lépine (1990) explained that he was committing suicide "for political reasons." He stated that he had decided "to send the feminists, who have always ruined my life, to meet their maker."[4] He had decided to "stop those viragos." Looking into the future, Marc Lépine then said that "even if the media call me a Mad Gunman, I consider myself a rational, educated person." He reiterated that "feminists have always enraged me. They want to keep the advantages of women (e.g., cheaper insurance, extended maternity leave preceded by a preventive leave, etc.) while seizing those of men." Feminists were "so opportunistic that they do not fail to take advantage of the knowledge accumulated by men through the ages. Yet they try to misrepresent it whenever they can." He saw feminists as rewriting history and claiming that they played an equal part in wars. "A real *Casus Belli*," he said in the conclusion of his letter, suggesting that feminists' actions could start a war, the war he had decided to wage by murdering fourteen women. Referring to his list of nineteen names, he stated that those persons had "nearly died today. Lack of time (because I started too late) has allowed these radical feminists to survive. *Alea Jacta Est.*" The die was cast.

The killer was familiar with the site of the attack; he had been seen there at least nine times in the months before the shootings (Mario Bilodeau 1990: 33, 41). He had wanted to become an engineer and to study at the École Polytechnique. In April 1989, a few months before committing his crime, he had met with a woman who worked in the registrar's office, who had informed him that he had to complete at least two college-level courses before he could register. According to that employee, Marc Lépine had reacted very badly and had "spoken with bitterness about women and the ever-increasing place they were taking in the job market. He felt that wasn't normal" (Gagné 2008: 221; translation).

In spite of the premeditated nature of his actions and his explicitly anti-feminist declarations, there were debates in the media about the meaning of his act.[5] Feminists provided a political reading of the event. Other social actors (intellectuals, journalists, psychologists, etc.) preferred to see it as a symptom of mental illness or the consequence of too easy access to firearms. Out of these differences, a collective memory was constructed that was marked by contradictory interpretations.

Various ways of recalling the tragedy were also evident in the media on the tenth (1999–2000) and the twentieth (2009) anniversaries of the massacre. On the tenth anniversary, different forms of commemoration (silent reflection, unveiling of commemorative plaques and monuments, publication of articles, direct actions, lobbying and a national campaign against firearms, etc.) revived the debates that had taken place immediately after the mass murder. Almost twenty years after the tragedy, the release of the film *Polytechnique* gave rise to a rearticulation of the collective memory, leading to the construction of a meaning of the massacre that sought to be consensual: men had also been affected by the killer; they too were victims. References to declarations made by feminists shortly after the massacre, criticizing men as a whole, were enough to discredit any feminist interpretation of the events and even to claim that men had been victims of feminists.

Notes

1. I checked the number of people wounded, since different sources give different figures. The Francophone media reported eleven wounded; since I took my information from these sources, that figure appears elsewhere in my work. However, the numbers from Dr. Pierre Lapointe are reliable. The figure of fourteen wounded is also found in Mercier-Leblond (1990: 33, 41). Among the wounded, four were male (Mario Bilodeau 1990: 19–20).

2. The headline read: "Le meurtrier antiféministe avait sur lui une 'liste rouge' de 14 femmes connues." Note the error; there was a total of nineteen names, of whom eighteen were women.

3. The names of a few of these women were given in articles in *La Presse* in 1990 and in an article by Francine Pelletier (2005).

4. Trans. note: The excerpts from Marc Lépine's letter are translated from the French original.

5. Marc Lépine was at the École Polytechnique for more than an hour before he started to shoot (Bilodeau 1990: 32).

References

Bilodeau, Mario. 1990. "L'opération policière et les services de sécurité de l'École Polytechnique de l'Université de Montréal." In Robert De Coster (chair), *La tragédie du 6 décembre 1989 à l'École Polytechnique de Montréal*. Québec City: Ministère de la Sécurité publique du Québec.

Gagné, Harold. 2008. *Vivre: Dix-neuf ans après la tragédie de la Polytechnique, Monique Lépine, la mère de Marc Lépine, se révèle*. Montreal: Libre Expression.

Gagnon, Martha, and Marcel Laroche. 1989. "Le meurtrier antiféministe avait sur lui une 'liste rouge' de 14 femmes connues." *La Presse*, December 8.

Gracia, Agnès. 1990. "La police reconnaît qu'elle a manqué de leadership lors de la tuerie à Poly." *La Presse*, January 26.

La Presse. 1989. "La police a été lente, estiment des rescapés." December 11.

Le Devoir. 1989. "Une étudiante a tenté de raisonner Lépine." December 9.

Lapointe, Pierre. 1990. "Les services préhospitaliers et hospitaliers d'urgence." In Robert De Coster (chair), *La tragédie du 6 décembre 1989 à l'École Polytechnique de Montréal*. Québec City: Ministère de la Sécurité publique du Québec.

Lépine, Marc. 1990. "Je me considère comme un érudit rationnel." *La Presse*, November 24.

Mercier-Leblond, Gabrielle. 1990. "Les interventions psychosociales." In Robert De Coster (chair), *La tragédie du 6 décembre 1989 à l'École Polytechnique de Montréal*. Québec City: Ministère de la Sécurité publique du Québec.

Pelchat, Martin, and Josée Boileau. 1989. "Un forcené tue 14 étudiantes de Polytechnique et se suicide." *Le Devoir*, December 7.

____. 1990. "La lettre de Marc Lépine: une clé importante pour comprendre la fusillade de l'École Polytechnique." *La Presse*, November 24.

____. 2005. "Je me souviens: Polytechnique." In *La Vie en rose*, special issue: 34–37. Montreal: Remue-ménage.

Chapter 9

FROM MARGINALIZATION TO DISPARAGEMENT OF FEMINIST DISCOURSES

Mélissa Blais

From: *"I Hate Feminists!" December 6, 1989 and Its Aftermath*, pp. 50–73 (reprinted with permission).

The reality of women as a social group is constantly being denied: as soon as it is alluded to as such, it no longer exists, it gets lost in the particularities. (Colette Guillaumin 1991)

In addition to giving only a marginal place to feminist discourses on the massacre, the newspapers disseminated other discourses that were directly or indirectly opposed to feminism. From 1989 to 1999, there were seven different types of discourses in the newspapers that marginalized, dismissed, co-opted or disparaged feminist analyses:

- the need to forget;
- silence and contemplation;
- generalized violence;
- the phenomenon of mass murders;
- public security;
- gun control; and
- the killer's psychology ("the mad killer").

The often conflictual relationship between these discourses and feminist discourses had the effect of producing a shifting, changing, multiple collective memory, certain elements of which encouraged the formation or maintenance of hierarchical sexual identities and denied the political differences between gender categories.

DISCOURSES THAT MARGINALIZED FEMINIST PARADIGMS

Collective memory is a stake in political struggle. As historian Patrice Groulx has shown in a study of the collective memory of Dollard des Ormeaux, Aboriginal people in the seventies changed the status of that "hero" (Groulx 1998: 355) by exposing his murderous actions in the context of European colonialism, transforming the collective memory of this man so that he is no longer celebrated as a hero in Québec today.[1]

Feminists attempted — starting immediately after the mass murder — to establish their understanding of the event, presenting Marc Lépine as a misogynist and anti-feminist. Non-feminist and anti-feminist discourses used very different social frameworks of memory and proposed other interpretations of the killer's act to orient the social uses that would be made of that memory, in explicit or implicit opposition to the desire for change expressed by the feminists. These different interpretations of the causes of the massacre coexisted in a power relationship that was unfavourable to the feminists, both quantitatively and qualitatively. Explicitly feminist texts were in the minority and were relegated to spaces such as the letters to the editor, while the feminists' adversaries expressed themselves on the editorial pages and enjoyed a more prestigious status as politicians and experts, whose words are generally considered credible.

While feminist analyses were repeated many times during commemorations and mobilizations, those who did not support those analyses also hastened — starting immediately after the attack — to organize official (religious and governmental) commemorative events that ignored the political meaning of the massacre. Such haste was necessary for both sides, because "without commemorative vigilance, history would soon sweep [sites of memory] away. These bastions buttress our identities, but if what they defended were not threatened, there would be no need for them" (Nora 1996: 7). Given the multiple and conflictual nature of the collective memory of December 6, 1989, it goes without saying that various coexisting discourses competed to become established through the commemorative events.

The media mainly covered the commemorations organized by student, religious and government bodies. Although these bodies were heterogeneous and included feminists in their ranks, their spokespersons' discourses were not feminist. Unlike the feminists' memorial expressions, those I will analyze in this chapter often received an official seal of approval, giving them a credibility that permitted them to establish their models of representation in physical space (through a commemorative plaque, for example, or through access to places of influence and prestige, such as the ceremonies that took place at Notre-Dame Basilica).

The Need to Forget

The first type of discourse rejected outright all work of memory, demanding that the tragedy be forgotten. Wieviorka (2005: 71; translation) explains the terrible consequences of the collective forgetting of a social tragedy:

> Must we not, in order to live together, erase what has been … a web of terrible violence? Some countries have therefore made the choice not to expose a recent event, sometimes in order to protect the perpetrators but also, in other cases, to move forward into the future while avoiding reopening wounds that are still very fresh … But beyond the fact that silence and forgetting in the name of the common interest obviously work in the interest of the perpetrators or the guilty and not necessarily that of the victims, experience suggests that a country that decides to do the work on itself called for by a recent past of extreme violence and mass crimes fares better than a country that does not.

As Elena de la Aldea points out with respect to the memory of the dictatorship in Argentina, forced forgetting leads to a damaging social silence (de la Aldea 2005: 341). In the case of the École Polytechnique massacre, silence may have contributed to muzzling feminists by allowing men especially and Québec society in general to avoid asking themselves questions that were, to say the least, awkward. The strategy of forgetting, according to Joël Candau, "can also be an advantage that permits the person or group to construct or restore a self-image that is on the whole satisfactory" (Candau 1996: 83; translation), in this case, the self-image of men with respect to women.

Appeals to forgetting with regard to the École Polytechnique massacre were thus aimed at maintaining the status quo in gender relations. Like Stuart Hall, we can see operating here one of the roles of the mass media, that is, to align the general interests of the population with those of a particular class or power (that of men in this case). "Once this system of equivalences has been achieved, the interests of the minority and the will of the majority can be 'squared' because they can both be represented as coinciding in the consensus, on which all sides agree. The consensus is the medium, the regulator, by means of which this necessary alignment (or equalization) between power and consent is accomplished" (Hall 1982: 86–97).

Sometimes, the project of memory of the massacre was challenged in the name of consensus or social cohesion, as in the case of the opposition to remembrances of the massacre. On December 1, 1990, *La Presse* editorialist Alain Dubuc asked:

"Why not try to forget, as the director of the Poly has suggested?" He added: "But the Poly is also a collective tragedy, which has traumatized all Québecers and, even more so, all Québec women, which has marked our society and raised difficult questions that have not all been answered" (Dubuc 1990; translation). These difficult questions seemed to justify forgetting. Thus, Louise Choquet (1990; translation) would have preferred that the government pay no attention to this sad event, since it was important to maintain harmony between the sexes:

> Recognizing the desperate actions of one individual as having national scope, the government has endorsed the symbolism of "violent, dangerous masculinity." Half the population has thus been able to identify with the persecutor and the other half with the victims, and society as a whole is unable to put the parts back together again to make a harmonious whole.

We see here the idea of a memory that divides society rather than helping it transcend the tragedy. By choosing forgetting, we would convince ourselves that the interests of men and women were the same, thus preserving "a harmonious whole" and maintaining male privilege.

While some were seeking consensus and social harmony, family and friends of the victims were speaking out in the large-circulation newspapers in favour of preserving the memories of the tragedy, saying that it was important not to forget the deaths of their daughters, sisters and spouses (Fortin 1989a; Poirier and McKenna 1989).[2]

Silence and Contemplation

The second type of discourse, while it did not encourage forgetting, demanded silent contemplation out of respect for the victims' loved ones. For example, immediately after the massacre, the Québec government declared a collective mourning for the fourteen victims (Descôteaux 1989). Many institutions adopted this approach: Father Aumont of the Catholic Church stated, "Faced with suffering ... often the best attitude is silence" (Béliveau 1989; translation). While they did not oppose the work of memory, these calls for silence, like the appeals to forget, sought to produce a social consensus based on national identity (the unified "we" of Québec) or Christian values.[3] Cardinal Paul Grégoire asked the population to "stand together" in order to "forge the solid ties that unite us in the Lord" (*Le Devoir* 1989b; translation).

Journalists also adopted this type of discourse. On December 9, 1989, editorialist Claude Masson of *La Presse* wrote of the importance of rediscovering Christian faith. The *Globe and Mail* also encouraged silent mourning out of respect for the victims. Journalist Lise Bissonnette seemed disappointed by what she described as the deafening noise and voyeurism of the media; in her opinion, the rare moments of respect were the minutes of silence during a vigil organized by Polytechnique students on December 7, 1989 (Bissonnette 1989). *Le Devoir* editorialist Benoît Lauzière wrote, "It should be enough for us to share the pain and distress of the family and friends of the victims. This should be done primarily in silence and in the greatest respect" (Lauzière 1989; translation). Some writers specified what they meant by respect, such as Jean-V Dufresne, who praised silent contemplation as opposed to public declarations, including those expressing "acrimony between men and women" (J.-V. Dufresne 1990; translation). Thus, some of the appeals for silence were accompanied by reactions against feminism, which was considered disrespectful of the fourteen dead women.

Journalists covering religious commemorations such as the one at Notre-Dame Basilica on December 11, 1989, spoke of these appeals for silence. They took up the words of Cardinal Grégoire, who, in contrast to the feminists, called for "forgiveness" so as to "build a brotherly world" (J. Boileau 1989b; translation). Father Delage called on members of the Christian community to forgive Marc Lépine during a ceremony in memory of Maryse Laganière (Poirier 1989). Many journalists similarly reported the appeals for silence to a community people wished to see as unified (Proulx 1990; "La Tuque").

In addition to the religious commemorations, there were official commemorations by the École Polytechnique and the government that took the form of minutes of silence (Descôteaux 1989), liturgies (Proulx 1990), a public visitation attended by some ten thousand people (Doré 1989) and the unveiling of a commemorative plaque (Léger 1990). All these events united the victims and the killer in silence and mourning. On the first anniversary of the massacre, at the unveiling of a marble plaque on which the names of the fourteen murdered women were inscribed, Jean-Pierre Proulx reported "a single reference, if that, to Marc Lépine: during the Prayer of the Faithful, the people in attendance prayed 'for those who suffer and those who are discouraged'" (Proulx 1990; translation).

The student community of the Université de Montréal called for silence as well, in *Le Continuum*, in order to ensure comfort and contemplation for the mourners. Françoise Beaudoin of the executive committee of the federation of student associations of the Université de Montréal summed up this desire as follows: "At times like this, when everyone is seeking a little comfort above all, all are entitled to contemplate the memory of the deceased in peace, silence and respect for their pain" (Beaudoin 1990; translation). Similarly, *Le Continuum* chose as the front page of the issue following the massacre a "page of silence," that is, a blank page (*Le Continuum* 1990; translation).

In an article with the evocative headline "Polytechnique wants to remember in 'respect and contemplation'" (Léger 1990; translation), Marie-France Léger reported on the commemorations at the École Polytechnique. She quoted the director of the school, André Bazergui, who expressed his desire to show respect and spoke against the publication of Lépine's letter. Representatives of student communities also took part in several official commemorations and had the benefit of an important media platform with respect to the events that had occurred in the school. In both the Francophone press and the *Globe and Mail* (see, for example, Malarek 1989a), journalists covering the student commemorations emphasized the speeches that favoured the contemplation and silence associated with respect for mourning (*Globe and Mail* 1989a; J. Boileau 1989a; Béliveau 1989). An analysis of the messages of condolence sent to the École Polytechnique, carried out by Lévy, Samson and Sansfaçon, also reveals that "the messages from Université de Montréal students had more of an emotional or religious dimension" than those from students of other universities (Sansfaçon et al. 1994; translation).

Journalists at the *Globe and Mail* mentioned the Université de Montréal students' request for silent contemplation. In an article entitled "Students' silence part of debate over killings," Michelle Lalonde also spoke of feminists' reactions to that silence, saying that many of them were dismayed by the fact that the students and the administration of the École Polytechnique had been completely silent on violence against women (Michelle Lalonde 1990b; Picard and Lalonde 1990). Some women engineers made the same observation, stating in a press release published in the *Globe and Mail*: "We have been silent too long and deeply regret if by our silence we have fostered a climate which does not actively discourage hostile acts or attitudes toward women" (Quinn Dressel Associates 1989).

Generalized Violence

The discourses focusing on the many forms of violence did not specify the gender of the persons targeted by the killer. There was abundant condemnation of violence in elementary and high schools, violence on television, and breaking and entering in homes, without any recognition of the fact that violence against women is a specific phenomenon that it is important to analyze as such in order to orient prevention and awareness campaigns, and to better understand the December 6, 1989, massacre.

In an article on the National Assembly's decision to declare a collective mourning, *La Presse* reported on statements by the members of the National Assembly discussing the elimination of various forms of violence and the social integration of people with difficulties (Normand 1989a; *Le Devoir* 1989a). *Le Continuum* ran articles condemning various forms of social violence without specifying the gender of the victims (Plourde 1990). *La Presse* published a list of crimes that had taken place the same year as the massacre, from violent acts (including that of Lépine) to tax fraud (Binsse 1989). Similarly, Timothy Appleby reported on an increase in homicides, including the December 6, 1989, massacre (Appleby 1990). Other writers speculated about the channels of transmission of social violence. Journalists such as Michèle Ouimet presented the opposing camps in the debate on the influence of violence on television; she indirectly took a position in favour of changes in television programming by beginning her article with a denunciation of the inaction of the television networks after the shooting (Ouimet 1989b). Finally, a short piece in the *Globe and Mail* reported that, according to the police, Lépine liked war movies, and added that a movie about a terrorist act in a school had been shown on television two days before the tragedy (*Globe and Mail* 1989b).

The articles that talked about a possible link between exposure to violence on television and Lépine's act focused on the psychological causes of the massacre. But, as sociologist Richard Poulin points out, "Lethal male violence is commonly associated with serious psychological disorders; the connection is undeniable, but it says nothing about — and may even serve to conceal — the social dynamics involved. Such violence is tied to the oppression of women and based on a conception of masculinity and a social construction that foster the appropriation of women by men" (Poulin and Dulong 2010: 56–57). In fact, discussions of violence usually do not deal with the oppression of women and do not specify that this is male violence.

Violence against women is not exactly in the same category of social problems as breaking and entering, a war or Bugs Bunny's brutality toward Daffy Duck. Before the modification of the *Civil Code* in 1964 and the removal of the obligation for a wife to obey her husband, men in Québec had the right to beat their wives (Canada, Department of Justice 2013). What remains today of men's ancestral right to beat their wives with impunity?

In no instance was the concept of male privilege included in the discourses focusing on generalized violence. However, as the engineer Karen L. Tonso pointed out, Lépine in fact used violence to defend a hierarchical society and claim his privileged place as a man, in opposition to the women who were working to take it from him (Tonso 2009: 1270). As sociologist Colette Guillaumin (1991: 11) says of December 6, 1989:

> These murders [of women] did not even lead people to ask questions; they were not seen as social acts of a collective nature as the others were; they did not even enter public consciousness ... These acts then did not mobilize public opinion, did not call forth any public protest ... But the fact is that racism is outlawed, even if it is practiced by many, while sexism is the substratum of the law, the normal state of a society which is plainly based on the physical and mental *availability* of women.

The journalists who promoted the discourse of generalized violence discounted the responsibility of the active social subject (Marc Lépine) and the fact that he belonged to a gender class (males), as did his targets (females), while assigning responsibility for social violence to a producer of discourse (television). In addition to denying the responsibility of the killer, such a discourse ignored the phenomenon of violence against women.

The Phenomenon of Mass Murders

Journalists from the major daily papers were quick to compare the École Polytechnique massacre with mass murders that had occurred in the United States and Europe. On December 7, 1989, *La Presse* ran the headline "Aucun pays n'est épargné par ce genre de tuerie" ["No country is spared this kind of massacre"]. Under it was a list of massacres committed mostly in the United States, without any mention of the categories of persons targeted. Sociologist Yanick Dulong states, "Since the late 1980s in the United States ... there have been some 10 mass killings in which sex acts were committed on the victims, for the most part women and little girls." These data did not lead journalists to consider that "women are often the victims of mass murderers, if we take into account the male murderers who target women and children in their own families, something which is overlooked in the scientific literature" (Poulin and Dulong 2010: 76–77).

La Presse and *Le Devoir* instead drew a parallel between Marc Lépine and Corporal Lortie, who in 1984 had entered the National Assembly armed and intending to murder sovereignist members of the legislature (*La Presse* 1989; Normand 1989a; Cauchon 1989a; Gingras 1989a). (This kind of analysis seems to have been absent from the student newspaper *Le Continuum*.) All the articles that made this type of comparison invoked the supposed insanity of the murderers. Martin Pelchat pointed out that in trying to identify Lépine's motives, police officers made comparisons with similar spectacular crimes (Pelchat 1990c). Journalists who report on mass murders talk very little about the motives of the murderers, but rather emphasize their presumed loss of contact with reality. According to Poulin and Dulong (2010: 72), "Insanity is often the core explanation given for mass killings, but most killers are not madmen divorced from reality." The explanation for multiple murders must be sought "not in the murderer himself, his insanity or his childhood traumas, but in his chosen targets: his victims. This change of perspective allows us to understand the political and social dynamics of multiple murders and casts an entirely new light on something which at first glance seems inexplicable apart from the presumed insanity of the killer" (Poulin and Dulong 2010: 12).

Comparisons between the Polytechnique massacre and various other collective crimes were particularly prominent in the *Globe and Mail*. However, they differed somewhat from the comparisons in the Francophone dailies. These differences included the use of quotations from social scientists emphasizing the sociological causes of psychological problems (Valpy 1989). And on the whole, the journalists from the *Globe* who placed Lépine's crime in the context of serial murders and mass crimes stressed the gender of the victims more often than their colleagues at the *La Presse* and *Le Devoir*, emphasizing this distinctive aspect of the event (MacLeod 1989). But this was not sufficient to allow us to conclude that there was a greater openness to feminist analyses at the *Globe and Mail*. The impact of these details was often cancelled out by the flood of information on other mass murders that did not target only women and by the absence of any explanation of Lépine's motives. Like the analyses that denounced generalized violence rather than violence against women, the discourse on mass murders ignored any understanding of the event based on an analysis of gender relations. This approach could even lead to surprising results: on February 28, 1990, close to three months after the massacre, *Le Devoir* published an article that was actually entitled "La police ne trouve pas ce qui a déclenché le geste de Lépine à Poly" ["The police have not found what triggered Lépine's act at the Poly"] (Pelchat 1990c).

Public Security
Much was written about the failures in the response of the police and emergency services. Journalists tried to determine if lives could have being saved if the police response had been different. The discourse on public security did not look at the causes of the massacre, but tried instead to find responsible parties (mainly the police) other than those identified by feminists (men as a historical group). According to *La Presse* and *Le Devoir,* some students at the École Polytechnique felt that the police took too long to respond (more than twenty minutes) (*La Presse* 1989c; *Le Devoir* 1989f). These articles then explained that the killer had time to fire 300 bullets, suggesting a causal link between the slowness of the police response and the number of victims. Lysiane Gagnon demanded an explanation from the Montreal Urban Community police, which still had not offered one on January 11, 1990 (L. Gagnon 1990). The chief of police admitted mistakes by the department first at a press conference on January 26, 1990 (Gracia 1990; Pelchat 1990b), and a second time on May 25, after a second report was produced (Lortie 1990c; C. Montpetit 1990). That did not seem sufficient because, on the first anniversary of the massacre, journalists again recalled the slowness of the police response (Colpron 1990a). The *Globe and Mail* asked the police for further details on the killer and the massacre (Malarek 1989b) rather than questioning them on the shortcomings of their response, which did not seem to interest the newspaper.[4]

Jean-Claude Leclerc in *Le Devoir* called for a public inquiry, because he felt that the police report by Alain St-Germain did not explain all the problems with the police response. He asked in particular how a killer could be neutralized before committing irreparable damage (Leclerc 1990). In response to this request, which was also made by parents of some of the victims (Pelchat 1990e), the minister of public security, Sam L. Elkas, ordered a study of how to improve emergency services (De Coster 1990). The study did not examine the motives of the killer or the specific nature of these murders, focusing instead on the recommendations of coroner Teresa Z. Sourour with respect to emergency communications, police operations, etc. The ambulance service was also criticized by journalist Suzanne Colpron (1990b) and others. Michèle Ouimet asked about the possibility of improving security on campuses, citing the case of the Université du Québec à Montréal, which has about twenty entrances and is accessible by subway. Unlike her colleagues, she advocated a change in attitudes:

> For Susan Addario, personal safety officer at the University of Toronto, high-tech equipment such as video cameras and access cards alone cannot prevent a Marc Lépine: "We can hardly build a wall around the university. We have to change attitudes. At the engineering school, for example, there is a sexist tradition that we want to fight." (Ouimet 1990; translation)

Most feminists did not seem opposed to the discourse on improvements to emergency services, improvements that could be beneficial for women, even though that discourse, like all those examined in this chapter, ignored the killer's motives and the political implications of his act.

Gun Control

There was a perceptible bias in the press in favour of the mobilizations for gun control.[5] It is surprising that in spite of the École Polytechnique students' association's petition for stricter gun control, only a single article in *Le Continuum* dealt with the subject, and only indirectly, in a report on efforts by the student community of the Université de Montréal to counter violence (Plourde 1990). The lack of articles on firearms is a response to the explicit desire of *Le Continuum* — discussed above — to observe silence on the tragedy in order to ease mourning for people.

In contrast, the firearm used by the killer was repeatedly presented as a problem by journalists at the *Globe and Mail* as well as *La Presse* and *Le Devoir*. Barely two days after the murders, *La Presse* described the .223-calibre Ruger Mini-14 used by Lépine. Jean-Paul Soulié tried to find out how easy it was to obtain this type of semi-automatic weapon and emphasized the fact that it was a weapon of war, not a hunting rifle (Soulié 1989). *La Presse* quickly took a position against access to these weapons, and began talking about gun control on December, 8, 1989 (April 1989a). There was a drawing of a semi-automatic weapon with an X over it in *La Presse* of December 9, 1989 (p. A11). The *Globe and Mail* of December 8, 1989, discussed the Conservative government's promises to legislate on gun control (Cleroux and McInnes 1989).

The corollary to this explicit position was favourable coverage of the mobilization for gun control. *La Presse* of December 10, 1989, announced that the minister of justice, Doug Lewis, did not intend to prohibit semi-automatic weapons (April 1989b), although the mobilization against them had substantial support, with 550,000 people signing a petition (M. Cornellier 1990) and a large number of letters on the subject published in the daily papers (for example: Sherkey 1989; McLaughlin 1989; Couto 1989).

It is impossible, however, to know whether the media covered this mobilization so extensively because it was so broad or if the mobilization was so broad because the media covered it so extensively. *La Presse, Le Devoir* and the *Globe and Mail* wrote about gun owners (for example, Gingras 1989), gun murders (for example, *La Presse* 1990b; Moon, 1990) and petitions (for example, J. Boileau 1990), and there were also many articles on amendments to the laws and on the gun control bill (Lortie 1990f; Gruda 1990; *La Presse* 1990d; "Canadian gun control under fire" 1989; French 1990). These papers closely followed the details of the mobilization and the political reactions to it. *La Presse* of January 13, 1990, reported on the support following the launch of the petition (*La Presse* 1990a). *Le Devoir* of January 18–19, 1990, stressed the mobilization of the municipalities in favour of changes to the law on firearms (Pelchat 1990a; *Le Devoir* 1990a). *La Presse* of June 27, 1990, reported on the pressure on the minister, Kim Campbell (*La Presse* 1990e). These newspapers criticized the federal government's slowness in passing the law (Pelletier 1990c; *Le Devoir* 1990b) and recalled the existence of the gun control petition (Dubuisson 1990; Francoeur 1990).

At the same time, Jeanne Maranda of Évaluation-Médias said she was having difficulty finding support for setting up a campaign to raise consciousness on violence against women in the schools. She obtained no financial support and only gathered 2,500 signatures on her petition asking the government to legislate against sexism and violence in the media, while the gun control petition had obtained 300,000 signatures, as reported in an article in *La Presse* on February 15, 1990. An interesting fact: that article was the only one that mentioned — at the very end — the petition against violence against women (Lortie 1990a).

In short, the media bias in favour of gun control as a way to try to prevent a repetition of this type of mass murder diverted attention from the true causes of the massacre to the instrument used (the weapon), ignoring the problem of inequality between the sexes. Paradoxically, even the words of the murderer — who chose this type of weapon — were almost totally ignored in analyses of the causes and the solutions proposed to prevent such attacks.

The Killer's Psychology ("The Mad Killer")

Analysis of the French-language corpus shows four forms of the psychological discourse: first, the use of psychologists' reports by journalists, editorialists and others, who thus justified their bias in favour of a psychological explanation for the massacre; second, direct statements by experts in the field and the important place given to them in the newspapers; third, the appropriation of this type of expert opinion by journalists and police; and fourth, the repetition by journalists of statements made on the killer's mental health during the commemorative events on the first anniversary of the massacre. All these expressions complemented each other to establish a psychological explanation of the massacre.

In an article entitled "Échos de la profession. 6 décembre 1989: retour sur l'événement" [Echos from the profession. December 6, 1989: A look back at the event], criminologist Marie-Andrée Bertrand criticized the fact that many analysts of the event sought explanations in the criminal and in him alone. She pointed out that the police made diagnoses without having real expertise (see, for example, Gagnon and Laroche 1989a). This reveals a conflict between two groups, men and women: men, as a privileged group, had an interest in ignoring the political aspect of the murder and formulating individualistic psychological explanations (Bertrand 1990).

The police were not the only ones to play psychologist despite their lack of expertise in that field. Journalists from La Presse and Le Devoir regularly explained Lépine's motives with psychologizing analyses. On the day after the attack, the front page of La Presse stated, "Un tireur fou abat quatorze femmes" [A mad gunman kills fourteen women]. Almost all the journalists at Le Continuum also adopted this approach. Calling on women not to give up the idea of studying at the École Polytechnique, Nicolas Plourde said, "We must above all not allow an isolated lunatic alone in his madness to divert them from one of the most beautiful careers they could dream of" (Plourde 1990; translation). In the same issue, the editorialist explained, "The action of this man was an isolated act, the act of a sick person, no doubt, but an act from which we cannot draw any major philosophical or other conclusions" (Braconnier 1990; translation).

Playing their roles as experts in psychology, journalists denied the feminist views. Furthermore, as Colette Beauchamp observes, they "place[d] the blame for so-called conjugal violence on the personal problems of the authors of the violence and turn[ed] women from victims into guilty parties" (Beauchamp 1998: 212; translation). Journalists from La Presse and Le Devoir actively sought the causes of the killer's violence in his personal difficulties with women, thus making them responsible for his supposed emotional problems. The front page of La Presse of December 8, 1989, described Lépine's failures, saying, "His main preoccupation was women. In spite of his efforts, he was not able to form friendships with them.

The accumulation of disappointments seems to have produced a great frustration in him that even became an obsession" (Gagnon and Laroche 1989b).

In their coverage of the commemorations, journalists again took part in the construction of the collective memory by emphasizing the words of students who adopted a discourse on the killer's mental health. For example, Marc Doré of *La Presse*, who covered the tribute to the victims by more than ten thousand people at the public visitation in the main building of the Université de Montréal, chose to quote people who spoke of Lépine's suffering. Similarly, Gérard Leblanc quoted Louise Leclair, the mother of one of the victims, who said that Lépine must have been suffering a great deal to do such a thing (1989a). However, other relatives and friends of the victims adopted a completely different analysis of the massacre, putting more emphasis on the situation of the women than on their killer. This was the case for Jean-François Larivée, the husband of Maryse Laganière, who asked,

> What is gained for women? That they take their place in the labour market, but with lower pay? That they be subject to all kinds of mockery if they ask to be respected? ... That the police now take seriously the violence against them? That they now have shelters where they can go and hide? ... The truth is that women have not gained everything. And the small gains they have made through hard struggle are constantly under threat. (quoted in Bélanger 1997: 63; translation)

Some journalists used the same filter when covering the minute of silence at Cégep du Vieux-Montréal. Michèle Ouimet wrote of "emotion mixed with incredulity and a certain aggressiveness toward the person responsible for this massacre. 'The killer was right to commit suicide. He was a sick man,' explained a female student. 'He was disturbed,' said another" (Ouimet 1989a; translation).

A conference on the prevention of violence was organized at the Université de Montréal on the first anniversary of the massacre. Patrick Grandjean covered the event, focusing on a talk by psychologist Guy Corneau, who explained that "in the absence of the father and without support from peers — Lépine was rejected by the army and the Poly — this man 'was never confirmed in his identity as a man'" (Grandjean 1990; translation). Grandjean reported on Corneau's lecture in the lead of his article, and only discussed the presentation by his feminist colleague Francine Pelletier further down, in just a few lines. This bias in favour of the psychological discourse was confirmed in the headline of the article, "Marc Lépine: a case of 'absent father, lost son,'" which referred to the title of Corneau's book.

Psychologists and psychiatrists went further, trying to understand the massacre by looking at Lépine's behaviour, family history and development. A few articles suffice to show the importance placed on them in the Francophone newspapers.

In *La Presse* of December 1, 1990, Marie-Claude Lortie (1990e) compiled various hypotheses put forward by Dominique Scarfone, a psychoanalyst and psychiatrist; Hifzija Bajramovic, a psychiatrist; Renée Fugère, a psychiatrist; Lorne Yeudall, a neuropsychologist; and J. Dankwort, a researcher in social work. In technical language that was difficult for the uninitiated to understand, these experts explained the killer's act in terms of a psychotic disorder. Their views took up most of the article and were discussed starting in the lead. Only a few lines at the very end of the article discussed the views of the only expert who said he was suspicious of the diagnoses made (Lortie 1990e).

Psychiatrists were often consulted by *La Presse* journalists to create a portrait of Lépine.[6] Readers learned of the family violence he was subjected to, his failure to be accepted in the army and his dropping out of school (Lortie 1990b; Colpron 1989; Boisvert 1989; *La Presse* 1989b; Ouimet 1989a). It is interesting to note that the majority of these psychological analyses focused on Lépine's interactions with his environment such as family and school; macrosociological considerations such as gender dynamics and the psychosocial development of a man in a misogynist society marked by inequality between the sexes were ignored. On December 8, 1989, *Le Devoir* published a column by Paul Cauchon referring to the hypothesis of Yves Lamontagne, director of the Louis-Hippolyte-Lafontaine research centre — who had not met with the murderer or read his letter (which was still confidential at that time) — that Lépine had an anti-social personality disorder (Cauchon 1989).

Unlike many experts who expressed their views in the media, Marie Chabot, a psychologist in mental health and consultant to the Ministry of Public Security, had access to confidential information on the murderer. She concluded her report by saying, "We have to go beyond thinking about concrete preventive measures, which, of course, are necessary. It is important to ask questions about violence, its consequences and the roles of men and women in our society and the family to really understand Lépine's act. We are all concerned, but nothing will change without disruption" (Mercier-Leblond 1990: 53; translation). But newspapers refused to raise questions about Québec society and gender relations and persisted in quoting psychologists and psychiatrists who, without carrying out a clinical examination, sought the causes of the massacre in their assessment of Lépine's mental health. For example, *Le Devoir* printed a comment by Michèle Brunet, a pediatrician, that concluded, "This man, this Gamil Gharbi, known as Marc Lépine, had everything that was biologically necessary to carry out such an act" (Gagnon-Brunette 1989; translation).

The psychological discourse was also abundantly repeated by the *Globe and Mail* (for example, Appleby 1989). However, the field of expertise favoured was not the same as in the Francophone newspapers. The journalists of the *Globe* (for example, Valpy 1989) quoted anthropologists and sociologists, who highlighted the sexist nature of the crime. Elliot Leyton, an anthropologist at Memorial University in Newfoundland, and James Fox, a criminologist, felt that the murders were exceptional, since it is very rare for mass murderers to target women.[7] They added that Marc Lépine had chosen his victims because of the specific nature of the place, which, according to Fox, suggested that Lépine did indeed want to attack feminist advances. Fox felt that if he had simply wanted to kill women, Lépine would have chosen a traditionally female workplace. Both of them finally maintained that Lépine's act was based on machismo or male chauvinism (MacLeod 1989), which is confirmed by Poulin and Dulong (2010).

While the *Globe and Mail* seemed at first glance to show interest in the specific nature of the murders, many of the journalists and most of the experts who expressed their views in its pages were far from favouring a feminist analysis. For example, Michael Valpy reported criminologist Jean-Paul Brodeur's view that "half of us are crazy and half of us are waiting to be" (1989). While they emphasized the gender of the victims, Brodeur and Valpy agreed that Lépine's motives were psychological. Although they talked about social factors in their analysis of the killer's mental health, they still did not take into account the power dynamics discussed by many feminists, even when they mentioned the misogynist nature of the murder. The search for causes that would explain the crime remained confined to the broad domain of psychology.[8]

This choice gave rise to many contradictions. As Poulin and Dulong point out, "A difficult childhood, setbacks and traumatic incidents are certainly no justification for mass murder, for the majority of people who have been injured by life do not become murderers" (Poulin and Dulong 2010: 72). Lépine's mother, Monique Lépine, a nurse, expressed a similar view, saying that she was not responsible for her son's choices and that "not all children who lack love commit murders" (quoted in Gagné 2008: 97; translation). The killer's sister, Nadia Gharbi, a victim, like Lépine, of their father's violence, committed suicide with an overdose of cocaine in 1996. Unlike her brother, "she went quietly, without any noise" (Gagné 2008: 228; translation), and without murdering anyone.

Other contradictions appeared in Martin Pelchat's article quoting Lieutenant Gauvreau of the Montreal police, who was still trying, three months after the attack, to understand the murderer's motives. In contradiction to the diagnoses of the experts quoted by the journalists, Gauvreau's study showed that "Marc Lépine had no criminal past ... And despite all the searching through his life and his relationships with people, there was nothing that would make him a murderer. 'His behaviour was the same as that of a lot of people'" (Pelchat 1990s; translation). According to the officer in charge of the investigation, André Tessier, Marc Lépine was "a model of calm. He seemed to be in full possession of his faculties. He wanted to go down in history" (Gagné 2008: 248; translation).

I previously quoted an article in *La Presse* from December 8, 1989, saying that Lépine was not able to make friends with women (Gagnon and Laroche 1989b). However, Suzanne Colpron of *La Presse* questioned José Lopez, a chemistry teacher at Cégep du Vieux-Montréal who had taught Lépine, who stated: "As far as I knew, he had no problems. He worked with a girl as a lab partner. She wasn't very good and he did all the work without complaining. He was very nice to her" (Colpron 1989). According to one of his friends, although Lépine was shy with women, he regularly took his break with his female colleagues during his shifts at St. Jude Hospital. His mother recounted that Marc Lépine had kissed a girl. This said one of his friends, Érik Cossette, confirmed that Lépine was prejudiced against women: "He was convinced that they should stay in the home and take care of their families. He thought it was ridiculous for them to become police officers, a job he felt should be reserved for men" (quoted in Gagné 2008: 54; translation). The fact remains that, like other men, he behaved like "a gentleman" with women he liked and was capable of setting aside his anti-feminist discourse in their presence (Gagné 2008: 173; translation).

Like many others, an article in *Le Devoir* of December 9, 1989, said that "nothing in his previous history distinguished Lépine from other men" (*Le Devoir* 1989) and that he had no learning difficulties in school. One teacher even called him a diligent student. His mother and his friends also believed he had higher than average intelligence. According to Monique Lépine, he "was a good little boy who had no psychiatric problems. He was a gifted student who got a hundred per cent in his math exams in college" (quoted in Gagné 2008: 221, 35; translation). According to the *Globe and Mail*, the merchant who sold him the gun said that Lépine did not look any crazier than anyone else ("After the Montreal massacre (2)" 1990).

In addition to these examples, the discourse of the police officers also included certain contradictions. Wendy Hui Kyong Chun of Brown University in the United States observes that the police claimed, on the one hand, that Lépine's act was incomprehensible, that nothing in their investigations permitted them to reconstruct its logic and that the December 6 massacre was an isolated act, and on the other hand, that the desire to kill feminists was present in a segment of the population and that it was important to stop the investigations so as not to encourage acts of anti-feminist violence (Chun 1999: 113). How could an isolated act at the same time be reproduced by a segment of the population?

There were also inconsistencies in the solutions considered in order to prevent a repeat of this type of crime. For example, *La Presse* of December 8, 1989, reported on a proposal by Claude Ryan, the minister of education and higher education, that "these people" be "supervised so that they cannot cause harm socially and can be integrated as much as possible into society" (quoted in Normand 1989b; translation). This proposal suggested that Marc Lépine's main motives were intrinsically related to his supposed social, emotional and academic problems. But, given the fact that he was a good student, capable of behaving well with women while harbouring contempt for feminism and admiration for Adolf Hitler (Gagné 2008: 55), would it not be more appropriate to "supervise" anti-feminists and fans of Nazi Germany so that they could not "cause harm socially"?

Given these contradictions, how can we explain the importance placed on the psychological discourse on the École Polytechnique massacre? Indeed, while the family and friends of Lépine "[could] not give a diagnosis of his act, others, without any evidence, persisted in considering him crazy" (Boudreau 1996: 89; translation). Andrée Côté criticized the predominance of psychologizing discourse in the media in a speech at the Union française on December 13, 1989. She said, "At the outset, Marc Lépine was designated as "a 'sick man,' a 'mad killer,' a 'maniac.' Having characterized him in this way, one could dismantle the political impact of his crime" (A. Côté 1991: 67). The use of this type of expert opinion permitted journalists to reduce Lépine's act to an individual action and to present the event as exceptional. Comparisons of different crimes committed specifically against women and analyses seeking explanations in social relations were set aside or submerged by the comments of (mostly male) experts in psychology. The large number of articles dealing with Lépine's family difficulties and emotional problems thus encouraged readers to adopt the psychological discourse in analyzing the causes of December 6, 1989.

FROM CO-OPTATION TO ANTI-FEMINISM

In addition to statements reacting indirectly to feminist analyses, the newspapers that were studied as creators and vehicles of collective memory contained explicitly anti-feminist discourse. Most of the writers voicing this discourse were men (82 percent) according to Boudreau (1996: 109). They included writers who used strategies of co-optation, defined by El Yamani as

> procedures that turn feminist terms upside down, for example, representing the oppressor as a victim … They reverse the roles of oppressor and oppressed that underlie all relationships of domination in our society, shifting responsibility for the act (the attack) onto the shoulders of the victims (feminists). (El Yamani 1998: 230; translation)

This reversal of the relationship of domination was mainly used by one category of anti-feminists: masculinists. Bouchard, Boily and Proulx say that the anniversary of the École Polytechnique massacre was one of the events that served as a support or referent for masculinist discourse (Bouchard, Boily and Proulx 2003: 12). Many journalists also adopted the strategy of reversal of power dynamics, particularly when the causes of the massacre were reduced to the killer's psychological problems.

Co-optation of Feminist Analyses

Masculinists directly attack feminists, accusing them of causing harm to boys and men, who are said to suffer from the feminization of schools and the justice system, and to experience a loss of identity references and male models (Dupuis-Déri 2005). To reach these conclusions, masculinists claim that there is oppression of men by women. Co-opting the terminology associated with feminist analyses, psychologists and psychiatrists displaced the asymmetry criticized by feminists: Lépine became the victim of an unjust society, or more specifically, of feminists, who have overturned men's references.[9]

A letter published in the *Globe and Mail* talked about the problems Lépine supposedly experienced as a man, given the absence of primary male models in his life (Christensen 1990). A letter published in *Le Continuum* suggested that the attacker was a "victim" (Blais 1990). Similarly, Mario Fontaine used the words of criminal lawyer Pierre Landreville to defend the idea that the massacre

> also illustrates some of our social and cultural relations. Power relations are changing, women are becoming liberated and many men feel threatened ... As was shown in those open-line shows after the event, when men swore they were against the mass murder but said they understood the killer. *Men feeling at a loss faced with the changes taking place, looking for a symbolic defence.* (Fontaine 1989; emphasis added; translation)

According to psychologist Shawn Johnson, men had a greater feeling of insecurity at that time, given the progress of the feminist movement (*Le Devoir* 1989e). In *Le Devoir*, Jean-Claude Leclerc expressed his concern for the losers in the feminist struggle; the feminist movement had created male victims who needed therapy because of the changes (Leclerc 1989). Similarly, F. M. Christensen (1990) criticized the tendency of "extremist" feminists to hate men, which, according to him, explained Lépine's emotional problems. *La Presse* of December 13, 1989, summed up a discussion between urban planner Christophe Caron and journalist Gérard Leblanc about the difficulty men have in showing their emotions. They maintained that "Marc Lépine [was] the product of his father's violence, but also the product of his mother, a victim, like him ... [Because] it is not always easy for men to live in the interregnum of the transition from violence to tenderness" (G. Leblanc 1989b). Rick Groen claimed that Lépine was a victim of other people's violence (Groen 1990). In short, the feminist analysis was co-opted, usually by experts and journalists who diverted it to the advantage of a historically privileged gender (men).

Disparagement of Feminism and Feminists

The co-optation of feminism is often accompanied by foul language and hostile reactions, sometimes even toward individual feminists. "Demagogic and fanatical intentions" are attributed to feminists, and "they are called, among other things, hysterical and extremist" (Boudreau 1996: 70–71; translation). These kinds of statements found a place in the large-circulation daily papers. According to Beauchamp, "the press does not talk much about what women do, say or think, and when it does, it speaks ill of them, often with ridicule, but it takes huge pleasure in anti-feminism" (Beauchamp 1998: 209; translation).

We must take care, however, not to confuse misogyny and anti-feminism. Michelle Perrot makes the following distinction between them: misogyny is more related to social representations, and anti-feminism to a movement. According to her, anti-feminism "is connected to feminism, for which it aims to provide the antidote and the exorcism" (Perrot 1999; translation). However, the anti-feminism in the media concerning December 6, 1989, was not completely organized. At that time, the masculinist movement was emerging and beginning to create a structure for itself (Blais and Dupuis-Déri 2008). The attack against the fourteen women, moreover, was a key event

> that actually led to a certain loss of legitimacy of feminist demands. The media coverage was marked by a thinly veiled anti-feminism, sometimes even coming from influential members of our intellectual elite. This tragedy was, for some, the outlet for frustrations that had accumulated over the last twenty years. Finally they could say out loud what they thought of feminists, of women in general and their demands. (Bélanger 1997: 43; translation)

This explicit anti-feminism was expressed in particular at the time of the publication of Roch Côté's *Manifeste d'un salaud* [Manifesto of a scoundrel], which was written in reaction to the feminist analyses of the École Polytechnique massacre. Roch Côté attacked feminists and their discourses both in his manifesto and in the media. In addition to directly attacking prominent feminists Lorraine Pagé and Armande Saint-Jean, he denounced what he considered a taboo imposed by a small group of doctrinaire feminists who blamed men. He accused feminists of being narcissistic, saying that their discourse on violence was unfounded, since there was no longer violence in Québec society (R. Côté 1990a: 63; R. Côté 1990b). Côté's anti-feminism was widely echoed, including in the *Globe and Mail*, where a student said he agreed with his complaints (Michelle Lalonde 1990b).

Anti-feminists accused feminists of co-opting the massacre for their own benefit and trying to give it a political meaning. As early as December 8, 1989, even

Lorraine Pagé, of the Centrale de l'enseignement du Québec [Québec federation of teachers' unions], took a position on this:

> The fact that women were specifically targeted in this lethal attack must not lead to a demagogy that would serve no one, neither women nor men. Without excusing or justifying any action, we must refrain from a fanaticism that could further deepen the difficulties men sometimes experience when women take their rightful place in society. (L. Pagé 1989)

She warned feminists against the effects of their discourse.[10]

Richard Fortin, in *La Presse*, welcomed the fact that the religious tributes to the victims of December 6, 1989, had resisted "all attempts at ideological co-optation" (1989b; translation). Again in *La Presse*, an editorial on December 9, 1989, by Marcel Adam stated that "feminists of both sexes wasted no time in interpreting this event through their ideological lens." He added: "Experts have pointed out that in the last few years, feminism has given rise to many acts of violence against women, particularly in the United States. How could it be otherwise?" (Adam 1989; translation). Thus, feminism was seen as the cause of this murderous behaviour.[11] Gérard Leblanc criticized what he called the ideological purism and rigid taboos of feminists (1989c). Jean-Paul Desbiens claimed that "feminism has indecently co-opted the massacre at the École Polytechnique. Indecently and clumsily" (1989; translation). *Le Devoir* published the views of Pierre Desjardins, who claimed that Lépine had not committed a sexist act and added, "Such an association is misplaced and even hides the real stakes of the problem" (P. Desjardins 1990; translation).

The discourse accusing feminists of attempting to co-opt the massacre was also taken up in the student press. According to Wendy Hui Kyong Chun, a part of the student community denounced feminism, accusing it of having purposes similar to those of Lépine, saying that feminist activism encouraged massacres of this kind (1999: 124). Nathalie Provost, a survivor of the massacre, went further: "Feminism sounds like racism, sexism and all those 'isms' that suggest great causes and holy wars. It sounds anti-men" (quoted in F. Montpetit 1990; translation). Of the small number of articles on the massacre published in the student newspapers, most dealt with the subject in reaction to feminism. Anne-Marie Braconnier, an editorialist with *Le Continuum*, stated, "These actions are political before being liberating ... Attempting to give this act a major social dimension is nothing but co-optation" (1990).

In summary, the newspapers studied included a substantial proportion of men — and to a lesser extent women — expressing anti-feminist views, whether in editorials, articles, columns or letters to the editor. To some, feminists were not the only ones causing men's misfortune, since all women who transgressed the limits of the conjugal home were responsible for the violence against them. As a reader of *Châtelaine*, Marc Duby, said, "there are too many women in the public sphere and not enough in the home. That is why," he continued, "there are so many divorces and so much conjugal violence" (Duby 1990; translation)

There was another form of anti-feminist discourse in the newspapers, one that arose from identification with Lépine. Thus, Francine Pelletier (1989b) received a call from a man who claimed he identified with the killer. Almost a year later, in an interview in *La Presse*, Pelletier stated that many men seemed to approve of the killer's act (*La Presse* 1990f).[12] This approval sometimes came from her journalist colleagues: "As evidence, this snatch of conversation the day after the massacre among three Radio-Canada employees … 'The guy's not so bad, after all. I've always dreamed of doing that!'" (Pelletier 1989a; translation) With respect to masculinist rhetoric on the bias of the justice system in favour of women, Emil Sher quoted a police officer: "Assaulted women like being beaten. I tell the guy to hit harder. If they go to court, these men have no chance. There is no justice. Feminists and Stalinists have influence on the judges" (Sher 1989).

Violent men saw themselves in the killer's act. A short piece in *Le Devoir* reported that a coordinator of a program to help violent men said, "Many of [the violent men] said they identified with him. Perhaps not to the point of going to buy a weapon, but it's that kind of rage and hatred they felt toward women" (*Le Devoir* 1989g; translation). Novelist Danielle Charest said that when she drove a taxi, she had overheard one of her clients, who had come out of a brothel, say of Lépine, "Ha, he got them, rata tat tat" (collected by Alias and Rose-Marie). Stevie Cameron (1989) of the *Globe and Mail* spoke of threats by a man who made a threatening call to the National Action Committee on the Status of Women, saying that Marc Lépine was not alone. Francine Pelletier reported the incendiary speech of a participant in a debate on violence against women at the Université de Montréal: "You're murderers! You feminists all deserve the firing squad!" (quoted in Pelletier 1990b; translation). Pelletier was concerned about the anti-feminists' actions, pointing to a list drawn up by the Comité antiféministe de Montréal of "the 140 injustices by women in general and feminists in particular of which men are victims" (Pelletier 1990b; translation). A few years later, in 1995, newspapers mentioned celebrations organized on December 6 in honour of Marc Lépine (including one in 1991) by soldiers in the airborne regiment in Petawawa; after dinner, the soldiers fired fourteen gunshots, a reminder of Lépine's victims (*La Tribune* 1995).[13]

The media covered these instances of parroting of Lépine. This type of article on the massacre did not show journalistic bias in content or structure, but the events reported revealed the existence of sympathy for the killer on the part of some men. Journalists covered a threat by a student at Cégep de Valleyfield on March

8, 1990 — International Women's Day — to kill a woman student in an office automation class; armed with a pistol, he declared that it was the technical college's turn (Bisson 1990; Picard 1990). Graffiti expressing hatred of women were found in the Engineering Faculty of the University of Toronto; messages such as "Kill all the feminists or I'll kill them myself" were signed "Marc Lépine II" (*La Presse* 1990c; translation). The authorities at Queen's University tried to deny that a law student had mimed the École Polytechnique shootings the day after the tragedy (Cameron and French 1989). The *Globe and Mail* reported that male members of the Vancouver Sports Club parodied the École Polytechnique massacre; dressed as butchers spattered with blood and carrying plastic pistols, they harangued women to take their revenge on Lépine (Matas 1990). A man armed with an ice pick was arrested in front of Notre-Dame Basilica on the day of the commemorative mass on the first anniversary, and he was carrying a photograph of the fourteen victims (for more details, see Proulx 1990).

The newspapers also covered manifestations of violence against women and feminists. Engineering students at the University of Alberta shouted "Shoot the bitch!" at a woman student in the program (French 1990). Engineering students at the same university were accused of making sexist remarks in editorials of the newspaper *The Bridge* (French 1989). The *Globe and Mail* reported that on November 27, 1990, letters threatening rape were slid under the doors of three hundred women students in the dormitory at the University of British Columbia by twenty-two male students, an act that was seen by sociologist Dawn Currie as an imitation of Lépine's actions (Bryson 1990).

Feminist Responses
Feminists first of all responded to the disparagement and negation of their words, and then refuted the attacks against them. However, many of their responses were confined to the opinion pages of the major newspapers. El Yamani notes the consequences of this:

> These isolated articles were important, but with the flood of reports and accounts in the media, they ended up being diluted. The relevance of these reflections on violence in our society, gender relations and hatred of women who dare to be proud was destroyed by the uninformative information overload in the media. (El Yamani 1998: 220–21; translation)

The Francophone newspapers — except for *Le Continuum* — published some of these feminist responses. There were also criticisms of the disparagement of feminist discourse in the media made by journalists with a feminist sensibility, such as Francine Pelletier. This type of analysis, however, was absent from the *Globe and Mail*, which contained few expressions of discontent by feminists, despite the fact that Anglophone feminists were targeted by journalists as much as their Francophone counterparts and were even attacked by certain students (Cameron and French 1989). Did Toronto feminists use other channels of communication, or did they feel less targeted by the killer (the nineteen women and pro-feminists on Lépine's list all lived in Québec)? Whatever the explanation, the result was that in the *Globe and Mail,* feminists expressed themselves on the murder of the fourteen women or on their mobilizations instead, without discussing the anti-feminist prejudices of the media.

The Francophone dailies presented a few criticisms of anti-feminism, such as that of writer Nicole Brossard (1991): "Reading *La Presse* and *Le Devoir* lately, I wondered if Marc Lépine would soon attract more sympathy than his victims, dead and wounded." As well as criticizing the sympathy for the killer, feminists took issue with the marginalization of their discourse. As Brossard explained:

> It is true that a certain exploitation of women is acknowledged, that too many women are beaten and raped but, at the same time, feminist analysis is not tolerated and nor is their deep reflection, their anger or their particular sadness ... To show solidarity with feminists is to recognize that men have dug an unbelievable death trench with their misogynist lies, their phallocratic privilege, and the "commonplace" intimidation that exists between women and men. (Brossard 1991: 32–33)

The feminist Nancy Jackman stated that it was "just about impossible for women to make the headlines with their fight for equal rights" (Cameron 1989). Louise Malette agreed with Beauchamp's analysis (Beauchamp 1998: 212–13) and said in a "letter to the media":

> Feminists have never had good media coverage. In the years when feminism was really a hot topic, the media didn't miss a chance to denigrate the feminist struggle and show their contempt for it. We have never benefited from the direct support of the media, and those women who did not hide their sympathy for the feminist movement paid for it with their jobs. (Malette 1991)

Ariane Émond went further in December 1990:

> That's what saddens me the most on the eve of this sad anniversary. Beyond necessary and fair criticism, is this the time to reduce to a caricature a movement that, beyond its excesses of language, has given back to thousands of women a dignity that is still fragile? (Émond 1990; translation).

While questioning the rejection of feminist discourse, many women discussed the hostility they said they were targets of. Francine Pelletier spoke of this in an article on conjugal violence: "There is another reason to keep quiet. Violence against women is a subject that irremediably divides us, men and women ... All this to tell you that it's a subject I personally find difficult to deal with. (I am unpopular enough as it is!)" (Pelletier 1990a; translation).

Other feminists expressed the difficulty they had in making a critical analysis of gender relations. Isabelle Bédard shared her feeling of sadness at being misunderstood by some men in her circle:

> It's not easy being a feminist when you're still dreaming of Prince Charming. Since the murder of fourteen of my sisters, I have had to explain to many of my male friends why I feel so concerned, why I'm in so much pain. They say I'm being paranoid, that I'm dramatizing the situation, that you can't take anything from that act since it was done by a madman. That there's nothing to understand ... But they're the ones who don't understand. And these same men are the ones I would want to love, and who I would want to love me ... I'm afraid it's going to be harder than I thought. (Bédard 1989; translation)

Pro-feminists, such as Brian K. Murphy in the *Globe and Mail*, criticized men who attacked the victims of male privilege (Murphy 1990). Feminists in turn responded to statements denigrating pro-feminist men. In her reply to Roch Côté, Armande Saint-Jean (1990) denounced him for his view that "the feminists' 'fellow travellers' are not responsible men whose views are worthy of interest; ... [that] they are 'traitorous dogs who follow good causes like others follow caravans.' According to him, those men have been duped." Saint-Jean's letter to *La Presse* in response to Roch Côté a year after the attack was endorsed by fourteen women, women's groups and organizations, including UQAM's services to communities. In it, Saint-Jean explained:

> Roch Côté accuses us of "taking advantage" of the Polytechnique massacre to "put all men on trial." As we were last year, we are accused of "co-opting" an event that some persist in wanting to surround with mystery, to see as a "private tragedy," the tragedy of the families of fourteen École Polytechnique students killed. (Saint-Jean 1990; translation).

CONCLUSION

Thus, feminists responded to various types of discourse that had in common the dismissal, marginalization, co-optation and sometimes even disparagement of their analyses of the tragedy. The purpose of all these discourses was to avoid any consideration of the issues raised by the feminists and the changes they proposed.

Finally, the case of the École Polytechnique massacre shows how rapidly the social actors sought to establish non-feminist representations of the tragedy in the collective memory. The work of memory that emerged from this type of discourse aimed to maintain the status quo or, as the historian and philosopher Krzysztof Pomian says when discussing the relation between memory and history, to maintain a stable dimension of a past that is evoked (Pomian 1999: 338) — a stable dimension and a social cohesion that suggest that the interests of the dominant are the same as those of the dominated, that "harmony" between the sexes is possible only on condition that we keep quiet about the oppression, domination and exploitation of women.[14]

Notes

1. The Patriotes have replaced Dollard des Ormeaux as the historical figures celebrated on the Monday preceding May 25 each year.
2. The parents of the murdered women also mobilized to ask for a public inquiry; see Pelchat 1990e; Pelchat 1990d.
3. There was a series of discussions around the Catholic Church in the opinion section of *Le Devoir*. For example, see *Le Devoir* December 15, 1989, p. 6, and the collection of letters published January 3, 1989, p. 7.
4. I found only one article on this topic: Poirier 1990. This subject was not dealt with in *Le Continuum*.
5. See the section "The Double Dtandard" in Blais (2014: Ch 1).
6. Many psychiatrists and psychologists also gave their opinions on the appropriateness of publishing Lépine's letter. For example, Marie-Claude Lortie reported the opinion of psychiatrist Jacques Lesage from the Philippe Pinel Institute, who felt that some people reading the letter could identify with the killer and emulate his actions (Lortie 1990d).
7. This observation is disputed, however, by Richard Poulin and Yanick Dulong in their study of serial and mass murders (Poulin and Dulong 2010).
8. Letters to the editor also adopted this type of discourse; for example, Walker 1990.
9. Jeanne d'Arc Jutras (1990) described the process of co-optation used on open-line radio shows in which men were presented as victims of feminist struggles.
10. *Le Devoir* also reported on Pagé's fears; see *Le Devoir* 1989c.
11. Similarly, a former student at Cégep de Saint-Laurent said that there was a "feminist hysteria" there during the time when Lépine was studying at the college (Foglia 1989; translation).
12. Other articles dealt with expressions of sympathy for the killer on open-line shows. See

Jean-V. Dufresne 1989; Saint-Jean 1991; Jutras 1990.

13. The soldier who organized these celebrations was suspected of belonging to a white supremacist group.

14. This desire for social cohesion is expressed in many other projects of memory construction, such as the collective memory of World War I, as shown by Djebabla-Brun (2004).

References

Adam, Marcel. 1989. "Quand une tragédie culpabilise une société et fait désespérer d'elle." *La Presse*, December 9.

Appleby, Timothy. 1989. "Card depicts gun lobby's view of life." *Globe and Mail*, December 15.

___. 1990. "No police slain again last year, 649 homicides recorded." *Globe and Mail*, February 24.

April, Pierre. 1989a. "Le contrôle de la vente des armes refait surface." *La Presse*, December 8.

___. 1989b. "Pas question d'interdire les fusils et les carabines semi-automatiques." *La Presse*, December 10.

Beauchamp, Colette. 1998. *Le silence des médias: Les femmes, les hommes et l'information*. Montreal: Remue-ménage.

Beaudoin, Françoise. 1990. "Le 6 décembre 1990. Un peu d'humanité." *Le Continuum*, December 3.

Bédard, Isabelle. 1989. [untitled]. *La Presse*, December 13.

Bélanger, Nicole. 1997. "Féminisme et antiféminisme: De la reconnaissance par les institutions à l'émergence d'un nouveau discours basé sur les 'exagérations' du féminisme." MA thesis (political science), Québec City: Université Laval.

Béliveau, Jules. 1989. "La gente étudiante se regroupe dans la tristesse et la réflexion." *La Presse*, December 8.

Bertrand, Marie-Andrée. 1990. "Écho de la profession. 6 décembre 1989: retours sur l'événement." *Sociologie et sociétés*, XXII, 1: 193–213.

Binsse, Lisa. 1989. "1989, une année marquée par la violence faite aux femmes." *La Presse*, December 28.

Bisson, Bruno. 1990. "Un étudiant armé menace de tuer en pleine classe." *La Presse*, March 9.

Bissonnette, Lise. 1989. "The self-centred hype of Montreal massacre." *Globe and Mail*, December 16.

Blais, Marcel. 1990. "Blessure d'être et d'existence humaine." *Le Continuum*, January 29.

Blais, Mélissa. 2014. *"I Hate Feminists!" December 6, 1989 and its Aftermath*. Halifax/Winnipeg: Fernwood Publishing

Blais, Mélissa, and Francis Dupuis-Déri (eds.). 2008. "Introduction: Qu'est-ce que le masculinisme?" In Mélissa Blais and Francis Dupuis-Déri (eds.), *Le mouvement masculiniste au Québec: L'antiféminisme démasqué*: 11–32. Montreal: Remue-ménage.

Boileau, Josée. 1989a. "Les rescapés pansent leurs blessures psychologiques." *Le Devoir*, December 9.

___. 1989b. "Ultime adieu en silence." *Le Devoir*, December 12.

___. 1990. "L'attitude des étudiants de Poly a beaucoup changé." *Le Devoir*, January 6.

Boisvert, Yves. 1989. "La tuerie à Polytechnique: le père de Marc Lépine le battait régulièrement." *La Presse*, December 9.

Bouchard, Pierrette, Isabelle Boily and Marie-Claude Proulx. 2003. *School Success by Gender: A Catalyst for the Masculinist Discourse*. Ottawa: Status of Women Canada.

Boudreau, Julie. 1996. "Étude du processus de construction du sens dans les médias: Le cas de la tragédie de l'École Polytechnique en 1989." MA thesis (French studies), Université de Sherbrooke.

Braconnier, Anne-Marie. 1990. "Féminin Polyriel." *Le Continuum*, January 8.

Brossard, Nicole. 1991. "The killer was no young man." In Louise Malette and Marie Chalouh (eds.), *The Montreal Massacre*: 31–33. Charlottetown: Gynergy Books.

Bryson, Mary. 1990. "When sexism stalks the campus." *Globe and Mail*, November 27.

Cameron, Stevie. 1989. "Hundreds in Toronto mourn killing of 14 women." *Globe and Mail*, December 8.

Cameron, Stevie, and Orland French. 1989. "Tension grows at Queen's over sexism controversy." *Globe and Mail*, December 12.

Canada, Department of Justice. 2013. "Important dates in the history of the civil law of Quebec." <justice.gc.ca/eng/rp-pr/csj-sjc/ilp-pji/hist/index.html>.

Candau, Joël. 1996. "Mémoire et amnésie collectives." In *Anthropologie de la mémoire*: 56–87. Paris: PUF.

Cauchon, Paul. 1989. "Un cas isolé … qui peut se produire partout." *Le Devoir*, December 8.

Charest, Danielle. 1999. *L'échafaudage*. Paris: Librairie des Champs Elysées.

Choquet, Louise. 1990. "Québec rongé de culpabilité." *Le Devoir*, August 16.

Christensen, F.M. 1990. "Hypocrisy, sexism and feminists." *Globe and Mail*, May 19.

Chun, Wendy Hui Kyong. 1999. "Unbearable witness: Toward a politics of listening." *Difference: A Journal of Feminist Cultural Studies*, 11, 1: 112–149.

Cleroux, Richard, and Craig McInnes. 1989. "Opposition MPs demand long-promised gun control amendments." *Globe and Mail*, December 8.

Colpron, Suzanne. 1989. "Marc Lépine était un premier de classe." *La Presse*, December 9.

____. 1990a. "Poly: qu'a retenu la police du drame?" *La Presse*, December 1.

____. 1990b. "Malgré des ratés à Poly, Urgences Santé n'a pas modifié ses procédures d'intervention." *La Presse*, May 16.

Cornellier, Manon. 1990. "Kim Campbell souhaite un meilleur contrôle des armes." *Le Devoir*, December 19.

Côté, Andrée. 1991. "The art of making it work for you." In Louise Malette and Marie Chalouh (eds.), *The Montreal Massacre*: 67–70. Charlottetown: Gynergy Books.

Côté, Roch. 1990a. *Manifeste d'un salaud*. Montreal: du Portique.

____. 1990b. "Le grand tabou féministe, ou comment l'on fait le procès des hommes." *La Presse*, November 17.

Couto, Maria L. 1989. "PM's duty to solve gun problem." *Globe and Mail*, December 30.

De Coster, Robert (chair). 1990. *La tragédie du 6 décembre 1989 à l'École Polytechnique de Montréal*. Québec City: Ministère de la Sécurité publique du Québec.

De la Aldea, Elena. 2005. "Le cas argentin: La mémoire et les mémoires." In Micheline Labelle et al. (eds.), *Le devoir de mémoire et les politiques du pardon*: 333–43. Sainte-Foy: PUQ.

Desbiens, Jean-Paul. 1989. "La consommation de l'horreur." *La Presse*, December 21.

Descôteaux, Bernard. 1989. "Québec décrète un deuil collectif." *Le Devoir*, December 8.

Desjardins, Pierre. 1990. "Marc Lépine n'a pas commis un geste sexiste." *Le Devoir*, January 10.

Djebabla-Brun, Mourad. 2004. *Se souvenir de la Grande Guerre: La mémoire plurielle de 14–18 au Québec*. Montreal: VLB.

Doré, Marc. 1989. "10 000 personnes rendent hommage aux victimes de la tuerie de Polytechnique." *La Presse*, December 11.

Dubuc, Alain. 1990. "Pourquoi parler de Polytechnique?" *La Presse*, December 1.

Dubuisson, Philippe. 1990. "Des représentants de Poly demandent aux députés de restreindre le port d'armes." *La Presse*, December 19.

Duby, Marc. 1990. "Les 'vrais' hommes." *Châtelaine*, June: 8.

Dufresne, Jean-V. 1989. "Les étudiants de Polytechnique replongent dans leurs bouquins." *Le Devoir*, December 14.

____. 1990. "Engelure d'âme." *Le Devoir*, December 12.

Dupuis-Déri, Francis. 2005. "Féminisme et réaction masculiniste au Québec." In Maria Nengeh Mensah (ed.), *Dialogues sur la troisième vague féministe*: 157–73. Montreal: Remue-ménage.

El Yamani, Myriame. 1998. *Médias et féminismes: Minoritaires sans paroles*. Montreal: L'Harmattan.

Émond, Ariane. 1990. "Poly: là où le bât blesse." *Le Devoir*, December 5.

Foglia, Pierre. 1989. "Quel monstre?" *La Presse*, December 9.

Fontaine, Mario. 1989. "C'est le moment ou jamais pour les Québécois de procéder à un sérieux examen de conscience." *La Presse*, December 9.

Fortin, Richard. 1989a. "La tuerie à Polytechnique: je ferai ses examens, j'aurai son diplôme … Stéphane Brochu, l'ami de Michèle Richard." *La Presse*, December 9.

____. 1989b. "Des adieux émouvants et grandioses: une foule recueillie offre son appui aux parents accablés." *La Presse*, December 12.

Francoeur, Louis-Gilles. 1990. "Quoi contrôler: l'arme ou le Rambo? Un an après Polytechnique et 500 000 pétitionnaires, rien, ou presque, n'a bougé." *Le Devoir*, December 4.

French, Orland. 1989. "Students' newspaper warned to end sexism." *Globe and Mail*, December 13.

____. 1990. "Engineering students discuss gun laws." *Globe and Mail*, January 12.

Gagné, Harold. 2008. *Vivre: Dix-neuf ans après la tragédie de la Polytechnique, Monique Lépine, la mère de Marc Lépine, se révèle*. Montreal: Libre Expression.

Gagnon, Lysiane. 1990. "Le silence de la police." *La Presse*, January 11.

Gagnon, Martha, and Marcel Laroche. 1989a. "Le meurtrier antiféministe avait sur lui une 'liste rouge' de 14 femmes connues." *La Presse*, December 8.

____. 1989b. "Le tueur avait trois obsessions: les femmes, la guerre et l'électronique." *La Presse*, December 8.

Gagnon-Brunette, Michèle. 1989. "Au-delà de la folie. Ce n'est pas l'antiféminisme qui monte, c'est la violence." *Le Devoir*, December 12.

Gingras, Pierre. 1989. "Les Québécois possèdent plus de deux millions d'armes de chasse: 'Dite arme de chasse, l'arme de Lépine est en fait arme de guerre.'" *La Presse*, December 16.

Globe and Mail. 1989a. "Thousands of mourners wait in silence to pay final respects to slain women." December 11.

Globe and Mail. 1989b. "Violent film on terrorists preceded tragedy." December 9.

Gracia, Agnès. 1990. "La police reconnaît qu'elle a manqué de leadership lors de la tuerie à Poly." *La Presse,* January 26.

Grandjean, Patrick. 1990. "Marc Lépine: un cas de 'père manquant, fils manqué.'" *La Presse,* December 3.

Groen, Rick. 1990. "A year after the trauma, the answers and insights still go begging." *Globe and Mail,* December 4.

Groulx, Patrice. 1998. *Pièges de la mémoire: Dollard des Ormeaux, les Amérindiens et nous.* Hull: Vents d'Ouest.

Gruda, Agnès. 1990. "Montréal tentera de faire interdire les armes militaires et paramilitaires." *La Presse,* January 18.

Guillaumin, Collette. 1991. "Madness and the social norm." Translated by Mary Jo Lakehead. *Feminist Issues* 11, 2: 10–15.

____. 1992. *Sexe, race et pratique du pouvoir: L'idée de Nature.* Paris: Côté-femmes.

Hall, Stuart. 1982. "The Rediscovery of 'Ideology': Return of the Repressed in Media Studies." In M. Gurevitch, T. Bennett, J. Curran and S. Woollacott (eds.), *Culture, Society and the Media*: 56–90. London: Methuen.

Jutras, Jeanne d'Arc. 1990. "Incompréhensif parce qu'avachi." *Le Devoir,* August 31.

La Presse. 1989a. "Aucun pays n'est épargné par ce genre de tuerie." December 7.

____. 1989b. "La tuerie à Polytechnique: Lépine ne répondait pas aux normes de l'armée." December 9.

____. 1989c. "La police a été lente, estiment des rescapés." December 11.

____. 1990a. "Pétition des étudiants pour le contrôle des armes à feu." January 13.

____. 1990b. "La prolifération des armes à feu inquiète les autorités policières: les Canadiens ne semblent plus avoir peur des armes." February 28.

____. 1990c. "Des graffiti signés Marc Lépine II à la Faculté d'ingénierie de l'U. de Toronto." April 11.

____. 1990d. "Ottawa dépose la loi sur les armes à feu." June 26.

____. 1990e. "Fini les armes automatiques." June 27.

____. 1990f. "Francine Pelletier: je ne crois pas qu'il soit dangereux d'avoir une fenêtre dans la tête de Marc Lépine." November 26.

____. 1995. "Commémoration annuelle du massacre de l'École Polytechnique: Tout le monde était au courant au sein du Régiment aéroporté, soutient un militaire." November 6.

Lalonde, Michelle. 1990b. "Students' silence part of debate over killings." *Globe and Mail,* December 4.

Lauzière, Benoît. 1989. [untitled]. *Le Devoir,* December 8.

Le Continuum. 1990. "Une page de silence. 6 décembre 1989." December 3.

Le Devoir. 1989a. "L'Assemblée nationale ajourne ses travaux en signe de deuil." December 7.

____. 1989b. "L'archevêque bouleversé." December 8.

____. 1989c. "Réactions de tous les milieux. La CEQ horrifiée." December 8.

____. 1989d. "Aucun antécédent particulier ne distinguait Lépine des autres." December 9.

____. 1989e. "La plupart des hommes ont pu un jour en vouloir aux féministes selon un psychologue." December 9.

____. 1989f. "Des survivants estiment que la police a mis trop de temps." December 11.

____. 1989g. "Plusieurs hommes disent se retrouver en Marc Lépine." December 12.

____. 1990a. "Blais n'envisage pas bannir les armes semi-automatiques." January 19.

____. 1990b. "Projet de loi sur le contrôle des armes à feu d'ici un mois." March 17.

Leblanc, Gérald. 1989a. "Elles ne sont pas mortes pour rien." *La Presse*, December 11.

____. 1989b. "Morbides symptômes de l'interrègne." *La Presse*, December 13.

____. 1989c. "Neuf rappels de 1989." *La Presse*, December 22.

Leclerc, Jean-Claude. 1989. "Les raisons d'une tragédie. Sommes-nous en face d'un terrorisme antiféministe?" *Le Devoir*, December 11.

____. 1990. "La police à Polytechnique. Le rapport du chef de police Alain St-Germain n'explique pas tout." *Le Devoir*, January 27.

Léger, Marie-France. 1990. "Polytechnique veut se souvenir dans 'le respect et le recueillement.'" *La Presse*, November 29.

Lépine, Marc. 1990. "Je me considère comme un érudit rationnel." *La Presse*, November 24.

Lortie, Marie-Claude. 1990a. "300 000 personnes ont signé la pétition de Poly sur le contrôle des armes." *La Presse*, February 15.

____. 1990b. "Lépine, le portrait type du meurtrier de masse suicidaire: c'est ce que révèle le rapport du psychiatre remis au coroner." *La Presse*, May 15.

____. 1990c. "Poly: la police reconnaît son incurie." *La Presse*, May 25.

____. 1990d. "Publier ou ne pas publier la lettre de Lépine? la tragédie de Poly, un drame majeur, sensationnel et ... commercial." *La Presse*, November 24.

____. 1990e. "Psychose? Blessures au cerveau? Les spécialistes n'ont pas encore résolu l'énigme Marc Lépine." *La Presse*, December 1.

____. 1990f. "Campbell dit vouloir une loi sur les armes." *La Presse*, December 6.

MacLeod, Robert. 1989. "Mass murders not increasing Canadian anthropologist says." *Globe and Mail*, December 8.

Malarek, Victor. 1989a. "3500 friends relatives bid a tearful farewell to murdered students." *Globe and Mail*, December 12.

____. 1989b. "Police refusal to answer questions leaves lots of loose ends in killings." *Globe and Mail*, December 13.

Malette, Louise. 1991. "Letter to the media." In Louise Malette and Marie Chalouh (eds.), *The Montreal Massacre*: 56–57. Charlottetown: Gynergy Books.

Masson, Claude. 1989. "La solidarité de tout un peuple." *La Presse*, December 9.

Matas, Robert. 1990. "Sports club apologizes over offensive skit, video." *Globe and Mail*, April 28.

McLaughlin, Claire. 1989. "Restrict access to guns." *Globe and Mail*, December 28.

Mercier-Leblond, Gabrielle. 1990. *Les interventions psychosociales*. In Robert De Coster (chair), *La tragédie du 6 décembre 1989 à l'École Polytechnique de Montréal*. Québec City: Ministère de la Sécurité publique du Québec.

Montpetit, Caroline. 1990. "Saint-Germain reconnaît que les policiers ont manqué d'initiative à Polytechnique." *Le Devoir*, May 25.

Montpetit, Francine. 1990. "Survivre. Quand on est passée à deux doigts de la mort, à quoi ressemble la vie? Rescapée de Poly, Nathalie Provost se raconte." *Châtelaine*, December: 55.

Moon, Peter. 1990. "Too many guns in Toronto, officer warns." *Globe and Mail,* February 9.

Murphy, Brian K. 1990. "Hyprocrisy, sexism and feminists." *Globe and Mail,* May 19.

Nora, Pierre. 1996. "General Introduction: Between Memory and History." In Pierre Nora and Lawrence D. Kritzman (eds.), *Realms of Memory: The Construction of the French Past,* Vol. 1: *Conflicts and Divisions:* 1–20. Translated by Arthur Goldhammer. New York: Columbia University Press.

Normand, Gilles. 1989a. "L'Assemblée nationale se rappelle l'affaire Lortie." *La Presse,* December 7.

____. 1989b. "Le Québec en deuil." *La Presse,* December 8.

Ouimet, Michèle. 1989a. "Des adieux émouvants et grandioses. Dans le silence des classes, l'incrédulité se mêle à une pointe d'agressivité." *La Presse,* December 12.

____. 1989b. "Émues, les télés refont un examen de conscience … et voilà: malgré l'émotion, personne ne songe à modifier sa programmation." *La Presse,* December 16.

____. 1990. "Comment protéger tous ces immenses campus?" *La Presse,* December 1.

Pagé, Lorraine. 1989. [untitled]. *La Presse,* December 8.

Pelchat, Martin. 1990a. "Montréal demande l'interdiction des armes militaires." *Le Devoir,* January 18.

____. 1990b. "La police de la CUM reconnaît ses ratés dans son intervention à Polytechnique." *Le Devoir,* January 26.

____. 1990c. "La police ne trouve pas ce qui a déclenché le geste de Lépine à Poly." *Le Devoir,* February 28.

____. 1990d. "Les parents des victimes de Poly réclament une enquête publique." *Le Devoir,* May 30.

____. 1990e. "Fusillade de la Polytechnique: des parents espèrent toujours une enquête." *La Presse,* November 25.

Pelletier, Francine. 1989a. "On achève bien les chevaux, n'est-ce pas?" *La Presse,* December 9.

____. 1989b. "Post-mortem." *La Presse,* December 16.

____. 1990a. "L'été meurtrier." *La Presse,* September 22.

____. 1990b. "L'antiféminisme: un nouveau phénomène." *La Presse,* December 8.

____. 1990c. "Adieu aux armes," *La Presse,* December 15.

Perrot, Michelle. 1999. "Préface." In Christine Bard (ed.), *Un siècle d'antiféminisme:* 7–20. Paris: Fayard.

Picard, André. 1990. "Teacher who faced armed man rejects hero status." *Globe and Mail,* March 10.

Picard, André, and Michelle Lalonde. 1990. "Montreal killings largely unnoticed by public." *Globe and Mail,* September 26.

Plourde, Nicolas. 1990. "Violence et sexisme. Que faire?" *Le Continuum,* January 8.

Poirier, Patricia. 1989. "1,000 fill church in Montreal to mourn victim of massacre." *Globe and Mail,* December 13.

____. 1990. "Reliance on coroner raises serious doubts about Montreal police." *Globe and Mail,* January 1.

Poirier, Patricia, and Barrie McKenna. 1989. "Quebec mourns slaying of women at university." *Globe and Mail,* December 8.

Pomian, Krzysztof. 1999. *Sur l'histoire.* Paris: Gallimard.

Poulin, Richard, and Yanick Dulong. 2010. *Serial and Mass Murder, Sociopolitical Dynamics.*

Translated by Michael J. Ustick. Montreal: Sisyphe.

Proulx, Jean-Pierre. 1990. "Le souvenir des 14 victimes 'demeurera toujours présent.'" *Le Devoir*, December 7.

Quinn Dressel associates. 1989. "Women in engineering." *Globe and Mail*, December 15.

Saint-Jean, Armande. 1990. "Se souvenir, comprendre, changer ... : une autre réplique cinglante à l'auteur du 'Manifeste d'un salaud.'" *La Presse*, December 7.

____. 1991. "Burying Women's Words: An Analysis of Media Attitudes." In Louise Malette and Marie Chalouh (eds.), *The Montreal Massacre*: 61–65. Charlottetown: Gynergy Books.

Sansfaçon, Daniel, Joseph J. Lévy and Jean-Marc Samson. 1994. "Rapports de sexe et violence contre les femmes: essai de reconstruction sociale du sens de la tragédie de la Polytechnique." *Revue sexologique* 2, 2.

Sher, Emil. 1989. "Speaking about the unspeakable." *Globe and Mail*, December 8.

Sherkey, J.A. 1989. "A small price to pay." *Globe and Mail*, December 23.

Soulié, Jean-Paul. 1989. "Diane Gamache s'étonne d'être encore en vie: le forcené l'a ratée deux fois." *La Presse*, December 8.

Tonso, Karen L. 2009. "Violent masculinities as tropes for school shooters: The Montréal massacre, the Columbine attack, and rethinking schools." *American Behavioral Scientist* 52, 9: 1266–85.

Valpy, Michael. 1989. "Systematic slaughter is without precedent." *Globe and Mail*, December 8.

Walker, Robin. 1990. "Investing in the future." *Globe and Mail*, January 6.

Wieviorka, Michel. 2005. "Les problèmes de la reconstruction identitaire." In Micheline Labelle et al. (eds.), *Le devoir de mémoire et les politiques du pardon*: 65–76. Sainte-Foy: PUQ.

MASCULINITIES

Chapter 10

UNDERSTANDING MEN

Gender Sociology and the New International Research on Masculinities

Raewyn Connell

From: *Gendered Intersections: An Introduction to Women's and Gender Studies,* *2nd edition,* pp. 116–120. Originally published in: Social Thought and Research 24, 2002 (reprinted with permission).

DEBATES ABOUT MEN AND BOYS

In the last decade there has been an upsurge of concern with issues about men and boys. In the public realm there have been social movements focused on the reform or restoration of masculinity, such as the "mythopoetic" movement, the Million Man March and the Promise Keepers (Messner 1997). In education there has been much talk of boys' "failure" in school and the need for special programs for boys (Connell 1996; Gilbert and Gilbert 1998). In health there has been increasing debate about men's health and illness (Sabo and Gordon 1995; Schofield et al. 2000), and a popular therapeutic movement addresses men's problems in relationships, sexuality and identity.

In a way this is surprising, because men remain the principal holders of economic and political power. Men make up a large majority of corporate executives, top professionals and holders of public office. Worldwide, men held 93 percent of cabinet-level posts in 1996, and most top positions in international agencies (Gierycz 1999). Men continue to control most technology and most weaponry; with only limited exceptions it is men who staff and control the agencies of force such as armies, police and judicial systems.

This used to be thought "natural," either prescribed by God or a consequence of biology. Essentialist views of gender are still popular and are constantly reinforced in the media. However, they are increasingly under challenge. The women's liberation movement, and the many feminisms that have followed on from it, have produced a massive disturbance in the gender system and in people's assumptions about gender. And what affects the social position of women and girls must also affect the social position of men and boys. Large numbers of men now acknowledge that their position is under *challenge*, that what they once took for granted must be re-thought. They may or may not like it, but they cannot ignore it.

THE "ETHNOGRAPHIC MOMENT": SIGNIFICANT CONCLUSIONS

We now have a growing library of ethnographic studies from around the world, across a number of the social sciences, in which researchers have traced the construction of masculinity in a particular milieu or moment.

Though each study is different, there are many common themes. Some of the most important findings of this research may be summarized in six theses:

1. Multiple Masculinities

Historians and anthropologists have shown that there is no one pattern of masculinity that is found everywhere. Different cultures, and different periods of history, construct masculinity differently. Equally important, more than one kind of masculinity can be found within a given cultural setting. Within any workplace, neighbourhood or peer group, there are likely to be different understandings of masculinity and different ways of "doing" masculinity.

2. Hierarchy and Hegemony

Different masculinities do not sit side-by-side like dishes in a smorgasbord; there are definite relations between them. Typically, some masculinities are more honoured than others. Some may be actively dishonoured, for example homosexual masculinities in modern Western culture. Some are socially marginalized, for example the masculinities of disempowered ethnic minorities. Some are exemplary, taken as symbolizing admired traits, for example the masculinities of sporting heroes.

The form of masculinity that is culturally dominant in a given setting is called "hegemonic masculinity." "Hegemonic" signifies a position of cultural authority and leadership, not total dominance; other forms of masculinity persist alongside. The hegemonic form need not be the most common form of masculinity. Hegemonic masculinity is, however, highly visible. It is likely to be what casual commentators have noticed when they speak of "the male role."

Hegemonic masculinity is hegemonic not just in relation to other masculinities, but in relation to the gender order as a whole. It is an expression of the privilege men collectively have over women. The hierarchy of masculinities is an expression of the unequal shares in that privilege held by different groups of men.

3. Collective Masculinities

The gender structures of a society define particular patterns of conduct as "masculine" and others as "feminine." At one level, these patterns characterize individuals. Thus, we say that a particular man (or woman) is masculine, or behaves in a masculine way. But these patterns also exist at the collective level. Masculinities are defined and sustained in institutions, such as corporations, armies, government, schools, workplaces, sports organizations and in informal groups, like street gangs. Masculinity also exists impersonally in culture. Video games, for instance, not only circulate stereotyped images of violent masculinity, but they require the player to enact this masculinity (symbolically) in order to play the game at all.

4. Active Construction

Masculinities do not exist prior to social behavior, either as bodily states or fixed personalities. Rather, masculinities come into existence as people act. They are accomplished in everyday conduct or organizational life, as patterns of social practice; that is, we "do gender" in everyday life. However, masculinities are far from settled. From bodybuilders in the gym, to managers in the boardroom, to boys in the elementary school playground, a great deal of effort goes into the making of conventional, as well as non-conventional masculinities. Recent research on homosexual men shows that for these men too, identity and relationships involve a complex and sustained effort of construction.

5. Internal Complexity

One of the key reasons why masculinities are not settled is that they are not simple, homogeneous patterns. Close-focus research on gender, both in psychoanalysis and ethnography, often reveals contradictory desires and logics. A man's active heterosexuality may exist as a thin emotional layer concealing a deeper homosexual desire. A boy's identification with men may co-exist or struggle with identifications with women. The public enactment of an exemplary masculinity may covertly require actions that undermine it. Masculinities may have multiple possibilities concealed within them.

6. Dynamics

Since different masculinities exist in different cultures and historical epochs, we can deduce that masculinities are able to change. That is, masculine identities are not fixed but are dynamic; particular masculinities are composed, de-composed, contested and replaced. Sometimes this process of contestation and change finds spectacular public expression in large-scale rallies or demonstrations. More often it is local and limited. Sometimes it becomes conscious and deliberate; at other times it is non-conscious.

CRITIQUE AND NEW DIRECTIONS

In masculinity research, there are real difficulties in defining "masculinity" or "masculinities" (Hearn 1996, 1998a; Clatterbaugh 1998). These terms are certainly used in inconsistent ways by different authors. They are often used in ways that imply a simplified and static notion of identity, or rest on a simplified and unrealistic notion of difference between men and women. Hearn and Clatterbaugh are both inclined to drop the concept of masculinities because they think the real object of concern is something else — "men." If, as Clatterbaugh (1998: 41) puts it, "talking about men seems to be what we want to do," why bother to introduce the muddy concept of "masculinities" at all?

But then, why would we talk about "men" in the first place? To talk at all about a group called "men" presupposes a distinction from and relation with another group, "women." That is to say, it presupposes an account of gender. And whichever conceptual language we use, we need some way of talking about men's and women's involvement in that domain of gender. We need some way of naming conduct that is oriented to or shaped by that domain, as distinct from conduct related to other patterns in social life. Hence the need for a concept of "masculinities."

In addition to problems of definition, research on the social construction of masculinities has placed a good deal of emphasis on the uncertainties, difficulties and contradictions of the process (Messner 1992; Thorne 1993; Connell 1995). Whether the outcomes are stable or unstable, mostly fluid or mostly fixed, is an empirical question, not one to be settled in advance by theory. There are some cases, both in research and in practice (e.g., in work concerning domestic violence), where patterns of masculinity are quite tough and resistant to change (Ptacek 1988). There are other situations where masculinities are unstable, or where commitment to a gender position is negotiable.

Recognizing this possibility raises important questions about when, and why, people hold on to a certain subject position, adopt or reject the possibility of movement.

Finally, the development of global social structures has meant an interaction between the gender orders of colonizers and colonized, sometimes resulting in hybrid or novel gender patterns. Globalization has further created new institutions which operate on a world scale, and which provide new arenas for the construction of masculinities: transnational corporations, global markets, global media, intergovernmental institutions.

In these complex and large-scale social processes, new patterns of masculinity may emerge. I call these "globalizing masculinities," appearing as they do on a global stage, oriented to a global gender order. Within the contemporary world gender order, the emerging hegemonic form seems to be a masculinity based in multinational corporations and international capital markets, which I call "transnational business masculinity" (Connell 1998).

Briefly, the most powerful group of men in the world are transnational businessmen and the politicians, bureaucrats and generals associated with them. The masculinities of these milieux are historically based on the bourgeois masculinities of the rich countries (Roper 1994; Donaldson 1998; Wajcman 1999). But some new patterns seem to be emerging: a shift towards mobile career structures with very conditional loyalties; a personalized rather than dynastic approach to marriage; the abandonment of commitments to social responsibility through the welfare state or corporate welfare.

While the embodiment of transnational business masculinity has yet to be studied in detail, two points leap to the eye. One is the immense augmentation of bodily powers by technology (air travel, computers, telecommunications), making this to a certain extent a "cyborg" masculinity. The other is the extent to which international businessmen's bodily pleasures escape the social controls of local gender orders, as their business operations tend to escape the control of the national state; along with globalization of business has gone the rapid growth of an international prostitution industry.

USES OF SOCIAL RESEARCH ON MASCULINITIES

Social research is useful at three levels: increasing understanding, solving practical problems, and guiding long-term change. A better understanding of masculinities and men's gender practices is worth having simply because gender is an important aspect of our lives. If we value living in knowledge rather than in ignorance, this subject is significant for education, research and reflection. If we are to think about it at all, we need to think about the whole of the gender equation and all the groups included in it.

There is also a hard practical purpose. Contemporary masculinities are implicated in a range of toxic effects including high levels of injury, such as those caused by road crashes; patterns of ill health and mortality resulting from poor diet, drug abuse, inadequate use of health services; high levels of victimization (men are the majority of victims of reported violence) and imprisonment (about 90 percent of prison inmates are men in countries like Australia and the U.S.). The toxic effects also impact the lives of others: rape and domestic violence against women, homophobic violence and racism (Hearn 1998; Tillner 1997). In dealing with these problems at a practical level, one is constantly led beyond the immediate situation; for instance, a campaign against men's violence against women is led towards issues of prevention as well as an immediate response.

Studies of men and masculinities may also help to identify men's interests in change. There have been two polar positions here: the idea that men share women's interest in changed gender relations, and the idea that men as the dominant group have no interest in change at all. The real position is more complex. Men as a group gain real and large advantages from the current system of gender relations. But some men pay a heavy price for living in the current system, as the observations just made on toxicity go to show. Particular men, or particular groups of men, share with certain women and interest in social safety, in prevention of discrimination, in more inclusive and less hierarchical economies. It is possible to define, for many issues, bases for coalitions for change. More generally, research on multiple forms of masculinity may help people to recognize the diversity of masculinities, and the open-ended possibilities in gender relations — and thus to see alternatives for their own lives.

In the growing gender disparities of the former communist countries, and the decline of the welfare state in the West, we see examples of decline, not advance, in gender equity. But history is not a one-way street. A more democratic gender order is possible, and some groups of men are working towards it (Segal 1997; Pease 1997). If we are to realize democracy in the gender order, many men must share the burden, and the joy, of creating it.

References

Clatterbaugh, Kenneth. 1998. "What is Problematic about Masculinities?" *Men and Masculinities* 1, 1.

Connell, R.W. 1995. *Masculinities.* Cambridge: Polity Press.

_____. 1996. "Teaching the Boys: New Research on Masculinity, and Gender Strategies for Schools." *Teachers College Record* 98, 2.

_____. 1998. "Masculinities and Globalization." *Men and Masculinities* 1, 1.

Donaldson, Mike. 1998. "The Masculinity of the Hegemonic: Growing Up Very Rich." *Journal of Interdisciplinary Gender Studies* 3, 2.

Gierycz, Dorota. 1999. "Women in Decision-Making: Can We Change the Status Quo?" In Ingeborg Breines, Dorota Gierycz and Betty A. Reardon (eds.), *Towards a Women's Agenda for a Culture of Peace.* Paris: UNESCO.

Gilbert, Rob, and Pam Gilbert. 1998. *Masculinity Goes to School.* Sydney: Allen & Unwin.

Hearn, Jeff. 1996. "Is Masculinity Dead? A Critique of the Concept of Masculinity/ Masculinities." In M. Mac an Ghaill (ed.), *Understanding Masculinities*. Philadelphia: Open University Press.

____. 1998. "Theorizing Men and Men's Theorizing: Varieties of Discursive Practices in Men's Theorizing of Men." *Theory and Society* 27, 6.

McMahon, Anthony. 1999. *Taking Care of Men: Sexual Politics in the Public Mind*. Cambridge: Cambridge University Press.

Messner, Michael A. 1992. *Power at Play: Sports and the Problem of Masculinity*. Boston: Beacon Press.

____. 1997. *The Politics of Masculinities: Men in Movements*. Thousand Oaks: Sage.

Pease, Bob, 1997. *Men and Sexual Politics: Towards a Profeminist Practice*. Adelaide: Dulwich Centre Publications.

Ptacek, James. 1988. "Why Do Men Batter their Wives?" In Kersti Yllo and Michele Bograd (eds.), *Feminist Perspectives on Wife Abuse*. Newbury Park: Sage.

Roper, M. 1994. *Masculinity and the British Organization Man since 1945*. Oxford: Oxford University Press.

Sabo, Donald, and David Frederick Gordon (eds.). 1995. *Men's Health and Illness: Gender, Power, and the Body*. Thousand Oaks: Sage.

Segal, Lynne, 1997. *Slow Motion: Changing Masculinities, Changing Men*, second edition. London: Virago.

Thorne, Barrie. 1993. *Gender Play: Girls and Boys in School*. New Brunswick: Rutgers University Press.

Tillner, Georg. 1997. "Masculinity and Xenophobia." Paper to UNESCO meeting on Male Roles and Masculinities in the Perspective of a Culture of Peace. Oslo.

Wajcman, Judy. 1999. *Managing Like a Man: Women and Men in Corporate Management*. Sydney: Allen & Unwin.

Walker, Linley, Dianne Butland and Robert W. Connell. 2000. "Boys on the Road: Masculinities, Car Culture, and Road Safety Education." *Journal of Men's Studies* 8, 2.

Chapter 11

MEN, MASCULINITY AND CRIME

Rod Earle and Deborah H. Drake

From: *Marginality and Condemnation: A Critical Introduction to Criminology*, third edition, pp. 350–370 (reprinted with permission).

In May 2011 one of the most powerful white men in the world, Dominique Strauss-Kahn, was arrested in New York and taken to the city's notorious Rikers Island prison. The world's media focused on his detention because he was the managing director of the International Monetary Fund and a prospective candidate for the French presidency. He was detained under suspicion that he had raped the black woman whose job it was to clean his hotel room. He was released after a few days and the charges were dropped.

In June of the same year, serious rioting broke out in several English cities following the shooting death of a black man by police officers on the edges of a London housing estate where he was suspected of leading gangs and drug dealing. Amidst widespread looting and arson over several days, five people were killed. In the following weeks and months, thousands of young men were arrested and charged with a variety of criminal offences. Many were jailed.[1] Women were also involved in the riots, although official figures based on arrest data indicate only 10 percent of those taking part were women. Some young women were jailed as a result, but the riots prompted two widely respected feminist sociologists (Cockburn and Oakley 2011) to comment on the relationship between violence, crime and cultures of masculinity:

Today is the International Day for the Elimination of Violence Against Women. The phrase "violence against women" calls for comment. It names the victims but not the perpetrators. The fact that men are mainly responsible for violent and health-harming behaviours, not only against women and children but also against each other, is so taken for granted that it slips beneath the radar of commentators and policymakers.

The two events, the arrest for rape in the U.S. of Dominique Strauss-Kahn and the English Riots, are completely unconnected if you think questions of gender, race, class and power should be excluded from attempts to understand what crime is and how it is controlled.

RE-INTEGRATIVE NAMING? BRINGING MASCULINITY BACK IN

Concern about crime as a problematic feature of social life rose dramatically in the second half of the twentieth century in most Western countries (Garland 2001). As crime rates started to peak in the late 1980s and early 1990s, some feminist scholars and activists (Heidensohn 1987) began to characterize the problem of crime in gender terms. They challenged the discipline of criminology to account for the "facts of crime" that consistently revealed men's pre-eminent position. Across different countries, and over any time scale, and in all forms of measurement, men outnumber women in crime statistics by a ratio of up to 10:1 (Newburn and Stanko 1995).

In Britain, after a series of urban disorders and moral panics in the early 1990s, the feminist journalist and activist Bea Campbell (1993: 319) suggested that "the great unspoken in the crime angst of the 80s and 90s was that it is a phenomenon of masculinity." In her analysis of urban disorder, Campbell identified aspects of masculine, working-class culture that were, according to her viewpoint, inextricably linked with their subjugated position within the economic system and thus their social status. Men found in criminal activity, she argued, the social status they were denied by their social positioning. Moreover, with respect to the problem of crime, Campbell (1993: 319) suggested that "crime and coercion are sustained by men. Solidarity and self-help are sustained by women. It is as stark as that." Though she was subsequently accused of over simplification and further fuelling the accelerating demonization of the working class in general, and working class men in particular, her more careful qualifications were frequently overlooked:

This is not to say that boys and men are bad and girls and women are good, it is simply to repeat the obvious, *that men and women do something dramatically different with their troubles.*" (Campbell 1993: 319, emphasis added)

Examining the actions of men and women and their troubles as arising from the social processes of gender relations, rather than the innate characteristics of men and women, has been, and continues to be, the exception rather than the norm, both in everyday understandings of social life (as expressed between people as well as in media and popular culture) and in many areas of academic study.

The hostile critical reaction to Campbell's analysis reveals a common and continuing difficulty in discussing men's involvements and investments in crime and crime control. In policy making, criminal justice practice and academic criminology, there is a tendency to disassociate the concept of masculinity from that of gender. Additionally, in societies that are heavily divided along class lines, such as Britain, there is often a corresponding but ironic insensitivity and blindness to the enduring and embedded nature of class hierarchies among those most privileged by it. As is the case with white people and the dynamics of racialization, those with the most power are least likely to recognize its privileging effects. So it is with gender.

When talking about masculinity we are not talking simply "about men" as such. Far from being just about men, the idea of masculinity engages, inflects and shapes everyone (Sedgwick 1985). It works across hierarchies of class, gender relations, race and ethnicity. Naming men as gender players, as agents of gendered power, need not efface or overshadow the ways in which these other features of social and personal interaction structure the possibilities of life. However, in this chapter, we argue that it is helpful for gender to be brought firmly within what might be called a critical, intersectional gaze.

An intersectional perspective insists on the indivisibility of the interactive constituents of class, race and gender in social life at the same time as recognizing their distinctive features (see Anthias 2013). An analogy might be made in the way that knowing water is composed of two hydrogen atoms to every oxygen atom allows for a certain kind of knowledge, but identifying the chemical composition of water does little to appreciate its wetness. In order to provide a detailed and textured understanding of the interaction between men, masculinity and crime, we build on Comack's (2015) analysis of gender by turning our attentions to examining how criminology first emerged in nineteenth century Italy as a science fascinated by gender and difference. We then go on to look at how twentieth century theorists of crime in the U.S. also noted the particularity of men's behaviours, but abandoned any account of the significance of gender or masculinity because they lacked the conceptual tools, and insights, to integrate either systematically into their analysis.

Our analyses then cross the Atlantic to consider the way studies of working-class young men preoccupied British subcultural theorists in the 1970s and 1980s. Having laid this ground work, we go on to investigate the emergence of critical masculinity perspectives within criminology at the end of the twentieth century by engaging with the contributions of James Messerschmidt and Tony Jefferson, among others. We then conclude the chapter with a short vignette that considers a kind of "paradigmatic prison masculinity" to illuminate the personal tragedies and sociological conundrums they so frequently embody.

CESARE LOMBROSO AND THE NEW SCHOOL BOYS: THE ORIGIN OF THE SPECIES

Conventional accounts of the origins of criminology identify the emergence of two perspectives associated with the European Enlightenment: classicism and positivism (Young 1981). The distinction between the two is neatly expressed by Hamel (1906: 265, cited in Young 1981): "The Classical School exhorts men to study justice; the Positive School exhorts justice to study men." It is only with the privilege of hindsight and the theoretical insights of feminism that we may recognize the unintended gender dimensions of Hamel's remark. Taken as a gender-specific observation, it neatly encapsulates the challenges that continue to confront contemporary criminology.

Positivism in criminology is most powerfully associated with the nineteenth-century work of Cesare Lombroso. Lombroso's work was widely read and popularized across Europe. His studies proposed that criminals were a different class of human, a throwback to more primitive types of "early human," almost a separate species of sub-human. This remains a powerful, if sometimes implicit, theme of some strands of criminology and forensic psychology.

According to Lombroso (and, to be fair to him, the dominant currents of thought at the time), the fit and healthy white male represented the apex of evolution, while women and criminals were closer to their "primitive origins."

Lombroso is sometimes referred to as "the father of modern criminology" (Newburn 2007: 122). His symbolic influence can be gauged by the fact that David Garland's (2001) revision of the intellectual trajectory of criminology over two centuries identifies the current resurgence of the discipline in the convergence of its two dominant streams of thought: "the governmental project" (effectively, if loosely, classicism) and "the Lombrosian project" (broadly, positivism). The Lombrosian project, according to Garland, is all about establishing categorical differences between "criminal-types" and "non-criminal-types."

Lombroso's interests were enthusiastically developed by his Italian contemporaries, Enrico Ferri and Raffaele Garofalo, who together became known as The Italian School after Ferri's 1901 book *The Positive School of Criminology*. Their influence in establishing the idea of a "criminal type of man" is a lasting one, as Garland suggests, and although it is tempting to dismiss the cruder notions of biological gender difference they deploy, it reminds us of the importance of situating social and scientific theories in their cultural and historical contexts (Valier 2001). Lombroso and his contemporaries in the Positive School had no effective social theory of gender and sought to explain difference in the powerful slipstream of the intellectual revolution of Darwinism because it offered such radically new perspectives on humanity's place in the world. It might appear crude and deterministic now, but at the time it was the height of theoretical sophistication and the cutting edge of innovation. Many of the Italian positivists were social radicals, associated with the socialist and communist movements in Italy and abroad. Though we might not wish to rescue Lombroso's theories, it is just as important to avoid what the historian E.P. Thompson (1963) calls "the enormous condescension of posterity" when reviewing earlier efforts to make sense of the social world and shape its destiny.

BORN IN THE USA: DELINQUENT BOYS, TYPICAL GIRLS

In the United States, the search for a more sociological, less biologically deterministic, explanation of crime was spurred on by Robert Merton's (1938) creative adaptation of Durkheim's theory of anomie. Merton was inspired by the effects of the American Dream as a form of capitalist development, and its first major crisis in the 1929 Crash and subsequent Depression years of the 1930s. Merton's theory of deviance is credited as being "the single most influential formulation in the sociology of deviance" (Clinard 1964: 10). His assertion that "a cardinal American virtue, ambition, promotes a cardinal American vice, deviant behaviour" (1949: 137) addressed the booming rates of crime that accompanied the explosive growth of American cities, most famously and most paradigmatically, Chicago.

The frustrations and adaptations Merton identified in the early twentieth century were not explicitly gendered but resonated most forcefully in the construction of working-class masculinities. Operating at the leading edge of capitalist development in the West, male employment and the breadwinner wage were central to these aspirational, industrial, U.S. masculinities. Structural unemployment in the 1930s challenged the much-idealized stability of the male breadwinner role and threatened the secure occupational identities around which conventional definitions of male self-esteem were increasingly gathered (Connell 1987, 1995).

The significance of the masculine life-course, and specifically the strains Merton identified, became central to what has come to be celebrated as The Chicago School of American sociology. Wide in scope, and profound in influence, Chicago School sociology was heavily pre-occupied with men and fascinated by deviance. Albert Cohen's (1955: 140) study of young men in New York, "Delinquent Boys," set both the tone and much of the agenda:

> The delinquent is the rogue male. His conduct may be viewed ... positively ... as the exploitation of modes of behaviour which are traditionally symbolic of untrammeled masculinity ... which are not without a certain aura of glamour and romance.

There is more than a hint of an echo of Lombrosian atavism in Cohen's reference to "untrammeled masculinity," as if masculinity was intrinsically wild, but his debt to Merton is clearer. He finds that the subculture among New York's marginalized young men was a solution to "problems of adjustment" which were "primarily problems of the male role." Developing into the male role included, first, overcoming the dependency of childhood and then becoming established within an appropriate work identity. With respect to middle-class boys, Cohen argued that there was a more prolonged dependence upon parental support that had to be confronted:

> Not only must the middle-class boy overcome an early feminine identification and prove his maleness, even the opportunities to assume the legitimate signs of maleness are likely to be denied him. (Cohen 1955: 166)

Within this analysis, the "breadwinner role," it was argued, established the basis (if only in principle and fantasy) for a lasting domestic symmetry with a steadfast, stay-at-home wife providing unwaged domestic labour (cooking, laundry, household maintenance and childcare), emotional comfort and sexual gratification. However, working class boys' earlier departure from the feminized home and entry into the (masculinizing) job market, by contrast, provided a distinctive dividend — they were able to accrue masculine (and often muscular) capital sooner.

Cohen's work is clearly sensitive to gender but shackled to the limitations of what is known as "sex-role theory." Cohen (1955) attributes middle-class male delinquency to "an attempt to cope with a basic anxiety in the area of sex-role identification; it has the primary function of giving reassurance to one's essential masculinity." Sex-role theory, as Connell (1987) argues, always tends to reinforce, rather than challenge, naturalized gender categories. The working-class male, according to Cohen, is more likely to be secure in his masculine identity through his earlier transition from the feminizing influence of the domestic space of home to the male-dominated spheres of work. His troubles, specifically his delinquency, arise from the difficulties of "adjustment in the area of ego-involved status differences in a status system defined by the norms of respectable middle class society" (Cohen 1955: 168). In other words, his masculine aspirations for power do not correspond with his class opportunities.

Albert Cohen can be credited with putting masculinity in the criminological picture, but he is hampered by the prevailing assumptions of biologically determined natural differences between men and women that took the form of complementary breadwinning and domestic roles. As such they were regarded as peripheral to the more determining forces of class stratification.

An unintended gender perspective comes across strongly in a section of Cohen's

Delinquent Boys headed "What About Sex Differences?" that candidly reveals Cohen's personal reading of his own natural, "representative" masculinity:

> My skin has nothing of the quality of down or silk; there is nothing limpid or flute-like about my voice. I am a total loss with needle and thread. My posture and carriage are wholly lacking in grace. These imperfections cause me no distress — if anything they are gratifying — because I conceive myself to be a man and want people to recognise me as a fully-fledged representative of my sex. (Cohen 1955: 138)

Albert Cohen's revealing, reflexive meditations and his sensitivity to the empirical realities of gender differences are a welcome exception to the more conventionally and casually gender-blind approach of a lot of mainstream criminology, both then and now.

An emerging concern about the significance of gender relations is also evident in Richard Cloward and Lloyd Ohlin's (1961) work, *Delinquency and Opportunity: A Theory of Delinquent Gangs*. With hindsight it is easy to see the constraints imposed on them by the sex-role paradigm, as it was with Cohen's work. The tension between a cultural faith in the notion of fixed gender identities despite empirical evidence of their fluidity, variation and instability is a consistent feature of any historical study of masculinities (Harvey and Shepard 2005). Responding to such empirical realities and theoretical difficulties, Cloward and Ohlin (1961: 51) record their doubts about "the distribution of the masculine-identity crisis" and indicate that "there is no firm agreement among theorists as to where in the social structure this problem occurs most frequently or in most acute forms". It is illuminating to note Cloward and Ohlin's early engagement with this tension and the popular belief that the "wayward" behavior of some men, and any empirical evidence of such behavior, denoted an alarming crisis in masculinity. Equally, despite these persistent misgivings about masculinity, it tended to remain underresearched, and the structures of masculine authority were left relatively untouched.

The lack of theoretical consensus around the relationship between men, masculinity, deviance and crime, or the contours of various crises facing men, sociology or capitalism, was not confined to the U.S. in the 1960s. On the other side of the Atlantic, broadly similar men in similar academic institutions studied corresponding cohorts of men a little younger than themselves in British cities and they began to generate further theoretical innovations (Dorn and South 1982).

NEVER MIND THE CHICAGO SCHOOL, HERE'S THE U.K. SUBCULTURALISTS

London and Birmingham, rather than Chicago, provided the backdrop for the development of the new subcultural studies that emerged in the U.K. David Downes (1966) adapted and inverted the conventions of his U.S. contemporaries by asserting that conformity to norms, rather than rejection and rebellion, was the hallmark of British working-class masculine subcultures. Pride in, and possession of, working-class values, such as solidarity and group identity, provided the young men Downes studied with positive resources rather than a sense of deficit, a solution to predicaments imposed on them by the deeply embedded class hierarchy of British society.

Subcultural sociologists like Phil Cohen (1972) and Paul Willis (1977) found inspiration in the vitality and diversity of working-class young men's cultures in a country moving across the cusp of the postwar gloom through to the 1960s boom and subsequently into the crash of the OPEC high oil price–induced recession of the 1970s (Hobsbawm 1995). In a country whose labour movement prided itself not only on its postwar achievements in establishing the world's first welfare state, but also its traditions as the first industrial proletariat, the forward march of labour was halted in its tracks (Hobsbawm 1978). The Cold War stand-off between the capitalist West and the Rest (i.e., the Soviet Union, the developing countries of the global south and China) was eventually lost to a triumphant neo-liberal order. Its threatening shadow chilled the hopes and aspirations of the postwar generation, stilling the tide of progressive liberalization after 1945 that rode on the back of the economic consensus delivered by Keynesianism in Britain. The Cold War ground out the contours of the reaction to come in the late 1980s as the Berlin Wall fell and Soviet power financialized itself in the image of Chicago's finest criminal icons and free-market gurus.

British popular culture in the 1960s and 1970s expressed an appetite for young white men in black leather jackets on motorbikes (rockers), or khaki parkas and Lambretta scooters (mods). Skinheads were perhaps the most aggressively masculine, assertively white and working class of these subcultures. As skinheads, young men reduced their dress code and self-presentation to a simple, masculine, no-frills essence: tight denim jeans, high Doc Marten boots, cropped or shaved heads and a T-shirt. Their neo-brutal minimalist fashion aesthetic co-existed with a paradoxical affection for the sensuous rhythms of Jamaican ska and reggae that was crossing the Atlantic in the 1960s with the Caribbean immigrants brought over to the British Isles during the postwar era, when the British welfare state was being built.

Although the distinctive aspects of white men's working-class cultures in Britain, and those of its emerging Black and minority ethnic groups, propelled correspondingly distinctive theoretical development from those in the U.S. (see Hall et al. 1978; Gilroy 1987), the analysis of gender remained much closer to Albert Cohen's, rather than offering new and distinctive insights. Hall and Jefferson (1975: 60), for example, re-state Cohen's thesis that "middle class youth remains longer than their working class peers 'in the transitional stage,'" living in the shelter of their (feminizing) families while working-class young men depart earlier to the masculinizing culture of work.

Paul Willis's *Learning to Labour* is considered the landmark ethnographic study of this generation in Britain, the subtitle "How Working Class Kids Get Working Class Jobs" providing a succinct account of the narrative, while obscuring the fact that it is almost exclusively a story about boys and young men. His account is a compelling one. Willis vividly describes a process of class differentiation occurring in the second or third year of secondary school (i.e., ages fourteen to fifteen), prior to which all the boys who would become "lads" (loosely, delinquents) could be described as "ear 'oles" (loosely, conformists because an "ear hole" was British slang for someone who listens). The lads accomplish their differentiation by a conscious process of identification with clothes, smoking, drinking, fighting and sex, which Willis insightfully collects under the young men's own collective term of "having a laff." Willis artfully presents the "'boys' secret and delicious joy in defying authority, celebrating their own values, and most important, confirming both, getting away with it" (Willis 1975: 6).

The tragic irony Willis apprehends is that the means of transcending school through their triumph over boredom, and their investment in time-wasting leavened with heavy and physical humour, only accelerates the young men's incorporation into dead-end jobs. These jobs are themselves recognized as such by the lads as mere instruments to the maintenance of an independent working class culture that pits (masculine) authenticity, subterfuge and humour against the duplicity of a meritocratic (i.e., middle class) work ethic, a kind of avowedly working-class consciousness but one that is more passive-aggressive than revolutionary.

Willis's work is innovative for including an explicit analysis of the articulation of capitalism with patriarchy but, according to Connell (1983), it is constrained by its orientation to an inflexible structuralist Marxism. In other words, in Willis's analysis, class is privileged at a fundamental, functional and structural level. The modes of production and the complex particularities of the young men's relation to physical and mental labour are so cleverly revealed in Willis's meticulous ethnography that they are inevitably reduced to a homogenous class experience. As Connell (1983: 225) points out:

> The fieldwork doesn't react on the conceptions of the social structure. Indeed, in the gradual elaboration of an analysis of patriarchy, we can

see the structuralist approach taking over the new material as it arrives. The eventual result is an abstract theory of social reproduction, not a theory of what the field material so beautifully demonstrates, sexual power structure.

Willis is eloquent in his appreciation of the injuries of class, hidden, self-inflicted or otherwise, but relatively silent about the boys' casual misogyny, fear of domesticity and horror of effeminacy. Angela McRobbie (1980) shares Connell's critique of Willis's attempt at theoretical synthesis, concluding that, unfortunately, as with Albert Cohen, masculinity in this and other subcultural accounts rarely achieves any theoretical purchase on the young men's presence in the narrative. However, both note and welcome the way masculinity registers positively, if only at the level of description. For McRobbie, the rich qualitative traditions of ethnographic research to be found in subcultural studies on both sides of the Atlantic should not now be dismissed for its gender blinkers, but revisited "so that questions hitherto ignored or waved aside in embarrassment become central" (1991: 17). Recognition of the need to bring a stronger theoretical grip to the study of masculinity and crime to prevent it slipping below the analytical radar or out of the storyline altogether has since become a major preoccupation for some critical criminologists.

THEORIZING CRIME AND MASCULINITY

In the history of criminology, it sometimes seems as if masculinity takes the position that the French novelist Gustav Flaubert recommended for the "authorial voice" in a novel — that is, to be everywhere present but nowhere fully identifiable. Feminist scholars' insistence throughout the 1970s and 1980s on the salience of gender across all the social sciences has forced the pace of change, and Frances Heidensohn (1987: 23) indicates its emerging effect in criminology:

> Gender is no longer ignored ... but it is consigned to an outhouse, beyond the main structure of the work and is almost invariably conflated with women; males are not seen as having gender; or if their masculinity does become an issue, it is taken-for-granted and not treated as problematic.

Until relatively recently in criminology, there has been little enthusiasm for explicitly studying masculinity, but there are signs this is changing. (For a critical account, see Collier 1998.) Bringing masculinity into the story at a more coherent theoretical level has been significantly advanced by Raewyn Connell's account of gender and power. For Connell (1983, 1987, 2002), appreciating the emergence of a historical consciousness of gender is critically important. She suggests that gender is a structure of social relations, is open to social reform and has been slower to emerge than the same corresponding knowledge of class. However, now that gender has emerged, it cannot be placed back in the box of biology from whence it came. That hitherto reliable alibi for inequality and privilege has been blown, just as it has for race (Hall 1992). Connell argues that we have passed "a horizon of historicity" in relation to gender, and although it crossed this horizon by focusing on the subordinate position of women, it now includes men and masculinity, in particular.

For Tony Jefferson (1993: 73; 1994, 1996, 1997), the task facing criminology is to account for "the near perfect fit between the mortice of masculinity and the tenon of crime," to understand why crime is overwhelmingly a male pursuit. In Canada, 95 percent of those admitted to federal custody are men, with very similar proportions sentenced in provincial and territorial courts. Likewise, 80 percent of the young people who are processed through youth courts are young men (Comack 2008). In the U.K., where detailed crime data is routinely collected through both self-report surveys and police-generated data, men persistently account for eight out of every ten people cautioned by the police (representing those people diverted away from formal prosecution but who nevertheless accept they have committed a crime, albeit usually a relatively minor one). Nearly nine out of ten people found guilty for indictable (relatively serious) offences are men. Men are responsible for 92 percent of violent crimes against the person and 97 percent of burglaries. In prisons, 96 percent of the population is made up of men, mostly young men. The modal ages of the male prison population are twenty-five and twenty-six (Newburn 2007). Despite some fluctuations in recorded crimes committed by adult or young women in some countries, the empirical data across most jurisdictions suggests that it is adult or young men who are most frequently convicted of criminal activity.

These figures inevitably tend to reflect the traditional selective concerns of criminal justice system agencies, such as the police, and government priorities on public order and private property. They neglect the less thoroughly policed sections of the social hierarchy, occupied by figures like Dominique Strauss-Kahn, but it seems highly likely that if they were, a range of harmful and criminalizable activities could be identified. A theoretical toolkit has begun to take shape that helps to understand these enduring gender dimensions of the crime equation, tools that can analyze the hitherto invisible "joint" Jefferson describes.

As Comack (2008, 2015) argues, such a toolkit is necessary to "bring masculinity into view." Significantly for the study of masculinity in relation to crime, Raewyn Connell's work provides a vocabulary and conceptual map that offers a framework for systematically examining and understanding masculinities. Connell identifies how the vast constellations of the different ways of being a man secure a distinctive pattern of social relations. This pattern is dynamic and contested within certain defining limits, prompting Connell to use the term "hegemony." Hegemony denotes a dominant and dominating pattern of social relations secured by a combination of consent, habit and the exclusion of alternatives. For Connell, it captures the way multiple masculinities operate around certain organizing principles of masculinity that privilege some ways of being a man over others, while maintaining an overall pattern of domination over women (Connell 1987, 1995, 2002, 2005, 2008).

A recurring theme of hegemonic masculinity is that it is heterosexual and closely connected, at least symbolically, if not always in practice, to the institution of marriage. The changing balance of forces in gender relations is closely mapped through patterns of family form, childcare and wage-labour relations. Despite significant legislative reform in many Western democracies, male homosexuality remains the kind of masculinity most antithetical to hegemonic form. Subordinated masculinities are those forms of masculinity, such as homosexuality, that are most discredited or oppressed in the culture, and are commonly marked as feminine.

Connell identifies the notion of "protest masculinities" to capture the pressures hegemonic masculinity exerts on men to conform to its organizational and experiential principles and some of the more resistant masculinities that develop as a result. These are often the ill-fitting masculinities associated, in the West, with adolescence as young men feel the attractions of their potential for power, status hierarchies and the benefits available to them in the conventions of the gender order (Connell 2005). Connell stresses the fluid and contested nature of this order as a historical composition, always in process, always unfinished but dynamically reproducing itself as a pattern of gender relations that tends toward the privileging of men and the subordination of women. By using the term hegemony, Connell reminds us that gender is a struggle, not a fact of nature. Masculinity is a form of politics rather than of biology. The persistent historical recurrence of concerns about "crisis" in relation to men's identities, of masculinity in crisis, underlines this dynamic feature of the gender order (see Tosh and Roper 1991; Tosh 1999, 2005).

The contemporary problematics of masculinity are profiled in the crime statistics that became so prominent and public in many Western societies in the closing quarter of the twentieth century. Complex varieties of empirical evidence back up what the English social reformer Barbara Wootton observed in 1959: "If men behaved like women, the courts would be idle and the prisons empty (Wootton 1959: 32). At the start of the twenty-first century, criminal courts are busier than ever and prisons are full, multiplying and expanding in size. Even though the rate of women's imprisonment is accelerating faster than it is for men, the gender gap remains a compelling, undertheorized and overlooked feature of crime and criminal justice systems. We urgently need new answers to the question of why "men and women do something dramatically different with their troubles."

DOING GENDER AND DOING CRIME — JAMES MESSERSCHMIDT

James Messerschmidt (1993, 1997, 2005) has been at the forefront of efforts to account for the masculinity of crime, and has collaborated with Connell (2005) to consolidate a theoretical framework that can account for men's pre-eminent position in the gender dimensions of crime.

Messerschmidt concentrates on the way in which men position themselves in relation to hegemonic masculinity and how their identities are framed in a broader social context. Messerschmidt suggests that men's social and emotional investments in crime can be better understood by examining more closely the situations and masculine dynamics in which they are involved. That is, for Messerschmidt, "doing crime" becomes an equivalent to "doing masculinity." Men's accomplishment of various diverse criminalized activities provides them with masculine resources and status, which may be as much emotional as material. As Comack's (2008) work with young men in Canadian prisons shows, the struggle of young men to align themselves with tough guys, sports, school (in)discipline, hardness, gang activity and drugs forms part of a series of activities that help make them feel they are men or becoming a man. As Comack's interviews so poignantly demonstrate, their crimes often feed a hunger for authentic masculine "truths" that are almost impossible to satisfy and that they are poorly resourced to pursue. More commonly, their aspirations for achieving a particular version of masculinity propels them, instead, into descending spirals of destructive (often self-destructive) and harmful actions. Nevertheless, the way these activities make men feel like they are men, in a social and personal context, is central to their attraction.

Messerschmidt borrows from Robert Merton's strain perspectives (see Comack 2015), arguing that the social structures of capitalism block legitimate opportunities for working-class men to secure many of the privileges associated with conventional hegemonic masculinities and, furthermore, that these blockages are compounded by racism. Black, minority and Aboriginal men are thus more highly represented in the crime statistics because they are more likely to have to draw from a narrower and less highly valourized repertoire of masculine opportunity. They don't, won't or can't talk the talk of the powerful white men at the top of the social hierarchy any more than they walk the walk of their corporate boardrooms. Unlike men at the top of the social hierarchy, men like Dominique Strauss-Kahn, mentioned at the start of this chapter, their struggles to establish a viable trajectory to their life are ringed ever closer with criminal justice and welfare agencies that increasingly monitor and track every wayward impulse. Likewise, returning to the other vignette that we started this chapter with, many of the men who looted shops, attacked police and created mayhem on the streets of England in 2011 were quickly arrested and thousands were prosecuted with the full force of the criminal law. Many ended up in prison, serving long sentences and will now carry the burden of criminal convictions that will weigh down any further effort to move beyond their positions at the social and economic margins of society once they are eventually released.

Messerschmidt uses a series of detailed case studies to argue that the general patterns of masculine practice that constitute hegemonic masculinity, such as competitiveness, physical toughness, emotional hardness and heterosexuality, are always personally configured according to circumstance and the structured opportunities of particular men. These features of masculine practice, these ways of being a man, are recognizable throughout the social hierarchy, but the contexts in which they occur for any one man, the opportunities that each man can capitalize on and generate, are structurally constrained by their class position and experiences of racialization. Masculinity is always lived in the plural as these variable combinations take shape and are shaped in each man's life and relationships. There are many masculinities, but they do not randomly occur in haphazard combinations.

According to Messerschmidt (1993: 84), "Particular types of crime can provide an alternative resource for accomplishing gender, and therefore, affirming a particular type of masculinity." Street crime, corporate crime, sexual harassment, domestic violence and rape are thus conceived as both the accomplishment and fulfillment of various types of masculinity that collectively collaborate in securing men's structural power over women. As with other masculinity scholars, Messerschmidt does not confine the problematics of male power to crime and criminalized activity because, as he points out in a series of detailed case studies, they are as equally evident in activities as diverse as the decisions that led to the disastrous launch of the Challenger space shuttle in 1986 and the lynching of Black men by white men in the nineteenth century. In the former case, masculine pride in risk-taking behavior and the desire for prestige resulted in the neglect of evidence that launch safety systems were radically compromised, leading to the catastrophic and fatal explosion of Challenger. According to Messerschmidt's analysis, key technicians in the Challenger team were so heavily invested in "doing masculinity," asserting their virility and masculine prowess, that they were prepared to abandon the safety of the flight crew. Similarly, in the nineteenth century, white men's conflicted investments in their own virility was counterposed by their fear of Black men's sexual potency. They combined to sanction the savagery of lynching because it provided both a collective affirmation of their insecure desires and a cathartic release for the emotional blockage their fear generated.

The problematics of male power that we opened this chapter with and which link the arrest in New York of a middle-aged white man of the cosmopolitan elite to the Black and white men living precariously in the urban margins of north London (Standing 2011) are not reducible to crime, but, if we care to examine them, the dynamics involved can tell us a lot about crime, men, gender and power.

What keeps one kind of man out of prison and throws many of another kind of man into prison — that deepest recess of the criminal justice system — should be at the forefront of criminological enquiry. The stark racialized patterning of the prison population is one starting point, and so too are its gender dynamics. Prison is a particularly revealing place to pursue these enquiries. Although, as Don Sabo (2001) remarks, "Prison is a hyper-masculine place where no-one speaks about masculinity."

PRISON LIFE, PRISON MASCULINITIES?

The academic study of men's prison life in the United States was first embarked upon by Donald Clemmer in 1940. Since then a number of in-depth studies of men's prisons have been undertaken in a variety of penal settings (for example, *inter alia* Sykes 1958; Irwin 1970; Morris and Morris 1963; Jacobs 1977; Sparks, Bottoms and Hay 1996; Liebling and Arnold 2004; Drake 2012). The main theoretical models that aim to explain and understand prison social life include a deprivation model, an importation model and those that integrate aspects of the two. In the deprivation model, it is argued that prison life is shaped by the coercive nature of the prison environment. The purest branch of this model argues that any differences in the organization of prison establishments are irrelevant because the experience of total institutions is so coercive that it homogenizes prisoner responses to their environment (see Goffman 1961; Sykes 1958). By contrast, a more situational model argues that prisoners' responses to prison life are situationally dependent on institutional characteristics (Grusky 1959; Wilson 1968). Broadly speaking, these perspectives are deprivation models because they seek to explain prison life and prisoners' adaptations to it as responses to the pains of imprisonment and the deprivations associated with the loss of liberty.

In response, and in contrast to, these explanations, an importation model to understanding prison life emerged. Importation models argue that the social environment of prison life is shaped by the imported characteristics of the prisoner group and that these originate in the subcultures to which prisoners belong prior to their entry into prison (Irwin 1970; Irwin and Cressey 1962). Further studies of prison life have proposed slight deviations from these models (e.g., Dilulio 1987; Useem and Kimball 1989). However, much contemporary prison literature tends to present integrated versions of prison social life that draw on aspects of both importation and deprivation models (Toch and Adams 1989; Liebling and Arnold 2004; Harvey 2007; Crewe 2009).

Despite the recognition amongst prison researchers that men's prison life is best understood by examining both the characteristics men bring with them into the prison environment and the peculiarities of the total institutions in which they are confined, there has been relatively little attention given to the way these experiences are gendered *as masculine*. Although numerous studies of women's imprisonment expose the specific dynamics of gender (Carlen 1983) that result in differential and differentiating experiences of prison, little corresponding work has been done with men that acknowledges their gender specificities. For example, men's specific relations to liberty and movement, to public and private space, to time structured by the labour process, and so on, remain largely unexamined through the gender lens that is routinely brought to bear on women in prison.

For all too many men, the journey from the harsh economic margins of society to prison is a cumulative and sometimes tragically terminal experience. It can be the result of patterns of behaviour or exceptional ruptures in established ones, as well as differential and discriminatory policing. Attending to how men make sense of their life in an institution that deprives them of so much that is conventionally central to masculine status, such as heterosexual relations and work, is strangely underdeveloped within criminology. Why are these "emasculations" regarded as so central to the process of punishment when masculinity is so thinly theorized in the critical literature? Men's prisons are, as Sabo observes, hypermasculine places where cultures of machismo may flourish, and be taken for granted, among staff cultures and prisoners alike, but the cliché of the macho-man does little to shed light on the complex ways in which men make sense of themselves and their lives in prison. Men are complex and diverse, even as prison forces them into its narrow correctional molds.

UNPACKING MEN IN CRIMINOLOGY — A VIGNETTE, A MAN

Drawing from recent work in English prisons, we present below a short composite case study that seeks to capture some of the issues at stake in men's imprisonment. Recent psycho-social approaches to criminology (Gadd and Jefferson 2007; Maruna and Matravers 2007) have pioneered a more personal and biographical approach to the study of crime. It is an approach that counters the tendencies of crude categorization and aggregation that criminology can be prone to.

Both crimes and prisons succeed in generating the driest of data and the most numbing forms of analysis, whilst also remaining utterly compelling to the imagination. The reasons for this are undoubtedly complex, but one of the most unsettling features that both authors of this chapter have encountered in our prison research is how ordinary most of the men there are. Far from being beasts or monsters, men in prison are very much like the men or boys we have met at school, or at work, or in the streets where we live. It is another cliché to say they are all different, and each have their own story to tell, but it seems these stories are rarely told, barely register in popular consciousness and are relentlessly outshone by the dazzling fictions of films, television series and novels. Either that or they are erased by statistical and scientific reports oblivious to their detail. The vignette below is not intended to be representative, or even deeply illustrative. It is little more than a thumbnail sketch designed to convey some basic features of a man's life in crime. Drawn from research experiences in English prisons, it functions as a device to insist that we take crime personally, to recall the person into the picture and to deal with people, not criminals. Finding a way of taking masculinity seriously can involve engaging, as Gadd and Jefferson suggest, more thoroughly with the details of men's biographies rather than their categorical characteristics.

JOHN: A CRIMINALIZED MAN

John is a middle-aged white man who grew up in a social housing block in the English midlands where unemployment was high, where there were few opportunities for young people to make the transition from school to work and where there were high levels of crime and vandalism. His parents divorced when he was twelve, and he went to live with his father, who worked full time in a factory and was not around for much of the day or the evenings. He was good at sports and enjoyed the time he spent with other boys and the sports coaches. When he was thirteen he met a girl who introduced him to cannabis and to other boys who were beginning to get into dealing drugs. Soon his involvement with drugs and the new-found independence he got from low-level drug dealing began to pull him away from sports and school. By the time he was fifteen, John was a physically big lad and had a developing reputation as someone who people could rely on to supply drugs (mostly cannabis) and who other (more powerful) drug dealers could call on to ensure that people paid up what they owed. His intimidating stature ensured that people would not mess with him. Due to John's increasingly late nights and chaotic lifestyle, his dad threw him out of the house when he was sixteen, and John turned to "the lads" he knew from the street. John's life became a mixture of drug dealing, acting as an enforcer for drug debts owed to other dealers and the occasional mugging or robbery to maintain his own growing drug dependency. These activities and the friends he was associating with, however, provided John with opportunities to gain a reputation and a status that felt meaningful to him. He felt he was working hard to achieve notoriety amongst his peer group, and by the time he was nineteen, few people were willing to challenge or stand against him. When John was twenty-two, he and one of his mates went to collect on a debt owed to them by another drug dealer. They knew going into the confrontation that they would be evenly matched and so they each brought along a knife. Perhaps they suspected the other man would be armed with one, perhaps they thought they could be useful for intimidation. The usual reasons men give for carrying weapons are "defensive," in both senses. A fight ensued, and the man they wanted to overpower was stronger than either of them anticipated. The fight ended, however, when John and his mate drew their knives and killed the person they went to collect their money from.

Both John and his mate were given mandatory life sentences for murder, each with a minimum term of eighteen years.

John's entry into the prison world was not a difficult one. His reputation preceded him to some extent, and he found he could slot in well to prison social life and the prisoner hierarchy. He found similar value systems on the inside to those he had encountered and subscribed to on the outside. Moreover, prison life afforded John some of the basic needs he had had difficulty securing on the outside, such as a roof over his head, regular meals and overcoming his addiction to drugs.

John's relationships with women were tangled in his unstable domestic circumstances. He may have fathered children, but if so, he had no sense of himself as a father. His relationships with women tended to be brief. He kept in touch with his mother only intermittently. His father refused to see him.

Whilst the punishing aspects of prison were difficult to endure, at times, John learned to cope with the rules and deprivations of prison, and, as a "lifer," John was able to maintain his reputation and status as a "hard man." It was not until John had served the majority of his minimum term and began to face the prospect of possible release that he began to realize he had no idea how he would fit in on the outside. He was now getting close to forty and nearly half of his life had been spent in prison. He recognized that although being a lifer had placed him at the top of the prisoner hierarchy, once he was released, as an ex-prisoner who had a murder conviction on his record, his status would completely reverse and he would enter a world where he was a social outcast, an ex-prisoner who would have to continue to live for the rest of his life under licence conditions. One false move and he could wind up straight back inside prison. At the same time, John realized he would likely have significant difficulties finding a place to live, finding a job, finding a partner or making new friends. John was unable to see any way he might fit in to society again and he realized he had never really fit into it in the first place. Six months prior to his release, after seventeen years in prison, John took his own life.

John's story illustrates a relatively common set of circumstances for men who find themselves in prison. The "prisoner society" and the constitution of prisons as places of power, control and punishment, in many ways, replicate the hierarchical, status-oriented and, often brutal, life that many men experience before they enter prison. Moreover, prisoner society is often replete with the same *sub rosa* economies and masculine value systems that governed men's lives on the outside — as Sim (1994) notes, "To speak in terms of normal and abnormal men … is to miss the fundamental point, namely that normal life in male prisons is highly problematic — it reproduces normal men".

On both sides of the prison walls there is a valourization of strength and fearlessness, an impossible identification with masculine invulnerability. One has only to think of the bizarre character traits played out to cartoon proportions by Hollywood heroes from John Wayne (*Rio Bravo*) to Sylvester Stallone (*Rambo*), Bruce Willis (*Die Hard*) to Robert Downey Jr. (*Iron Man*) to recognize how durable, pervasive and profitable this identification is (Pfiel 1995). In this value system, men award other men status and respect according to their willingness and capacity to exploit vulnerability and inflict harm rather than extend empathy and consideration toward each other. The omnipotent hero is the singular individual, a culturally iconic form of masculinity, no less influential than the calculating risk-taking individual (man) of conventional liberal economics. Men inside and outside prison adhere to negotiated codes on how to earn and maintain respect (Bourgeois 1995), how to be a man in a man's world, but they are no more born to do it than they are doomed to it.

For John, above, the accomplishment of his masculinity and the absence or neglect of viable alternatives that might displace his continuing investments in narrowing social and economic prospects proved ultimately as fatal to him as it did to his victim. The irony and the paradox is that having made himself a successful prisoner in the homo-social, ultra-masculine prison world, he cannot face the journey back into a more complex, unstable and gender-variegated world. It's a man's world in prison, but that was no longer so much the case beyond its walls. It makes the journey back all the more challenging for men and the journey back into prison more likely.

Studying the inner life of prisons brings to light a stark picture of the pernicious and deeply ingrained structures of men's social and personal lives and their orientations to domesticity, intimacy and care. It tells us something of what men do with their troubles and what becomes of troubled men. Violence features as prominently in the "solutions" as the problems. Examining the connections between this penal inner life and the inner life of men can tell us more about the relationships between men, masculinity and crime. It forges the connections suggested in Oakley's observation:

> Criminality and masculinity are linked because the sort of acts associated with each have much in common. The demonstration of physical strength, a certain kind of aggressiveness, visible and external proof of achievement, whether legal or illegal — these are facets of the ideal male personality and also much of criminal behaviour. Both male and criminal are valued by their peers for these qualities. Thus, the dividing line between what is masculine and what is criminal may at times be a thin one. (1972: 64, revisited in 2011 with Cockburn)

As the French filmmaker and feminist activist Virginie Despentes (2011) commented in reaction to the media focus on Dominique Strauss-Kahn's predicament, and its neglected contexts:

> If anything is as disgusting and incomprehensible as rape, it's prison: this rape by the state, this abject useless destruction of humanity. What does prison create? It is no solution, just the face of inhumanity, the dirty mirror reflecting how poorly we live together, how we only know how to respond to violence by unleashing more violence ... Whether it is called rape or jail, we need to ask ourselves how we developed the sordid habit of considering either one as part of the landscape, or as tolerable.

Note

1. For a full account, see <http://www.theguardian.com/uk/series/reading-the-riots>.

References

Anthias, F. 2013. "Moving Beyond the Janus Face of Integration and Diversity Discourses: Towards an Intersectional Framing." *The Sociological Review* 61: 323–343.

Bourgeois, P. 1995. *In Search of Respect: Selling Crack in El Barrio.* Cambridge: Cambridge University Press.

Campbell, B. 1993. *Goliath: Britain's Dangerous Places.* London: Methuen.

Carlen, P. 1983. *Women's Imprisonment.* London: Routledge & Kegan Paul.

Clemmer, D. 1940. *The Prison Community.* New York: Holt, Rinehart and Winston.

Clinard, M. 1964. "The Theoretical Implications of Anomie and Deviant Behaviour." In M. Clinard (ed.), *Anomie and Deviant Behaviour.* New York: Free Press.

Cloward, R.A., and L.E. Ohlin. 1961. *Delinquency and Opportunity: A Theory of Delinquent Gangs.* London: Routledge:

Cockburn, C., and A. Oakley. 2011. "The Culture of Masculinity Costs All Too Much to Ignore." *Guardian*, 25 November. <http://www.guardian.co.uk/commentisfree/2011/nov/25/dangerous-masculinty-everyone-risk> accessed January 2012.

Cohen, A.K. 1955. *Delinquent Boys.* New York: Free Press.

Cohen, P. 1972. "Sub-Cultural Conflict and Working Class Community." Working Papers in Cultural Studies 2: 5–52. Centre for Cultural Studies, University of Birmingham.

Collier, R. 1998. *Masculinities, Crime and Criminology.* London: Sage.

Comack, E. 2008. *Out There: In Here – Masculinity, Violence and Prisoning.* Winnipeg: Fernwood Publishing.

____. 2015. "The Sex Question in Criminology." In C. Brooks and B. Schissel (eds.), *Marginality and Condemnation: A Critical Introduction to Criminology*, third edition. Halifax/Winnipeg: Fernwood Publishing.

Connell, R.W. 1983 *Which Way Is Up – Essays on Sex, Class and Culture.* Sydney: Allen & Unwin.

____. 1987. *Gender and Power: Society, the Person and Sexual Politics.* Cambridge: Polity Press.

____. 1995. *Masculinities*. Cambridge: Polity Press.

____. 2002. *Gender*. Cambridge: Polity Press.

____. 2005. "Growing Up Masculine: Rethinking the Significance of Adolescence in the Making of Masculinities." *Irish Journal of Sociology* 14, 2: 11–28.

____. 2008. "A Thousand Miles from Kind: Men, Masculinities and Modern Institutions." *Journal of Men's Studies: A Scholarly Journal about Men and Masculinities* 16, 3: 237–252.

Crewe, B. 2009. *The Prisoner Society: Power, Adaptation and Social Life in an English Prison*. Oxford: Clarendon Press.

Curtis, Anna. 2014. "'You Have to Cut It off at the Knee': Dangerous Masculinity and Security Inside a Men's Prison." *Men and Masculinities* 17, 2.

Despentes, V. 2011. "A Game Only One Side Plays." *Guardian*, 23 May: 17.

Dilulio, J. 1987. *Governing Prisons: A Comparative Study of Correctional Management*. London: Collier Macmillan.

Dorn, N., and N. South. 1982. "Of Males and Markets: A Critical Review of 'Youth Culture' Theory." Research Paper 1, Centre for Occupational and Community Research. London: Middlesex Polytechnic

Downes, D. 1966. *The Delinquent Solution: A Study in Subcultural Theory*. London: Routledge, Kegan and Paul.

Drake, D.H. 2012. *Prisons, Punishment and the Pursuit of Security*. Basingstoke: Palgrave Macmillan.

Gadd, D., and T. Jefferson. 2007. *Psychosocial Criminology: An Introduction*. London. Sage.

Garland, D. 2001. *The Culture of Control: Crime and Social Order in Contemporary Society*. Oxford: Clarendon.

Gilroy, P. 1987. *There Ain't No Black in the Union Jack*. London: Routledge.

Goffman, E. 1961. "On the Characteristics of Total Institutions." In D. Cressey (ed.), *The Prison: Studies in Institutional Organization and Change*. New York: Holt, Rinehart and Winston.

Grusky, O. 1959. "Organizational Goals and the Behavior of Informal Leaders." *American Journal of Sociology* 65 (July): 59–67.

Hall, S. 1992. "New Ethnicities." In J. Donald and A. Rattansi (eds.), *"Race," Culture and Difference*. London: Sage.

Hall, S., C. Critcher, T. Jefferson, J. Clarke and B. Roberts. 1978. *Policing the Crisis: Mugging, the State and Law and Order*. London: Macmillan.

Hall, S., and T. Jefferson (eds.). 1975. *Resistance through Rituals: Youth Subcultures in Post-War Britain*. New York: Holmes and Meier.

Harvey, J. 2007. *Young Men in Prison: Surviving and Adapting to Life Inside*. Cullompton: Willan.

Harvey, K., and A. Shepard. 2005. "What Have Historians Done With Masculinity? Reflections on Five Centuries of British History, Circa 1500–1950." (Editorial Introduction.) Special Issue on History and Masculinity, *Journal of British Studies* 44: 274–280.

Heidensohn, F. 1987. "Women and Crime: Questions for Criminology." In P. Carlen and A. Worrall (eds.), *Gender, Crime and Justice*. Milton Keynes, Open University Press.

Henry, R. 2013. "Social Spaces of Maleness: The Role of Street Gangs in Practicing Indigenous Masculinities." In K. Anderson and R. Innes (eds.), *Indigenous Masculinities in a Global Context*. Winnipeg, MB: University of Manitoba Press.

Hobsbawm, E. 1978. "The Forward March of Labour Halted?" *Marxism Today* (Sept.) CPGB.

Irwin, J. 1970. *The Felon*. Englewood Cliffs, NJ: Prentice-Hall.

Irwin, J., and D. Cressey. 1962. "Thieves, Convicts and the Inmate Culture." *Social Problems* 10: 145–147.

Jacobs, J.B. 1977. *Stateville: The Penitentiary in Mass Society*. Chicago: University of Chicago Press.

Jefferson, T. 1993. "Crime, Criminology, Masculinity and Young Men." In A. Coote (ed.), *Families, Children and Crime*. London: IPPR.

____. 1994. "Theorising Masculine Subjectivity." In T. Newburn and E. Stanko (eds.), *Just Boys Doing Business*. London: Routledge.

____. 1996. "Introduction to British Journal of Criminology Special Issue on Masculinities, Social Relations and Crime." *British Journal of Criminology* 36, 3: 337–347.

____. 1997. "Masculinities and Crimes." In M. Maguire et al., *The Oxford Handbook of Criminology*. Oxford: Clarendon.

Liebling, A. (assisted by H. Arnold). 2004. *Prisons and Their Moral Performance*. Oxford: Clarendon.

Maruna, S., and A. Matravers. 2007. "N=1: Criminology and the Person." *Theoretical Criminology* 11, 4: 427–442.

McRobbie, A. 1980. "Settling Accounts with Subcultures: A Feminist Critique." *Screen Education* 39.

____. 1991. *Feminism and Youth Culture: From Jackie to Just Seventeen*. London: Macmillan.

Merton, R.K. 1938. Social Structure and Anomie. *American Sociological Review* 3: 672–682.

____. 1949. "Social Structure and Anomie: Revisions and Extensions." In R. Anshen (ed.), *The Family*. New York: Harper Brothers.

Messerschmidt, J. 1993. *Masculinities and Crime: Critique and Reconceptualisation of Theory*. Maryland: Rowman & Littlefield.

____. 1997. *Crime as Structured Action: Gender, Race, Class and Crime in the Making*. Los Angeles, CA: Sage.

____. 2005. "Men, Masculinities and Crime." In M. Kimmel, J. Hearn and R.W. Connell (eds.), *Handbook of Studies on Men and Masculinities*. London: Sage.

Morris, T., and P. Morris. 1963. *Pentonville*. London: Routledge and Kegan Paul.

Newburn, T. 2007. *Criminology*. Cullompton: Willan.

Newburn, T., and E. Stanko. 1995. *Just Boys Doing Business*. Abingdon: Routledge.

Oakely, A. 1972. *Sex, Gender and Society*. London: Temple-Smith.

Oliffe, J., C. Han, M. Drumand, E. Maria, J. Bottorff and G. Creighton. 2014. "Men, Masculinities, and Murder-Suicide." *American Journal of Men's Health* 1,13.

Pfiel, F. 1995. *White Guys – Studies in Postmodern Domination and Difference*. London: Verso.

Sabo, D., T. Kupers and W. London (eds.). 2001. *Prison Masculinities*. Philadelphia: Temple University Press.

Sedgwick, E.K. 1985. *Between Men: English Literature and Male Homosocial Desire*. New York: Columbia University Press.

Sim, J. 1994. "Tougher than the Rest: Men in Prison." In T. Newburn and E. Stanko (eds.), *Just Boys Doing Business*. Abingdon: Routledge.

Sparks, R., A.E. Bottoms and W. Hay. 1996. *Prisons and the Problem of Order*. Oxford:

Clarendon Press.

Standing, G. 2011. *The Precariat: The New Dangerous Class*. London: Bloomsbury.

Sykes, G. 1958. *The Society of Captives: A Study of a Maximum-Security Prison*. Princeton: Princeton University Press.

Thompson, E.P. 1963. *The Making of the English Working Class*. London: Penguin.

Toch, H., and K. Adams. 1989. *Coping: Maladaptation in Prisons*. Piscataway: Transaction Publishers.

Tosh, J. 1999. *A Man's Place: Masculinity and the Middle-Class Home in Victorian England*. New Haven, CT: Yale University Press.

____. 2005. "Masculinities in an Industrialising Society, 1800–1914." *Journal of British Studies* 44: 330–42.

Tosh, J., and M. Roper (eds.). 1991. *Manful Assertions: Masculinities in Britain Since 1800*. Abingdon: Routledge.

Useem, B., and P. Kimball. 1989. *States of Siege: US Prison Riots, 1971–1986*. Oxford: Oxford University Press.

Valier, C. 2001. *Theories of Crime and Punishment*. Oxford: Longman.

Willis, P. 1977. *Learning to Labour – How Working Class Kids Get Working Class Jobs*. Farnborough: Saxon House.

Wilson, T.P. 1968. "Patterns of Management and Adaptations to Organizational Roles: A Study of Prison Inmates." *American Journal of Sociology* 74: 146–57.

Wootton, B.F. 1959. *Contemporary Trends in Crime and Its Treatment*. London: Clarke Hall.

Young, J. 1981. "Thinking Seriously About Crime – Some Models of Criminology." In M. Fitzgerald et al. (eds.), *Crime and Society: Readings in History and Theory*. London: Routledge & Kegan Paul/The Open University Press.

EQUALITY RIGHTS

Chapter 12

EQUALITY RIGHTS AND JUSTICE

Marilou McPhedran

From: *Pursuing Justice: An Introduction to Justice Studies*, pp. 188–214 (reprinted with permission).

This chapter explores the concept of equality as an essential component of justice at the provincial, national and international levels. Examples are provided and topics for thought and discussion are introduced to help integrate the notion of equality with that of justice and human rights and to assess the usefulness of the concept of equality in the pursuit of justice. Until the 1980s, the term "Constitutional equality rights" was unknown in this country. The human rights we now associate with the *Canadian Charter of Rights and Freedoms*, Part 1 of the *Constitution Act, 1982*, and provincial/territorial human rights codes were introduced conceptually in the human rights parlance of the founding of the United Nations (U.N.), following the atrocities of World War II. But the concept of "rights" goes much further back. In 1817, the philosopher Hegel observed:

> Whether what is called ancient *right and constitution* is actually right or not cannot depend on its antiquity. For the abolition of human sacrifice, of slavery, of feudal despotism and innumerable other infamies was also the abolition of what had been an ancient right. (cited in Habermas 1973: 122)

Hurlbert (2011) discusses the advent of human rights as articulated in the first and overarching policy of the U.N. — the *Universal Declaration of Human Right* (UDHR). Although the Declaration is not legally enforceable, because it is a high-level policy statement, or "declaration," it has had tremendous influence in the thinking behind legal definitions of rights, considered essential to building civilized societies sustained by the rule of law. Dating back to the *Magna Carta* (1215), the rule of law is part of the British common-law tradition, adopted in Canada and other countries — particularly members of the British Commonwealth — holding that law should be written down and applied consistently rather than at the whim of monarchs or governments. For 115 years (from 1867 to 1982) Canada operated with a common-law constitution and without a constitutionally entrenched bill of rights that defined equality.

WHAT IS EQUALITY?

Hurlbert and Mulvale (2011) encourage us to set aside our normative thinking and reach for a deeper understanding of justice. Similar "rules of engagement" apply in the study of equality. Since we generally think within the confines of our own values, norms and experiences, we must honestly acknowledge our own centrism, especially within our social context (for example, ethno-centrism). For instance, a legal challenge must approach the issue of a provincially appointed marriage commissioner who refuses to officiate at same-sex marriage ceremonies from more than one perspective, since both freedom of religion and freedom from discrimination on the basis of sexual orientation are covered by section 15 of the Charter and provincial human rights statutes. Perspectives to consider include local and international human rights norms and questions such as whether it is necessary to fire the marriage commissioner in order to enforce the rights of the same-sex couple.

Since majority viewpoints do not always resemble justice, equality analysis must reach beyond personal experience to consider the perspectives and lived experiences of members of marginalized populations — both *within* the particular population and *between* that population and society-at-large: for example, as a woman member of the Muslim community in Regina, Saskatchewan, Canada; and as a Muslim in Regina compared to other populations in Regina, in Saskatchewan and in Canada.

A thorough study of equality cannot be limited to the law. Equality has meaning and is a concept "beyond the law," and our understanding of equality is informed by other disciplines, including philosophy, history, economics, sociology, religious studies and criminology.

Formal versus Substantive Equality

In *Ethica Nichomacea*, Aristotle concluded that equality was achieved by treating likes alike and unlikes unalike. Aristotle's reasoning is at the root of what we today consider to be the principle of "formal equality." The Aristotelian-derived formula of "same = equal" has proven problematic — particularly for equality seekers. Clearly, women are different from men, persons living with a disability are different from those who do not, and Aboriginal Canadians are a different people than non-Aboriginal Canadians. So, according to Aristotle, do their differences define them as "unlike" and therefore they are to be treated unequally? Does inequality mean different treatment for likes, same treatment for unlikes? Perhaps the best known application of the Aristotelian approach is found in the American Constitutional Fourteenth Amendment terms, which require equality claimants to be "similarly situated" before they will be considered eligible to pursue their equality claim. MacKinnon (2006: 107) challenges this approach:

> But what if social life is unequal? Legal equality then becomes a formula for reinforcing, magnifying, and rigidifying the social inequalities it purports to be equalizing and might have rectified.

While "formal" equality requires that claimants must be "similarly situated," the approach in international human rights law is different and can be seen as a strong influence in the first Canadian Charter cases, decided under Chief Justice Brian Dickson in the 1980s, which led to the distinction between "formal" and "substantive" equality (Young 1990: 199–200). "Substantive" equality requires recognizing the inherent value of each individual human being, and assessing the impact of alleged discrimination demands more thought and inquiry than the formulaic approach where judges apply the same formal equality analysis to all cases.

Constitutional Equality in Canada

Constitutions are considered to be the supreme law of the land for defining the limits of governmental powers. The Canadian Constitution is the source for legally defining the division of powers among federal, provincial, territorial and municipal governments — such as which level of government can tax what, which has responsibility for health care and which is responsible for the military. When defining a liberty or freedom, the Constitutional question is whether there are any explicit limits on the power of governments to constrain certain liberties that are particularly important to people, such as the freedom to practise their religion or freedom of expression.

Prior to passing the *Constitution Act, 1982*, with its entrenched Charter, there were few national legally enshrined rights guarantees in Canada. The British common-law position on people's liberty is that individuals are free to do whatever the law does not prohibit — which may suit most people as long as their government does not pass oppressive laws. However, the common law does not explicitly guarantee that governments must respect certain individual rights and freedoms. Compared to an explicit Constitutional guarantee of a freedom (for example, freedom of expression/speech), the common-law scope of an individual's freedom is that we have as much liberty as remains *after* we obey any laws that governments may have enacted to restrict that freedom. In the common-law tradition, governments would not be acting outside their power if they took away certain freedoms or rights because there are no clear rules or principles that forbid such governmental actions. Constitutional rights may be described as legally protected "spaces" in the justice system that allow people to claim freedoms that are considered essential to a democracy — in other words, to have choices and to be able to live their rights.

Rights are used to defend our liberties. Historically, rights were not guaranteed widely; civil rights and liberties were available to those privileged enough to own property. The right of African Americans in the southern United States to vote was a major organizing focus of the social movement against racial segregation, which gained momentum in the 1960s, commonly known as the "civil rights movement." This focus on civil rights raised awareness worldwide about the connections between citizenship and the basic human rights set out in 1948 in the *Universal Declaration of Human Rights*. Therein, rights are defined as *equal* and *inalienable*, meaning that they are the inherent rights of *every* human, *because* they are human and *regardless* of their immutable personal characteristics, such as race. The first lines of the preamble to the UDHR state:

Whereas recognition of the inherent dignity and of the equal and inalienable rights of all members of the human family is the foundation of freedom, justice and peace in the world...

Balancing Individual and Collective Rights

When Alberta made photographs on drivers' licences mandatory, members of the Hutterian Brethren of Wilson Colony, who sincerely believed that the second of the Ten Commandments of the Christian/Judaic faiths prohibits them from having their photographs willingly taken, began proceedings against the Alberta government, alleging breach of their religious freedom. The Supreme Court of Canada (SCC) in *Hutterian Brethren of Wilson Colony v. Alberta* (2009) overruled the decisions made in the Alberta courts that had decided in favour of the Hutterian members. Balancing competing interests, the SCC concluded that Alberta's universal photo requirement did not limit freedom of religion more than was required to meet the important goal of minimizing identity theft. Using the language of section 1, the SCC held that this infringement was a "reasonable limit prescribed by law" and was "reasonably justified" in Canada as "a free and democratic society."

Legal rights are rights recognized by law and therefore enforceable in courts. In Canada today, legal rights include equality rights. But what is the connection between constitutions, rights and liberties or freedoms? In everyday terms, liberty or freedom means the ability to do something if we want to do it, as long as it does not hurt others and is not illegal; this includes the freedom *not* to do something, not to be subjected to certain governmental requirements. Judges are tasked with trying to balance rights in the best interest of our society, and they often reach different conclusions as to which governmental actions are unconstitutional.

DOES EQUALITY INCLUDE ECONOMIC AND SOCIAL RIGHTS?

The UDHR introduced the idea of economic, social and cultural rights, such as the freedom to work; the right to an adequate standard of living, which includes food, clothing, shelter, medical care and social services; the right to education; and the right to cultural life in the community (Articles 22–27). While the Charter does guarantee equality rights, specific social and economic rights are not listed in section 15. Canadian judicial decisions where aspects of poverty have been central to the issues to be decided have not been encouraging to the notion that Canadians have social and economic rights or that protection from discrimination on the basis of "poverty" should be included as a section 15 equality right in the Charter. The "five faces" of oppression, often mirrored in poverty, include exploitation, marginalization, powerlessness, cultural imperialism and violence (where violence against a particular group is accepted more than when directed to more advantaged groups) (Young 1990: 199–200).

Human Rights and Poverty in Canada

Three of the more compelling examples of Canadian judicial reasoning on poverty that demonstrate a judicial "disconnect" to the reality of those who live "below the poverty line" are *Gosselin v. Québec (Attorney General)* (2002), *Federated Anti-Poverty Groups of B.C. v. Vancouver* (2002) and *Masse v. Ontario (Ministry of Community and Social Services)* (1996). In the Gosselin and Masse cases, one from Québec and the other from Ontario, poor citizens argued that their Charter rights were violated because their governments kept social assistance benefits below subsistence levels. The judges favoured the governments — in Masse, government cutbacks were found to be acceptable; and in Gosselin, the claimant lost because she was under thirty and did not participate in a provincial workfare program for youth. In *Federated Anti-Poverty Groups of B.C. v. Vancouver (City)*, the British Columbia Supreme Court upheld a Vancouver bylaw restricting areas where panhandling was allowed, finding that it did not violate the rights of poor people who begged to their freedom of expression under section 2 of the Charter or to their access to fundamental justice under section 7)

Brodsky and Day (2002: 200) argue that it is incumbent on the Canadian government to observe and implement the rights set out in both the *International Covenant on Social and Cultural Rights* (ICESCR) and the *International Covenant on Civil and Political Rights* (ICCPR) because one set of rights cannot be implemented without the other. Essentially, civil and political rights for disadvantaged Canadians are not achievable unless they have the capacity to be full citizens, which comes with economic and social rights. Conservative Senator Noel Kinsella (2008: 16) writes that there is already a de facto "charter of social rights" in Canada, achieved through combining the 1999 federal/provincial/territorial Social Union Framework Agreement (SUFA) goal to "ensure access for all Canadians ... to essential social

---

Equality under International Law

Social and economic rights are not very "popular" with most governments. Of the three parts of the U.N. *International Bill of Rights* (IBR), the rights defined in the *International Covenant on Economic, Social and Cultural Rights* (ICESCR) are the least implemented. This gap in implementation is primarily due to the financial implications on government budgets and policies of the broad sweep of ICESCR guarantees, including:

- equal rights for men and women (article 3),
- right to work, and just and favourable work conditions thereof (articles 6, 7),
- right to social security and social insurance (article 9),
- right to an adequate standard of living (article 11),
- right to the highest attainable standard of physical and mental health (article 12)
- right to education (article 13).

Also a part of the IBR, the *International Covenant on Civil and Political Rights* (ICCPR) offers a range of equality protections, such as "the equal right of men and women to the enjoyment of all civil and political rights set forth in the present Covenant," including:

- right to determine political status and pursue economic, social and cultural development Article 1(1)),
- right to life (Article 6),
- freedom from torture, cruel, inhuman and degrading treatment (Article 7),
- right to liberty and security (Article 9),
- right to dignified, human and respectful treatment (Article 10),
- freedom of movement (Article 12),
- equality before courts and tribunals (Article 14(1)),
- freedom of thought, conscience and religion (Article 18),
- freedom of association (Article 22),
- right to participate in public affairs, vote and be elected, and become a member of the public service (Article 25), and
- equality before the law and entitlement to equal protections under the law (Article 26).

programs and services of reasonably comparable quality" with section 36 of the Constitution. SUFA commits to:

- promoting equal opportunities for the well-being of Canadians;
- furthering the economic development to reduce disparity in opportunities; and
- providing essential public services of reasonable quality to all Canadians.

Amartya Sen (1988: 57–68), a Nobel Laureate in economics, observed that poverty is often not the failure of economic production but rather of "entitlement systems," whereby the rights claimed by the most vulnerable in society to such basics as food and housing are devalued relative to the property-oriented rights claimed by more privileged people, with more capacity to actualize their own rights.

As discussed in Hurlbert and Mulvale (2011), John Rawls in his 1971 book, *A Theory of Justice,* proposed a new version of social contract theory, stating that we must rethink what a just society is from the ground up, putting aside our individual interests. In the Canadian context, Pierre Elliott Trudeau, who identified the federal-provincial Constitutional reform process as a priority when he became justice minister in 1968, was influenced by the ideas of his law professor Frank Scott. While neither used the term "equality rights," Scott taught and wrote (prior to Rawls and Sen) about his vision of Canada and the need for rights to be applied equally — describing the "just society" that can be found in Trudeau's later reform arguments.

In the 1980s and 1990s, arguments were increasingly made that traditional theories of social justice failed to address the necessity of confronting sexism (for example, Baines and Eberts 1981; MacKinnon 1991); building tolerant, multicultural societies (for example, Taylor 1994a, 1994b; Kymlicka 1995) and racism (Razack 1998)).

MADE IN CANADA EQUALITY RIGHTS

An understanding of how equality rights came to be in the Charter begins with a discussion of the longstanding leadership of Canadian women on the issue. After decades of battles in courts and parliaments, much of what women gained in the articulation of sex equality extended the notion of "equality rights" to include and benefit other equality seeking groups in Canadian society. The examination of women's struggle for equality in the Canadian political sphere must recognize that the federation model of government was not imported to Canada. Aboriginal self-government was well developed when Europeans immigrated. For example, the Iroquois Confederacy, in which women held significant positions of authority, straddled what we now see as the American border and served as a model for some aspects of Canadian federalism.

With the 1982 patriation of Canada's Constitution and the advent of the Charter, equality seekers — including advocates for women, people with disabilities, Aboriginal peoples and other racialized minorities, such as Japanese-Canadians interned in World War II — successfully pressured parliamentarians to ensure that the Charter committed to more than mere formal equality and individualistic rights. Dobrowolsky (2009: 205) notes:

> Women's rights groups, in particular, were celebrated for both tightening up the wording and broadening the intent of section 15, as well as adding an entirely new equality provision, section 28, to Canada's *Charter of Rights and Freedoms.*

But the quest of Canadian women's rights advocates for equality began long before the Constitutional negotiations of the 1970s and 1980s. In what has come to be known as the Persons Case (*Edwards v. Canada (Attorney General),* [1929]), the first court battle focused on the exclusionary definition of "persons" that the scc applied to wording in the *British North America Act* (bna) of 1867:

> Unlike the Iroquoian model of federal governance, women had been excluded when the "Fathers of Confederation" met in Charlottetown to craft the bna. Litigating to secure a fairer place in the affairs of the nation, more than eighty years ago five women launched the Persons Case and what has been termed a "tradition of Canadian women using the judicial system to advance equality rights." (Falardeau-Ramsay 1998: 8)

Early Fighters for Equality: The Famous Five in the Persons Case
In 1916, Emily Murphy (not a lawyer) presided over the new Women's Police Court as the first woman police magistrate in the British Empire until a male lawyer challenged her jurisdiction to hear his case because, as a woman, she could not have been lawfully appointed. On August 27, 1927, Murphy called on four other Alberta-based women — Nellie McClung, Henrietta Muir Edwards, Louise Crummy McKinney and Irene Parlby — to sign a petition under the *Supreme Court of Canada Act,* asking for the Supreme Court's answer to a crucial question, which eventually became worded as: "Does the word 'person' in section 24 of the *British North America Act, 1867,* include female 'persons'?"

On April 24th, 1928, Chief Justice Anglin, for a unanimous scc, answered in the negative, holding that the bna was limited by the period in which it had been passed, noting the exclusive use of male pronouns and that there was no English precedent of women appointed to the British House of Lords. He concluded:

> Women are not eligible for appointment by the Governor General to

---

Persons Case Commemoration

October 18 is now officially celebrated in Canada as Persons Day, commemorated by the annual awarding of a governor general's medal to five long-time activist women (as well as an award for youth leaders) and Legal Education and Action Fund (LEAF) Breakfasts across Canada.

---

the Senate of Canada under section 24 of the *British North America Act, 1867,* because they are not "qualified persons" within the meaning of that section (*Reference as to the Meaning of the Word "Persons" in section 24 of the British North America Act, 1867,* [1928]. S.C.R.276)

The only recourse open to the five women petitioners was to convince the government to legislate in their favour or, since at that time the SCC was subject to the judicial review of the Judicial Committee of the Privy Council of England, to appeal. On October 18, 1929, Lord Chancellor Sankey of the British Privy Council provided a significantly different unanimous answer, overruling the SCC:

> And to those who would ask why the word [persons] should include female, the obvious answer is, why should it not?" (*Reference as to the Meaning of the Word "Persons" in section 24 of the British North America Act, 1867,* [1928] S.C.R.276, reversed in *Edwards v. Canada (A.G.),* [1930] A.C.124 (P.C)).

Canadian Bill of Rights, 1960

The *Canadian Bill of Rights* (CBR 1960, c.44) was a "recognition and declaration of the rights and freedoms" championed by one of the few prime ministers from western Canada, the Rt. Hon. John G. Diefenbaker of Saskatchewan. Following World War II, numerous women subsumed personal frustrations, having experienced considerable autonomy in the war years. Soon their economic and social grievances surfaced, creating an environment where Canadian women in the mid-1960s were asking questions about their lives and about their "status" as women. In response to pressure from women's organizations and questioning commentary in the media, Prime Minister Lester B. Pearson appointed the Royal Commission on the Status of Women in the early months of Canada's centennial year, 1967, asking the commissioners to

> inquire into the status of women in Canada and to recommend what steps might be taken by the Federal Government to ensure for women equal

opportunities with men in all aspects of Canadian identity. (CBC Radio and Television Archives n.d.: 14)

Expectations that "justice" included women's equality were rising, as was optimism that the CBR (which is still a law in Canada) would deliver. Section 1 of Part I of the CBR states:

> There have existed and shall continue to exist without discrimination by reason of race, national origin, colour, religion or sex, the following human rights and fundamental freedoms, namely ... the right of the individual to equality before the law and the protection of the law.

However, judicial interpretation was largely cautious and unhelpful to equality seekers who tried to claim their rights under the CBR. The following decisions under the CBR delineate differences between interpretations of "justice" and the "law."

Aboriginal Women and the Indian Act

Aboriginal women married to non-Aboriginal men felt the unfair sting of the CBR in *Canada (Attorney General) v. Lavell*, when federal *Indian Act* provisions denying status were upheld in a 1974 SCC decision. Counsel for Jeanette Lavell and Yvonne Bédard argued that s.12(1)(b) discriminated on the basis of sex against women of Indian status, who lost that status upon marriage to a non-Indian, but permitted a status man to extend status to his non-Indian wife and in turn to their children.

This decision prompted a dramatic activist response involving a group of Aboriginal women who left the Tobique Reserve in New Brunswick with their small children, fathered by non-status men, to walk in protest to Ottawa. One of their leaders, Sandra Lovelace (now Senator Lovelace-Nichols), a Maliseet woman of the reserve, gained international attention when she petitioned the United Nations Human Rights Committee, alleging violations by Canada under the *Optional Protocol to the International Covenant on Civil and Political Rights,* to which Canada had just acceded (G.A. Res. 2200 (XXI), 1966). Canada defended the legislation. Embarrassed internationally by the U.N. finding that the federal law contravened the rights of Aboriginal women (*Lovelace v. Canada,* 1981), Canada moved slowly, even with sustained lobbying from a wide range of women's groups. Nearly ten years after the march from Tobique, in 1981 the government enacted partial redress, leaving Aboriginal women's rights at the discretion of bands, which could ask the government to exempt them from s.12(1)(b) (Bayefsky 1982).

Women's "Routine" Work

In *Murdoch v. Murdoch* [1975], dismissing more than twenty-five years of ranching with her husband in Alberta, the SCC awarded Irene Murdoch just $200 a month, agreeing with the trial judge that the "routine" work of "any ranch wife" was not enough to create a legal claim to the matrimonial property. Women across Canada identified with Murdoch and mobilized to demand their property rights. By 1980 every province and territory had passed family law amendments as a result of women discovering and flexing their collective political "muscle."

Gender Neutral Pregnancy?

Stella Bliss lived in British Columbia when she was fired because she was pregnant. After her baby was born, she actively sought, but did not find, appropriate employment, and so, having determined that she met the regular criteria, applied for unemployment insurance benefits. The Unemployment Insurance Commission refused her application because she had been pregnant when she lost her job and she did not meet the more stringent criteria applied to pregnancy benefits in the legislation. In *Bliss v. A.G. Canada,* (1979), Bliss's *pro bono* lawyers argued before the Federal Court of Appeal and the SCC that the higher legislative bar for pregnant women discriminated on the basis of sex. To the dismay of women's groups, both courts rejected this argument in favour of the Aristotelian formal equality notion that all pregnant women were equally denied regular benefits due to a legitimate gender neutral distinction based on nature — not between men and women, but between pregnant and non-pregnant persons.

Reacting to Losses under the CBR

When Prime Minister Trudeau announced his determination to "bring home" the Canadian Constitution and to entrench within it a charter of rights and freedoms, the platform for women's Constitutional activism had already been framed by the judicial use of the CBR to deny the discrimination rampant in women's daily lives. When the draft charter was released in 1980, the federally appointed members of the Canadian Advisory Council on the Status of Women launched a public education campaign on the Constitution, led by its president, Doris Anderson. British Columbia, Alberta, Saskatchewan, Québec, New Brunswick, Nova Scotia, Newfoundland and the Yukon had all enacted new laws or amendments to their family property regimes in 1979–80, preceded by the Northwest Territories, Ontario and Manitoba. So, when a women's Constitutional battle broke out in January 1981, prompting Doris Anderson to resign in a very public manner, many grassroots women had a sense that making politicians respond was an achievable prospect, and the women's movement had both human and organizational infrastructure in place and on the alert. In her article on the impact of the "ad hoc" women's Constitutional conference and lobby that sprang up in early 1981, Collins (1981: 22) reported:

> The issue — whether women would have a share in the future of the nation ... As Linda Ryan-Nye says, there seemed to be a peculiar readiness to speak with one voice: "A lot of us sensed it and not just in the organized women's movement. It had been building ... this shoddy treatment of a strong and honest woman at the same time as denying us our rights as citizens ... Boom."

CANADIAN CONSTITUTIONAL TRIALOGUE ON EQUALITY

So how did Canadians end up with equality rights guaranteed in a bill of human rights entrenched in the supreme law of the land — the Constitution? It is important to remember that governments make laws and governments are made up of people. Constitutions are built by people — but only certain people. It's helpful to understand the background and context to the introduction of the Charter and how it took years from when the first draft charter, with "non-discrimination" provisions, was introduced in 1968 at a federal/provincial first ministers' conference until more than a decade later, when "equality rights" became a topic of broad public concern and televised debates and were introduced into the proposed Charter in 1981. Journalist Graham Fraser (2002) offers this retrospective on events leading up to the Charter:

> In April 1968, a year after becoming justice minister, Trudeau was prime minister and the agenda he had had as justice minister acquired a new importance. Within three years, a Charter ["Victoria Charter"] had been written and quietly negotiated with Québec's new Liberal premier, Robert Bourassa. Fundamental liberties would be guaranteed and language rights would be protected in every province. But the Victoria Charter ultimately failed when Bourassa withdrew his support.

The Struggle for Equality Rights in the Charter

Prime Minister Pierre Trudeau envisioned a statement of rights and freedoms as part of the new Constitution that would provide "guarantees" for people in Canada (mostly Canadian citizens, with some exceptions) in a stronger manner than in the 1960 *Canadian Bill of Rights,* which was limited to federal laws, was not applicable to provincial statutes and could be amended at any time, because it was not an entrenched part of the Constitution. However, "equality rights" was not a term used in any of the drafts of the Charter developed by government officials or political leaders from the 1960s through to 1981, although one of the arguments for accepting the Trudeau government's "people's package" for Constitutional reform was that an entrenched charter would apply to governments across Canada and thus rights would be equally available. Equality rights in the charter came out of the grassroots mobilization of people and groups in Canada — mostly women's rights organizations and representatives of people living with disabilities.

Accounts of this struggle vary; perspectives differed depending on the position of the participant in the Constitution-building processes. Initially, the Trudeau government was not prepared to "open up" the process, but public pressure convinced the government to name a special joint committee of the Senate and of the House of Commons on the Constitution in 1980, with members drawn from all the parties of both houses of Parliament — co-chaired by M.P. Serge Joyal from Québec and Senator Harry Hays from Alberta. For the first time in Canada, a parliamentary committee was televised, and millions of Canadians paid attention to what was happening at the hearings. Senator Hays made news when he addressed the National Action Committee on the Status of Women (NAC) executives (with this author present) in the following manner:

> I want to thank you girls (*sic*) for your presentation. We're honoured to have you here. But I wonder why you don't have anything in here for babies or children. All you girls are going to be working and who's going to look after them? (in Watson and Barber 1988: 141)

After months of presentations by concerned citizens and their organizations to the Special Joint Committee, Attorney General Jean Chrétien announced major changes to section 15 in January 1981. Dawson (2006: 31) and Lepofsky (1998: 156) wrote firsthand accounts of what went into these changes, including altering the title to "equality rights," creating an opening for non-enumerated or analogous grounds of discrimination, reversing the order of "age" and "sex" and adding another enumerated ground — "mental or physical disability." The attorney general attributed the title change to "Equality Rights" to a (now defunct) federal body called the Canadian Advisory Council on the Status of Women (CACSW), then chaired by Doris Anderson, with Mary Eberts acting as her legal counsel (Senate and House of Commons 1981).

The "spark" that galvanized Canadian women's Constitutional activism was when Doris Anderson abruptly resigned in January 1981, in public protest against what she considered to be government interference in the women's Constitutional conference being organized by the CACSW. Again, perspectives on what happened vary, but the aptly named Ad Hoc Committee of Canadian Women on the Constitution ("Ad Hoc Committee" or "Ad Hockers") took responsibility for organizing an alternative conference — to be surprised when more than 1,300 women found their way to Ottawa on Valentine's Day in 1981. Run by consensus, the conference produced resolutions that guided ensuing months of lobbying for amendments to the draft Constitution to strengthen equality rights (Kome 1983).

It was this unprecedented public engagement in the 1980s Canadian Constitution building process that gave rise to the term "trialogue" to describe and validate citizens and their organizations as key contributors. Constitutional scholars Hogg and Bushell (1997, also see Hogg, Bushell and Wright 2007) used the term "Charter dialogue" to describe the bilateral dynamic between legislators in drafting and adopting the Charter, complemented by judges using their authority under the Charter to interpret what the written words actually meant when applied to real-life problems and challenges to the Charter brought before the courts. In arguing for a more inclusive understanding of how the Canadian Constitution was built and is sustained, McPhedran (2005: 14) introduced the "trialogue" metaphor to acknowledge the ongoing engagement and influence of social movements in the drafting of Constitutional text and in securing equality rights in sections 15 and 28 of the Charter:

> Too often, judges and politicians fail to appreciate that Canadians invested in an equality-based constitutional democracy — often engaging directly through interventions in Parliament and in the courts — have turned the dynamic into a *trialogue*; surely one of the most significant outcomes of the s.15 impact on Canadian society.

The *Canadian Charter of Rights and Freedoms* is a bill of rights consisting of 34 sections entrenched within the *Constitution Act, 1982,* which, in effect, reintroduced all of Canada's statutory Constitutional law, including the *British North America Act, 1867.* Prime Minister Pierre Elliot Trudeau stated at the proclamation ceremony for the *Constitution Act, 1982,* on April 17, 1982:

> We now have a Charter which defines the kind of country in which we wish to live, and guarantees the basic rights and freedoms which each of us shall enjoy as a citizen of Canada. It upholds the equality of women, and the rights of disabled persons. (Library and Archives Canada n.d.)

Women's determination to strengthen Charter equality rights was honed by the harsh fact that the cases brought by women in the 1970s seeking equality protections under the *Canadian Bill of Rights* were all lost. In the early 1980s, when the new *Constitution Act* and the Charter were being drafted to effect patriation to Canada, Canadians watched as American women were losing their battle to include the "Equal Rights Amendment (ERA)" in their Constitution. Canadian women saw how Canadian judges followed American judges (using the Fourteenth Amendment equal protections for race- and sex-based discrimination) in foisting notions of formal equality on women. The ultimate wording of the equality sections of the Charter was substantially different from the drafts that had caused such concern.

Efforts to ensure that the new Constitutional equality rights actually made a difference in the daily lives of equality seekers took many forms after the *Constitution Act, 1982,* was activated. Since section 32 of the Charter imposed a three-year moratorium on people being able to use section 15, during the moratorium, from 1982 through 1985, a number of preparations were made, including publication of the first textbook on equality rights (Bayefsky and Eberts 1985) and the formation of a new organization, LEAF (the Women's Legal Education and Action Fund) — launching what Manfredi (2004: 49) describes as the women's "microconstitutional campaign for substantive equality." LEAF — founded in 1985 by some of the "Ad Hockers" — has been involved in more equality cases than any other non-governmental organization in Canada, attempting to ensure that equality is interpreted by the courts through a "gender impact lens" even when the case has not focused on women. For example, in 1989, the first major Supreme Court decision interpreting section 15, *Andrews v. Law Society of British Columbia* [1989], was brought by a white male lawyer, but LEAF was granted intervener status to make arguments that became reflected in the Court's decision that section 15(1) and (2) of the Charter should benefit those who have been historically disadvantaged, thus preventing arguments, based on American cases of "reverse discrimination," from those who traditionally benefited from legislation developed by privileged classes. Five principles that continue to frame Canadian discussions of Constitutional equality were established in the *Andrews* decision.

First, the Court emphasized that equality cannot be reduced to sameness of treatment. Laws that treat everyone the same — laws that are "facially neutral" — may be discriminatory in their impact. This is referred to as "adverse effects discrimination." Second, the American "similarly situated" test based on the Aristotelian notion of formal equality, was rejected as a reliable guide to the interpretation of section 15. Third, the actual effects of a challenged law or practice should be the focus of the analysis. It is not necessary to establish intentional or purposeful discrimination. Fourth, to make out a violation of section 15, the claimant must establish differential treatment that amounts to discrimination on the basis of a personal characteristic that is either listed as a prohibited ground of discrimination in section 15 ("enumerated") or that is analogous to the listed grounds (as eventually happened in the equality cases brought on the basis of sexual orientation). Fifth, a personal characteristic will be accepted as an analogous ground if it shares the essential features of the personal characteristics listed in section 15.

Ten years after *Andrews,* in its 1999 decision in *Nancy Law v. Canada (Minister of Employment and Immigration)*, the Supreme Court of Canada unanimously reformulated the *Andrews* test, stating that burdensome differences in treatment on the basis of prohibited grounds are discriminatory *only if they can reasonably be said to violate "human dignity."* Although the term "dignity" is nowhere to be found in the Charter, it figures prominently in the international human rights treaties and has become significant in many Canadian judicial interpretations of equality.

Unfortunately, many of those decisions have gone against the equality seekers who brought their claims to the courts (Petter 1987). Nancy Law was married to

Equality Protections and Limitations in the *Charter*

Equality Protection	Limitations of Equality Protection
Equality of Women and Men Preamble Whereas respect for the dignity of human beings, equality of women and men, and recognition of their rights and freedoms constitute the foundation of justice, liberty and peace;	Reasonable Limits s.1 The *Canadian Charter of Rights and Freedoms* guarantees the rights and freedoms set out in it subject only to such reasonable limits prescribed by law as can be demonstrably justified in a free and democratic society.
Equality before and under Law and Equal Protection and Benefit of Law s.15 (1) Every individual is equal before and under the law and has the right to the equal protection and equal benefit of the law without discrimination and, in particular, without discrimination based on race, national or ethnic origin, colour, religion, sex, age or mental or physical disability. Affirmative Action Programs s.15(2) Subsection (1) does not preclude any law, program or activity that has as its object the amelioration of conditions of disadvantaged individuals or groups including those that are disadvantaged because of race, national or ethnic origin, colour, religion, sex, age or mental or physical disability. Rights Guaranteed Equally to Both Sexes s.28 Notwithstanding anything in this Charter, the rights and freedoms referred to in it are guaranteed equally to male and female persons.	Exception s.32(2) Notwithstanding subsection (1), section 15 shall not have effect until three years after this section comes into force. Exception where Express Declaration s.33(1) Parliament or the legislature of a province may expressly declare in an Act of Parliament or of the legislature, as the case may be, that the Act or a provision thereof shall operate notwithstanding a provision included in section 2 or sections 7 to 15 of this Charter. Operation of Exception s.33(2) An Act or a provision of an Act in respect of which a declaration made under this section is in effect shall have such operation as it would have but for the provision of this *Charter* referred to in the declaration.

a man quite a bit older, and when he died, she relied on the protection in s.15(1) against discrimination on the basis of age, because the benefits allowed to her as a spouse under the age of thirty-five were less than for those over that age. Nancy Law lost her case. This one decision has generated hundreds of pages of commentary and speculation. Through its *Nancy Law* decision, the Court established a tougher test for claimants — requiring the additional step of proving to the Court that their human dignity has been impaired — as an addition to the *Andrews* principles summarized above. The Court still applied a comparative test, but it came down to being what the Court decided a "reasonable person" in the position of the claimant would/should feel about their dignity being impaired, not necessarily what the claimant actually did feel about the impact of the alleged discrimination.

Petter (1987: 857, 860), a "Charter critic," expressed the following years before the *Nancy Law* decision:

> The argument is that, while sold to the public as part of a "people's package," the *Canadian Charter of Rights and Freedoms* is a regressive instrument more likely to undermine than to advance the interests of socially and economically disadvantaged Canadians … The negative nature of Charter rights combined with this selective view of state action remove from Charter scrutiny the major source of inequality in our society — the unequal distribution of property entitlements among private parties.

In *R. v. Kapp* (2008 SCC, 41), the Supreme Court changed its approach again — described by Ryder (2008) as "Taking Section 15 Back to the Future" — and returned to the test in the *Andrews* case of almost two decades earlier, prompting cautious optimism among equality rights advocates.

When Is a Charter Guarantee Not a Guarantee?

When section 1 of the draft Canadian Constitution was introduced, deep concern was expressed before the Special Joint Committee and in the media that it did not protect rights, allowing governments to place too many limitations on rights. Many names were given to section 1 to illustrate that it was a problem, including the "Mack Truck clause" and the "bathtub clause" because it would make it too easy for politicians to "run over" or "pull the plug" on human rights. Justice Minister Chrétien introduced a number of changes to the section until it reached its current wording:

> The *Canadian Charter of Rights and Freedoms* guarantees the rights and freedoms set out in it subject only to such reasonable limits as are generally accepted in a free and democratic society with a parliamentary system of government.

Opting Out of Charter Rights — Section 33 Override

Ironically, section 33 of the Charter, introduced much later in the Constitutional negotiations, gave to governments a much clearer authority to opt out of rights than the much-scrutinized section 1. The Latin term for a clause like section 33 of the Charter is *non obstante*, or "notwithstanding," because this clause functions like an optional legislative "override" on the rights specified in s.33(1) of the Charter — all of the fundamental freedoms in section 2, all of the legal rights in sections 7 through 14 and the equality rights in section 15 (but not the sex equality guarantee in section 28). Section 33 makes it clear that there is no tight "guarantee" in the face of this governmental power.

How did the so many rights in the Charter become potentially "unentrenched"? One of the earliest suggestions for such a clause came from Harvard-based Canadian law professor Paul Weiler (1980: 231), who urged:

> We should entrench our fundamental rights in the Canadian Constitution in order to give them the legal and symbolic authority which would be conducive to their flourishing. But we should include in the Constitutional Bill of Rights the kind of *non obstante* provision now contained in our statutory bill ... In typical Canadian fashion, I propose a compromise, between the British version of full-fledged parliamentary sovereignty and the American version of full-fledged judicial authority over Constitutional matters.

The fundamental difference between section 1 and section 33 is that section 1 requires balancing of the rights and freedoms identified in the Charter with the needs and values of a free and democratic society, but section 33 empowers governments to decline to respect specific rights and freedoms listed in the Charter.

However, Hogg and Bushell (1997: 75) assessed the likelihood of section 33 being used often by governments as slim, even though there is nothing in law to stop them, "because of the development of a political climate of resistance to its use." Another possible contest between *non obstante* powers in the Charter has yet to unfold — there is another override still operative: the sex equality guarantee in section 28, which is not subject to section 33 in the way that equality rights in section 15 are, but a case is yet to arise (Kome 1982).

Statutory

Federal, Provincial and Territorial Human Rights

In 1947, Saskatchewan became the first North American government to enact a general human rights statute — soon after the United Nations was founded in 1945, at the close of World War II. Now human rights mechanisms, created by statute, such as human rights commissions and tribunals, operate nationally and in every province and territory in Canada, each with its own enabling legislation. For example, the national legislation, the *Canadian Human Rights Act*, prohibits discrimination on eleven grounds: disability, race, national or ethnic origin, colour, religion, age, sex, sexual orientation, marital status, family status and conviction for which a pardon has been granted.

Complaints on the specified grounds in the federal/provincial/territorial legislation are initially addressed through related bodies and their quasi-judicial tribunals, while complaints related to the Charter are addressed through the courts. Thus, jurisprudence (reports on the facts and outcomes of judicial and quasi-judicial decisions on cases brought to these tribunals and courts) for statutory human rights mechanisms is different from decisions by courts in Constitutional Charter cases. However, when a human rights tribunal decision is challenged, then the appeal moves into the same court system as the Charter complaints — underscoring the importance of Canadian judges at every level being well educated in human rights, including equality rights, regardless of the jurisdiction (federal, provincial or territorial).

LIVED EQUALITY

The complexity of the pursuit of equality rights in Canada is the topic of extensive commentary. The Chief Justice of the Supreme Court of Canada, the Right Honourable Beverley McLachlin (2001: 17), concluded:

> The *Canadian Charter of Rights and Freedoms* guarantees a panoply of rights … And like most modern bills of rights, it guarantees equality. Of all the rights, this is the most difficult.

How do citizens of the world turn promises on paper — in constitutions, local and international laws — into "lived rights" that make a positive difference in their daily lives? This chapter discusses how grassroots engagement altered the *Canadian Charter of Rights and Freedoms* and Canadian Constitutional jurisprudence. Real life examples of "equality lived" through active section 15 claims, based on the protected grounds specified in section 15 equality rights, as well as the analogous ground of sexual orientation, which was "read in" by the Supreme Court, demonstrate the complexity and imperfections in the pursuit of justice based on equality rights. However, these setbacks should not be taken as a message to "give up" on justice or equality. Consider the alternatives. In the examples that follow, look for information that gives a practical perspective on how important it is for information and evidence — from the perspective of the equality seekers — to be presented to judges in the course of a hearing, before they make their decision. Because judges are supposed to make their decisions only on the evidence presented to them, this is a challenging but crucial aspect of the strategic litigation undertaken by sophisticated equality-focused organizations like Egale, the Council of Canadians with Disabilities, the Native Women's Association of Canada and most frequently, LEAF, often in collaboration with other equality-seeking groups.

The importance of judges having the best available evidence on which to base their decisions is unlikely to draw debate. But the value of equality-based organizations being allowed by judges to bring information and evidence in their role as "interveners" in key cases (because they are not one of the parties to the case) is less settled. A notion that frontline expertise provided to the Court through interventions should be invalidated as that of "special interest" groups — such as Constitutional rights advocates — seems to be gaining ground. Such a notion is derived from an elitist perspective. Rights are just words on paper unless they can be beneficially experienced — unless they can be lived. Interventions before the Court are a form of inclusion that is consistent with Canadian Charter values, and this produces knowledge that is essential in equality cases — if only because judges are among our most privileged and protected of citizens.

The interconnection of rights guarantees in the Charter and in statutory human rights law has emerged in case after case. In the examples of "lived rights" that follow, the relationship between equality rights and other rights and freedoms in the Charter exposes how inequality is compounded by other prohibited grounds of discrimination, such as Aboriginal status, disability or sexual orientation.

Aboriginal People
The following excerpt from a speech by Senator Lillian Quan Dyck (2007 n.p.), one of two Aboriginal women senators in Canada at the time, captures the tension inherent in Charter promises and the different reality often experienced:

> I am proud to be a Canadian. Canadians have much to be proud of; our nation believes it and passes legislation that provides for basic fundamental freedoms and equality of its citizens. On the one hand I know this to be true, yet at the same time I know for some of us it is not necessarily true. As I look at the history of federal legislation and how it affected my family and others like me, the ideals of our country and the reality of our lives do not necessarily match up. There is a political and cognitive dissonance.

Senator Dyck went on to speak of how her mother, an Aboriginal woman, qualified as a "Status Indian" under the *Indian Act,* but Canadian law dictated that she lost her status when she married a non-Indian. This is an illustration of how the intersection of rights and personal characteristics — in this case, gender, race and culture — necessitates a balancing with Aboriginal sovereignty.

When she was national speaker of the Native Women's Association of Canada

(NWAC), Gail Stacey-Moore (1991) noted how Aboriginal women's equality advocates often experienced significant resistance from influential leaders within a number of important bodies, such as governments, academia and the media, and how Aboriginal women have been legally, politically and socially subordinated by the federal government and by Aboriginal governments. Canadian legal scholar Douglas Sanders (1985: 569), soon after the *Canadian Charter of Rights and Freedoms* was activated in the early 1980s, reasoned:

> If Canadians are serious about cultural autonomy for aboriginal collectivities, then sexual discrimination should be acceptable so long as it authentically reflects the continuing traditions of the communities.

By contrast, some twenty years later, then National Chief Phil Fontaine (2001) of the Assembly of First Nations stated:

> The strength, knowledge, and capacity of our women leaders must be heard and honoured by all First Nations, and all Canadians.

Disability

The most significant recent success for equality seekers came in *Council of Canadians with Disabilities v. VIA Rail Canada Inc.* [2007], "which affirms the universal application of human rights principles and the right to equality for people with disabilities" (Manitoba Human Rights Commission 2007). However, counsel for the Council of Canadians with Disabilities (CCD), David Baker and Sarah Godwin (2008: 61) caution that the success of the case almost bankrupted the CCD and that governmental resistance does not seem to have been reduced by the decision.

In an earlier turning point for disability rights, *Eldridge v. British Columbia (Attorney General)* [1997], the CCD intervened, as did LEAF, in coalition with the Disabled Women's Network of Canada, to convince the Supreme Court that the government was obligated to fund sign language as part of its promise to provide medical services to all residents of the province.

Sexual Orientation

Until 1969, the *Criminal Code of Canada* contained an offence that effectively criminalized homosexuality. Now, the human rights architecture in Canada (federal, provincial, territorial and, in some places, municipal) holds that sexual orientation is not an acceptable ground of discrimination and complaint mechanisms are provided — but nowhere in the Charter will you find an explicit protection against discrimination on the basis of sexual orientation. The answer to this Constitutional puzzle lies in the open wording of section 15 and the section 24 "remedies" power given to Canadian judges in the Charter to decide on appropriate remedies, including what has come to known as "reading in rights" that are not specifically listed in section 15.

Douglas Elliott (2006: 98), counsel in a number of sexual orientation cases, including *Hislop v. Canada (Attorney General)* (2007), which extended same-sex pension benefits, observed how the shift in society toward equality rights for lesbian, gay, bisexual and transgendered (LGBT) Canadians was influenced by the Charter:

> So long as growing public support did not move the politicians, the only way to move them would be through the courts ... All of these cases accepted that sexual orientation was an analogous ground, but most of the early cases ended in failure ... The public began to conceive of the issues in terms of the human rights model, and countervailing arguments based on the "sin" or "medical" models began to be viewed as antiquated at best and bigoted at worst ... The question of sexual orientation as an analogous ground finally reached the Supreme Court of Canada in the famous Egan case. A majority of the Court found that discrimination against same-sex couples was an infringement of section 15(1) ... However, a different majority upheld the impugned law under section 1. It would be the last time that section 1 would be relied upon to reach that result, but it was a bitter blow at the time.

In 1996, the Alberta Court of Appeal ruled against Delwin Vriend, a teacher who was fired when it was discovered that he was gay. The Alberta *Individual Rights Protection Act* did not include "sexual orientation," so Vriend sued the Alberta government, arguing that the appropriate remedy was for "sexual orientation" to be read into the Alberta statute. The Supreme Court agreed, overruling the Alberta Court of Appeal:

> As a remedy, the words "sexual orientation" should be read into the prohibited grounds of discrimination in these provisions. (para. 497)

Although his government fought Vriend at every stage of the case, Alberta premier Ralph Klein surprised many when he announced in 1998 that he would not use his legislative majority to override the Court by activating section 33 of the Charter, and he acceded to the requirement that his province's human rights legislation should prohibit discrimination on the basis of sexual orientation. Elliott (2006: 112–3) describes the importance of the wide-ranging political and legal battle over the legalization of same-sex marriage in the federal government's Bill C-38:

> Parliament relented and passed Bill C-38, but only after a long and difficult

political battle ... in the process, we had moved the political goalposts ... Canadians had firmly embraced the human rights model embodied in the Charter.

Sex Equality

The world over, in courts and beyond, control over women's bodies is the crux of equality struggles. Much of the equality jurisprudence has been related to sexual assault. In *R. v. Seaboyer* [1991], legislation that women fought for — known as the "rape shield" — was struck down, but this loss in court galvanized public concern and paved the way for subsequent pro-victim legal amendments by Parliament — another example of the crucial contribution citizens make to law reform. In *O'Connor* [1995] (a Catholic priest who sexually assaulted Aboriginal women under his authority in residential school and as their employer), the compelling dissent from Justice L'Heureux-Dubé led to major amendments expanding the understanding of Constitutional rights beyond those who are accused of sexual crimes. *R v. Ewanchuk* [1999] generated the "no means no" legislation on sexual assault when an Alberta appeal court judge (ironically, the grandson of Nellie McClung, one of the Famous Five in the Persons Case) was overruled by a stinging opinion penned by Justice L'Heureux-Dubé. Public mobilization was triggered by personal and professional criticism of her by prominent defence counsel and Judge McClung in the media. In *R. v. Darrach* [2000] — another challenge to rape shield provisions in the *Criminal Code* — women's Constitutional equality rights figured prominently, but the protective legislation was upheld. The various "sides" have different perceptions of fundamental rights in the Charter, but all sides have passionately engaged the criminal legal system in these cases. It has been an exhilarating and exhausting series of steps forward and back. More often than not, public engagement has had real impact in broadening the courts' and Parliament's perspectives on just whose rights and freedoms are at stake in sexual assault cases and what constitutes a truly "fair trial."

Assessments on the extent to which section 15 equality rights in the courts have been the source of progress for women are mixed. Dobrowolsky (2009) and Bashevkin (2009) determine the political sphere to be equally as important as the courts for women's equality gains.

EQUALITY RIGHTS AND JUSTICE

As in the pursuit of justice, the path to equality is not only through the courts and the Charter. Following the *Nancy Law* case, most equality-seeking claims were lost before the Supreme Court. Soon after that decision, Beverly Baines (2000: 71–73) predicted that the Court's unusually unanimous decision in *Law* would create additional barriers through which equality-seeking litigants would have difficulty passing. Broad judicial latitude for subjective assessment of others' reality is exposed in the split decision in *Gosselin v. Québec (Attorney General)* 2002 S.C.C. 84, where the Chief Justice (para. 68), for the majority, applied the *Law* test in dismissing a class action on behalf of the majority of young, entrenched unemployed in Québec: "This is not a case where the complainant group suffered from pre-existing disadvantage and stigmatization."

In the *Canadian Foundation for Children, Youth and the Law v. Canada (Attorney General)* [2004] — the "spanking" case on assaults by parents protected under the *Criminal Code of Canada*, the Court held that such assaults on children — which would be illegal if committed on other adults — were not a violation of children's section 15 rights. On the other hand, in *Dickie v. Dickie* [2007], the Supreme Court held that parents who refuse to comply with family court orders for support of their

---

Ethical Considerations

"Two central issues for ethical analysis of equality are: Why equality? Equality of what? The two questions are distinct but thoroughly interdependent. We cannot begin to defend or criticize equality without knowing what on earth we are talking about, i.e., equality of what features (incomes, opportunities, wealths, achievements, freedoms, rights)" (Amartya Sen 1980: 256).

Unequal Distribution of Wealth — In *World Poverty and Human Rights: Cosmopolitan Responsibilities and Reforms* (2002), philosopher Thomas Pogge argues that individuals from affluent countries were directly or indirectly responsible for the millions of annual preventable deaths of individuals in developing countries arising from an inability to access the requisite resources. The unequal distribution of wealth within societies raises a heatedly debated ethical question. Do affluent individuals and countries have an ethical obligation to instill elements of substantive equality into society?

Affirmative Action for Substantive Equality — Affirmative action (sometimes called reverse discrimination in the United States), defined in s.15(2) of the Charter, is allowed to rebalance the effects of inequality that arise from discrimination of historically disadvantaged groups to provide members of these groups with substantively equal opportunities for success in education, business, politics and other realms of life.

Resolving Competition between Rights — Although rights and freedoms are guaranteed under the Charter, guaranteeing one right or freedom for a certain individual can infringe on the enjoyment of rights and freedoms for others. For instance, a juror who exercises his or her freedom of expression by discussing the trial in progress could infringe the right to a fair trial for the accused. Reconciling competing outcomes of the enjoyment of rights and freedoms is a delicate balance that judges must decide within the ethical and legal framework of the Constitution.

families (about 97 percent being men) can be held in contempt of court. It is clear that the Charter has changed Canada — section 15 equality rights and section 15 equality values intersect with Canadian perceptions and concerns. A Trudeau Foundation poll (Environics 2006) found that 49 percent of the population felt immigrants should be free to maintain their religious and cultural practices in Canada, but the vast majority (81 percent) also felt that gender equality "trumps" multiculturalism — an opinion shared almost equally across demographic, income, education, age and gender lines. The Charter is a contract between Canadians and their governments. Another Trudeau Foundation poll (Environics 2010) revealed an intergenerational difference in viewing responsibility for justice — 70 percent of young adults believed that current Canadian governments are responsible for addressing human rights violations committed by previous governments, compared with only 47 percent of Canadians sixty and over.

Nevertheless, there is concern that a negative shift in the impact of how the courts are dealing with equality rights is emerging — from constructive to damaging — from section 15 acting as a beacon to illuminate and value the struggles against inequality in ordinary lives, to section 15 becoming the laser that burns away access to justice.

ACKNOWLEDGEMENTS

I dedicate this chapter to my "Charter babies" Jonathan Jacob and David Kitson, with thanks to my teachers on equality: Bev Baines, Mary Eberts, Peter Hogg, Claire L'Heureux-Dubé, Michele Landsberg, Catharine MacKinnon, Nancy Ruth and LEAF, Bruce Ryder; to my former colleagues at U. of Saskatchewan College of Law: Norm Zlotkin and Mark Carter, to Margot Hurlbert for inviting and editing this chapter, and to my indefatigable research tag team over two years: Sarah E. Sharp, Adele Domenco, Aaron Swanson and Christina Szurlej.

References

Aristotle. 1985. *Nicomachean Ethics: The Various Types of Justice.* (H. Hachett, trans.) Indianapolis, IN: Terence Irwin.

Baines, B., and M. Eberts. 1981. "Women, Human Rights and the Constitution." In A.D. Doerr and M. Carrier (eds.), *Women and the Constitution in Canada* (p. 31). Ottawa, ON: Canadian Advisory Council on the Status of Women.

Baker, D., and S. Godwin. 2008. "All Aboard! The Supreme Court of Canada Confirms that Canadians with Disabilities Have Substantive Equality Rights." *Saskatchewan Law Review* 71, 1: 39–77.

Bashevkin, S. 2009. *Women, Power, and Politics: The Hidden Story of Canada's Unfinished Democracy.* Toronto, ON: Oxford University Press.

Bayefsky, A. 1982. "The Human Rights Committee and the Case of Sandra Lovelace." *Canadian Yearbook of International Law* 120: 244–46.

Bayefsky, A., and M. Eberts. 1985. *Equality Rights and the Canadian Charter of Rights and Freedoms.* Toronto, ON: Carswell.

Brodsky, G., and S. Day. 2002. "Beyond the Social and Economics Rights Debate: Substantive Equality Speaks to Poverty." *Canadian Journal of Women and the Law* 14, 1: 185–220.

CBC Radio and Television Archives. "Equality First: The Royal Commission on the Status of Women." Retrieved 26 August 2010, from <http://archives.cbc.ca/politics/rights_freedoms/topics/86>.

Collins, A. 1981." Which Way to Ottawa? A Special Report on the Women's Conference on the Constitution." *Homemaker's Magazine* 22.

Dawson, M. 2006. "The Making of Section 15 of the Charter." *Journal of Law & Equality* 5, 25: 31.

Dobrowolsky, A. 2009)=. *Women and Public Policy in Canada: Neoliberalism and After?* Toronto, ON: Oxford University Press.

Dyck, L.Q. 2007)=. *Debates of the Senate* (Hansard), February 13, 1st Session, 39th Parliament, Volume 143, Issue 69, Debate on second reading of Bill S-4, to amend the Constitution Act, 1867 (Senate tenure).

Elliott, D. 2006. "Secrets of the Lavender Mafia: Personal Reflections on Social Activism and the Charter." *Journal of Law and Equality* 5: 98.

Environics Poll. 2006. "Complete Poll Results." Conducted from Sept. 18–Oct. 12, 2006 for the Trudeau Foundation. Retrieved August 20, 2010 from <www.trudeaufoundation.ca>.

Falardeau-Ramsay, M. 1998. "Gender Equality and the Law." *Canadian Woman Studies* 19, 1–2: 52–53.

Fraser, G. 2002. "The Fight for Canada's Rights." *Toronto Star*, April 14. Retrieved June 27, 2010 from <vigile.quebec/archives/ds-federation/docs/02-4-14-fraser-3-1982.html>.

Habermas, J. 1973. *Theory and Practice.* Boston: Beacon Press.

Hogg, P.W., and A.A. Bushell. 1997. "The *Charter* Dialogue Between Courts and Legislatures (or Perhaps the *Charter* of Rights Isn't Such a Bad Thing After All)." *Osgoode Hall Law Journal* 35: 75–124.

Hogg, P.W., A.A. Bushell and W.K. Wright. 2007. "*Charter* Dialogue Revisited — Or 'Much Ado About Metaphors.'" *Osgoode Hall Law Journal* 45: 1–65.

Hurlbert, M. 2011. "Human Rights." In M. Hurlbert (ed.), *Pursuing Justice: An Introduction to Justice Studies.* Halifax and Winnipeg: Fernwood Publishing.

Hurlbert, M. and J. Mulvale. 2011. "Defining Justice." In M. Hurlbert (ed.), *Pursuing Justice: An Introduction to Justice Studies.* Halifax and Winnipeg: Fernwood Publishing.

Kinsella, N. 2008. "Can Canada Afford a *Charter* of Social and Economic Rights? Toward a Canadian Social Charter." *Saskatchewan Law Review* 71, 1: 7–22.

Kome, P. 1983. *The Taking of Twenty Eight: Women Challenge the Constitution.* Toronto, ON: Women's Press.

Kymlicka, W. 1995. *Multicultural Citizenship: A Liberal Theory of Minority Rights.* New York: Oxford University Press.

Lepofsky, M.D. 1998. "The Charter's Guarantee of Equality to People with Disabilities: How Well Is It Working?" *Windsor Yearbook of Access to Justice* 16, 55: 156.

MacKinnon, C. 1991. *Toward a Feminist Theory of State.* Cambridge: Harvard University Press.

____. 2006. *Are Women Human? And Other International Dialogues*. Boston: Harvard University Press.

Manfredi, C.P. 2004. *Feminist Activism in the Supreme Court: Legal Mobilization and the Women's Legal Education and Action Fund*. Vancouver, BC: University of British Columbia Press.

Manitoba Human Rights Commission. 2007. *Council of Canadians with Disabilities v. Via Rail Canada: Decision Ensures Equality and Freedom From Discrimination*. March 23. Retrieved July 4, 2010 from <manitobahumanrights.ca/publications/news_releases/pdf/2007_03_23_1.pdf>.

McLachlin, B. 2001. "Equality: The Most Difficult Right." *Supreme Court Law Review* 14, 2d: 17.

McPhedran, M. 2005. "Reflections on the 20th Anniversary of Section 15: The Impact of s. 15 on Canadian Society Equality Rights: Beacon or Laser?" *National Journal of Constitutional Law* 19: 7–29.

Petter, A. 1987. "Immaculate Deception: The Charter's Hidden Agenda." *The Advocate* 45: 857–867.

Pogge, T.W. 2002. *World Poverty and Human Rights: Cosmopolitan Responsibilities and Reforms*. Cambridge: Polity Press.

Rawls, J. 1971. *A Theory of Justice*. Cambridge: Harvard University Press.

Razack, S. 1998. *Looking White People in the Eye: Gender, Race and Culture in Courtrooms and Classrooms*. Toronto, ON: University of Toronto Press.

Ryder, B. 2008. "Taking Section 15 Back to the Future." *The Court*. Toronto: Osgoode Hall Law School. Accessed February 28, 2011 from <thecourt.ca/2008/07/r-v-kapp-taking-section-15-back-to-the-future/>.

Sanders, D. 1985. "The Renewal of Indian Special Status." In A. Bayefsky and M. Eberts (eds.), *Equality Rights and the Canadian Charter of Rights and Freedoms* (p. 529). Toronto, ON: Carswell.

Sen, A. 1980. "Equality of What?" In S. McMurrin (ed.), *Tanner Lectures on Human Values*. Cambridge: Cambridge University Press. Retrieved August 10, 2010 from <http://philosophy.ucsd.edu/faculty/rarneson/Courses/SENeqofcapacity.pdf>.

____. 1988. "Property and Hunger." *Economics and Philosophy* 4: 57–68. Reprinted in W. Cragg and C. Koggel (2005), *Contemporary Moral Issues* (fifth edition), p. 402, Toronto, ON: McGraw-Hill Ryerson; and in S. Boyd, G. Brodsky, S. Day and M. Young (2007), *Poverty, Rights, Social Citizenship and Legal Activism* (p. 77), Vancouver, BC: University of British Columbia Press.

Senate & House of Commons. 1981. *Minutes of Proceedings and Evidence of the Special Joint Committee of the Senate and of the House of Commons on the Constitution of Canada*. January 12. 32nd Parliament, 1st Sess., issue no. I.

Stacey-Moore, G. 1991. "Aboriginal Women, Self-Government, the Canadian *Charter* of Rights and Freedoms, and the 1991 Canada Package on the Constitution." *An address to the Canadian Labour Congress*, Ottawa, ON.

Taylor, C. 1994a. *Multiculturalism and the Politics of Recognition*. Princeton, NJ: Princeton University Press.

____. 1994b. "The Politics of Recognition." In A. Gutmann (ed.), *Multiculturalism: Examining the Politics of Recognition* (pp. 25–73). Princeton: Princeton University Press.

United Nations. 1948. *Universal Declaration of Human Rights*. GA Res. 217A (III), 3d Sess. Supp. No.13, U.N. Doc. A/810. December 10. Retrieved June 28, 2010, from <un.org/en/universal-declaration-human-rights/>.

Weiler, P.C. 1980. "Of Judges and Rights, Or Should Canada Have a Constitutional Bill of Rights?" *Dalhousie Review* 205 (Summer).

Williams, P.J. 1991. *The Alchemy of Race and Rights*. Boston, MA: Harvard University Press.

Young, I.M. 1990. *Justice and the Politics of Difference*. Princeton: Princeton University Press.

Legislation

British North America Act, 1867, 30-31 Vict., c. 3 (U.K.).

Canadian Bill of Rights, 1960 CBR, c.44

Canadian Charter of Rights and Freedoms, Part 1 of the *Constitution Act, 1982,* being Schedule B to the *Canada Act 1982,* (U.K.), 1982, c. 11.

Charter of the United Nations, 26 June 1945, Can. T.S. 1945 No. 7 (entered into force 24 October 1945) and annexed Statute of the International Court of Justice, 26 June 1945, Can. T. S. 1945 No. 7 (entered into force 24 October 1945).

Constitution Act, 1867, (U.K.), 30 & 31 Victoria, c. 3.

Constitution Act, 1982, being Schedule B to the *Canada Act 1982* (U.K.), 1982, c. 11

Criminal Code, R.S.C. 1985, c. C-46.

Indian Act (1876).

Universal Declaration of Human Rights, G.A. Res 217A (III), U.N. Doc. A/810 (Dec. 10, 1948 [UDHR]

Legal Cases

A.G. Canada v. *Lavell* [1974] S.C.R. 1349.

Alberta v. Hutterian Brethren of Wilson Colony, 2009 SCC 37, 2 S.C.R. 567

Andrews v. Law Society of British Columbia, [1989] 1 SCR 143

Bliss v. Canada (Attorney General) [1979] 1 S.C.R. 183

Canadian Foundation for Children, Youth and the Law v. *Canada (Attorney General),* 2004 SCC 4, [2004] 1 S.C.R. 76.

Council of Canadians with Disabilities v. VIA Rail Canada Inc., 2007 SCC 15, [2007] 1 S.C.R. 650.

Dickie v. *Dickie,* 2007 SCC 8, [2007] 1 S.C.R. 346.

Edwards v. *Canada (Attorney General),* [1928] S.C.R. 276, 1928 Carswell Nat 35 (S.C.C.), reversed (1929), [1930] A.C. 124, 1929 Carswell Nat 2 (Canada P.C).

Eldridge v. *British Columbia (Attorney General),* [1997] 3 S.C.R. 624, 151 D.L.R (5th) 577.

Federated Anti-Poverty Groups of B.C. v. *Vancouver (City)* [2002] B.C.J. No. 493.

Gosselin v. *Quebec (Attorney General)* [2002] 4 S.C.R. 429.

Hislop v. *Canada (Attorney General),* [2007] 1 S.C.R. 429

Lovelace v. Canada (1981), Report of the Human Rights Committee, GAOR 36th Sess., Supp. No.40 (AQ/36/40), Annex XVIII, 166.

Masse v. Ontario (Ministry of Community and Social Services) (1996), 134 D.L.R. (4th) 20, 35 C.R.R. (2d) 44 (Ont. Div. Ct.); leave to appeal to C.A. denied [1996] O.J. No. 1526; leave to appeal to S.C.C. denied [1996] S.C.C.A. No. 373.

Murdoch v. Murdoch, [1975] 1 S.C.R. 423.

Nancy Law v. Canada (Minister of Employment and Immigration) [1999] 1 S.C.R. 497.

R. v. Darrach, [2000] 2 S.C.R. 443

R. v. Ewanchuk, [1999] 1 S.C.R. 330

R. v. Kapp, [2008] 2 S.C.R. 483, 2008 SCC 41

R. v. O'Connor, [1995] 4 S.C.R. 411

R. v. Seaboyer; R. v. Gayme, 1991 [1991] 2 Superior Court Report. 577.

Reference as to the Meaning of the Word "Persons" in Section 24 of the British North America Act, 1867, [1928]. S.C.R.276

Vriend v. Alberta, [1998] 1 S.C.R. 493, [1998] S.C.J. No. 29, 156 D.L.R. (4th) 385.

SEXUAL ASSAULT

Chapter 13

"SEX WAS IN THE AIR"

Pernicious Myths and Other Problems with Sexual Violence Prosecutions

Karen Busby

From: *Locating Law: Race/Class/Gender Connections*, third edition, pp. 257–293 (reprinted with permission).

It must be acknowledged that the parties met in what can only be described as "inviting" circumstances. At 2:30 on a summer morning two young women, one of which was dressed in a tube top without a bra and jeans and both of whom were made up and wore high heels in a parking lot outside a bar, made their intention publicly known that they wanted to party … the accused was led by the circumstances to conclude that sex was in the air. (*R. v. Rhodes* 2011: sentencing 73–75)

Justice Dewar of the Manitoba Court of Queen's Bench convicted Kenneth Rhodes of sexually assaulting C.P., an Indigenous woman half his size and sixteen years his junior, in the woods off a secluded highway in Northern Manitoba. Justice Dewar noted that C.P.'s testimony evidenced that she feared for her life, asking Rhodes whether he planned to kill her. He also noted that when the complainant objected to vaginal penetration, Rhodes replied that "it would only hurt for a while." Justice Dewar found that Rhodes continued to penetrate her in various ways without taking any reasonable steps to ascertain whether she was consenting. Yet in his reasons for conviction and for sentencing, Justice Dewar minimized the assault on the complainant. He observed that the complainant and her friend's appearance and behaviour were a "provocation" and "enticement" of the accused and he described the defendant as a "clumsy Don Juan."

By these observations, Justice Dewar revived the long discredited myth that an aroused man is entitled to sexual release and that rapists are just bad lovers. Rhodes was given a conditional sentence of two years' house arrest and was ordered to write an apology to the complainant. The conviction was overturned by the Court of Appeal because, as will be discussed in more detail, Justice Dewar only stated in his decision that he preferred the complainant's evidence but failed to explicitly say that he was satisfied beyond a reasonable doubt of the defendant's guilt.

Over the last three decades, the feminist anti-rape movement has helped us to understand sexual violence as a pervasive, systemic method of creating and sustaining male dominance over women, which also exacerbates other manifestations of social inequality such as racism (see Backhouse 2008). In the 1980s and 1990s governments became more responsive to recognizing sexual violence as systemic and gendered, and in response to feminist calls for change they amended criminal laws to give effect to this understanding. Still, some criminal justice personnel, especially judges and defence lawyers, resist implementing the spirit and intent of these changes. As Justice Dewar's reasoning in *Rhodes* demonstrates, sexual attacks are still viewed by some as private, individual matters stemming from either unfortunate but isolated encounters with strangers or as the natural, but uncontrollable and therefore non-culpable, responses of men to the seductive powers of loose women. Elizabeth Comack and Gillian Balfour (2004: 118) interviewed defence lawyers and concluded that they "resist legislative reforms intended to constrain the influence of rape myths" because they "see the amendments as politically motivated and thus contrary to the principles of fundamental justice." Comack and Balfour (2004) also found that "the strategies adopted in sexual assault cases" by some of these lawyers "are based on a purposeful defiance of the legislative reforms."

Sexual violence laws were founded on rape myths, and while some of these laws have been changed, the *Rhodes* case demonstrates that these myths remain deeply insinuated in some judges' opinions about sexual violence. The most egregious myth — that women and children frequently lie about sexual violence out of malice or delusion — underpins all of the others (L'Heureux-Dubé 2012). The myth is sustained even though there is no evidence in Canada that the incidence of false reports is higher for sexual offences than for other offences. In its decision-making and without referring to evidence or context, the Supreme Court of Canada conjures up and relies upon old and new versions of the myth, such as the spectre of therapy-induced memories (*R. v. O'Connor* 1995; *R. v. Carosella* 1997), vengeful wives (*R. v. J.A.* 2011), or women hiding behind their niqabs (*R. v. N.S.* 2012). Judicial pronouncements, especially when they emanate from Canada's highest court, have a special power for lawyers. Quite simply, if a judge says something is true, then it is.

Feminists are, at best, ambivalent about relying on a coercive state to counter violence against women and recognize the potential for the system to minimize the problem of male violence through processes that deny its existence. Complainants fear for their safety and risk loss of privacy (Perreault and Brennan 2009; Vandervort 2012). Moreover, as some argue, "The very legal process ... creates its own order of damages for the abused child or woman. It is glaringly obvious that the criminal law does not provide a remedy to sexual abuse; it is increasingly obvious that it causes harm" (Smart 1989: 161; see also Comack and Peter 2005). A recent well-publicized case, where a fifteen-year-old was allegedly assaulted by four young men at a party, demonstrates these harms. After photographs of the assault were spread throughout her school and community, she and her parents decided to go to the police. Police told the family that no charges would be laid, as it was a case of "he said, she said." After enduring a year of investigations to no avail, the young woman committed suicide (CBC News Nova Scotia 2013).

Sexual assault is the least likely offence to be reported (Statistics Canada 2005). Charges are less likely to result from these complaints than for any other type of complaint, and, even if charges are laid, the charges are more likely to be stayed, guilty pleas are uncommon, and, for the small percentage of cases that do go to trial, the conviction rate is the lowest of any offence. In 2009, only 3 percent of sexual assaults were reported to police, and of those 3 percent, less than 20 percent were brought to trial. Rates of sexual assault reports increased slightly in 2010 and remained constant throughout 2011 (Sinha 2013). Once failure to complain, to charge and to convict are taken into account, the likelihood that someone who commits a sexual assault will be convicted of an offence is less than 1 percent (Statistics Canada 2010, 2011a, 2011b).

Even where a conviction is obtained, conditional sentences are more likely to be entered into for sexual assault than for any other violent crime (Statistics Canada 2012). Despite legislative reforms in 2007 that made conditional sentences unavailable to individuals convicted of sexual assaults, cases such as *Rhodes*, where the assault occurred prior to the changes, still allow judges to enter conditional sentences (*R. v. Rhodes* 2011: sentencing; *R. v. Arcand* 2010). Feminists must now be concerned with "the ways in which conditional sentences are justified in sexual assault cases," and ask, "do rape myths operate in the legal narratives of restorative justice sentencing practices?" (Balfour and Du Mont 2012). Long terms of incarceration are not the solution to the gendered inequalities present in sexual assault prosecutions. However, if rape myths and stereotypes are ever to be eradicated from the criminal justice system, they must not be allowed to re-emerge in sentencing decisions.

Why is it so difficult to get convictions in sexual assault cases? In this chapter I examine the legal rules (especially as set out by judges in their reasons for decision) and the processes used to determine the Official Version of the "truth" in sexual violence trials (see Comack 2014). The rules and processes composing the Official Version are such an integral part of the methodology of legal professionals that it is unquestioned. While non-lawyers are more likely to recognize the contingencies and other flaws in law's account of itself, they run the risk of being branded by legal professionals as uninformed, unfair and even hysterical if they question the fairness of the process. But as it turns out, various legal principles — including foundational rules governing all criminal proceedings, laws on what acts constitute sexual offences, and evidentiary and procedural rules specific to sexual offences — work *against* the likelihood of securing a conviction in sexual violence cases. In particular, I examine the interaction between these principles, which foster partial and incomplete fact-finding, and rape mythologies (old and new), which perpetuate inequalities. I also look at how feminist-inspired law reforms have fared in courts in the three decades since Parliament started on sexual assault law reform.

Reviewing written reasons for decision (case law) to reveal not just legal principles but also to identify underlying patterns of thinking has various limitations, two of which should be noted. First, reasons for decision are not released in print form in the vast majority of cases; rather, the judge typically releases oral reasons and these are not usually transcribed. Without more information, it cannot be determined whether the case under discussion is an outlier or common thinking. Where available, I have noted more comprehensive case law reviews or other research, such as qualitative research with criminal justice system actors. Second, while the complainant's and the defendant's gender are always apparent in reasons for decision, other aspects of the parties' identity or social location, such as race, indigeneity, sexual orientation, disability or class, are rarely apparent in the written reasons. Thus, it is not usually possible to determine from a case law review whether or how discriminatory thinking related to identity or social location is manifest in sexual violence cases. There are, however, exceptions. In the *Rhodes* case we do know that the complainant is Indigenous because the media reported this fact and a careful read of the sentencing transcript (which is prepared for the appeal and then, in this case, was made publicly available) shows the Crown attorney referring to the complainant's "*kokum*," the Cree word for "grandmother."

FOUNDATIONAL RULES OF CRIMINAL LAW

Underpinning the Official Version of Canadian criminal procedural law are two important principles: criminal convictions are extremely serious and therefore should only be obtained if there is a very high degree of certainty that an offence was committed; and the state, especially the police, should be restrained from using coercive tactics during investigations. To back up these principles, three foundational rules apply in all criminal cases: the person charged (the defendant) is presumed innocent until the charge is proved; the Crown must prove the offence "beyond a reasonable doubt"; and the defendant has the right to silence and the right to full answer and defence.

Presumption of Innocence

Anyone charged with a criminal offence is presumed to be innocent. The Crown has the burden of proving both that the defendant did the acts that amount to an offence and that the defendant intended to commit the acts. To satisfy the intention element in sexual assault cases, the Crown must prove not only that the defendant intended to commit a sexual act but also that he intended to do it in the absence of consent. (Because it is, overwhelmingly, men who commit acts of sexual violence, I use male pronouns to describe defendants. I use female pronouns to describe complainants, because most criminal prosecutions in sexual violence cases involve female complainants and the rules specific to sexual violence prosecutions develop out of beliefs about women and girls.) Evidentiary gaps or weak evidence on any element of the offence will result in an acquittal. Conversely, there is no presumption that the complainant is telling the truth. As one judge said, "One cannot be the victim of the assaultive conduct of an accused until the accused has been found guilty beyond a reasonable doubt," and therefore the use of the term "victim" is inconsistent with the presumption of innocence (*R. v. Seaboyer* 1991: 648).

Proof beyond a Reasonable Doubt

The Crown is also held to a strict standard in proving the case: the judge or jury must be convinced "beyond a reasonable doubt" when all the evidence is assessed together that the defendant committed the alleged acts. As Justice Bacchus of the Ontario Court of Justice observed, "It is not enough for me to believe that the defendant is possibly or even probably guilty. Reasonable doubt requires more. As a standard, reasonable doubt lies far closer to absolute certainty than it does to a balance of probabilities" (*R. v. Woldemichael* 2011: 10). If there is a doubt, the defendant must be acquitted. In civil cases, such as those in which an injured person seeks financial compensation from the person responsible for the injury, the standard of proof is "balance of probabilities"; that is, which of the parties is to be believed more. In contrast, criminal cases are *not* to be decided on the basis of who is more believable.

The Supreme Court of Canada held in *R. v. W.(D.)* (1991) that when a complainant gives evidence that the defendant denies, the judge or jury is to weigh the evidence using these tests:

> First, if you believe the evidence of the defendant, obviously you must acquit. Second, if you do not believe the testimony of the defendant but you are left in reasonable doubt by it, you must acquit. Third, even if you are not left in doubt by the evidence of the defendant, you must ask yourself whether, on the basis of the evidence which you do accept, you are convinced beyond a reasonable doubt by that evidence of the guilt of the defendant. (*R. v. W.(D.).*1991: 758)

These tests are strictly applied. In the *Rhodes* case (2010), after Justice Dewar had reviewed the evidence and found the defendant guilty, Crown counsel sought to ensure that the judge had, in fact, turned his mind to the *W.(D.)* test. She asked:

> During the course of your reasons you made comment that you preferred the testimony of the complainant to the accused and I'm sure you intended to say that you had rejected ... the evidence of the accused and ... you found no reasonable doubt based on it, in accordance with the test in *W.(D.)*. (*R. v. Rhodes* 2010: 26)

Justice Dewar responded, "I have rejected the evidence of the accused primarily in part." The Court of Appeal found that Dewar's choice of words failed to satisfy the requirements of *W.(D.)* as it suggested that the decision was made "on the basis of a credibility contest between the complainant and the accused" (2011). The test in *W.(D.)* requires the trial judge to consider whether or not the evidence of the defendant raises a reasonable doubt as to the defendant's guilt, which Justice Dewar failed to do.

The "reasonable doubt" standard in sexual violence cases falls well short of a positive response to the question "Is she lying?" Rather it approaches, "Are you convinced about her version of the events?" Therefore, the defendant's lawyer will try to undermine the complainant's credibility by casting doubts about her character or motive; or the defence will try to make the case that a different interpretation of the events is possible by pointing to inconsistencies in her accounts of the events, or by finding evidence that suggests there was a chance that she was consenting to the activity.

The case of *R.C.H.* (2012) demonstrates how defence counsel can aggressively attack a complainant's credibility by revealing inconsistencies and omissions. The defence's arguments included that the complainant failed to report to the police that (1) the defendant had attempted to force the complainant to perform oral sex at the time of the assault; (2) the defendant had attempted to "dirty dance" with her days before the assault; (3) the presence of other people at her home on the days preceding the assault; (4) the kitchen light was on at the time of the assault; and (5) she did not attempt to avoid the assault by grabbing onto her kitchen doorframe. The Manitoba Court of Queen's Bench found that the complainant had valid justifications for these omissions and that there was no reasonable doubt as to the defendant's guilt. In other cases, inconsistencies between police reports and testimony, similar to those in *R.C.H.,* have been enough to raise a reasonable doubt in the mind of the judge, who has then been forced to acquit the defendant.

In some historical abuse cases (that is, cases in which the events giving rise to the charge occurred years before the charges were laid) it is not unusual for the judge to state that he or she believes the complainant's evidence but nonetheless has some doubt arising from the defendant's sworn denial and the absence of evidence independently corroborating the complainant's story. The defence strategy in historical cases is to argue that, because of the passage of time, the evidence is too weak to satisfy the reasonable doubt standard. In *R. v. Sanichar* (2012), the appellate court overturned the defendant's conviction because the trial judge had failed to self-instruct on the dangers of convicting the defendant in a historical sexual assault case. The trial judge had found that the complainant was sincere, honest and truthful and had rejected a portion of the complainant's evidence where he found it was insufficient to convict. Nonetheless, a majority of the Court of Appeal stated:

> Memory is fallible. Courts have long recognized that even an apparently convincing, confident and credible witness may not be accurate or reliable … In [cases] evolving out of allegations of distance events, including allegations involving historical acts of physical and sexual abuse — particular caution and scrutiny are called for in approaching the reliability of evidence. (*R. v. Sanichar* 2012: para 35–38)

A complainant's reliable testimony cannot, without more, provide enough evidence to prove beyond a reasonable doubt that a sexual assault occurred in the distant past. Some judges have acknowledged that "such a result is often unsatisfying but is unavoidable" (*R. v. Finley* 1998). In 2013, the Supreme Court of Canada overruled the Court of Appeal's decision in *Sanichar,* stating that self-instruction is not necessary, but can be left to the trial judge's discretion. While it is not essential for trial judges to acknowledge the dangers of conviction in historical sexual assault cases, it is still within their ability to do so and acquit on such grounds.

Right to Silence and Full Answer and Defence

All defendants have the right to silence and cannot be incriminated by exercising that right. In *R. v. P.A.A.* (2012), the defendant's conviction was overturned on appeal. The court cited *R. v. Turcotte* (2005: para 55) to explain the connection between the defendant's right to silence and determination of guilt:

> Silence in the face of police questioning will, therefore, rarely be admissible as post-offence conduct because it is rarely probative of guilt. Refusing to do what one has a right to refuse to do reveals nothing. An inference of guilt cannot logically or morally emerge from the exercise of a protected right. Using silence as evidence of guilt artificially creates a duty, despite a right to the contrary, to answer all police questions. (*R. v. P.A.A.* 2012: para 18)

A defendant cannot be compelled to testify at his own trial, nor can evidence he has given in a previous proceeding be used against him. Moreover, no adverse inference can be drawn from the failure to testify, unless it is the uncommon case in which the defendant is in the unique position of offering an explanation about an unusual fact. Evidence obtained in violation of the right to silence rule cannot be used at trial even in very serious cases (such as murder), except in rare circumstances.

The right to silence extends to the investigative stages of the proceedings. Thus, for example, any statements made by the defendant to the police (or others in authority) will be scrutinized to ensure that they were made voluntarily and taken only after the defendant was advised of the right to a lawyer. If there is any hint that the police used coercion or deception in taking the statement, the statement will be rejected. In *R. v. S.G.T.* (2010) the trial court refused to admit the defendant's police confession to sexually assaulting his stepdaughter because the police had conveyed that the charges were not serious and that the case would not proceed if the defendant simply apologized to his family. However, the trial court did admit the apology letters that were sent to the mother of the complainant. The Supreme Court of Canada upheld the decision to admit the letter because inadmissibility of confessions is only a contentious issue when the confession is made to a "person of authority," not to an ordinary person.

Every defendant also has the right to full answer and defence, which includes a defendant's right to counsel, to cross-examination and to full disclosure by the Crown. These rights override the interests of the complainant at trial because "Society's interest in encouraging the reporting of sexual assault offences should not prohibit the defendant from making full answer and defence" (*R. v. K.C.* 2005). In *R. v. N.S.* (2012), the defendant's right to full answer and defence interfered with the complainant's right to freedom of religion (the wearing of a niqab). The case arose out of a preliminary inquiry judge's decision to have N.S. remove her niqab to testify. The decision was appealed twice, subsequently reaching the Supreme Court of Canada. The Court ruled in favour of the defendant's rights, affirming that the religious and moral integrity of the complainant must be secondary to the defendant's interests, but stating that removal must be determined on a case-by-case basis. In 2013, the new preliminary inquiry was heard by the Ontario Court of Justice. Despite acknowledging the negative impacts upon the reporting of sexual assault generally, as well as N.S.'s religious autonomy, the court ordered the complainant to remove her niqab.

Few feminists would disagree with the principles underlying the foundational rules of the presumption of innocence, proof beyond a reasonable doubt, and the right to silence and to full answer and defence given the abuses that could flourish in the absence of such rules. At the same time these rules also have the effect of creating a truth-seeking process, including the trial, which both favours the defendant and only permits part of the story to be told. The process by which law arrives at the "truth" falls well short of the methodological standards required by other disciplines.

THE ROLES FOR CROWN ATTORNEYS AND COMPLAINANTS

Crown attorneys represent the state; they do not represent complainants. With the exception of personal records applications (discussed later in this chapter), complainants do not have the status of being a party to the proceedings and, even if they could afford it, complainants cannot have independent legal representation in court in criminal cases. While some Crown attorneys are sensitive to the experience of trauma that complainants have undergone, it is not their role to counsel complainants. Moreover, many Crown attorneys have such high caseloads that they have little time to prepare witnesses for trials (often they only see the file the night before the trial), and even less time to keep complainants informed about the progress of the prosecution.

Complainants, especially minors but also adults, have little control over whether charges are laid. If a third party (such as a social worker or medical personnel) initiates police involvement, a complainant may only find out about the charges *after* they are laid (see, for example, Comack and Peter 2005). Plea bargains are agreements between the Crown attorney and the defendant's lawyer that the defendant will plead guilty if the Crown will drop some charges, reduce the charges or agree to recommend a lighter sentence than the offence might otherwise attract. These bargains are made without any input from complainants, and the complainant may not even be informed that a guilty plea has been entered and a sentence pronounced (McGillivray 1998).

The Crown attorney's role is not to obtain convictions (Public Prosecution

Service of Canada 2013). It is to ensure that the evidence in the case is presented fairly. Police lay charges if they have information that suggests there are reasonable and probable grounds to believe that an offence has been committed. The standard for taking a case to trial is higher: the Crown attorney can only proceed when there is a reasonable chance of conviction based on admissible evidence. If Crown attorneys are of the view that this higher standard is not met, they must stay the charges and cannot proceed to trial even when, for example, a complainant wants the case to be heard. If an acquittal is entered, the complainant has no say in determining whether it should be appealed, and if an appeal is made she cannot participate in the appeal. In criminal proceedings, a complainant is merely a witness to a crime. She has no control over whether or how the process unfolds and no specific interest in the outcome of criminal proceedings.

Complainants may be allowed to take part in the sentencing process by providing a victim impact statement. These statements were once touted as a process through which complainants could gain control and vindication in the prosecution of their assaulter. They were created to "relate to the sentencing judge the harm inflicted upon the victim by providing an assessment of the physical, financial, and psychological effects of the crime" (Ruparelia 2012). Many women believe that by making a victim impact statement, they will have a direct effect on the sentence of the defendant. In reality, victim impact statements are not meant to include any advice or opinion on sentencing (R. v. Gabriel 1999, cited in Ruparelia 2012). The statements are merely a process through which complainants may have their voices heard. Furthermore, the use of victim impact statements is not universal. A complainant may — or may not — be asked by the Crown to submit a statement for the sentencing hearing.

THE SPECIFIC ELEMENTS OF SEXUAL OFFENCES

Generally speaking, a defendant in a sexual violence case will be found guilty if the Crown proves beyond a reasonable doubt that 1) he (and not someone else) committed the offence, 2) the acts amounting to the offence with which the defendant has been charged did occur, and 3) the complainant did not consent to the acts. The defendant may be found not guilty if he can prove diminished responsibility arising from, for example, insanity. Sexual violence prosecutions in which the defence involves either the defendant's identity or sanity are uncommon. Whether the acts constitute an offence is sometimes in issue, particularly if the events giving rise to the charges occurred before the reforms enacted in 1983 and 1985. However, in most cases involving complainants over sixteen, consent is the contentious issue, and for offences involving those under sixteen, "nothing happened" or inaccurate memory is the usual defence.

1983 *Criminal Code* Amendments

The *Criminal Code* provisions on the precise acts necessary to a finding of criminal culpability in sexual offence cases were subject to revisions by Parliament in 1983, 1985, 1992, and 2008. Because the law that applies is the law in effect at the time that the acts giving rise to the charges were committed, the former laws continue to be applied to some historic cases. Thus, for example, for events occurring prior to 1983, proof of penile-vaginal penetration is a requirement in rape cases, and husbands cannot be charged with raping their wives. Some judges are of the view that a pre-1983 rape conviction requires not only an unwilling complainant but also forcible intercourse, which requires evidence that the complainant actively resisted the defendant's actions (*R. v. O'Connor* 1998; Lös 1994).

While a rape conviction required proof of penile-vaginal penetration prior to 1983, after the 1983 amendments the determination of sexual offences only required that there be some sexual element to the acts, so that proof of the acts themselves (apart from issues of credibility) is not usually problematic. For example, the New Brunswick Court of Appeal held, in *R. v. Chase* (1984), that grabbing a teenage girl's breasts did not constitute a sexual assault because breasts, "like a man's beard," were secondary sexual characteristics, and it overturned the previous conviction. The evidence had established that the forty-year-old man had entered the home of the fifteen-year-old girl, uninvited, and grabbed her. He said, "Come over here, don't hit me. I know you want it." She had prevented him from touching her genitals. This decision was overturned by the Supreme Court of Canada (in 1987), which held that a sexual assault is committed in circumstances of a sexual nature that involve a violation of the sexual integrity of the victim.

For the purposes of sentencing, judges classify sexual assaults as major or minor assaults. In *R. v. Arcand* (2010: para 169) the Alberta Court of Appeal confirmed that the starting point for major assault is a penitentiary term of three years. Major sexual assaults include, but are not limited to, vaginal or anal penetration, fellatio and cunnilingus. (But remember that Justice Dewar in *R. v. Rhodes* granted a conditional sentence even though he had assaulted her genitals repeatedly.) A sentencing judge can label an assault as major where it was reasonably foreseeable that the defendant's actions would "likely [cause] serious psychological or emotional harm, whether or not physical injury occurs" (*R. v. Arcand* 2010: para 171). Feminists argue that, by this definition, all sexual assaults should be defined as major sexual assault. Psychological or emotional harm is always done in the case of sexual assault and should always be foreseeable. (In August 2013, R. v. Arcand was appealled to the Supreme Court of Canada).

1985 *Criminal Code* Amendments

Until 1985, sexual offences against children focused on whether the complainant was "of previously chaste character" and applied, in most cases, only to females. The 1985 *Criminal Code* amendments, which mainly concerned offences against children, are gender-neutral and based on a combination of age, power dynamics and specific activities. For example, consent is not a defence to any sexual offence charge if the complainant is under sixteen; if the complainant is fourteen or fifteen, consent is not a defence unless the defendant is less than five years older than the complainant and is not in a position of trust or authority. (Note that the age of consent was raised from fourteen to sixteen in 2008.) A person in a position of trust or authority, or with whom the complainant is in a relationship of dependency or a relationship that is exploitative, who engages in sexual activity with someone between fourteen and seventeen commits an offence. "Procuring" and other prostitution-related offences attract harsher sentences if minors are involved.

In the cases where consent cannot be a defence, judges sometimes discount the harm flowing from the offence. For example, in *R. v. Bauder* (1997), involving a twelve-to-thirteen-year-old girl, the Manitoba Court of Appeal commented in a sentencing appeal that:

> The girl, of course, could not consent in the legal sense, but nonetheless was a willing participant. She was apparently more sophisticated than many her age and was performing many household tasks including babysitting the accused's children. The accused and his wife were somewhat estranged. (*R. v. Bauder* 1997: para 2).

This statement is even more shocking in that, because the defendant entered a guilty plea, the girl did not testify. All three of the appeal judges who heard the case had no problem simply agreeing with the defence counsel's unsupported assertion that the girl was a "willing participant." As Anne McGillivray (1998: 381) notes, "myths abounded" in the *Bauder* case:

> Sexual abuse does not hurt; children are not believable; children should be spared the trauma of testifying at whatever cost to the administration of justice and to their own sense of justice; and sophisticated little girls ensnare innocent men, jail-bait to the last: "willing," "sophisticated" and consenting, leading men on, playing grown-up, bullying them. That the law says they cannot consent factually or legally is a minor problem in myth making.

A more recent case shows that while judges are aware that the legal age of consent is sixteen they are still willing to consider the consent of the underage complainant in sentencing. In *R. v. B.B.* (2011), the complainant was fifteen and the defendant was twenty-two. The parties engaged in five sexual acts within three days, all of which fell under the category of major sexual assault. The starting point for major sexual assault of a child is four years; however, the Provincial Court of Alberta sentenced the defendant to a mere six months. The sentencing judge found that the assaults could not be defined as major sexual assaults because the complainant had consented, despite her legal inability to do so, and there was little to no proof of harm.

1992 *Criminal Code* Amendments

When consent or "nothing happened" is the defence, the defence lawyer's likely strategy will be to raise doubt about whether the complainant is telling the truth. A complainant's credibility can be undermined by, for example, showing bias, prejudice, bad character, inconsistent previous statements, impaired capacity to recall or possibly false memories. While feminists have attempted to limit how credibility attacks can be mounted against complainants, another strategy has been to redefine the legal meaning of "consent" by imposing positive obligations on parties to obtain voluntary agreements and imposing age restrictions on certain activities.

The 1992 amendments to the *Criminal Code* (often referred to as Bill C-49) redefined the "consent" element in sexual assault law to be the voluntary agreement of the complainant to engage in specific sexual activity at a specific time, rather than, for example, whether she offered a sufficient degree of resistance or whether she consented on a previous occasion. This amendment is intended to shift the factual and legal issue at trial away from what the defendant might have thought to what the complainant actually said or otherwise communicated at the time of the incidents. By this law, to assume consent, initiators of sexual activity should no longer be able to rely upon stereotypes or fantasies about women or even their knowledge of specific complainants' sexual lives. Rather they should have the positive obligation of determining whether the real, present woman is agreeing on the particular occasion to sexual activity. For greater specificity, the 1992 amendments also provide that no consent is obtained if a third party purports to make the agreement; the complainant is incapable of consenting; the defendant induces consent by abusing a position of trust, power, or authority; or the complainant expresses by word or conduct a lack of agreement to engage or to continue engaging in the activity.

The Crown is required to prove that the defendant knew that the complainant was not consenting or that he was being reckless about whether she consented or not (*R. v. Sansregret* 1985). Therefore defendants can rely on the "honest-but-mistaken belief in consent" defence: the defendant testifies that he "honestly" believed that the complainant was consenting to the acts in question. Prior to

1992 the test was whether the defendant himself honestly believed this, and his belief could be based on, for example, his information about the sexual history of the complainant or even his own ideas about the "kinds" of women who would consent. While there had to be an "air of reality" to his assertion, it was irrelevant whether the woman in question was, in fact, not consenting or what a "reasonable person" watching the events would have believed about consent. The 1992 amendments limit the mistaken-belief defence by restricting it to situations in which the defendant actually took "reasonable steps" to ascertain that the complainant was consenting. This change places the burden on the defendant to substantiate his claim of belief in consent. The Act also eliminates the defence altogether when the defendant was intoxicated or wilfully blind to the complainant's non-consent.

Early research by Colin Meredith, Renate Mohr and Rosemary Cairns Way (1997) on the first three years of Bill C-49 and sexual assault cases could not identify any impacts of the consent defence amendments. Later, however, in *R. v. Ewanchuk* (1999), the Supreme Court of Canada made it clear that an offence is committed unless the defendant explicitly obtained the complainant's clear consent to sexual activity at the time the activity took place. That case involved a seventeen-year-old girl who repeatedly said "no" to Ewanchuk's sexual advances during what had been purported to be a job interview. Despite the complainant's objections, Ewanchuk argued that there had been implied consent to the sexual touching. The Supreme Court of Canada rejected Ewanchuk's defence, stating that implied consent could not exist in the context of sexual assault. After reviewing the post-*Ewanchuk* decisions by trial and appeal courts on consent and mistaken belief, Lise Gotell (2006: 21) concludes, "There is a strong indication of a meaningful shift in the law of consent and in the standards for mistaken belief."

In *R. v. Rhodes* (2010), the trial judge held that the defendant could not rely on mistaken belief in consent because no reasonable steps had been taken by him to obtain consent. However, in sentencing, Justice Dewar still discussed stereotypical evidence that was supposed to have been eradicated by the 1992 reforms. He relied on the complainant's dress, location and social cues to justify the defendant's actions and reinforce the myth that, for some women, no means yes:

> I'm sure that whatever signals there were that sex was in the air were unintentional. But that does not change the fact that they were there, more than just a manner of dress, more than the fact that she was a woman. And they are a relevant, mitigating factor. (*R. v. Rhodes* 2011: sentencing 79)

Decisions such as *Rhodes* call into question whether or not the 1992 amendments have truly altered judges' perceptions of sexual assault cases, or whether they have merely forced judges and defence counsel to be more creative in the ways they use character and sexual history evidence. Two recent cases (discussed below) demonstrate how the 1992 changes to consent laws are being implemented by some judges. Interestingly, in both of these cases a majority of the Supreme Court of Canada sustained a conviction, but a majority of all judges who ruled on culpability (trial and appeals) would not have entered convictions — thus demonstrating that there is still some uncertainty among judges as to the full impact of the 1992 changes.

In *R. v. Stender* (2004), the complainant had recently ended an intimate relationship with the defendant. He threatened to distribute electronically nude photos of her unless she had sex with him, and as a result she did. The trial judge described the defendant's conduct as "reprehensible," but stated that he was not sure that Parliament had intended to criminalize this situation and he was not sure that the defendant's conduct amounted to extortion that would vitiate the complainant's consent. The Court of Appeal overturned the acquittal (a decision affirmed by the Supreme Court of Canada), stating that the defendant clearly coerced the complainant into doing something that she otherwise would not have voluntarily chosen to do. Therefore it could not be said that she had voluntarily consented to have sex with the defendant.

In *R. v. J.A.* (2011), the complainant was consensually strangled (or erotically asphyxiated) by her partner, the defendant, into unconsciousness. When she awoke, she was on her knees, with her hands tied behind her back, and the defendant was inserting a dildo into her anus. The trial court convicted the defendant of sexual assault on the grounds that a party cannot give advance or prior consent to sexual activity that takes place while unconscious. On appeal, a majority of the Ontario Court of Appeal found that there was insufficient evidence to determine, beyond a reasonable doubt, that the complainant had not consented to the insertion of the dildo. After a second appeal, the Supreme Court of Canada reinstated the conviction. Five out of nine judges hearing the case found that the intention of the legislature was not to allow prior consent, but to ensure that reasonable steps were taken to confirm consent and that an individual's consent could be obtained or revoked at any point. If an individual is incapable of consenting because of her state of consciousness, the defence cannot argue that the activity was consensual or that the defendant had a mistaken belief. The four dissenting judges of the Supreme Court of Canada would have upheld the appellate court decision. The dissent held that the defendant and the complainant had engaged in consensual, sexual activity and that the majority's decision deprived women of autonomy to participate in "sexual adventures" which "involve no proven harm to them or others" (*R. v. J.A.* 2011: para 73).

GENERAL EVIDENCE RULES

As the *Rhodes, Stender* and *J.A.* cases demonstrate, some of the facts that need to be proved in sexual violence cases include the basic elements of the offence, such as "Did he obtain her voluntary agreement?" and "Did he take reasonable steps to ascertain whether she was consenting?" As well, in law's Official Version the credibility of a witness is also something that can be proved or disproved, and is always an issue. Information is admissible in court if it is relevant and reliable. While there is usually a high degree of consensus on what information is relevant, it must nonetheless be recognized that this determination, especially on credibility issues, will be influenced by a judge's experience and social location. Judges in Canada are still predominately male and have upper-middle-class origins. Overwhelmingly, they are white, heterosexual and able-bodied (except for age-related disabilities, such as visual impairments). As the Women's Legal Education and Action Fund (LEAF) argued in its brief in *R. v. N.S.* (2012: para 44), "Courts have repeatedly acknowledged that 'groundless myths and fantasized stereotypes' about rape victims have improperly informed the assessment of complainants' credibility in sexual assault trials, thus perpetuating women's inequality and undermining the truth seeking function of the criminal trial."

How do experience and common sense inform credibility findings? In *R. v. J.A.,* the fact that the complainant had previously consented to participate in "sado-type behaviour ... 'the aggressive type' ... the kinky behaviour" (2008: para 4) and had discussed the possibility of anal penetration with the defendant led the Court of Appeal to find that the evidence on lack of consent was too weak to convict. The Court of Appeal ignored the requirement of affirmative consent that arose from *Ewanchuk*, instead deciding that the prior sadomasochistic interests of the complainant and the defendant created a reasonable doubt as to the complainant's non-consent even though she was unconscious. The majority of the court assumed that because the complainant had consented to "the kinky behaviour" before, there was insufficient evidence in her testimony to conclude that she had not consented to it on the night in question. The Supreme Court of Canada, while maintaining silence on the use of sexual history evidence, held that prior consent is not valid if a complainant is unconscious regardless of sexual history.

The issue at trial in *R. v. N.S.* was whether or not the applicant had to remove her niqab to testify as a complainant at a preliminary inquiry to a sexual assault trial. Interveners argued that the issue of whether or not removal was necessary was founded upon the incorrect stereotype that women in sexual assault trials were lying and vindictive. Post-9/11 distrust of minorities, in addition to the classic myth that women falsely report sexual assault, underpinned the inherent assumption that the complainant would lie and jeopardize the right to a fair trial if the judge could not see her face. The Supreme Court of Canada decided that whether or not removal was necessary would have to be decided on the facts of each case. Where non-removal posed a risk to a fair trial and the defendant's right to full answer and defence, which it would in most if not every sexual assault case, the complainant should be required to remove her niqab.

So what role did experience and common sense play in the *J.A.* and *N.S.* cases? No evidence was tendered in either case on issues such as bondage-domination-submission-sado-masochism (BDSM) practices or erotic asphyxiation or the science of reading a face for clues as to veracity. In *J.A.* all of the judges hearing the case incorrectly assumed that the objective of erotic asphyxiation is to achieve unconsciousness, and they did not understand the practice of using safe words to indicate non-consent. No judge recognized that the physical acts of strangulation and erotic asphyxiation are identical — pressure on the veins carrying oxygenated blood to the brain — and more than one judge described the practice as unharmful. In *N.S.* the Court simply and unreflectively expressed confidence that judges knew how to recognize credible witnesses by viewing their faces and ignored reams of research reports demonstrating the fallibility of this belief.

Reliability

Various evidence rules have been developed to evaluate the reliability or competence of witnesses, that is, their ability to tell the truth. Until recently, courts would not deem children under fourteen or adults with mental disabilities capable of testifying unless it was first established that the individual understood some notion of a moral obligation to tell the truth and had the capacity to perceive, remember and communicate events. In *R. v. D.A.I.* (2012), the Supreme Court of Canada found that where a child under fourteen or an individual with a mental disability can communicate events and promises to tell the truth, they must be deemed competent to testify. In the rare cases in which a mature minor or adult has a mental disability that affects his or her reliability, expert witnesses may be called upon to give evidence about the impact of the disability on perception, memory or ability to communicate. However, Janine Benedet and Isabel Grant (2013) argue that the use of expert witnesses may be detrimental to credibility determinations if the expert does not have a prior familiarity with the complainant. When an expert provides a statement about a complainant's abilities that is summarized merely from reports and impressions of the complainant during trial testimony, the expert will often underestimate the abilities of the individual.

In cases where the complainant's reliability is at question, the Crown may also seek to admit hearsay evidence (that is, information conveyed by a third party, not a direct observer). If the judge allows the application, the Crown may call an adult that the complainant has confided in, for example, a teacher, caretaker, parent or doctor, to give evidence of what the complainant told them about the assault. An analysis of cases seeking to rely on such witnesses showed that they result in mixed success (Benedet and Grant 2007). Where a complainant is found competent to testify, whether under oath or promise, it is unlikely that the court will allow impact testimony from a third party.

Relevance: Prior Convictions

General evidence rules exclude information that may be relevant if the probative value (that is, light that the evidence might shed on the case) is outweighed by a competing concern flowing from its use in criminal proceedings. Thus, for example, the Crown cannot enter evidence of a defendant's prior convictions or character unless the defendant testifies or otherwise raises these issues, for example by having others testify that the defendant was not the sort of person who could have committed the acts. How does the law justify this rule? That the defendant has committed crimes in the past or that he is generally regarded as a bad person is of little relevance, for it does not tell the judge or jury much about whether he committed the specific acts at issue. Moreover, it is unfair to require the defendant to account in the course of a criminal trial for every previous wrongdoing. Finally, such an inquiry would lengthen trial proceedings considerably. However, if a conviction is obtained, prior offences are relevant to the issue of what is an appropriate sentence, and therefore such evidence can be received at a sentencing hearing.

Even if the defendant does testify and thereby puts his own credibility in question, the judge can restrict questioning on character, including criminal record. What is law's justification for this rule? As the trial judge in *R. v. Last* explained:

> The theory of the law is that if an accused has been convicted of prior offences and testifies, those convictions can be brought out for the purpose of assessing his credibility as a witness, nothing more. You cannot infer from those that he was guilty on these charges before us today because of those prior convictions. (*R. v. Last* 2005, cited in *R. v. Last* 2008: para 41)

However, repeated violence against a complainant may be admitted to assist the judge in comprehending the patterns of abuse and violence that have led up to the current charge, including, for example, to explain a delay in reporting. Without allowing such evidence at trial, it may be more difficult for the trier of fact to fully comprehend the nature of the assault. In *R. v. J.A.*, for example, the trial judge was not informed of J.A.'s violent past — even though he had only recently been released from jail having been convicted a second time for assaulting the complainant — until after the court had convicted the defendant (Busby 2012). The Crown did not attempt to introduce evidence of the defendant's thirteen prior assault convictions, some of which involved the complainant, until the sentencing hearing. Such evidence, had it been tendered at trial, might have brought into question whether the complainant was viciously strangled or erotically asphyxiated by the defendant. Crown attorneys often shy away from introducing this evidence, probably because they want to avoid provoking a mistrial if the evidence is misused.

The rules on character evidence do not apply with the same force to other witnesses, including complainants. The defence frequently uses character evidence, including cross-examination on criminal records, to undermine complainants' and other witnesses' credibility. Law justifies this double standard on the ground that witnesses are not being tried and therefore do not risk the serious consequences of a criminal conviction.

Relevance: Similar Fact

Evidence that the defendant has on other occasions committed acts that are similar to the subject matter of the charge before the court (known as "similar fact evidence") is generally not admissible, for two reasons. First, by law's account, the evidence is not relevant because the fact that someone has committed other acts of sexual violence does not tell us much about whether he committed the assault that is the subject of the charge. Second, like evidence on the defendant's character, similar fact evidence has the severely prejudicial effect of inducing the jury to think of the defendant as a "bad" person who has a propensity to commit such acts. There is an exception to this rule: the evidence can be received if the similar acts "are so unusual and strikingly similar that their similarities cannot be attributed to coincidence" (*R. v. C.(M.H.)* 1991) and if the relevance of the evidence is not outweighed by its prejudicial effect.

Similar fact evidence can be vital in domestic sexual assault cases to understand the context and history of the abusive partnership. Two cases have admitted similar fact evidence in abusive domestic relationships: *R. v. F.(D.S.)* (1999) and *R. v. P.S.* (2007). In *F.(D.S.)*, the Court of Appeal found that similar fact evidence must be admitted to assist the jury in understanding the defendant's motive and to explain why there had been a delay in disclosure from the complainant. The judge found that not admitting the evidence would have given the jury an "incomplete and possibly misleading impression of the relationship" (*R. v. F.(D.S.)* 1999: para 22). In *P.S.*, the appellate court clarified the admissibility of similar fact evidence in spousal abuse cases, stating that the evidence can only be admitted where the similar facts arose within the same long-term abusive relationship with the complainant and where the evidence shows that the defendant had a strong predisposition to perform the alleged assault. Despite the principles set down in these two cases, similar fact evidence is rarely admitted in spousal abuse cases, as is evidenced by *J.A.*

A typical example of the similar fact rule occurred in *R. v. Handy* (2002), where the issue was whether the complainant consented to anal intercourse with the defendant. The Supreme Court of Canada rejected testimony from the defendant's former wife that he had a propensity to inflict painful sex, including anal intercourse, and that he often refused to take "no" for an answer. The Court did not think this evidence was unusual or strikingly similar, and it therefore could not be admitted as similar fact evidence. As well, the incidents recounted by the former wife were more reprehensible than the actual charge in the case and were therefore seriously prejudicial to the defendant.

R. v. Shearing (2002) is a rare case in which similar fact evidence was admitted at a sexual assault trial. The defendant was charged with sexually assaulting numerous teenaged girls who were members of a small religious cult that he led. His defence to most of the charges was consent. The girls (now women) gave evidence that he groomed them for sexual gratification by exploiting the cult's beliefs on how to attain certain spiritual goals. In particular, the girls all gave similar accounts of the defendant's use of distinctive "spiritualist imagery (achieving higher states of awareness) and horror stories (invasion of young girls by disembodied minds), and the supposed prophylactic power of the appellant's sexual touching to ward off these horrific threats" (R. v. Shearing 2002: para 55). The Court recognized that the evidence was exceptionally prejudicial to the defendant because it involved a spiritual leader taking sexual liberties with minors and justifying these actions with an overlay of spiritual cant. Nonetheless, it held that the evidence met the "so unusual and strikingly similar" test and that its probative value, in all the circumstances, outweighed its prejudicial effects.

The Shearing (2002) case is exceptional because similar fact evidence is rarely found to be admissible in child sexual abuse cases (including historical and recovered memory cases). For example, the evidence is unlikely to be received to show that the modus operandi of the defendant is the same, because it is unlikely that the modus will be significantly different from that used by many abusers (for example, "He told me never to tell anyone"; "It only happened when Mom was not home"). Therefore, the evidence is not probative. On the other hand, if the "so unusual" test for the modus is met, its bizarreness could be cause for heightened concern about its credibility. In R. v. Burke (1996), the Supreme Court of Canada said that similar fact evidence should not be admitted if there is a possibility for collaboration to concoct the evidence between the complainants or a complainant and another witness giving similar fact evidence. Such contact opportunities would be the norm rather than the exception, because they would include, for example, cases in which the complainants are relatives, are participating in civil actions, were involved in the same organizations or institutions, or come from the same geographical area. In Shearing, the Court may have watered down the strict test of Burke because it was satisfied, on the facts, that even though some of the complainants were in contact with each other, there was no direct evidence of collaboration. However, even in *Shearing* the judge had to remind the jury of the specific evidence supporting the possibility of concoction and expressly warn them that they needed to fully consider this possibility before allowing the evidence to influence their verdict. The risk of collusion is still considered by judges when admitting similar fact evidence, as can be seen in R. *v. Wheeler* (2013: para 38) and R. *v. Gibson* (2012: para 149).

SPECIAL EVIDENCE RULES FOR SEXUAL VIOLENCE CASES

For centuries the special evidence rules have applied to sexual violence cases. The rules, as formal principles or by judicial application, have permitted far greater range for attacking the complainant's credibility than is permitted in other criminal cases. Law's Official Version for justifying these rules may well seem surprising to a twenty-first-century reader, but what is even more surprising is the tenacious hold that these discredited justifications retain over how judges and other criminal justice personnel use the rules.

John Wigmore (1970: 736), whose treatise on evidence law has been considered the single most famous work in any field of law, stated:

> Modern psychiatrists have amply studied the behavior of errant young girls and the women coming before the courts in all sorts of cases. Their psychic complexes are multifarious and distorted ... One form taken by these complexes is that of contriving false charges of sexual offences by men. The unchaste mind finds incidental but direct expression in the narration of imaginary sex incidents of which the narrator is the heroine or victim ... The real victim, however, too often in such cases is the innocent man.

Wigmore went on to advocate that sexual offences ought not to be prosecuted unless a psychiatrist had testified as to the complainant's ability to tell the truth.

Wigmore's assertion was not good science (Bienen 1983) when it was first stated in 1934, and although this particular paragraph was repeated in all subsequent editions of the work, the psychiatric examination of complainants did not become a general requirement for sexual violence prosecutions, as suggested. However, the thinking underlying his proposition — that women and children frequently lie about sexual violence out of delusion or malice — remains deeply ingrained in sexual violence law. Until the 1983 *Criminal Code* amendments, for example, the law required that, for some sexual violence offences, a complainant's testimony had to be corroborated (that is, directly supported by independent evidence) before a conviction could be entered. For other sexual offences a judge had to warn a jury that it was dangerous to convict in the absence of corroboration. While corroboration is no longer required specifically for any sexual offences, *R. v. F.C.* (2012) demonstrates that the absence of corroborative evidence is often fatal to a prosecution. The trial judge failed to find the evidence of either the complainant or the defendant credible as he stated, "I am unable to decide who to believe." Without corroboration, the evidence of the complainant was not enough to convince the judge, beyond a reasonable doubt, of the defendant's guilt.

Until 1983 the law also provided that if a complainant failed to tell someone about a sexual assault at the first reasonable opportunity after it occurred, the "recent complaint" doctrine required judges to tell juries that this failure supported a strong presumption of unreliability. The belief underlying this rule — and freely described as such by judges in law's Official Version — was that women would fabricate complaints if given time to think them up in order to protect their reputations against allegations of consensual but extramarital sex.

The "recent complaint" law has been formally repealed, and the Supreme Court of Canada has vigorously asserted that "a delay in disclosure, standing alone, will never give rise to an adverse inference against the credibility of a complainant" (*R. v. D.D.* 2000: para 65). Nonetheless Comack and Balfour (2004) reveal how defence lawyers continue to draw upon the recent complaint doctrine in their efforts to discredit complainants' credibility in sexual assault cases. In *R. v. Crampton* (2004), the Court of Appeal set aside the conviction of the defendant partially because of a delay in disclosure. The defence purported that the delay was evidence of consent because the complainant had only decided to make a complaint after she had spoken with her boyfriend about the assault. In *R. v. R.G.B.* (2012: para 63), an appellate court acknowledged that the trial judge had incorrectly relied upon a delay in disclosure to acquit the defendant. In the reasons for acquittal, the trial judge rationalized, "Slow reporting and returning to the environment in which the alleged incidents occurred are matters which could be inconsistent with the allegations." However, the appellate court did not overturn the acquittal. Despite a reliance on the stereotype that "real victims" report incidents of assault immediately, the appellate court did not find the error serious enough to allow the Crown's appeal.

A delay in police reporting is not the only stereotype courts rely on to determine the credibility of the complainant. In *R. v. Shearing* (2002), a majority of the Supreme Court of Canada gave credence to another variation on recent complaint by accepting the assertion of the defence that a teenage complainant's failure to record repeated sexual abuse in her diary could support a conclusion that the assault did not occur.

While the abolition of the formal discriminatory evidence rules on corroboration and recent complaint has probably made a practical difference in some (perhaps many) sexual violence cases, the effects of these rules linger on. The most egregious special evidence rules are those permitting defence lawyers to question complainants about their sexual history and obtain access to their personal records, and, as we shall see, the impacts of these rules remain pervasive and significant.

Sexual History Evidence

At common law, a complainant in a sexual violence case could be questioned about her sexual history because, according to law's Official Version, this information was relevant. Unchaste women, for instance, were considered to be less worthy of belief, and therefore sexual history evidence was probative of a complainant's general credibility. As well, unchaste women were more likely than were chaste women to consent to the acts giving rise to the charge, and therefore the evidence was probative of consent. These two uses of sexual history — often now referred to as the "twin myths" — and the discriminatory logic underlying them were so firmly embedded in Canadian law that it took specific legislative amendment in 1983 to remove them from the law. Even then, these amendments were subjected to a constitutional challenge in the *Seaboyer* (1991) case. While the Supreme Court of Canada also repudiated the laws on the "twin myths" of sexual history evidence in *Seaboyer*, the Court nonetheless left the door wide open to other uses of sexual history evidence.

The Seaboyer Case

In *R. v. Seaboyer* (1991) the Court struck down the 1983 *Criminal Code* amendment that restricted the admissibility of evidence on the complainant's sexual history to three circumstances: testimony by someone other than the defendant stating that it was he (and therefore not the defendant) who committed the acts in question; to give evidence of sexual activity on the same occasion to support a mistaken belief defence; or to rebut evidence adduced by the Crown on the complainant's sexual reputation (for example, she is a nun and therefore would not have consented). The Court now stated that the complainant's sexual history might be relevant and admissible in other, additional situations.

By way of illustration only, the Court gave these examples: to explain the complainant's physical condition; to prove bias or motive to fabricate; to establish similar fact conduct on the part of the complainant; and to support a mistaken belief defence. The Court predicted that it would be an exceptional case in which the evidence would be admitted and expressed confidence that judges were now free of the biases that characterized an earlier age. But the guidelines were so open-ended that they not only encouraged defence attempts to admit the evidence but also helped to ensure the success of such attempts.

The *Seaboyer* (1991) decision outraged people across Canada, and that outrage mobilized demands for Parliament to act (McIntyre 1994). Parliament responded with the 1992 amendments (Bill C-49), which stated in the preamble that a complainant's sexual history is rarely relevant and its admission should be subject to particular scrutiny, bearing in mind the inherently prejudicial character of such evidence. The Act makes it clear (again) that the evidence cannot be used to support the inference arising from the twin myths respecting character and consent. It also stated that the evidence had to be of specific instances of sexual behaviour, relevant to an issue at trial, and of significant probative value that was not substantially outweighed by the danger of its prejudicial effects. A special hearing (called a *voir dire*) on admissibility without the jury present must be held to determine whether the case is one of the rare cases in which the evidence should be permitted.

The Darrach Case

Defence lawyers immediately challenged the constitutionality of this amendment, asserting that it violated defendants' right to fully answer criminal charges. While the Supreme Court of Canada upheld the law in *R. v. Darrach* (2000), its analysis proved disappointing. The drafters of Bill C-49 had gone to lengths to ensure that judicial decisions on whether to admit sexual history evidence would consider the prejudicial effects of this evidence, including how it reinforced gendered inequalities. Yet the Court failed to refer to these parts of the Act, much less give them any meaning, or to encourage lower court judges to evaluate these factors. It also stated that in cases in which it was unclear whether the evidence should be admitted, the judge should admit the evidence.

Gotell's (2006) research on sexual history applications after *R. v. Darrach* (2000) reveals that lower court judges have taken their lead from the Supreme Court, because there is not a single case in which a lower court judge has seriously considered gendered inequality or the prejudicial effects of sexual history evidence. Her research also reveals that judges have permitted sexual history evidence in 53 percent of the cases in which defence counsel sought to have it admitted, belying the Court's prediction in *Seaboyer* that the evidence would only be admitted in exceptional cases.

Until 1983, it was not legally possible for a husband to be convicted of sexually assaulting his wife. Despite statutory restrictions on use of this evidence, defence lawyers continue to argue that sexual history must be admitted in the context of long-term relationships. While the law has been reformed, the stereotype remains; a partner who has consented to sexual acts in the past must have consented to the act in question. As one defence lawyer describes it, "consent is continuous and persisting in intimate relationships" (Lazar 2010: 340). Another defence lawyer in this study stated:

> In a domestic relationship … access to sexuality is a part of it and therefore of course an episode of sexuality has to be judged differentially than

people on a first date or strangers because it's part of their history that sexuality would be accessed. So for the prosecutors to complain that there is something unfair simply makes no sense. They want to treat each case as if there was no history between the parties, that's wrong — that's wrong in principle and that's wrong as a matter of *common sense*. (Lazar 2010: 343)

In *R. v. J.A.,* described earlier, the appeal court came to the conclusion that the complainant had consented to anal penetration while unconscious because of the complainant's prior participation in sadomasochistic sexual activities and an unresolved issue as to whether or not she had willingly participated in anal sex previously. The appeal court noted that:

The complainant acknowledged that the appellant had choked her in this way on prior occasions ... [S]he said they had engaged in the behaviour somewhere between three and ten times ... [T]he complainant confirmed that having her hands tied behind her back was not uncommon; the couple experimented with bondage on several prior occasions ... Concerning being penetrated in the anus with a dildo, the complainant said ... that was something new they were trying ... However, after being confronted with a portion of her evidence at the appellant's bail hearing, she adopted her prior testimony that anal penetration with a dildo had happened once before and confirmed that she consented. (*R. v. J.A.* 2010: para 12–19)

The appeal court's decision was overturned by the Supreme Court of Canada on the basis that an unconscious person could not consent to sexual activity. Sexual history evidence in *J.A.* was admitted without a *voir dire* on admissibility, yet no court hearing the *J.A.* case commented on the propriety of ignoring the *Criminal Code* dictate that a *voir dire* must be held. This is not uncommon for sexual assault cases involving prior BDSM between the parties. Since 1995, all but two BDSM sexual assault cases have had "evidence either [creep] in without a section 276 application (as in *J.A.*) or it was easily admitted when an application was made on the ground that its absence would render the defendant's evidence inherently improbable" (Busby 2012: 353).

While sexual history evidence is particularly pervasive in spousal assault and BDSM cases, these are not the only contexts in which it is admitted. In *R. v. Antonelli* (2011) the trial judge found a history of sexual *inactivity* admissible to allow the defence to argue that the complainant was more likely to have fabricated the allegations. The defence sought to establish that the complainant had a strong motivation to lie about consenting to sexual activity with a stranger because the complainant and her fiancé had chosen to remain abstinent prior to their wedding. The admittance was justified by reasoning that section 276 of the Criminal Code only applied to sexual activity, not sexual inactivity. The judge stated that while the prejudicial value of sexual activity must be considered before it is admitted, there is no prejudicial value to sexual inactivity. "Negative stereotyping about sexually active women is not an issue when the evidence to be adduced is of the complainant's sexual *inactivity*" (R. v. Antonelli 2011: para 13). The defence sought, and succeeded, to admit the evidence to create a new sexual assault myth: Women who were previously chaste are more likely to fabricate complaints.

Indirect Uses of Sexual History

In some situations, defence counsel does not need to solicit direct evidence on a complainant's sexual history, but rather can rely on stereotypes held by judges and juries about the credibility of certain "kinds" of women. In other words, what does information about a complainant's work, dress, motherhood or marital status, disability, attitude and demeanour, or abuse history suggest about her credibility?

In the *Rhodes* sentencing hearing, Justice Dewar minimized the defendant's assault of the complainant on the basis of her appearance, location and inebriation. Despite the complainant having blatantly rebuffed the defendant's advances, the trial judge concluded that "sex was in the air." By heavily relying on the complainant's appearance and behaviour in his decision for a conditional sentence, he fuelled a powerful sexual assault myth: women are at fault for sexual assaults. The inappropriately trivial sentence also reinforced the common misconception that some women are less worthy of protection under the law than others.

In *R. v. Ewanchuk* (1998: para 2), one appeal court judge stated, "It was a hot summer day and both [the complainant and the defendant] were wearing shorts and T-shirts. Underneath her shorts and T-shirt, the complainant wore a brassiere and panties." Later he sarcastically stated that the complainant did not present herself for the job interview offered to her by the defendant "in a bonnet and crinolines." Other wholly irrelevant details about the complainant's sexual life managed to find their way into the judgment, including the information that she was a seventeen-year-old mother of a six-month-old baby and shared an apartment with her boyfriend and another young couple. On appeal to the Supreme Court of Canada, the majority decision failed to examine the stereotypes and myths that influenced the appeal court judges.

As *Rhodes* and *Ewanchuk* illustrate, complainants often do not meet the judiciary's expectations of a "real" survivor of sexual assault (Randall 2010). Case law reveals that prosecutorial success depends in part upon whether or not the complainant fulfills the role of the "ideal victim" (Comack and Peter 2005). The role is a narrow one, as Melanie Randall (2010: 414) describes it:

"Ideal" or "real" victims of sexual assault, then, are not women who are assumed to be highly sexualized, such as prostitutes or so-called "promiscuous" women, are not women who are intoxicated or use drugs, are not women engaged in so-called "high risk" lifestyles, but, ironically, nor are they women who are "wives" of their attackers.

"Real victims" of sexual assault are those who the judiciary find to be blameless and worthy of legal protection. The legal system relies on a wide variety of character evidence to define the ideal victim. For example, judges often note that a complainant did not appear to be vindictive, which supposedly adds to the complainant's credibility (for example, *R. v. J.E.W.* (2013), in which the appeal court deemed the testimony of the complainant's mother to be corroborative because it was not vindictive or embellished, and *R. v. D.B.R.* (2004)). Implicit in such comments is that if complainants, or corroborative witnesses, fail to maintain an appropriate demeanour — a presentation fraught with gender, race, and class implications — under cross-examination, they may be perceived as vengeful.

In *R. v. Sanichar* (2012), the majority of an appellate court overturned the defendant's conviction because of the trial judge's inadequate examination of credibility in light of the historical nature of the abuse and the anger of the complainant. The sexual assaults occurred when the complainant was a young teen. The complainant had reported the abuse to the police, a Children's Aid Society worker and a school counsellor, and the defendant had faced prior charges for the assaults. After the abuse, as a young adult, the complainant wrote a letter to the defendant that the defence argued provided motive for fabrication of the complaints:

> The letter epitomizes the hatred the complainant bears towards [the accused] and that hatred provides the true motivation for what [the accused] argues are the false charges against him. While the letter does refer to some allegations of physical and sexual abuse, it is more or less venomous in other respects as well. (*R. v. Sanichar* 2012: 23)

In its decision, the Court alluded to the letter and how the complainant's dislike for the defendant may have been reason to fabricate the complaints. Without a better determination of the complainant's credibility, the Court could not be satisfied beyond a reasonable doubt because, "[Evidence] may become contaminated. Life experiences can colour and distort the memory of what occurred." The Court held that the trial judge should have addressed "the worry that the simple vicissitudes and influences of life over a long period can have an impact on such things as motive and reliability," and that "the complainant's detailed memory of things that happened to her in the distant past might be a by-product of the influence of the complainant's life experiences on her memory" (*R. v. Sanichar* 2012: para 38–43). The complainant was too vindictive and distressed with the defendant to fit the role of the "ideal victim." While the appeal court's decision was overturned by the Supreme Court of Canada (in 2013), the decision is still evidence of the pervasive judicial attitude towards victim demeanour. Vengeance as evidence of fabrication is also frequently used in sexual assaults of women with disabilities.

The infantilization of women with mental disabilities also plays a detrimental role in credibility determinations. Descriptions of women with mental disabilities as childlike are commonplace in the courtroom (Benedet and Grant 2007). In *R. v. D.A.I.*, for example, the court described the twenty-three-year-old complainant as having the mental capacities of a three- to six-year-old.

The comparison of disabled women to children is further supported by section 16 of the Canada Evidence Act (1985), which provides the same rules of admissibility for individuals with mental disabilities and individuals under fourteen whose competency to testify has been challenged. By infantilizing women, courts ignore the differences in development between children and disabled individuals. While it may be appropriate to protect young children from sexuality, preferring them to be sheltered and asexual, it is not appropriate to expect the same from women with disabilities. For example, Benedet and Grant (2013) note that it would be entirely acceptable for a nineteen-year-old female to discuss sexuality with her peers, while it would not be acceptable for a six-year-old to do the same. The issue in these descriptions is that women with mental disabilities are more often than not equated with the six-year-old. When a disabled woman is likened to a child but does not meet the sexual expectations of a child, she is labelled as "too friendly" or "hypersexual" and, as a result, is blamed for tempting the defendant and bringing the assault upon herself. Any prior sexual activity is labelled as "inappropriate" and "can be used to question the complainant's behaviour during the encounter at issue, to question whether she consented to sexual activity, and to question whether the defendant knew she was not consenting" (Benedet and Grant 2007: 522).

Following the passage of Bill C-49 in 1992 and increasingly after the *Darrach* case of 2000, defence counsel have been seeking evidence of prior sexual abuse in order to back up some highly questionable inferences. Sometimes the evidence is used to show that, because the complainant has been proven in a criminal court to have been abused, she has a disordered sexual perception that could lead to misinterpretations, overreactions and false criminal accusations. Alternatively, the defence seeks such evidence to be entered to show that the complainant has made allegations of prior abuse that did not result in a criminal conviction. According to this faulty inference, the absence of a conviction regarding these allegations indicates her tendency to lie. Thus, argues defence counsel, any evidence of the prior sexual abuse should be used to compromise a complainant's credibility. Moreover, defence counsel assert — and judges accept — that evidence of prior sexual abuse is not being used to question the sexual morality of the complainant, but rather more generally to show why her general credibility is compromised.

In the case of *J.T.* (2010), for example, the trial court allowed cross-examination of witnesses on the topic of past sexual abuses to determine whether the corroborative memories and accusations of two of the six sibling complainants against a family acquaintance were reliable — or — whether the two siblings had simply transferred memories of their father's abuse onto the accused. For one of the complainants, the court justified this examination because she "described certain sexual assaults by her father that are strikingly similar to her recollection of sexual acts Mr. T. has allegedly committed ... As a result, there is an issue as to whether S.G.'s memory of the of [sic] events involving her father and Mr. T. may be conflated or commingled or perhaps transferred from her father to Mr. T." (*R. v. J.T.* 2010: para 8). For the other complainant, the court relied on the fact that the sexual abuse of the complainant's father and J.T. had temporally overlapped, which "increases the potential for there to be conflated or commingled memories or even transferred memories" (para 9). When judges accept these arguments, as they often do, the procedural protections of Bill C-49 (notably the special hearing to determine the admissibility of sexual history evidence) are not applicable because the evidence is not sexual history evidence.

As we have seen in the case of character evidence and similar fact evidence, courts exclude evidence that could lead to improper inferences when its probative value is low. Ironically, most people in Canada believe that a complainant cannot be questioned about her sexual history — and they celebrate this legal breakthrough. Yet, notwithstanding Parliament's clear intent that sexual history evidence should only be used rarely because it is not relevant and it supports improper inferences — and the Supreme Court of Canada's prediction that this would be the case — such evidence is frequently used in one way or another in sexual violence proceedings. In light of the heavy burden placed on the Crown (proof beyond a reasonable doubt), defence lawyers' direct and indirect uses of sexual history evidence remain a powerful tool to undermine the credibility of the Crown's chief (and, often, only) witness — the complainant.

Access to Personal Records

Despite Bill C-49's limited effectiveness, most defence lawyers were of the view that Bill C-49 went too far in restricting their ability to represent clients in sexual assault trials (Meredith, Mohr, and Cairns Way 1997). They lost little time in developing a tactic to counter the Bill: if they could not intimidate or undermine complainants by dragging their sexual lives into court, they would seek access to any personal records about a complainant that might contain other embarrassing or discrediting information, on the ground that defendants' constitutional right to make a full answer and provide a full defence to a criminal charge justified such access.

Access to personal records was almost unheard of before 1992, but by the late 1990s defence lawyers were routinely seeking access to sexual assault counselling records and child welfare records. Indeed, it seems as though every imaginable personal record has been the object of a defence application. Defendants have sought access not only to counselling, therapy and psychiatric records but also to records from abortion and birth control clinics, child welfare agencies, adoption agencies, residential and public schools, drug and alcohol abuse recovery centres, other doctors, employers, the military, psychiatric hospitals, victim/witness assistance programs, criminal injuries compensation boards, prisons and youth detention centres, social welfare agencies, immigration offices, the Crown on unrelated charges against the complainant, and criminal and young offender records, as well as personal diaries and reporters' notes (Busby 1997).

As Elizabeth Comack and Tracey Peter (2005) have vividly demonstrated, a complainant must be reasonable, responsible and rational, and she must maintain this status over time, even in the face of the incredible trauma that can arise from all the events giving rise to the charge or as a consequence of the charge (such as estrangement from family and overwhelming fear). If psychiatric and other records describing her actions (such as fleeing, attempts at suicide, self-blame or recantation) either before or after the events and the charges indicate that she is not "normal," she becomes unreasonable, irresponsible and irrational and therefore discreditable as a witness. Given that few sexual violence survivors can unfailingly appear to be normal, personal records have become a gold mine for defence counsel seeking any information to discredit a complainant.

The O'Connor Case

In 1995 the Supreme Court of Canada (by a bare majority of five judges) issued the infamous R. v. O'Connor decision, which raised personal records access to the status of a defendant's constitutional right to a fair trial. (In contrast, a minority of four judges held that records could be obtained in "the rarest of cases.") Many defence lawyers believe that the standard practice post-O'Connor should be to seek every possible record on a complainant in all sexual violence cases.

O'Connor was charged in the late 1980s with having committed various sexual offences in the early 1960s against four Indigenous women in their late teens. At the time of the offences, the women were students or recent graduates employed at the residential school where O'Connor was priest, teacher and principal. O'Connor's defence was that two of the women had consented to have sex with him and that nothing had happened between him and the two others.

A judge ordered the women to authorize the release to O'Connor of their entire residential school records (academic, medical and employment) and all therapy and medical records since the time they had left the school. None of these records were in the Crown's possession, and as the records covered a period of twenty to thirty years and some of the records had been destroyed, compliance with the order proved difficult. Consequently, O'Connor applied to have the proceedings stayed, and ultimately the trial judge ordered the proceeding stayed for failure to produce. The stay was appealed to the Supreme Court of Canada. While the Court overturned the stay, it gave exceptionally large scope to defence access to complainants' personal records held by third parties.

The majority decision in *R. v. O'Connor* (1995) paid lip service to notions of protecting a complainant's privacy "interests," but unlike the minority decision, it utterly failed to comprehend that the production of personal records was the latest manifestation of laws that reflect and perpetuate women's and children's inequality. For example, the judges accepted — without comment on this double standard — that records are sought in sexual violence cases, but not others. They failed to note that the Court has been quick to protect against access to the records of a witness in other criminal cases, yet that in sexual violence cases it has been satisfied with baseless and prejudicial rationales for access to records. The Court also failed to notice that the practice — which it has now elevated to a constitutional right — was then barely three years old and an obvious backlash to Bill C-49. The judges disregarded something that had been frankly admitted by defence counsel in other settings: that the production orders were sought not for information that would be relevant to the criminal proceedings but, rather, with the intent to intimidate complainants into refusing to continue to participate in the process (Kelly 1997; Feldthusen 1996).

Perhaps most egregiously, the Court simply ignored that what O'Connor was seeking were residential school records. Thus, it avoided having to consider whether records created in a system designed to destroy Indigenous cultures have any place in an attempt to discredit the very people subjected to that system. The Court refused to consider how records applications would have a disproportionate impact on women who have been subject to extensive record-keeping in contexts characterized by multiple inequalities, such as prisons, psychiatric hospitals or the child welfare system. They also avoided having to consider whether records written by the defendant himself (as the residential school records almost certainly were in *O'Connor*) are inherently unreliable. They paid little attention to the effects of the release of records on counselling relationships or the willingness of complainants to report sexual violence crimes to the police.

Every one of these issues was squarely before the Court based on the facts of the *O'Connor* (1995) case, and various interveners fully argued for constitutional equality rights. Yet the majority of members of the Court failed to deal with these issues. They do not even mention the equality rights section of the Charter. In contrast, the Court did refer to the newest rape mythologies — the beliefs that women falsely conjure up sexual abuse histories and then lay charges against innocent men and that counsellors use therapy to improperly influence complainants' memories — even though there was no evidence before the Court on such influences and none of the prosecutions in *O'Connor* involved recovered memories. Law's Official Version decides when and to whom it will be accountable; and judges ignore constitutional equality rights simply because they choose to do so, even when these rights plainly arise on the face of the case.

Bill C-46

Well in advance of the Court's *O'Connor* ruling, feminist organizations had been attempting to deal with the crisis experienced by complainants and record-keepers as a result of defendants' burgeoning demands for records disclosure. One strategy adopted by some record-keepers, particularly sexual assault counsellors, was to alter note-taking practices (remembering always that the defendant himself might read the record) and revise record retention policies. Another strategy was to engage in consultations with the federal Department of Justice to develop legislation to end the practice, a process that began months before the *O'Connor* decision was released.

By Bill C-46 (passed in 1997), Parliament required judges to take into account the issue on which the Supreme Court of Canada maintained a deafening silence in *O'Connor*: a reconciliation and accommodation of women's constitutional equality rights with the defendant's right to a fair trial. This law states that records cannot even be considered for release if the defence cannot establish that they are "likely relevant," and Parliament sets out examples of rationales that would *not* meet this test, including the fact of the person in question having seen a counsellor or the possibility that the record may contain information about the acts giving rise to the charge. Even records that cross the likely relevance threshold cannot be released either to the judge or to the defendant unless that judge has weighed a number of factors, including effects on counselling relationships or the potential for biases to operate. Complainants and record-holders have the right to be represented by counsel at the hearing of these applications, and some provinces have programs to ensure that lawyers will be made available to complainants who cannot afford to pay for them. While Bill C-46 did not prohibit all records production applications, it was written to significantly limit circumstances in which personal records can be released to a judge and to lead to even fewer cases in which they will be ordered released to defendants.

Within months of its passage, the Bill C-46 amendment was subject to numerous constitutional challenges. In *R. v. Mills* (1999) the Supreme Court of Canada upheld the constitutionality of the Act while at the same time watering down its most important features. The Court refused to interpret the Act as categorically prohibiting access to records based on discredited rationales and, instead, stated that the mere assertion of the rationale (such as, the complainant has seen a counsellor) was not enough to access the record unless there was some evidence to support that assertion. As well, as it did in *R. v. Darrach* (2000) regarding Bill C-49, the Court gave lip service to the requirement that women's equality and privacy rights should be balanced against the defendant's right to a fair trial, but gave no meaningful content to this balancing act. It stated that if there was any doubt, that doubt should be resolved in favour of producing the records.

Renate Mohr's study based on interviews with judges, defence counsel and Crown attorneys revealed that most respondents had never heard anyone making an equality-based argument in either a sexual history or a personal records case (Mohr 2002, cited in Gotell 2006). As in the case of applications to examine sexual history, trial judges are not engaging with any significant evaluation of complainants' equality rights. Therefore, perhaps not surprisingly given the resistance to equality-based arguments and the requirement that production is warranted if the judge is in doubt, defendants are gaining access to complainants' records in a significant number of cases. One study (Gotell 2006) found that these applications are successful 47 percent of the time.

In 2012, the Standing Senate Committee on Legal and Constitutional Affairs (2012) reported on the effectiveness of Bill C-46. The Committee found that inappropriate uses of record evidence placed complainants at a greater risk for re-victimization through the criminal justice system and reduced the likelihood that women who faced psycho-social or medical barriers would report sexual assault. The report contained eighteen recommendations to reduce the harms that flow from record admittance in sexual assault cases. The recommendations shed light on the injustices that still operate after Bill C-46. Recommendations which may help to eliminate these harms include Recommendation 9, that the complainant's right to personal security be considered by judges in the decision to admit records, and Recommendation 13, that judges inform the complainant of her right to independent counsel when there is an application for the admittance of third party records.

THE VICTIMIZATION CONTINUES

Despite the Official Version of Law's claim to be "an impartial, neutral and objective system for resolving social conflict" (Naffine 1990: 24), the combined effect of the legal principles applicable to all criminal cases and the specific rules applicable only to sexual violence cases makes it very difficult to obtain a conviction in sexual assault cases. Moreover, the pre-trial proceedings and the trial itself are ordeals for complainants. The trial process does little to affirm women's stories of male violence or to call into question the larger social forces that sustain a rape culture.

When complainants do come forward, they become powerless in a legal system that judges and categorizes them as the "ideal victim," the "vengeful wife," the "unchaste," the "consenting child" and the "desperate asexual woman." Women of all ages, sexual experiences and disabilities are blamed for their assaults. Where a woman was promiscuous she was enticing, where she was chaste she must be lying, where she was just a child she was sophisticated, where she is mentally disabled she was desperate for attention, and where she was a wife she was consenting. Despite years of legislative reform designed to change judicial interpretations of sexual assault, women and children continue to be victimized — by both the assault and the system.

A POSTSCRIPT ON RHODES

Kenneth Rhodes was retried in the spring of 2013. In a pre-trial motion, Rhodes opposed the admissibility of the statements he made to the police. After a four-day-long *voir dire*, the Manitoba Court of Queen's Bench admitted these statements. Once the trial began it was obvious why Rhodes had opposed admissibility. Seven years had passed since the assault occurred and between the police statements, the original trial and the new trial, Rhodes had defended himself in four different ways: (1) no sexual contact occurred; (2) some consensual contact occurred; (3) sexual contact occurred of the nature alleged but he had a mistaken belief in consent; and (4) all sexual contact that occurred on the night in question was consensual. While his story had changed significantly through time, the complainant's evidence remained almost identical. In her July 2013 judgment, Justice Spivak strictly followed the analysis set out in *W.(D.)* and, on considering the totality of both parties' evidence, held that there was no reasonable doubt as to Rhodes' guilt. In October 2013 Rhodes was sentenced to three years in prison.

Note

I am grateful for the excellent research assistance of Miranda Grayson, as well as the many students who have given me feedback on earlier versions of this chapter. While I was a member of the LEAF brief writing team for many of the Supreme Court of Canada cases noted in this chapter, the views in this chapter should not be attributed to LEAF. I also acknowledge the financial support of the University of Manitoba Legal Research Institute and the Centre for Human Rights Research.

References

Backhouse, Constance. 2008. *Carnal Crimes: Sexual Assault Law in Canada, 1900–1975.* Toronto: Irwin Law.

Balfour, Gillian, and Elizabeth Comack (eds.). 2006. *Criminalizing Women: Gender and (In) justice in Neo-liberal Times.* Halifax, NS: Fernwood Publishing.

Balfour, Gillian, and Janice Du Mont. 2012. "Legal and Rape Narratives in Conditional Sentencing." In Elizabeth A. Sheehy (ed.), *Sexual Assault in Canada: Law, Legal Practice and Women's Activism*. Ottawa: University of Ottawa Press.

Benedet, Janine, and Isabel Grant. 2007. "Hearing the Sexual Assault Complaints of Women with Disabilities: Evidentiary and Procedural Issues." *McGill Law Journal* 52, 3.

____. 2013. "More Than an Empty Gesture: Enabling Women with Disabilities to Testify on a Promise to Tell the Truth." *Canadian Journal of Women and the Law* 25, 1.

Bienen, Leigh. 1983. "A Question of Credibility: John Henry Wigmore's Use of Scientific Authority." *California Western Law Review* 19.

Busby, Karen. 1997. "Discriminatory Uses of Personal Records in Sexual Violence Cases." *Canadian Journal of Women and the Law/Revue "Femme et Droit"* 9.

____. 2012. "Every Breath You Take: Erotic Asphyxiation, Vengeful Wives, and Other Enduring Myths in Spousal Sexual Assault Prosecutions." *Canadian Journal of Women and the Law* 24, 2.

CBC News Nova Scotia. April 9, 2013. "Rape, Bullying Led to N.S. Teen's Death, Says Mom." <cbc.ca/news/canada/nova-scotia/story/2013/04/09/ns-rehtaeh-parsons-suicide-rape.html>.

Comack, Elizabeth. 2014. "Theoretical Excursions." In Elizabeth Comack (ed.), *Locating Law: Race, Class, Gender and Sexuality Connections*, third edition. Halifax, NS: Fernwood Publishing.

Comack, Elizabeth, and Gillian Balfour. 2004. *The Power to Criminalize: Violence, Inequality and the Law*. Halifax, NS: Fernwood Publishing.

Comack, Elizabeth, and Tracey Peter. 2005. "How the Criminal Justice System Responds to Sexual Assault Survivors: The Slippage Between 'Responsibilization' and 'Blaming the Victim.'" *Canadian Journal of Women and the Law* 17, 2.

Feldthusen, Bruce. 1996. "The Best Defence Is a Good Offence: Access to the Private Therapeutic Records of Sexual Assault Complainants under the *O'Connor* Guidelines and Bill C-46." *Canadian Bar Review* 75.

Gotell, Lise. 2006. "The Discursive Disappearance of Sexualized Violence: Feminist Law Reform, Judicial Resistance and Neo-liberal Sexual Citizenship." In Dorothy E. Chunn, Susan B. Boyd, and Hester Lessard (eds.), *Reaction and Resistance: Feminism, Law and Social Change*. Vancouver: UBC Press.

Kelly, Katharine. 1997. "'You Must Be Crazy If You Think You Were Raped': Reflections on the Use of Complainants' Personal and Therapy Records in Sexual Assault Trials." *Canadian Journal of Women and the Law* 9, 1.

L'Heureux-Dubé, Claire. 2012. "Still Punished for Being Female." In Elizabeth A. Sheehy (ed.), *Sexual Assault in Canada: Law, Legal Practice and Women's Activism*. Ottawa: University of Ottawa Press.

Lazar, Ruthy. 2010. "Negotiating Sex: The Legal Construct of Consent in Cases of Wife Rape in Ontario, Canada." *Canadian Journal of Women and the Law* 22, 2.

Lös, Maria. 1994. "The Struggle to Redefine Rape in the Early 1980s." In Renate M. Mohr and Julian V. Roberts (eds.), *Confronting Sexual Assault: A Decade of Legal and Social Change*. Toronto: University of Toronto Press.

McGillivray, Anne. 1998. "*R. v. Bauder*: Seductive Children, Safe Rapists, and Other Justice Tales." *Manitoba Law Journal* 25.

McIntyre, Sheila. 1994. "Redefining Reformism: The Consultations that Shaped Bill C-49." In Renate M. Mohr and Julian V. Roberts (eds.), *Confronting Sexual Assault: A Decade of Legal and Social Change*. Toronto: University of Toronto Press.

Meredith, Colin, Renate Mohr, and Rosemary Cairns Way. 1997. "Implementation Review of Bill C-49." *TR1997-1e*. Ottawa: Department of Justice, February.

Naffine, Ngaire. 1990. *The Law and the Sexes: Explorations in Feminist Jurisprudence*. London: Allen and Unwin.

Perreault, Samuel, and Shannon Brennan. 2009. "Criminal Victimization in Canada, 2009." *Juristat* 30, 2.

Public Prosecution Service of Canada. 2013. "About the Public Prosecution Service of Canada." <ppsc-sppc.gc.ca/eng/bas/index.html>.

Randall, Melanie. 2010. "Sexual Assault Law, Credibility, and 'Ideal Victims': Consent, Resistance, and Victim Blaming." *Canadian Journal of Women and the Law* 22, 2.

Ruparelia, Rakhi. 2012. "All That Glitters Is Not Gold: The False Promise of Victim Impact Statements." In Elizabeth A. Sheehy (ed.), *Sexual Assault in Canada: Law, Legal Practice and Women's Activism*. Ottawa: University of Ottawa Press.

Sinha, Maire (ed.). 2013. *Measuring Violence Against Women: Statistical Trends*. Ottawa: Statistics Canada. <statcan.gc.ca/pub/85-002-x/2013001/article/11766-eng.pdf>.

Smart, Carol. 1989. *Feminism and the Power of Law*. London, Routledge.

Standing Senate Committee on Legal and Constitutional Affairs. 2012. "Statutory Review on the Provisions and Operation of the *Act* to amend the *Criminal Code* (production of records in sexual offence proceedings)." Ottawa.

Statistics Canada. 2005. "General Social Survey: Criminal Victimization (2004)." *The Daily* (November 24). <statcan.gc.ca/daily-quotidien/051124/dq051124b-eng.htm>.

____. 2010. "General Social Survey: Self-reported Victimization, by Type of Offence and Province, 2009." <statcan.gc.ca/pub/85-002-x/2010002/article/11340/tbl/tbl2-eng.htm#n1>.

____. 2011a. "Police-reported Crime for Selected Offences, 2009 and 2010." <statcan.gc.ca/pub/85-002-x/2011001/article/11523/tbl/tbl04-eng.htm#n2>.

____. 2011b. "General Social Survey: Time Use." *The Daily* (July 12). <statcan.gc.ca/daily-quotidien/110712/dq110712b-eng.htm>.

____. 2012. "Court, Adult Cases by Type of Sentence, Total Guilty Cases, by Province and Territory, 2010/2011."<statcan.gc.ca/tables-tableaux/sum-som/l01/cst01/legal22a-eng.htm>.

Vandervort, Lucinda. 2012. "Lawful Subversion of the Criminal Justice Process? Judicial, Prosecutorial, and Police Discretion in *Edmondson, Kindrat*, and *Brown*." In Elizabeth A. Sheehy (ed.), *Sexual Assault in Canada: Law, Legal Practice and Women's Activism*. Ottawa: University of Ottawa Press.

Wigmore, John. 1970. *Evidence in Trials at Common Law* (revised edition). (Ed. J.C. Chadbourne). Boston: Little Brown and Co.

Legislation
Canada Evidence Act, RSC 1985, c C-5
Criminal Code of Canada, RSC 1985, c C-46

Legal Cases

R. v. Antonelli, [2011] 280 CCC (3d) 96 (Sup. Ct.)

R. v. Arcand, [2010] 264 CCC (3d) 134 (CA)

R. v. B.B. [2011] 97 WCB (2d) 579 (Prov. Ct.)

R. v. Bauder (1997), MbJ (Q/L) No. 270 (CA)

R. v. Burke, [1996] 1 SCR 474

R. v. C.(M.H.), [1991] 1 SCR 763

R. v. Carosella, [1997] 1 SCR 80

R. v. Chase, [1984] 55 NBR (2d) 97 (C.A.), reversed (1987), 37 CCC (3d) 97 (SCC)

R. v. Crampton, [2004] 188 OAC 357

R. v. D.A.I. [2012] 1 SCR 149

R. v. D.B.R. [2004] 182 Man.R. (2d) 189 (QB)

R. v. D.D. [2000] 2 SCR 275

R. v. Darrach, [2000] 2 SCR 443

R. v. Ewanchuk, [1999] 1 SCR 330 reversing (1998) 57 AR 235

R. v. F.(D.S.), [1999] 43 OR (3d) 609 (CA)

R. v. F.C. [2012] OSC.J 6934 (CanLII)

R. v. Finley, [1998] OJ (Q/L) No. 974 (Ct. of Jus.)

R. v. Gibson 2012 ONSC 900 (CAN.LII)

R. v. Handy, [2002] 2 SCR 908

R. v. J.A. [2008] OJ (Q/L) No. 4814 (Ct. of Jus.), overturned [2010], 260 O.A.C. 248, trial
    decision affirmed [2011], 2 SCR 440

R. v. J.E.W. [2013] NSJ (Q/L) No. 76 (CA)

R. v. J.T. [2010] O.J. (Q/L) No. 4007 (Sup. Ct. of Jus.)

R. v. K.C. [2005] 65 W.C.B. (2d) 425 (Ct. of Jus.)

R. v. Last, [2008] 268 OAC 289

R. v. Mills, [1999] 3 SCR 668

R. v. N.S. [2012] 290 CCC (3d) 404 (SCC); (Factum of Intervener, Women's Legal
    Education and Action Fund);

R. v. O'Connor, [1995] 4 SCR 411

R. v. O'Connor, 1998. BCJ (Q/L) No. 649 (C.A.)

R. v. P.A.A. [2012]NLCA 40 (CanLII)

R. v. P.S. [2007] 223 OAC 293

R. v. R.C.H. [2012] 276 Man.R. (2d) 242 (QB)

R. v. R.G.B. [2012] MJ (Q/L) No. 17 (CA)

R. v. Rhodes, [2010], Man.CR08-15-00316(QB); [2011], MJ (Q/L) No. 67 (QB)
    (Sentencing Transcript), overturned [2011], 281 CCC (3d) 29 (CA), retried 2013
    MBQB 166 (CanLII), sentencing 2013 MBQB 251

R. v. S.G.T. [2010] 1 SCR 688

R. v. Sanichar, [2012]288 OAC 164, reversed [2013], 300 OAC 281 (SCC)

R. v. Sansregret, [1985] 1 SCR 570

R. v. Seaboyer, [1991] 2 SCR 577

R. v. Shearing, [2002] 3 SCR 33

R. v. Stender, [2004] 72 OR (3rd series) 223 (CA), affirmed (2005) 1 SCR 914

R. v. Turcotte, [2005] 2 SCR 519

R. v. W.(D.), [1991] SCR 742

R. v. Wheeler 2013 NLCA 36 (CAN.LII)

R. v. Woldemichael, [2011] OJ (Q/L) No. 6555 (Ct. of Jus.)

Chapter 14

A SELECTED HISTORY OF SEXUAL ASSAULT LEGISLATION IN CANADA, 1892–1983

Compiled by Constance Backhouse

From: *Gendered Intersections: An Introduction to Women's and Gender Studies,* second edition, pp. 293–295 (reprinted with permission).

In 1983, the Criminal Code was amended to replace rape and indecent assault with three types of sexual assault (levels one to three) in order to encourage victims to report sexual assaults to the police. In this new legislation, as a way of destigmatizing the crime, sexual assault was reconceptualized as a violent offence, so that the degree of physical violence, rather than its sexual nature, was taken into account. In addition, the legislation specified that victims of sexual assault could be both male and female, and that a spouse could be charged with sexual assault. During the first decade of the legislation, rates of reporting for level 1 sexual assault (the least level of violence) almost doubled, but from 1993 to 2007, they steadily declined; the rates for levels 2 and 3 sexual assault remained steady (Brennan and Butts 2008).

Getting a handle on statistics about sexual assault is notoriously difficult since most victims regard sexual assault as "a private matter" (Brennan and Butts 2008: 7). The *General Social Survey on Victimization* (2004) (GSS) shows that only one in ten victims report a sexual assault to the police, usually for levels 2 and 3. Based on 2004 GSS data, there were 1,977 incidents of sexual assault per 100,000; the vast majority of victims over the age of fifteen were women (3,248/100,000 as compared to 664/100,000 for men (Brennan and Butts 2008: 6). Despite widespread public awareness and almost four decades of activism by women's groups, sexual assault is still a major issue for women, children and some men.

Most of us don't know anything about the law governing sexual assault, until we unfortunately need to know. In connection with my book, *Carnal Crimes: Sexual Assault Law in Canada, 1900–1975* (2008), I have compiled selected statutes to help summarize the laws for the past century and subsequent amendments. What will strike you, as the reader, are the changes in language, the definitions of rape/sexual assault, the type of punishments and the length of prison terms. These changes represent alterations in attitudes toward women, patriarchal values and an understanding of women's rights in Canadian society. The questions that you have to ask yourself are "Is it enough?" and, if not, "What will it take so that women, children and men can live freely without the fear of sexual assault?"

A SELECTED HISTORY OF SEXUAL ASSAULT LEGISLATION IN CANADA, 1892–1983

The Criminal Code, 1892, S.C. 1892, c. 29, s. 266.

[Rape defined.]

266. Rape is the act of a man having carnal knowledge of a woman who is not his wife without her consent, or with consent which has been extorted by threats or fear of bodily harm, or obtained by personating the woman's husband, or by false and fraudulent representations as to the nature and quality of the act.

2. No one under the age of fourteen years can commit this offence.

3 Carnal knowledge is complete upon penetration to any, even the slightest degree, and even without the emission of seed. R.S.C., c. 174, s. 226.

[Punishment for rape.]

267. Every one who commits rape is guilty of an indictable offence and liable to suffer death, or imprisonment for life. R.S.C., c. 162, s. 37.

[Attempt to commit rape.]

268. Every one is guilty of an indictable offence and liable to seven years' imprisonment who attempts to commit rape.

An Act to amend the Criminal Code, S.C. 1919–1920, c. 43, s. 7.

[Penalty of whipping added.]

300. Every one is guilty of an indictable offence, and liable to seven years' imprisonment and to be whipped, who attempts to commit rape.

An Act to amend the Criminal Code, S.C. 1921, c. 25, s. 4.

[Punishment for rape.]
299. Every one who commits rape is guilty of an indictable offence and liable to suffer death or to imprisonment for life and to be whipped. 55-56 V., c. 29, s. 267.

Criminal Code, S.C. 1953–54, c. 51, s. 135.

[Rape.]
135. A male person commits rape when he has sexual intercourse with a female person who is not his wife,
    (a) without her consent, or
    (b) with her consent if the consent
      (i) is extorted by threats or fear of bodily harm
      (ii) is obtained by personating her husband, or
      (iii) is obtained by false and fraudulent representations as to the nature and quality of the act.

[Punishment for rape.]
136. Every one who commits rape is guilty of an indictable offence and is liable to imprisonment for life and to be whipped.

[Attempt to commit rape.]
137. Every one who attempts to commit rape is guilty of an indictable offence and is liable to imprisonment for ten years and to be whipped.

An Act to amend the Criminal Code in relation to sexual offences and other offences against the person and to amend certain other Acts in relation thereto or in consequence thereof, S.C. 1980-81-82-83, c. 125, s. 19.

[Assault]
244. (1) A person commits an assault when
    (a) without the consent of another person, he applies force intentionally to that other person, directly or indirectly;
    (b) he attempts or threatens, by an act or gesture, to apply force to another person, if he has, or causes that other person to believe upon reasonable grounds that he has, present ability to effect his purpose; or
    (c) while openly wearing or carrying a weapon or an imitation thereof, he accosts or impedes another person or begs.

[Application]
(2) This section applies to all forms of assault, including sexual assault, sexual assault with a weapon, threats to a third party or causing bodily harm and aggravated sexual assault.

[Consent]
(3) For the purposes of this section, no consent is obtained where the complainant submits or does not resist by reason of
(a) the application of force to the complainant or to a person other than the complainant;
(b) threats or fear of the application of force to the complainant or to a person other than the complainant;
(c) fraud; or
(d) the exercise of authority.

[Accused's belief as to consent]
(4) Where an accused alleges that he believed that the complainant consented to the conduct that is the subject-matter of the charge, a judge, if satisfied that there is sufficient evidence and that, if believed by the jury, the evidence would constitute a defence, shall instruct the jury, when reviewing all the evidence relating to the determination of the honesty of the accused's belief, to consider the presence or absence of reasonable grounds for that belief.

[Sexual assault]
246.1 (1) Every one who commits a sexual assault is guilty of
(a) an indictable offence and is liable to imprisonment for ten years; or
(b) an offence punishable on summary conviction.
[No defence]
(2) Where an accused is charged with an offence under subsection (1) or section 246.2 or 246.3 in respect of a person under the age of fourteen years, it is not a defence that the complainant consented to the activity that forms the subject-matter of the charge unless the accused is less than three years older than the complainant.

[Sexual assault with a weapon, threats to a third party or causing bodily harm]
246.2 Every one who, in committing a sexual assault,
(a) carries, uses or threatens to use a weapon or an imitation thereof,
(b) threatens to cause bodily harm to a person other than the complainant,
(c) causes bodily harm to the complainant, or
(d) is a party to the offence with any other person,
is guilty of an indictable offence and is liable to imprisonment for fourteen years.

[Aggravated sexual assault]

246.3 (1) Every one commits an aggravated sexual assault who, in committing a sexual assault, wounds, maims, disfigures or endangers the life of the complainant.

[Punishment]

(2) Every one who commits an aggravated sexual assault is guilty of an indictable offence and is liable to imprisonment for life.

Note

This compilation represents a selection of legislation governing rape and sexual assault. A complete history and more detail is at: <constancebackhouse.ca/fileadmin/website/index.htm>.

References

Backhouse, Constance. 2008. *Carnal Crimes: Sexual Assault Law in Canada, 1900–1975*. Toronto: Irwin Law.

Brennan, Shannon, and Andrea Taylor-Butts. 2008. *Sexual Assault in Canada: 2004 and 2007*. Ottawa: Canadian Centre for Justice Statistics, Statistics Canada. Ministry of Industry (Catalogue no. 85F0033M — No. 19).

TRANS

Chapter 15

COMPETING CLAIMS FROM DISADVANTAGED GROUPS

Nixon v. Vancouver Rape Relief Society

Joanna Harris

From: *Gendered Intersections: An Introduction to Women's and Gender Studies, 2nd edition*, pp. 462–466. Originally published in: Trans/forming Feminisms: Trans/Feminist Voices Speak Out, 2006, Krista Scott-Dixon (ed.), Toronto: Sumach Press (adapted and reprinted with permission).

The complex relationship between trans rights and women's substantive equality is exemplified by the case of *Nixon v. Vancouver Rape Relief Society* (hereafter referred to as *Nixon*) — a clear example of the dilemma caused when two concepts come into conflict.

ANTI-DISCRIMINATION LAW IN CANADA

In Canada, discrimination is addressed using various legal instruments: the *Charter of Rights and Freedoms* (part of Canada's Constitution) and federal, provincial or territorial human rights codes.[1]

Under the Charter, specifically section 15, a mere distinction drawn between two people does not in itself constitute discrimination. The distinction must be based on a specified or analogous ground; the grounds specified in the Charter are race, national or ethnic origin, colour, religion, sex, age and mental or physical disability. Analogous grounds have also been held to include, for example, sexual orientation. In subsequent case law, the Supreme Court of Canada established another overarching principle, namely, the prevention of violations of human dignity: they established a three-part test in order to determine whether discrimination occurred (*Law v. Canada* [*Minister of Employment and Immigration*] 1999, hereafter referred to as *Law v. Canada* or *Law*). The Court first considers if there is a formal distinction drawn, based on personal characteristics; second, if the law or action on the part of the government fails to take into account the claimant's already disadvantaged position within Canada based on an enumerated or analogous ground; and third, if this differential treatment discriminates in a substantive sense, which would defy the purpose of remedying prejudice, stereotyping and historical disadvantage.

The final step helps the Court consider whether a claimant's dignity has been infringed. Mr. Justice Frank Iacobucci, in the significant 1999 decision *Law v. Canada*, defines human dignity in the context of section 15:

> Human dignity means that an individual or group feels self-respect and self-worth. It is concerned with physical and psychological integrity and empowerment. Human dignity is harmed by unfair treatment and premised upon personal traits or circumstances which do not relate to individual needs, capacities or merits. (*Law v. Canada* 1999: 53)

In contrast to the *Charter* provisions, a finding of discrimination in the federal, provincial and territorial human rights legislation has not, at least historically, depended upon infringement of human dignity. While the human rights codes refer generally, by way of their preambles or statement of objectives, to the concept of preservation of human dignity (Tarnopolsky 2001: 4-100.3), the legal analysis has been analytically distinct from that laid out by Justice Iacobucci in the *Law* decision. The relevant test for a finding of discrimination in Canadian human rights codes was decided in the *Meiorin* decision (*British Columbia* [*Public Service Employee Relations Commission*] *v. B.C.G.E.U* 1997): when a distinction in treatment between two people is made directly, or by the effect of seemingly neutral requirement, discrimination is considered to have occurred prima facie (on its face), and the finding of discrimination will prevail until contradicted and overcome by other evidence. Therefore, the onus shifts to the alleged perpetrator who must defend their conduct based on a bona fide (genuine) occupational requirement that requires an employee to be accommodated to the point of undue hardship.

The distinction between the Charter dignity analysis and the *B.C. Human Rights Code* was at the crux of Vancouver Rape Relief's appeal to the Supreme Court of British Columbia on December 19, 2003, in the *Nixon* case. The B.C. Human Rights

Tribunal decision of January 17, 2002, did not adopt the Charter analysis, which considers the element of human dignity. Subsequently, the B.C. Supreme Court overturned this decision, holding that the *Charter* analysis should apply. However, the B.C. Court of Appeal reviewed this case and determined on July 12, 2005, that the "broad application of the *Law* framework in a case without governmental overtones" is inappropriate (*Vancouver Rape Relief Society v. Nixon* 2005: at para 39).

THE NIXON CASE

Kimberly Nixon is a post-operative male-to-female transsexual. In 1987, at age thirty, she attended the Gender Disorder Clinic at the Vancouver General Hospital. Three years later, she had sex-reassignment surgery and her birth certificate was subsequently amended to change the sex designation of birth from male to female. In 1992 and 1993, Kimberly experienced physical and emotional abuse in a relationship with a male partner. When this relationship ended she was referred to the services of Battered Women's Support Services (BWSS). In August 1995, she responded to a Vancouver Rape Relief Society advertisement calling for volunteers. All potential volunteers are pre-screened to ensure that they agree with Rape Relief's views as a feminist, pro-choice and lesbian-positive organization. Rape Relief also requires that volunteer peer counsellors be women. Men interested in volunteering at Rape Relief are offered positions on the fundraising committee.

After passing the pre-screening interview, Kimberly was invited to attend the peer-counsellor training session. When she attended the first night of her training, she was immediately recognized by the training facilitator as an individual who had not always been physically female. During the first break, the facilitator, Ms. Cormier, approached Kimberly and asked to speak with her in private. Their conversation confirmed that Kimberly had not been a woman since birth. Ms. Cormier asked that Kimberly leave the training group, and she complied.

The next day, Kimberly filed a complaint with the British Columbia Council of Human Rights. Following her removal from the Rape Relief training program, she testified that, due to the distress she felt, she returned to the support group at BWSS. In the fall of 1996, she applied and was accepted into the BWSS training program for volunteers. Kimberly ended her involvement with BWSS after she discovered that the members circulated what she considered to be "hate" literature about transsexuals. She worked briefly for Peggy's Place, a transition house for women who, in addition to dealing with male violence or battering, have mental-health issues. Kimberly was considered a very capable volunteer in her subsequent positions.

JUDICIAL HISTORY

The B.C. Human Rights Tribunal heard Kimberly's arguments that Rape Relief had discriminated against her on the basis of sex,[2] by denying her a service (a training program in counselling women who have experienced violence) and an employment opportunity (*Vancouver Rape Relief Society v. British Columbia* [*Human Rights Commission*] 2002). The tribunal ruled that the relationship between Rape Relief and its volunteers fell within the definition of employment and found that there had been prima facie discrimination — discrimination had occurred without having to provide any further evidence — against Kimberly on both accounts.

Thus, Rape Relief was required to justify this discriminatory treatment. Rape Relief argued that lifelong experience as a woman was a bona fide occupational requirement for peer counsellors and, in addition, Rape Relief had attempted to accommodate Kimberly by suggesting that she join its fundraising committee. In effect, Rape Relief argued that it had accommodated Kimberly up to the point of undue hardship for the organization. The tribunal rejected both of these claims. In addition, the tribunal rejected Rape Relief's argument based on section 41 of the B.C. *Human Rights Code*, which stipulates that it is not discrimination for a non-profit organization whose "primary purpose" is promoting the welfare and interests of the identifiable group. The tribunal ruled that the evidence did not establish that Rape Relief's primary purpose was "the promotion of women who fit their political definition of what it means to be a woman" (*Nixon v. Vancouver Rape Relief* 2002: 221). The tribunal also held that Rape Relief did not establish that it was necessary to exclude transsexuals in order to accomplish the organization's goals.

In a controversial and highly publicized decision, taken January 17, 2002, the tribunal ordered Rape Relief "to cease denying, for discriminatory reasons, to transsexual women the opportunity of participating in their training program and the opportunity, on completion of the training, for the same group of women of volunteering at Rape Relief" (*Nixon v. Vancouver Rape Relief* 2002: 231). In addition, an award in the amount of $7,500 was ordered for injury to Kimberly's dignity, feelings and self-respect. At the time of this decision, this was the highest amount in special compensation ever awarded in the tribunal's history.

LEGAL ISSUES AT THE TRIBUNAL AND BEFORE THE COURTS

Rape Relief petitioned to the B.C. Supreme Court for judicial review of the tribunal's decision. Issues considered by the court were the effect of section 41 of the Code, discrimination under the *Law* analytical framework and "dignity" under the *Law* framework.

The B.C. Supreme Court quashed the tribunal's order. Mr. Justice Edwards held that the tribunal was incorrect in not applying the *Law* analytical framework. The

tribunal's finding, that Kimberly's exclusion from Rape Relief's volunteer training was prima facie discrimination, could not stand up under the *Law* analysis.
Both Rape Relief and Kimberly characterized gender as a continuum rather than
a binary male/female concept. Justice Edwards accepted Rape Relief's submission that Rape Relief's community of women was located on the far end of the
female continuum.

The B.C. Supreme Court decision also held, as was implicit in the tribunal's
decision, that women who were born and raised as girls and women ("non-
transsexual" women) are entitled to form a group protected under the exemption
provisions of section 41 of the [Human Rights] Code. Justice Edwards held that
the tribunal failed to correctly interpret and apply the leading Supreme Court
of Canada decision on section 41 in *Caldwell v. St. Thomas Aquinas High School*
(1984, hereafter referred to as *Caldwell*). The Supreme Court of Canada found
that section 41 is a rights-granting provision, and as such, is not subject to the
restrictive interpretation generally applicable to legislative provisions which place
limitations on rights. The *Caldwell* decision also held that it was permissible to
make a preference of one member of the identifiable group over another, as long
as the distinction was made honestly, in good faith and in the sincerely held belief
that it is imposed in the interest of the adequate performance of the work, and if
it was related, in an objective sense, to the performance of employment (*Ontario
Human Rights Commission v. Etobicoke* 1982). Justice Edwards followed this
reasoning and allowed the preference of one member of the identifiable groups
over another, as long as the distinction was made for the benefit of the members
of the community served by Rape Relief. Further, Justice Edwards ruled that
Rape Relief did not have to prove its primary purpose had a political dimension
in light of the bona fide belief that only women born women were suitable peer
counsellors for female rape victims.

The final step with the *Law* approach to section 15 is meant to be both contextual and purposeful, and its objective is to prevent the violation of human dignity.
The test of whether dignity has been harmed is both subjective and objective. It is
therefore necessary to consider the context of the complainant from the standpoint
of a reasonable person.

Justice Edwards believed that Kimberly's exclusion from a "relatively small
obscure self-defining private organization cannot have the same impact on human
dignity as legislated exclusion from a statutory benefit program" (*Law v. Canada*
1999: 145). Because her exclusion didn't bear state approval, and hence some wider
public acceptance, it was therefore judged not to be a public indignity. Although
the court agreed that this was no less subjectively hurtful to Kimberly, the court
distinguished the issue of the objective impact on human dignity, which was held
to be unreasonably exaggerated. In particular, the court noted, "no reasonable

male to female transsexual, standing in Ms. Nixon's shoes, could plausibly" argue that they "can no longer participate in the economic, social and cultural life of the province" (*Law v. Canada* 1999: 151). Additionally, Christine Boyle, counsel for Rape Relief, argued that a reasonable person would take into account the needs of disadvantaged groups to understand their own experience.

In essence, the court characterized the nature of Rape Relief as a political organization and the nature of the dispute, essentially a political one over membership criteria (*Vancouver Rape Relief Society v. Nixon* 2005: 114). It was not the function of the [Human Rights] Code to provide a referee and impose "state-sanctioned penalties in political disputes between private organizations." Finally, Justice Edwards held that the reason Kimberly was attracted to the peer-counsellor training program was because it would vindicate her womanhood, because it was part of a women-only organization. Her participation was held to have a political dimension.

In the end, the tribunal's conclusion that Rape Relief's exclusion of Kimberly as discriminatory was found to be unreasonable and the order for Rape Relief to pay her $7,500 in compensation was set aside. The B.C. Supreme Court's decision leaves room, as the *Law* decision suggests, for different forms of disadvantage. The decision also allows and recognizes the experience of growing up as a girl and living as a woman to be a permissible basis for a group to exclusively associate.

The decision by the B.C. Supreme Court has been substantially upheld by the B.C. Court of Appeal. On July 12, 2005, Kimberly's appeal of Justice Edward's decision was dismissed. The Court of Appeal found that the test of "discrimination" under the *B.C. Human Rights Code* was met. Rape Relief was held to be exempt from the application of the Code by virtue of section 41.

VIOLENCE AGAINST WOMEN

Many women's groups, sexual assault centres and women's interval houses insist on a women-only membership. It is seen as "essential to the struggle to restore dignity to disempowered women" and "necessary conditions to self-empowerment in a socio-economic and cultural context where access to and mobility within public space is still largely controlled by men and where women's roles and opportunity are frequently defined against their own interests" (Denike and Renshaw 2003: 13). Members gathering from oppressed groups to organize against oppression is a well-recognized tactic of addressing the effects of oppression and forming strategies for change (Freire 1970, cited in Findlay 2003).

Most women's organizations, including Rape Relief, believe that gender exists along a continuum and none of the needs and desires of their groups are considered unique or exclusive to them, but given the systemic nature of such groups, identity must be a legitimate basis for organizing. "It is essential to the integrity and autonomy of these groups that they be able to define and control membership in their group." Rape Relief thus excluded Kimberly because of the unique role Rape Relief serves for women experiencing violence.

Notes

1. For non-government actors, the Charter does not apply. When discrimination occurs by a private actor, the complainant must seek redress under the applicable human rights code.
2. Rape Relief had applied to halt proceeding on the basis that the *B.C. Human Rights Code* did not specifically prohibit discrimination based on transsexualism or gender identity. Mr. Justice Davies disagreed and that "it would be wrong to interpret the prohibition against discrimination on the basis of sex in the Code as not also prohibiting discrimination against an individual merely because that person or group is not readily identifiable as being either male or female" (*Vancouver Rape Relief Society v. British Columbia (Human Rights Commission* 2002: 57).

References

Denike, Margaret, and Sal Renshaw. 2003. "Transgender and Women's Substantive Equality." Paper prepared at the National Consultation on Transgender and Women's Substantive Equality, National Association of Women and the Law.

Findlay, Barbara. 2003. "'Real Women': Kimberly Nixon v. Vancouver Rape Relief." *University of British Columbia Law Review* 36.

Tarnopolsky, Walter Surma. 2001. *Discrimination and the Law*. Scarborough: Carswell.

Legal Cases

British Columbia (Public Service Employee Relations Commission) v. B.C.G.E.U., 176 D.L.R. (4th) 1.35 C.H.R.R. D/257, [1997] 3 S.C.R. 3.

Caldwell v. St. Thomas Aquinas High School, [1984] 2 S.C.R. 603, (QL).

Law v. Canada (Minister of Employment and Immigration), [1999] S.C.R. 497 [Law].

Nixon v. Vancouver Rape Relief [2002] B.C.H.R.T.D. No 1 2001 B.C.H.R.T. 1 (QL).

Ontario Human Rights Commission v. Etobicoke (Borough of), [1982] 1 S.C.R. 202 (QL), 208.

Vancouver Rape Relief Society v. British Columbia (Human Rights Commission) [2002] B.C.H.R.T.D. No. 1, 57.

Vancouver Rape Relief Society v. Nixon 2005 BCCA 601 at para 39.

COLONIALISM

Chapter 16

COLONIALISM PAST AND PRESENT

Elizabeth Comack

From: *Racialized Policing: Aboriginal People's Encounters with the Police*, pp. 66–88 (reprinted with permission).

Colonialism is not simply a historical artifact that has no bearing on contemporary events. As Patricia Monture (2007: 207) advises, it is "a living phenomenon ... The past impacts on the present, and today's place of Aboriginal peoples in Canadian society cannot be understood without a well-developed historical understanding of colonialism and the present-day trajectories of those old relationships." Encounters with the police call for this same understanding, this same deep need for context. Nevertheless, as the Commissioners for the Royal Commission on Aboriginal Peoples (RCAP 1996: vol. 1 chap. 3) noted, "most Canadians are simply unaware of the history of the Aboriginal presence in what is now Canada." Many Canadians, the commissioners pointed out, have "little understanding of the origins and evolution of the relationship between Aboriginal and non-Aboriginal people that have led us to the present moment" (RCAP 1996: vol. 1 chap. 3).

Yet it is not so much the case that Canadians have *no* national memory of their history. Rather, as Amanda Nettelbeck and Russell Smandych (2010) point out, colonial societies such as Canada and Australia have developed particular "foundational narratives" about their histories of European settlement, including the role of frontier police forces in managing and containing the Aboriginal populations. One distinct feature of our collective imaginary — our sense of who we are as a nation — is that Canada is one of the few countries in the world to claim a police force as a national symbol. You need only visit a local tourist shop to find iconic images of the "Scarlet Riders" on everything from postcards to coffee mugs. As Peter C. Newman once proclaimed, "In Canada's case, the Mountie symbolizes not merely law and order but Canada itself" (cited in Brown and Brown 1978: 127). The officers of the Royal Canadian Mounted Police (RCMP) are so identified with the national interest that criticism of the force is akin to an unpatriotic act.

The precursor to the RCMP, the North West Mounted Police, has also been part of this national memory, especially in terms of its origins and purpose in relation to the Aboriginal people who populated the land that became known as the Northwest Territories. According to this foundational narrative, the NWMP was established in 1873 by a benevolent federal government to protect the Aboriginal population of the Northwest from whiskey traders and other outlaws and "to ensure that all the people of the Canadian North West — Indians and Métis, settlers and traders — might have the opportunity of living under a system of law impartially enforced and guaranteeing equal rights to all" (Brown and Brown 1978: 2). This Canadian experience of a benign and peaceful stance towards Aboriginal people is often contrasted to the Wild West of the U.S. experience, where the "Indians" were nearly wiped out and the law of the fast gun and lynch mob prevailed. As Nettelbeck and Smandych observe, historical sites across Western Canada keep the foundational story of the NWMP as a mediating and peacekeeping force alive. "In regional museums, monuments and murals," they say, a constant refrain is repeated: "that the NWMP provided protection to Indigenous peoples and brought law and order to the west" (2010: 369).

Apart from visiting museums and historical sites, most Canadians get their understanding of their nation's history — and of Aboriginal people — from movies and television and what they learned in school. In my own experience, early lessons about Aboriginal people came from watching Saturday-afternoon horse-opera movies and television shows featuring cowboys and Indians of the American Wild West. In this racialized narrative the cowboys were invariably the heroic "good guys" who always won out in the end against the "savage" Indians.

Other lessons came from my formal schooling. *Pages from Canada's Story* (Dickie and Palk 1957) was the text used for many years to teach countless numbers of Canadian students about our colonial past. The text presents the story of white settlement in unproblematic terms — and never mentions colonialism. When the book covers the settling of the Canadian West and the treaty process, for instance, it matter-of-factly informs students: "White settlers soon made their way in such numbers to the North-West Territories that the Indian could no longer claim the great prairie as his hunting-ground. Treaties were made with various tribes for the surrender of the land to the Government" (Dickie and Palk 1957: 374). At the time the lieutenant governor of the territories was David Laird, and, as the text would have it, "Mr. Laird dealt so fairly with the Indians, and explained the treaties to them in such an understanding way, that very little trouble resulted" (Dickie and Palk 1957: 374).

Pages from Canada's Story also introduces students to the role of the NWMP in the settling of the West. The officers were "messengers of law and order" (Dickie and Palk 1957: 371) known as "Red Coats." As the text explains, "The matter of uniforms was given special consideration. Someone who knew of the Indian's love of colour must have had a voice in the choice of the bright scarlet coat which later became known as the 'Queen's red,' and stood, in the eyes of the Indians, for order and justice" (Dickie and Palk 1957: 370). The book emphasizes the ostensibly benevolent and paternalistic role played by this paramilitary force. Commenting on the arrival of a NWMP detachment at Fort Whoop-Up in 1874, the text quotes none other than Chief Crowfoot, leader of the Blackfoot tribe, as saying that the Red Coats "have protected us as the feathers protect the birds from the frosts of winter" (Dickie and Palk 1957: 372). But it goes on: "The Indians early learned to respect the men who faced danger unafraid and whose word was never broken. 'Before you came,' said old Chief Crowfoot [who was actually only forty years old at the time] to Colonel Macleod, 'the Indian crept along. Now he is not afraid to walk erect'" (Dickie and Palk 1957: 372–73). Clearly, the impression left on young minds by this history lesson was that if it were not for the arrival of the white man and his police force, Aboriginal people would have simply disappeared into the annals of time.

While we would like to think that things have changed since I received my formative schooling so many decades ago, Aboriginal scholar Susan Dion (2005) suggests otherwise. Her work with elementary school teachers and students has led her to conclude that the Canadian educational system continues to reproduce a discourse that positions Aboriginal people as a "romantic, mythical and frequently inferior Other."

> The study of Aboriginal people by Canadian school children continues to focus on how we lived prior to European contact. When attention is given to Aboriginal people in the post-contact period, it is without serious consideration of events that led to current conditions. The perspective taken suggests that the Europeans were stronger, more advanced and therefore progressed, while Aboriginal people were victims of that progress. The Europeans are not shown to be in any way responsible for the impacts on Aboriginal people. (Dion 2005: 40)

To contextualize the contemporary situation of Aboriginal people and their encounters with police, then, we first need to clarify the historical record.

Sherene Razack (2007: 74) notes, "The national mythologies of white settler societies are deeply racialized stories." For instance, one of the enduring components of Canada's foundational narrative is that explorers and settlers arrived from Europe to a *terra nullius*, an "empty land," that could be claimed and used for their own purposes. In this decidedly Eurocentric account, the original inhabitants of the land were depicted as "savages" in need of the civilizing influences of the European newcomers. Missing from this account is any recognition of the sophisticated trading and commercial exchanges, and customs and traditions practised by the various tribes that populated the space now known as Canada. Also missing is a recognition of the forms of governance that prevailed. As AJI commissioners Alvin Hamilton and Murray Sinclair (1991: 54) note, "Before the arrival of the Europeans, Aboriginal peoples had their own laws and customary practices for maintaining peace and stability within their communities — including the use of force and ostracism to enforce social norms and the role of elders in administering those norms."

What transpired after that European arrival — which can best be described as colonialism — was, in the words of John McLeod (2000: 7), at its core "a lucrative commercial operation, bringing wealth and riches to Western nations through the economic exploitation of others." Developing especially through the late seventeenth and early eighteenth centuries, the seizing of "foreign" lands for settlement was in part motivated by the desire to create and control markets abroad for Western goods, as well as securing the natural resources and labour power of different lands and people at the lowest possible cost. As McLeod puts it, colonialism "was pursued for economic profit, reward and riches. Hence, colonialism and capitalism share a mutually supportive relationship with each other" (2000: 7). A key characteristic of colonialism is the effort to govern the indigenous inhabitants of the occupied lands. At its heart, therefore, is the construction of unequal relations of power between the colonizers and the colonized.

Colonialism is not just the work of capitalists or the state. Joyce Green (2006) points out that the primary motivation of those immigrating to the new lands was the prospect of economic opportunities and advancements (including cheap or free land) that were not available to them in their homeland. To this extent, *all* newcomers are complicit in the colonial project: "To different degrees every colonizer is privileged, at least comparatively so, ultimately to the detriment of the colonized" (Green 2006: 512).

COLONIALISM PAST

The project of colonizing the indigenous population and constructing a white settler society began in Canada in the seventeenth century. While Aboriginal people were initially valued for their skills and knowledge, as these were indispensable to the survival of the newcomers, this power balance began to shift as more and more Europeans arrived. "By the early 19th century, Eurocanadians had made Aboriginal people a minority in their own lands," Celia Haig-Brown states (cited in Dion 2005: 36). "Acting through the power of organized religion and colonial governments, Canadians insisted that Aboriginal peoples should abandon their ways, languages, spiritual and economic systems, seasonal movement to hunting and gathering places and most importantly their lands" (cited in Dion 2005: 36).

This colonial project involved a number of strategies, one of which was signing treaties that transferred large tracts of land over to the government. As the Royal Commission on Aboriginal Peoples (1996: vol. 1 chap. 8) notes, "Treaties and other agreements were, by and large, not covenants of trust and obligation but devices of statecraft, less expensive and more acceptable than armed conflict." Another colonial strategy was the passage of the *Indian Act* in 1876 — legislation that consolidated previous rulings and provided a national foundation "based unashamedly on the notion that Indian cultures and societies were clearly inferior to settler society" (RCAP 1996: vol. 1 chap. 8). The 1876 annual report of the Department of the Interior expressed the assimilationist and paternalistic philosophy that prevailed at the time. Indians were to be treated as "children of the state":

> Our Indian legislation generally rests on the principle, that the aborigines are to be kept in a condition of tutelage and treated as wards or children of the State ... The true interests of the aborigines and of the State alike require that every effort should be made to aid the Red man in lifting himself out of his condition of tutelage and dependence, and that is clearly our wisdom and our duty, through education and every other means, to prepare him for a higher civilization by encouraging him to assume the privileges and responsibilities of full citizenship. (Cited in RCAP 1996: vol. 1 chap. 8)

The *Indian Act* defined in law who was an "Indian" and specified how someone could lose status as an Indian. An Indian was legally defined as "any male person of Indian blood reputed to belong to a particular band, and any child of such person and any woman who is lawfully married to such a person" (Gibbins and Ponting 1986: 21). Under this definition, an Indian woman who married a non-Indian man ceased to be an Indian in legal terms, and both she and her children lost all claims associated with that status (for example, residence on a reserve, use of reserve property, and participation in band affairs). In contrast, a non-Indian woman who married an Indian man would gain legal status as an Indian, as would the children from that union. This provision in the *Indian Act* remained in effect until it was abrogated in 1985. Aboriginal people were also denied basic political rights; they did not have a legal right to vote in provincial elections in British Columbia and Newfoundland until 1949, in Québec until 1969, and in federal elections until 1960.

In addition to replacing traditional systems of governance by a restricted form of democracy in which only men had a voice and vote, the *Indian Act* gave considerable power to the Indian agents, who represented the Department of Indian Affairs. Hamilton and Sinclair state:

> Each agent had full authority to conduct trials anywhere in the country involving Indians charged with violating the *Indian Act* or with certain crimes under the *Criminal Code*. As a result, the Indian agent could direct the police to prosecute "troublemakers" and then sit in judgment. The agents effectively had power over all aspects of daily life. (1991: 64–65)

Aboriginal people also experienced considerable restrictions on their mobility. With the relinquishing of their land to the government under the treaty process, most tribes were relegated to smaller tracts of land as part of the reservation system. A pass system was imposed as early as 1885 under which Aboriginal people were prohibited from leaving their reserve without first securing written permission from the local Indian agent. While the pass system had no legislative basis and therefore could not be legally enforced, Indian agents could withhold rations for those who refused to comply, and those found off the reserve without a pass could be prosecuted for trespass under the *Indian Act* or for vagrancy under the *Criminal Code* (Hamilton and Sinclair 1991; RCAP 1996).

To further this colonial project the government also created a number of status offences that applied only to Aboriginal peoples. An 1884 amendment to the *Indian Act* outlawed the Potlatch (ceremonial gift-giving) and Tamanawas (medicine or healing ceremony) and imposed sanctions of two to six months' imprisonment for those found in violation. In 1885 another amendment outlawed Sun Dances, providing for imprisonment of two to six months for violators. As Andrea McCalla and Vic Satzewich (2002) note, missionaries — tasked with the "civilizing mission" of the colonial project — saw the persistence of these cultural practices as "devil worship." One Anglican missionary wrote to the Department of Indian Affairs about his first encounter with the Blackfoot people whom he was sent to convert:

> I arrived in July when that great heathen festival, the Sun Dance, was in full swing ... The fantastic costume, of the people, the paint and feathers, the then to me foreign tongue, made my heart sink within me, and

if I ever felt the hopelessness of a task set me to do it was then. (Cited in
Pettipas 1995: 97)

The giveaways associated with these cultural practices were inimical to the
capitalist ethic — respect for private property and pursuit of individual accumulation — that the government was endeavouring to instill in Aboriginal people. As
well, the hours taken to prepare for the ceremonies were considered to be time
that could be better spent engaging in more "legitimate" economic pursuits. Yet
Aboriginal people were not passive bystanders to these efforts to outlaw their
culture (McCalla and Satzewich 2002). Resistance took the form of holding
ceremonies in secret and altering the practices to make them seem more "acceptable" to European eyes.

One plank of the colonial project that was more difficult to resist was the residential school system, which was initiated in the 1880s with the specific objective
of assimilating Aboriginal people into mainstream Canadian society. Aboriginal
children were forcibly removed from their homes and transported — often some
distance away — to attend these large, racially segregated industrial schools.
Attendance was compulsory. Indian agents were empowered to commit children
under sixteen to the schools and to keep them there until they were eighteen. By
way of contrast, non-Aboriginal children were not subject to compulsory schooling. Manitoba, for instance, did not introduce compulsory schooling until 1916. In
addition, federal legislation passed in 1894 allowed for the arrest and conveyance
to school of truant Aboriginal children, and for fines or jail terms for parents who
resisted (Hamilton and Sinclair 1991).

The government delegated this civilizing project of the residential school system
to religious organizations and churches, which were given the task of transforming
the children from "savages" into "citizens" by inculcating the values of Christianity
and industry so that the youngsters could take up positions as "functioning"
members of the emerging capitalist society. As the 1889 Annual Report of the
Department of Indian Affairs explained:

> The boarding school dissociates the Indian child from the deleterious
> home influences to which he would otherwise be subjected. It reclaims
> him from the uncivilized state in which he has been brought up. It brings
> him into contact day to day with all that tends to effect a change in his
> views and habits of life. By precept and example he is taught to endeav-
> our to excel in what will be most useful to him. (Cited in Hamilton and
> Sinclair 1991: 68)

By the 1930s eighty residential schools were spread across the country, with
children registered from every Aboriginal culture (RCAP 1996: vol. 1 chap. 2).

Eventually, a total of 139 residential schools were in operation in Canada. Some 150,000 First Nation, Inuit and Métis children were forced to attend the schools.

Much has been written in recent times about the residential school system, especially in the wake of revelations by survivors about the harsh treatment received at the schools (see, for example, York 1990; Hamilton and Sinclair 1991; RCAP 1996; Milloy 1999; Knockwood 2001). What we now know from this work is that conditions at the schools were abysmal; they were built with the cheapest materials, employed untrained staff, and were overcrowded due to the government's financial inducements to increase enrolments (Blackstone and Trocmé 2004). The expressed goal was to produce educated graduates, but few of the children completed the full course of study. In 1945, for example, no students were enrolled beyond Grade 8 in any of the schools (RCAP 1996: vol. 1 chap. 2). Children were poorly fed and clothed; so many of them died from preventable diseases (such as malnutrition, smallpox and tuberculosis) that several of the schools even had their own grave-yards. Physical punishment was the norm. Children were beaten for speaking their indigenous languages; those who tried to run away were shackled to their beds. Suicide attempts by the children were common. Not only were physical abuse and neglect rampant, but so too was sexual abuse — something that was never cited in all of the major reports on the residential school system and only became public knowledge once survivors began to break the silence and tell their stories (RCAP 1996: vol. 1 chap. 2).

While the effort by the European colonizers to take control over the lives of Aboriginal people involved a number of strategies, including the signing of trea-ties, the *Indian Act* and the residential school system, the North West Mounted Police played an instrumental role in carrying out this colonial project or "civiliz-ing mission."

The North West Mounted Police

The primary role of the NWMP — like that of other frontier police forces — was "to ensure the submission of Indigenous peoples to colonial rule" (Nettelbeck and Smandych 2010: 357). While the foundational narrative of the NWMP posits that the force was brought into being in response to the Cypress Hills Massacre in May 1873, when U.S. whiskey traders murdered several Assiniboine peoples, Lorne and Caroline Brown (1978: 10) have a different view:

> This is true only in the sense that the massacre hastened the organiza-tion of the Force. The establishment of the Force had been planned and officially authorized prior to this, and the primary reason for establishing it was to control the Indian and Métis population of the North West.

Prime Minister John A. Macdonald had been making plans for the policing of the

Northwest since 1869. His main concern was to keep peace between Aboriginal people and settlers in order to encourage economic development.

The plans for the NWMP were approved by an order-in-council on April 6, 1870. The force was to march west with the Canadian military in 1870, but this plan was shelved with the passage of the *Manitoba Act,* which left the administration of justice in the hands of the new province. Plans continued, however, for controlling that part of the Northwest outside of Manitoba, particularly because government officials worried that the Métis of Manitoba would ally themselves with Aboriginal tribes farther west and take a stand against the federal government. There were also concerns that any unrest would interfere with the progress on the building of the Canadian Pacific Railway and limit plans to settle the area with immigrants. A military presence was therefore increasingly seen as necessary.

Officially established by an act of Parliament in the spring of 1873, the NWMP was "to be a semi-military body directly controlled from Ottawa, and not by the local government officials in the North West" (Brown and Brown 1978: 13). While an earlier proposal had called for the inclusion of Aboriginal people on the force (similar to what had transpired under British colonial rule in India), the Act made no special provisions for this condition. The events of the Red River "Rebellion" and the unrest following it had "convinced the authorities that the native peoples were not likely to become loyal servants of their colonial masters" (Brown and Brown 1978: 13).

While the force was not intended to be put into effect until 1874, the Cypress Hills Massacre caused the government to speed up its plans. The government's fear was that "the outrage in the Cypress Hills and other atrocities of this nature might provoke the Indians into open warfare against the whites" (Brown and Brown 1978: 13). Also of concern was the unrest generated by the prosecution of some of the activists in the Manitoba provisional government of 1869–70, with fears raised about the whereabouts and activities of Louis Riel and "the fanaticism of the French Canadian Half-breeds" (cited in Brown and Brown 1978: 14).

The first years of the NWMP were not without controversy. Members of the force encountered severe hardships — poor food, deplorable living conditions, delays in receiving wages, and bullying by officers — which led to a high rate of desertion. Concerns were raised about alcoholism and a high percentage of personnel suffering from venereal disease. In 1880 a member of Parliament from Manitoba reported on the sexual exploitation of Aboriginal women. Prostitution was apparently rampant in the vicinity of NWMP posts, and the police were spreading venereal disease among the Aboriginal population (Brown and Brown 1978: 16).

As Sarah Carter (1999: 129) notes, the NWMP "had powers that were unprecedented in the history of police forces." In addition to the power to arrest, the NWMP were granted magisterial powers: they were able to prosecute, judge and jail an accused. The force was also charged with implementing the government's policies towards Aboriginal people. As AJI Commissioners Hamilton and Sinclair (1991: 592) note:

> Whenever an Indian agent felt the need for assistance in enforcing government policy regarding Indian people, he called upon the Mounted Police. Indian children who ran away from residential schools were sought and returned by NWMP officers. Indian adults who left their reserves without a pass from the Indian agent were apprehended by the Mounted Police.

Given that the historical record was written largely by the white colonizers, the standpoint of Aboriginal people during this period of history remains in the shadows — and especially because Aboriginal people use oral as opposed to written narratives to communicate and learn from their own past (see RCAP 1996: vol. 1 chap. 3). Nevertheless, we do know that factors such as the virtual extinction of the buffalo, the arrival of increasing numbers of settlers, the impact of the infectious diseases that newcomers brought with them, the negative effects of the whiskey trade, and the threat of starvation all took their toll on the Aboriginal population. Due to these conditions, some of the people may well have welcomed the presence of the NWMP. Yet, as Brown and Brown (1978: 20) note, "a state of constant tension between the police and the Indian nations" was the norm, given that "the Force represented the interests who were rapidly destroying the Indian economy and way of life and was frequently called upon to protect those same interests."

This tension became even more pronounced during and after the Saskatchewan Rebellion of 1885. While the NWMP was not the cause of the rebellion (and repeatedly warned the government that unrest was likely to occur), the force participated along with regular military forces in suppressing it. The NWMP was also instrumental in apprehending and meting out punishment to the rebels, including sentences of imprisonment and the execution of Métis leader Louis Riel and eight others. Brown and Brown (1978: 22) write:

> The authorities punished Métis and Indians suspected of having supported the rebellion regardless of whether they had been tried for specific offences. They virtually wiped out the Métis as a distinct national and political group. They burned and looted their homes and destroyed their property. They withheld annuities from those Indian bands that had participated in the rebellion and confiscated their horses and arms. From that time on they made greater efforts to restrict Indians to the reserves and strictly regulated the sale of ammunition to them. Most of these punitive measures were carried out by the Mounted Police.

As Carter (1999: 161) notes, after 1885 a significant shift occurred in Euro-Canadian attitudes towards Aboriginal people: "If there was a shred of tolerance before, or the possibility of working towards a progressive partnership, it was shattered in 1885, as thereafter Aboriginal people were viewed as a threat to the property and safety of the white settlers." After 1885 government policies aimed at controlling and monitoring the lives of Aboriginal people were "pursued with great vigour" (Carter 1999: 162). During this period the pass system was implemented (accompanying the outlawing of practices and ceremonies such as the Potlatch and Sun Dance). The number of NWMP officers was greatly increased to enhance the effort to monitor and control Aboriginal people.

A tradition of active, armed violence was missing from the Canadian experience, which was notably different from that of the United States. Between 1866 and 1885 the U.S. West saw 943 military engagements (Ennab 2010: 161). By comparison, the Canadian Northwest saw only six or seven comparable clashes, most of them taking place in the two years prior to the Métis resistance of 1885. As Ennab (2010: 186) argues, overt physical violence was replaced with compulsion and coercion:

> It was through intimidation and broken promises along with the larger colonial disciplinary system that was shaping the rationalities of the inhabitants that a few red-coated Mounties were able to coerce Aboriginal people to stay on reserves. If it was not for this, the NWMP would have needed more investment in the ongoing, armed engagements, which they could not afford, thus jeopardizing the entire colonial enterprise. Most Aboriginal people recognized that even if the NWMP were not able to "destroy" them, they were able to push them on the side to starve.

Historians have uncovered many instances in which members of the NWMP acted with fairness and concern towards Aboriginal people. But as Brown and Brown (1978: 19) argue:

> That certain individuals in the Force sympathized with the plight of the Indians and attempted to carry out a disagreeable task in as humane a manner as possible does not alter the nature of the Force and their work. Most police officials knew whose interests they served and knew that to be "too soft on Indians" endangered their career in the Force.

As such, even though the conquest of the Canadian West was not nearly so bloody an affair as it was in the Western United States, and violence by the frontier police against the Aboriginal population was not as rife as it was in Australia (Nettelbeck and Smandych 2010), the NWMP did play a crucial role in implementing the Canadian colonial project. The NWMP, according to Brown and Brown (1978), was "a crucial part of a conscious scheme by which powerful economic and political interests destroyed the economy and way of life of entire peoples and wrested a vast territory from its inhabitants for a pittance." Moreover, these authors argue, "Anyone who describes the role of the NWMP during this period as constituting the 'glorious foundations of a great tradition' must surely be either hopelessly naïve or lacking in moral sensitivity" (Brown and Brown 1978: 23).

The name of the North West Mounted Police was changed to the Royal North West Mounted Police (RNWMP) in 1904 in recognition of the force's service to the Empire. As settlement of the West continued, with Saskatchewan and Alberta gaining provincial status in 1905, the RNWMP acted in the capacity of a provincial police force. The modern version of the force — the Royal Canadian Mounted Police — came into being in 1920 when the RNWMP was amalgamated with the Dominion Police. During the Great Depression of the 1930s, the RCMP expanded its scope. Some of the provinces and many smaller municipalities facing financial troubles disbanded their police forces and contracted the RCMP instead. This contractual relationship continues to the present day.

This history of the NWMP, then, has a direct connection to contemporary relations between Aboriginal people and the police. As AJI commissioners Hamilton and Sinclair note, memories of the treatment at the hands of the force "linger in many communities." The history of the relationship has "coloured the perceptions Aboriginal people hold of other police forces in the province. The impact of past wrongs has been reinforced by the negative experiences of today" (1991: 593).

Just as significant, the strategies of the colonial project laid down in the earlier period of Canadian history would have had profound and long-lasting impacts. The *Indian Act* of 1876 — with its decidedly paternalistic and assimilationist bent — continues to inform the lives of Aboriginal peoples. Although the Act has been repeatedly amended, its fundamental provisions have remained intact. It "still holds a symbolic but powerful grip on the thinking of Canadians" towards Aboriginal people (RCAP 1996: vol. 1 chap. 8). Similarly, residential schools had a profound and long-lasting impact. Although their phasing out began in the late 1940s, it was not until 1996 that the last federally run residential school was shut down (DIAND 2003). The generations of children who attended the schools were cut off from their families, their communities, and their cultural and spiritual teachings. Survivors were confronted with the difficult challenge of healing from years of abuse and neglect. Being deprived of healthy parenting role models also left them with diminished capacities as adults to raise and care for their own children. In the words of the AJI commissioners, "These policies have caused a wound to fester in Aboriginal communities that has left them diminished to this day" (Hamilton and Sinclair 1991: 505).

COLONIALISM PRESENT

Colonialism has not disappeared; it has just taken on new forms in contemporary times. One of the ways in which colonialism is perpetuated is through racialized discourse. While past discourses cast Aboriginal people as "savage," "inferior" and "child-like" (and therefore in need of a civilizing influence and the benevolent paternalism of the state), more contemporary discourses include the notions of the "welfare recipient," the "drunken Indian" and the "criminal Other" (and therefore in need of heightened surveillance and control). As with discourses generally, these racialized constructions have their basis in material conditions. In contemporary times, social exclusion, poverty, violence and alcohol use have dominated the lives of many Aboriginal people, and their overrepresentation in the criminal justice system has become a problem of large proportions.

Social Exclusion and Poverty

Social exclusion, as Grace-Edward Galabuzi (2009) notes, "is used to broadly describe the structures and the dynamic processes of inequality among groups in society, which, over time, structure access to critical resources that determine the quality of membership in society." These conditions define "the inability of certain subgroups to participate fully in Canadian life." The access to critical resources — whether social, economic, political, or cultural — arises "out of the often intersecting experiences of oppression relating to race, class, gender, disability, sexual orientation, immigrant status, and the like." Social exclusion is "also characterized by processes of group or individual isolation within and from Canadian societal institutions such as the school system, criminal justice system, health care system, as well as spatial isolation or neighbourhood segregation" (2009: 253–254).

Poverty is both a product and a cause of social exclusion, and it is also a racialized phenomenon in Canada. Being born Aboriginal means an increased likelihood of living in poverty. Almost 1.2 million people reported Aboriginal identity in the 2006 census, representing 3.8 percent of the total Canadian population (Statistics Canada 2008). In 2005, 18.7 percent of Aboriginal families and 42.8 percent of unattached individuals who identified as Aboriginal experienced low income, compared to 8.4 percent of families and 28 percent of unattached individuals who were non-Aboriginal (Collin and Jensen 2009). Children and youth account for just under half (48 percent) of the Aboriginal population, and some 35 percent of Aboriginal children live with a lone parent, which means that Aboriginal adults will often be on their own, providing for a larger group of dependants than is the case for non-Aboriginal adults (Smylie 2009: 291). The poverty gap is most pronounced in the Prairie provinces. In Saskatchewan, for instance, where Aboriginal people make up 15 percent of the population, an Aboriginal person is about three and a half times more likely to be poor than is a non-Aboriginal resident (Noël

2009: 8). While conditions vary by region, if we apply the United Nations Human Development index to Aboriginal communities in Canada, they would rank 68 out of 174 nations. By comparison, Canada as a nation ranks in the eighth position (Graydon 2008).

Living conditions on many reserves have been defined as a matter of crisis proportions. Substandard and overcrowded housing is one pressing issue. In 2006, 28 percent of First Nations people were living in a home in need of major repairs, compared with just 7 percent of the non-Aboriginal population; First Nations people were five times more likely than non-Aboriginal people to live in crowded homes (Statistics Canada 2008). Access to potable water, adequate sanitation and waste disposal services are resources that many Canadians take for granted. Yet in November 2010, 117 First Nation communities were under drinking water advisories (Campaign 2000 2010). Many reserve communities still do not have running water or sewer lines. These living conditions undermine the health of a community. Aboriginal people have shorter life expectancies and a higher risk of suffering from infectious diseases such as tuberculosis and chronic illnesses such as diabetes. The Royal Commission (RCAP 1996; vol. 3 chap. 3) found that rates of tuberculosis infection were forty-three times higher among registered Indians than among non-Aboriginal Canadians born in this country, and the incidence rate for diabetes was at least two to three times higher among Aboriginal than among non-Aboriginal people. These impoverished conditions generate a sense of hopelessness and despair. While the suicide rates vary widely among First Nations communities, the youth suicide rate in these communities is still between three and seven times greater than in Canada overall (Campaign 2000 2010).

Deteriorating social and economic conditions in many First Nations communities have prompted increased migration between First Nations communities and urban centres. As John Loxley (2010) notes, remarkably few Aboriginal people were living in urban centres such as Winnipeg up to the 1950s — perhaps "less than a dozen Indians" in 1901 "and only about 700 Métis in the city of 42,340." By 1921, 69 Indians lived in Winnipeg, and by 1951 only 210, in a city with a population of 354,000. "The Métis were invisible" (Loxley 2010: 151). As of 2006, however, over half (54 percent) of the Aboriginal population of Canada now live in urban centres (Statistics Canada 2008).

Conditions for Aboriginal people living in these urban settings are no better than on reserves. Aboriginal residents of urban areas are more than twice as likely to live in poverty as are non-Aboriginal residents. In 2000, for instance, 55.6 percent of urban Aboriginal people lived below the poverty line compared to 24.5 percent of non-Aboriginal urban residents (NCCAH 2009–10). In 2006 almost half (49 percent) of First Nations children living off-reserve and nearly one-third (32 percent) of Métis children were members of low-income families (Collin and Jensen 2009: 19). The highest concentration of urban Aboriginal people is in the inner-city communities of major cities in the Western provinces. Winnipeg has the highest concentration of Aboriginal people in Canada (Statistics Canada 2008), and most of them live in the inner city. While Aboriginal people make up 10 percent of Winnipeg's population, they constitute 25 percent of those living in poverty (MacKinnon 2009: 30). Unemployment explains some of this disparity. As RCAP (1996) notes: "Aboriginal people living in urban centres fare somewhat better than reserve residents in gaining employment, but their unemployment rate is still two and a half times the unemployment rate of non-Aboriginal people, and their total annual income from all sources lags behind by 33 per cent."

Jim Silver (2006a: 17) observes that "the spatial distribution of Aboriginal people in cities ... parallels their spatial distribution outside urban centres." That is, just as they have historically been confined to rural reserves, now in cities they are being set apart from mainstream Canadian life. Their "move to the city is too often a move from one marginalized community to another." Nevertheless, much like the assimilationist policies of an earlier era, the difficulties encountered by Aboriginal people who have migrated to urban centres are often interpreted as being not the result of their social exclusion but of their own failure to successfully integrate into mainstream capitalist society.

Colonialism has produced the social and economic marginalization of Aboriginal people in contemporary Canadian society — something that even the Supreme Court of Canada acknowledges: "Many aboriginal people are victims of systemic and direct discrimination, many suffer the legacy of dislocation, and many are substantially affected by poor social and economic conditions" (R. v. Gladue 1999: 20).

Violence and Alcohol Use

For Aboriginal communities one of the legacies of colonialism is inordinately high levels of violence. While many Canadians, especially women and children, encounter violence in their lives (Statistics Canada 2011; Johnson 1996), in the lives of Aboriginal people it is an even more pressing social issue. In interviews with 621 Aboriginal people living in four Canadian inner cities, Carol La Prairie (1994) found that 70 percent of the males and 75 percent of the females reported family violence in childhood. A study by the Ontario Native Women's Association (1989) found that eight out of ten Aboriginal women had experienced violence, many of them as young children. In the 2009 General Social Survey, 15 percent of Aboriginal women (compared with 6 percent of non-Aboriginal women) who had a spouse or common-law partner in the previous five years reported being a victim of intimate partner violence. Aboriginal victims of this violence were also nearly twice as likely than non-Aboriginal victims (60 percent versus 33 percent) to report the most serious forms of domestic incidents (being hit with an object, beaten, strangled, threatened or assaulted with a firearm or a knife, or forced to engage in an unwanted sexual act), and twice as many Aboriginal as non-Aboriginal victims (57 percent versus 29 percent) said they were injured as a result (Perreault 2011; see also Bopp, Bopp, and Lane 2003; Brownridge 2003; Canadian Panel on Violence Against Women 1993; Moyer 1992).

While studies that report on the incidence of particular types of abuse are useful in documenting the nature and extent of the violence encountered by Aboriginal people, several writers have noted that separating out and focusing on specific forms of abuse is highly problematic. Sharon McIvor and Teressa Nahanee (1998: 63) state: "Compartmentalizing 'types' of violence within Aboriginal communities into distinct categories of investigation is counter-productive. Sexual, physical, and emotional attacks are inter-related and inter-generational in our communities. Treating these acts as discrete events serves only to obscure our everyday lives." Similarly, Patricia Monture-Angus (1995: 171) tells us that "focusing on a moment in time or incidents of violence, abuse or racism, counting them — disguises the utter totality of the experience of violence in Aboriginal women's lives." Indeed, the violence experienced by Aboriginal people is systemic; it "has invaded whole communities and cannot be considered a problem of a particular couple or an individual household" (RCAP 1996: vol. 3 chap. 2).

One explanation often offered to account for the high levels of violence in Aboriginal communities is the use of alcohol. Sharon Moyer (1992), for instance, found that 70 percent of the homicide incidents involving Aboriginal people between 1962 and 1984 involved the use of alcohol. The General Social Survey found that violent crimes involving an Aboriginal victim were more likely (67 percent) than incidents with a non-Aboriginal victim (52 percent) to involve alcohol or illegal drug use of the perpetrator (Perrault 2011). Accordingly, alcohol use is often taken as a sign of "cultural difference" that marks Aboriginal people off from the rest of Canadian society. According to this view, excessive drinking has become commonplace in Aboriginal communities to the point at which it is now an accepted cultural practice that leads to "drinking parties" where violence is likely to break out (see Comack and Balfour 2004).

However, explaining violence in Aboriginal communities by pointing to the use of alcohol and, more generally, to the notion of "cultural difference" contains a number of problems. Many of the Aboriginal women interviewed for *Women in Trouble* (Comack 1996) indicated that they turned to alcohol and other drugs as a way of escaping their difficult pasts (see also McEvoy and Daniluk 1995). In this regard, these women are no different than many other Canadians who regularly turn to alcohol as a means of coping with distress in their lives. In the view of the Royal Commission (RCAP 1996), alcohol abuse is not a cause of violence but a parallel means of dealing with deep distress. In a similar fashion, AJI commissioners Hamilton and Sinclair (1991: 498) state: "Ultimately, it must be recognized that the presence and influence of alcohol and substance abuse in Aboriginal communities and among Aboriginal people are a direct reflection of the nature and level of despair which permeates that population."

Moreover, to say that violence in Aboriginal communities is the result of cultural differences raises another question: different from what? More often than not, it is the standards of the dominant white culture that are used as the measuring rod by which Aboriginal people are transformed into the deviant Other. Such an approach only works to reproduce the racism that prevails in the mainstream society. In this regard, centring explanations for violence in Aboriginal communities on the use of alcohol can align too easily with racist stereotypes, including the two most invidious of these, the "squaw" and the "drunken Indian" (see Sangster 2001; LaRocque 2000). As Emma LaRocque (2000) put it so powerfully to the Aboriginal Justice Inquiry, "The portrayal of the squaw is one of the most degrading, most despised and most dehumanizing anywhere in the world. The 'squaw' is the female counterpart of the Indian male 'savage' and, as such, she has no human face; she is lustful, immoral, unfeeling and dirty." LaRocque draws a direct connection between "this grotesque dehumanization" and the constant vulnerability of Aboriginal girls and women to serious physical, psychological and sexual abuse: "I believe that there is a direct relationship between these horrible racist/sexist stereotypes and violence against Native women and girls" (cited in Hamilton and Sinclair 1991: 479).

The racist stereotype of the "drunken Indian" works in a similar fashion. Bolstered by a dominant, regularly reinforced discourse that is content to explain private troubles as being rooted in individual circumstances (as opposed to systemic processes), the common view is to see Aboriginal people as being intoxicated and "out of control." Such representations merely function to objectify and devalue Aboriginal people. Ignored are the historical processes by which alcohol was introduced into Aboriginal life and the social conditions that have fostered its continued use, as well as the general use of alcohol as a socially sanctioned resource in contemporary society.

Explanations that rest on cultural difference to account for the prevalence of violence in Aboriginal communities, then, are highly suspect. Rather than cultural difference, the prevalence of violence and alcohol use in Aboriginal communities is more accurately located as a contemporary manifestation of colonialism. As the Canadian Panel on Violence against Women (1993: 173) argues, poverty is a key factor in the perpetuation of this violence: "The impact of poverty on the Aboriginal family and community is immeasurable. Poverty, in its severest form, is a fact of life for many Aboriginal people … It is the daily stress, financial hardship and chronic despair inflicted by poverty that contribute to the widespread abuse of Aboriginal women and children."

Overrepresentation in the Criminal Justice System

The volatile mixture of poverty, violence, and alcohol use that colonialism has perpetrated on Aboriginal individuals and communities also figures into the over-representation of Aboriginal people in the criminal justice system. The statistics are telling.

- Although Aboriginal people made up just 3 percent of the Canadian population in 2007–8, they accounted for 18 percent of admissions to provincial and territorial jails and 18 percent of admissions to federal prisons. This overrepresentation is most acute in the Prairie provinces. In Saskatchewan, Aboriginal people made up 11 percent of the population and a whopping 81 percent of provincial sentenced custody admissions in 2007–8. In Manitoba, Aboriginal people made up only 15 percent of the population yet represented 69 percent of provincially sentenced custody admissions (Perrault 2009).

- The overrepresentation of Aboriginal women is even more acute than it is for Aboriginal men. In 2007–8 Aboriginal women accounted for 24 percent of the female inmate population in provincial and territorial jails, while Aboriginal men accounted for 17 percent of the male inmate population (Perrault 2009).

- The number of Aboriginal people held in custody has been steadily increasing. Between 2001 and 2007, Aboriginal people admitted on remand increased by 23 percent, compared to a 14 percent increase for the general population. Aboriginal people are incarcerated at a rate of 1,024 per 100,000 population in comparison to 117 per 100,000 for the general population (Sapers 2007: 11–12).

- According to a one-day snapshot conducted in 2003, the Aboriginal youth incarceration rate was 64.5 per 10,000 population compared to 8.2 per 10,000 population for non-Aboriginal youth. Aboriginal youth were almost eight times more likely to be in custody than their non-Aboriginal counterparts. Aboriginal youth in Saskatchewan were thirty times more likely to be incarcerated than their non-Aboriginal counterparts. In Manitoba, Aboriginal youth were sixteen times more likely to be incarcerated than were non-Aboriginal youth (Latimer and Foss 2004).

La Prairie (2002) found that Aboriginal people's overrepresentation in the criminal justice system was not a uniform phenomenon. For one, studies showed that only a small proportion of incarcerated Aboriginal people committed their offences while on a reserve; most were living in an urban area at the time the offence was committed. For example, a one-day snapshot of Aboriginal youth in custody in Canada revealed that more than half (58 percent) of the Aboriginal youth were in a city when they committed or allegedly committed the offence for which they were currently being held (Bittle et al. 2002: 10–11). While offences by First Nations youth were mainly committed on-reserve in the Eastern provinces, they were mainly committed off-reserve in the Western provinces. For example, 67 percent of Aboriginal youth in Manitoba and 65 percent of those in Saskatchewan committed or allegedly committed the offence for their current admission in a city (Bittle et al. 2002: 85, 104).

For another, while urban areas contribute to the majority of incarcerated Aboriginal offenders, there are regional variations. La Prairie found that these variations could be accounted for by the degrees of disadvantage experienced by Aboriginal people. More specifically, Winnipeg, Saskatoon, Regina, and Thunder Bay contribute the most to Aboriginal overrepresentation. These are also cities with the largest percentage of Aboriginal people living in extremely poor neighbourhoods. According to La Prairie (2002: 202), therefore, the concentration of poor, single-parent, and poorly educated Aboriginal people living in the inner core of these cities explains their greater likelihood of involvement with the criminal justice system.

More recently, Samuel Perrault examined factors that contribute to the overrepresentation of Aboriginal people in the criminal justice system. According to the 2006 Census, 38 percent of Aboriginal people aged twenty years and over had not completed high school, compared to 19 percent of non-Aboriginal people. As well, the unemployment rate among Aboriginal people was 14 percent compared to 6 percent among non-Aboriginal people (Perrault 2009: 12). Nevertheless, Perrault found that while the level of education and employment status help to explain some of the overrepresentation of Aboriginal adults in custody, "the incarceration rates for Aboriginal adults aged 20 to 34 still remain higher than for their non-Aboriginal counterparts even when high school graduation and employment are considered." As such, Perrault concludes, "Other factors beyond education and employment, therefore, may also contribute to the representation of Aboriginal adults in custody" (2009: 14).

What are those other factors? Clearly, race and racialization come into play here. An inescapable connection exists between the historical forces of colonialism that have shaped contemporary Aboriginal communities and the overincarceration of Aboriginal people. Poverty, social exclusion, violence and alcohol use have become all too regular features in the lives of Aboriginal people, and prison — with all of its negative effects (see Comack 2008) — has become for many young Aboriginal people the contemporary equivalent of what the Indian residential school represented for their parents (Jackson 1989: 216). Still, explaining the disproportionate incarceration rates of Aboriginal people on crime-producing conditions in their families and communities tells only part of the story. Left out of the equation is the role of the criminal justice system in the production of crime.

THE PRODUCTION OF "CRIME"

While La Prairie directs our attention to the impoverished living conditions of Aboriginal people, she also suggests another possible factor to account for Aboriginal people's overrepresentation in the criminal justice system: "that the majority of offences (of incarcerated Aboriginal offenders) were committed off-reserve may be explained by the potential for the criminal justice system to *respond differently* to offenders on- and off-reserve" (LaPrairie 2002: 189; emphasis added). In other words, we need to acknowledge the role that the police — as the first point of contact with the criminal justice system — perform in the criminalization of Aboriginal people.

Despite the ways in which it is represented in public discourse and official statistics, "crime" is not an obvious or straightforward category. Like the idea of race, crime is a social construction that varies over time and place. As Wendy Chan and Kiran Mirchandani (2002: 14) note, "Definitions of crime and categories of criminality are neither fixed nor natural." Stuart Hall and his colleagues (1978: 188) make a similar point in saying that crime cannot be treated as a "given, self-evident, ahistorical, and unproblematic category." At the same time that crime cannot be separated from the social context in which it occurs,

> [it is also] differently *defined* (in both official and lay ideologies) at different periods; and this reflects not only changing attitudes amongst different sectors of the populations to crime, as well as real historical changes in the social organization of criminal activity, but also the shifting *application* of the category itself. (Hall et al. 1978: 189)

Like the process of racialization, the process of criminalization involves the exercise of a particular form of power; in this case, the "power to criminalize" or "to turn a person into a criminal" (Comack and Balfour 2004: 9). In the same way that racialization involves a "representational process of defining an Other" (Miles 1989: 75), criminalization involves establishing a binary between "the criminal" and "the law-abiding." This dualism reinforces the view that those who are deemed to be criminal are not like "the rest of Us" — not only in terms of what they have done, but also who they are and the social spaces in which they move. The net result is that the criminal justice system and policing reproduce "a very particular kind of order" (Comack and Balfour 2004: 9).

At its core the goal of criminalization is "to target those activities of groups that authorities deem it necessary to control, thus making the process inherently political" (Chan and Mirchandani 2002: 15). For instance, criminologists have long noted that the criminal justice system devotes far more resources to the policing of the poor and marginalized in society than it does to controlling the harmful activities of the wealthy and their corporations (Snider 2006; Reiman and Leighton 2010). Crimes that are promulgated "in the suites" of large corporations (price-fixing, tax evasion, environmental pollution, and workplace health and safety) have been documented as producing great harm in lives lost and financial costs incurred. Yet these actions receive far less attention in the criminal justice system than those that occur "in the streets" (assaults, robbery and theft). One result of this focus of criminal justice intervention is that measures taken to control and contain the threat posed by "crime" have resulted in the construction of particular racialized groups as troublesome "problem populations." Hence, the policing of Aboriginal people becomes racialized.

Similar to the role played by the NWMP in the colonial project of creating the white settler society, contemporary police forces in Canadian society have been assigned a central role in the management and containment of "problem populations." This is especially the case in the urban centres of the Prairie provinces. It falls to the police as "reproducers of order" to devote their considerable resources to the realization of that objective. In doing their surveillance of the racialized spaces of the inner city, police come to define Aboriginal people as "troublesome" and therefore in need of control. The result can be deadly.

References

Bittle, S., N. Quann, T. Hattem, and D. Muise. 2002. *A One-Day Snapshot of Aboriginal Youth in Custody Across Canada*. Ottawa: Department of Justice Canada. <publications.gc.ca/collections/Collection/J2-266-2002E.pdf>.

Blackstone, C., and N. Trocmé. 2004. "Community Based Child Welfare for Aboriginal Children: Supporting Resilience through Structural Change." <cwrp.ca/sites/default/files/publications/en/communityBasedCWAboriginalChildren.pdf>.

Bopp, M., J. Bopp, and P. Lane. 2003. *Aboriginal Domestic Violence in Canada*. Ottawa: Aboriginal Healing Foundation.

Brown, L., and C. Brown. 1978. *An Unauthorized History of the RCMP*. Toronto: James Lorimer.

Brownridge, D. 2003. "Male Partner Violence against Aboriginal Women in Canada: An Empirical Analysis." *Journal of Interpersonal Violence* 18, 1.

Campaign 2000. 2010. *Report Card on Child and Family Poverty in Canada: 1989–2010*. <campaign2000.ca/reportCards/national/2010EnglishC2000NationalReportCard.pdf>.

Canadian Panel on Violence Against Women. 1993. *Changing the Landscape: Ending Violence: Achieving Equality*. Ottawa: Minister of Supply and Services Canada.

Carter, S. 1999. *Aboriginal People and Colonizers of Western Canada to 1900*. Toronto: University of Toronto Press.

Chan, W., and K. Mirchandani. 2002. "From Race and Crime to Racialization and Criminalization." In W. Chan and K. Mirchandani (eds.), *Crimes of Colour: Racialization and the Criminal Justice System in Canada.* Peterborough: Broadview Press.

Collin, C., and H. Jensen. 2009. *A Statistical Profile of Poverty in Canada.* Ottawa: Library of Parliament. <parl.gc.ca/Content/LOP/ResearchPublications/prb0917-e.htm#a9>.

Comack, E. 1996. *Women in Trouble: Connecting Women's Law Violations to Their Histories of Abuse.* Halifax: Fernwood Publishing.

_____. 2008. *Out There/In Here: Masculinity, Violence, and Prisoning.* Halifax, NS: Fernwood Publishing.

Comack, E., and G. Balfour. 2004. *The Power to Criminalize: Violence, Inequality and the Law.* Halifax and Winnipeg: Fernwood Publishing.

DIAND (Department of Indian Affairs and Northern Development). 2003. *Backgrounder: The Residential School System.* Ottawa: Indian and Northern Affairs Canada. <ainc-inac.gc.ca/gs/schl_e.html>.

Dickie, D.J., and H. Palk. 1957. *Pages from Canada's Story.* Toronto: J.M. Dent and Sons.

Dion, S. 2005. "Aboriginal People and Stories of Canadian History: Investigating Barriers to Transforming Relationships." In C. James (ed.), *Possibilities and Limitations: Multicultural Policies and Programs in Canada.* Halifax, NS: Fernwood Publishing.

Ennab, F. 2010. "Rupturing the Myth of the Peaceful Western Canadian Frontier: A Socio-historical Study of Colonization, Violence, and the North West Mounted Police, 1873–1905." Master's thesis, Department of Sociology, University of Manitoba. <mspace.lib.umanitoba.ca/handle/1993/4109>.

Galabuzi, G.E. 2009. "Social Exclusion." In D. Raphael (ed.), *Social Determinants of Health: Canadian Perspectives,* second edition. Toronto: Canadian Scholars' Press

Gibbins, R., and R. Ponting. 1986. "Historical Background and Overview." In R. Ponting (ed.), *Arduous Journey.* Toronto: McLelland and Stewart.

Graydon, J. 2008. "Canadian Aboriginal Reserves in Crisis: Long-term Solutions Are Needed to Stop the Cycle of Poverty." <suite101.com/content/canadian-reserves-in-crisis-a78339>.

Green, Joyce. 2006. "From *Stonechild* to Social Cohesion: Anti-Racist Challenges for Saskatchewan." *Canadian Journal of Political Science* 39, 3.

Hall, S., C. Critcher, T. Jefferson, J. Clarke, and B. Roberts. 1978. *Policing the Crisis: Mugging, the State and Law and Order.* London: MacMillan.

Hamilton, A.C., and C.M. Sinclair (Commissioners). 1991. *Report of the Aboriginal Justice Inquiry of Manitoba. Volume 1. The Justice System and Aboriginal People.* Winnipeg: Queen's Printer.

Knockwood, I. 2001. *Out of the Depths: The Experiences of Mi'kmaw Children at the Indian Residential School at Shubenacadie, Nova Scotia* (third edition). Halifax: Rosewood.

La Prairie, C. 1994. *Seen But Not Heard: Native People in the Inner City.* Ottawa: Aboriginal Justice Directorate, Minister of Justice and Attorney General of Canada.

_____. 2002. Aboriginal Over-Representation in the Criminal Justice System: A Tale of Nine Cities." *Canadian Journal of Criminology* 44, 2.

LaRocque, E. 2000. "Violence in Aboriginal Communities." In K. McKenna and J. Larkin (eds.), *Violence Against Women: New Canadian Perspectives.* Toronto: Inanna.

Latimer, J., and L.C. Foss. 2004. *A One-Day Snapshot of Aboriginal Youth in Custody Across*

Canada: Phase II. Ottawa: Department of Justice Canada. <justice.gc.ca/eng/rp-pr/cj-jp/yj-jj/yj2-jj2/yj2.pdf>.

Loxley, J. 2010. *Aboriginal, Northern, and Community Economic Development: Papers and Retrospectives.* Winnipeg: Arbeiter Ring.

MacKinnon, S. 2009. "Tracking Poverty in Winnipeg's Inner City: 1996–2006." *State of the Inner City Report 2009.* Winnipeg: CCPA-MB.

McCalla, A., and V. Satzewich. 2002. "Settler Capitalism and the Construction of Immigrants and "Indians" as Racialized Others." In W. Chan and K. Mirchandani (eds.), *Crimes of Colour: Racialization and the Criminal Justice System in Canada.* Peterborough: Broadview Press.

McEvoy, M., and J. Daniluk. 1995. "Wounds to the Soul: The Experiences of Aboriginal Women as Survivors of Sexual Abuse." *Canadian Psychology* 36.

McIvor, S., and T. Nahanee. 1998. "Aboriginal Women: Invisible Victims of Violence." In K. Bonnycastle and G. Rigakos (eds.), *Unsettling Truths: Battered Women, Policy, Politics, and Contemporary Research in Canada.* Vancouver: Collective Press.

McLeod, J. 2000. *Beginning Postcolonialism.* New York: Palgrave.

Milloy, J. 1999. *A National Crime: The Canadian Government and the Residential School System, 1879 to 1986.* Winnipeg: University of Manitoba Press.

Monture, P. 2007. "Racing and Erasing: Law and Gender in White Settler Societies." In S. Hier and S. Bolaria (eds.), *Race & Racism in 21st-Century Canada.* Peterborough: Broadview Press.

Monture-Angus, P. 1995. *Thunder in My Soul: A Mohawk Woman Speaks.* Halifax: Fernwood Publishing.

Moyer, S. 1992. "Race, Gender and Homicide: Comparisons between Aboriginals and Other Canadians." *Canadian Journal of Criminology* 34.

National Collaborating Centre for Aboriginal Health [NCCAH]. 2009–2010. *Poverty as a Social Determinant of First Nations, Inuit, and Métis Health.* <nccah-ccnsa.ca/docs/fact%20sheets/social%20determinates/NCCAH_fs_poverty_EN.pdf>.

Nettelbeck, A., and R. Smandych. 2010. "Policing Indigenous Peoples on Two Colonial Frontiers: Australia's Mounted Police and Canada's North-West Mounted Police." *The Australian and New Zealand Journal of Criminology* 43, 2.

Noël, A. 2009. "Aboriginal Peoples and Poverty in Canada: Can Provincial Governments Make a Difference?" Paper presented at the Annual Meeting of the International Sociological Association's Research Committee 19, Montreal, August 20. <cccg.umontreal.ca/RC19/PDF/Noel-A_Rc192009.pdf>.

Ontario Native Women's Association. 1989. *Breaking Free: A Proposal for Change to Aboriginal Family Violence.* Thunder Bay, Ontario.

Perreault, S. 2009. "The Incarceration of Aboriginal People in Adult Correctional Services." *Juristat* 29, 3.

____. 2011. "Violent Victimization of Aboriginal People in the Canadian Provinces, 2009." *Juristat* (March).

Pettipas, K. 1995. *Severing the Ties that Bind: Government Repression of Indigenous Religious Ceremonies on the Prairies.* Winnipeg: University of Manitoba Press.

Razack, S. 2007. "When Place Becomes Race." In T. Das Gupta, C.E. James, R. Maaka, G-E. Galabuzi and C. Andersen (eds.), *Race and Racialization: Essential Readings.* Toronto:

Canadian Scholars' Press.

RCAP (Royal Commission on Aboriginal Peoples). 1996. *Report of the Royal Commission on Aboriginal Peoples*. Ottawa: Indian and Northern Affairs Canada. <aadnc-aandc.gc.ca/eng/1100100014597/1100100014637>.

Reiman, J., and P. Leighton. 2010. *The Rich Get Richer and the Poor Get Prison: Ideology, Class and Criminal Justice*, ninth edition. Toronto: Pearson.

Sangster, J. 2001. *Regulating Girls and Women: Sexuality, Family and the Law in Ontario, 1920–1960*. Toronto: Oxford University Press.

Sapers, H. 2007. *Annual Report of the Office of the Correctional Investigator 2006–2007*. Ottawa: Minister of Public Works and Government Services Canada. <oci-bec.gc.ca/cnt/rpt/pdf/annrpt/annrpt20062007-eng.pdf>.

Silver, J. 2006a. Building a Path to a Better Future: Urban Aboriginal People." In J. Silver (ed.), *In Their Own Voices: Building Urban Aboriginal Communities*. Halifax and Winnipeg: Fernwood Publishing.

Smylie, J. 2009. "The Health of Aboriginal Peoples." In D. Raphael (ed.), *Social Determinants of Health*, second edition. Toronto: Canadian Scholars' Press.

Snider, L. 2006. "The Disappearance of Corporate Crime." In E. Comack (ed.), *Locating Law: Race/Class/Gender/Sexuality Connections*. Halifax and Winnipeg: Fernwood Publishing.

Statistics Canada. 2008. *Aboriginal Peoples in Canada in 2006: Inuit, Métis and First Nations, 2006 Census*. <statcan.ca/census-recensement/2006/as-sa/97-558/pdf/97-558-XIE2006001.pdf>.

____. 2011. *Family Violence in Canada: A Statistical Profile*. Catalogue no. 85-224-X. <statcan.gc.ca/pub/85-224-x/85-224-x2010000-eng.pdf>.

York, G. 1990. *The Dispossessed: Life and Death in Native Canada*. London: Vintage.

Legal Cases

R. v. Gladue [1999] 1 S.C.R. 908

Chapter 17

POLICIES OF DISCRIMINATION

The Canadian Indian Act

Pamela Downe

From: *Gendered Intersections: An Introduction to Women's and Gender Studies,* second edition, pp. 447–451 (reprinted with permission).

In 1876, the Government of Canada passed the first *Indian Act* in an attempt to define who was an "Indian" and to control the mobility, economy and culture of Canada's diverse Aboriginal peoples. The objective was to promote an agenda of assimilation whereby culturally distinct Aboriginal communities would be eliminated and integrated into the larger and emerging European-based society of colonial Canada. The impact of this legislation on Aboriginal women, men and children cannot be overstated. As Bonita Lawrence (2000: 76) argues, "The *Indian Act* ... is much more than a set of regulations that have controlled every aspect of Indian life for over a century. It provides a way of understanding Native identity." The *Indian Act* of 1876 consolidated policies dealing with the "protection, civilization and assimilation" of Aboriginal peoples. The colonial racism that informs this legislation is clear. In a 1920 presentation to parliament, Duncan Campbell Scott, former Superintendent General of Indian Affairs, stated: "Our object is to continue until there is not a single Indian in Canada that has not been absorbed into the body politic and there is no Indian Question" (cited in Arnot 2000: 256).

The 1876 Act stipulated under what conditions someone could be defined as "Indian" and under what conditions Aboriginal people could be "enfranchised," losing Indian status. The discriminatory policies set forth in this Act had far-reaching implications. If an Aboriginal man or woman decided to pursue state-recognized and professional education, the *Indian Act* stipulated that s/he would lose Indian status (the racist logic being that there could be no formally recognized Indian educated in the same way as a Euro-Canadian citizen). Some traditional ceremonies were banned by the *Indian Act*: a paternalistic system of supervision was established through the creation of a federal Department of Indian Affairs, expressed most forcefully through the appointed "Indian Agents."

For "Indian" women, the *Indian Act* was extremely problematic for it denied them the right to vote in band elections or to participate in decisions about reserve land surrenders. If her husband died without leaving a will, a woman was required to be of "good moral character" (as judged by the Superintendent General of Indian affairs) in order to receive any of her husband's property. And if a woman married a man without Indian status, she lost her own official status as did her children. It was thought that a woman was to be subsumed in the identity of her husband, for when a non-Indian woman married an officially recognized "Indian" man, his status was then conferred to her and all subsequent children (see RCAP 1996).

The Act went through many revisions and permutations; each marked with specific gains towards First Nations self-determination as well as certain drawbacks that perpetuated the federal government's assimilationist agenda. The 1951 Act, for example, increased the imposition of provincial laws and standards on status Indians but it also removed cultural prohibitions banning certain ceremonies (Bartlett 1988). In 1985, the watershed Bill C-31 amendment repealed the policies that required "Indian" women and their children to lose status when those women married a non-status man. While this was an important victory, it is equally important to note that the Bill only reinstates "Indian" status to the enfranchised women and their children. Legal status is still not conferred to the grandchildren of enfranchised women. Therefore, rather than repealing the patriarchal assumptions that inform this policy, Bill C-31 only displaces them by two generations (RCAP 1996). It is also important to note that some women who regained status through Bill C-31 experienced tremendous discrimination by Aboriginal and non-Aboriginal communities alike. The legacy of their enfranchisement was stigmatizing and these women had to overcome many obstacles to reclaim a place for themselves as recognized "Status Indians." However, despite its limitations, Bill C-31 repeals all policies of enfranchisement, guaranteeing status to those First Nations people who may have once feared that it would be taken from them.

In April 2001, the Minister of Indian Affairs and Northern Development introduced the First Nations Governance Initiative (FNGI). In theory, the FNGI is an interim step towards self-governance putting "the power to handle community governance affairs where it belongs, in the hands of First Nations people themselves" (Indian and Northern Affairs 2002). However, as Anna Hunter (2011) explains so well, the FNGI does not adequately consider the specific gender- or class-based needs of those people it hopes to benefit. Moreover, there is a lack of "cultural fit" between the template of governance established by the federal government and the daily decision-making dynamics that characterize many First Nations communities.

As students and scholars of Women's and Gender Studies, we are faced with the important and necessary task of examining how influential policies discriminate against those most intimately affected by a collective colonial past. What follows are excerpts from two versions of the *Indian Act of Canada* as well as from Bill C-31. The language that is used and the context that is established reveals a great deal about the cultural assumptions held by policy-makers towards Aboriginal peoples, Aboriginal women and the power of the Euro-Canadian state.

The Indian Act, 1876
[...]
Terms
3.   The following terms contained in this Act shall be held to have the meaning hereinafter assigned to them ...:

(1) The term "band" means any tribe, band or body of Indians who own or are interested in a reserve or in Indian lands in common, of which the legal tide is vested in the Crown [...]

(3) The term "Indian" means

First. Any person of Indian blood reputed to belong to a particular band;

Secondly. Any legitimate child of such person;

Thirdly. Any woman who is or was lawfully married to such person.

(a) Provided that any illegitimate child, unless having shared with the consent of the band in the distribution moneys of such band for a period exceeding two years, may, at any time, be excluded from the membership thereof by the band, if [...] sanctioned by the Superintendent-General:

[...]

(c) Provided that any Indian woman marrying any other than an Indian or non-treaty Indian shall cease to be an Indian in any respect within the meaning of this Act

[...]

(d) Provided that any Indian woman marrying an Indian of any other band shall cease to be a member of the band to which she formerly belonged, and become a member of the band [...] of which her husband is a member:

(e) Provided also that no half-breed in Manitoba who has shared in the distribution of half-breed lands shall be accounted an Indian; and that no half-breed head of family (except the widow of an Indian, or a half-breed who has already been admitted into a treaty), shall [...] be accounted an Indian, or entitled to be admitted into any Indian treaty.

[...]

(5) The term "reserve" means any tract or tracts of land set apart by treaty or otherwise for the use of benefit of or granted to a particular band of Indians, of which the legal title is the Crown, but which is unsurrendered, and includes all the trees, wood, timber, soil, stone, minerals, metals or other valuables thereon or therein.

[...]

Protection of Reserves

11. No person [...] other than an Indian of the band, shall settle, reside or hunt upon, occupy or use any land or marsh, or shall settle, reside upon or occupy any road, or allowance for roads running through any reserve belonging to [...] such a band;

[...]

Privileges of Indians

64. No Indian or non-treaty Indian shall be liable to be taxed for any real or personal property, unless he holds real estate under lease or in fee simple, or personal property, outside of the reserve or special reserve, in which case he shall be liable to be taxed for such real or personal property at the same rate as other persons in the locality in which it is situate.

[...]

Disabilities and Penalties

72. The Superintendent-General shall have power to stop the payment of the annuity and interest money of any Indian who may be proved, to the satisfaction of the Superintendent-General, to have been guilty of deserting his family, and the said Superintendent-General may apply the same towards the support of any family, woman or child so deserted; also to stop the payment of the annuity and interest money of any woman having no children, who deserts her husband and lives immorally with another man.

[...]

Enfranchisement

86. Whenever any Indian man, or unmarried woman, of the full age of twenty-one years, obtains the consent of the band of which he or she is a member to become enfranchised [...] the local agent shall report [...] the name of the applicant to the Superintendent-General; whereupon the Superintendent-General [...] shall authorize some competent person to report whether the applicant is an Indian who, from the degree of civilization to which he attained, and the character for integrity, morality and sobriety which he bears, appears to be qualified to be [enfranchised]:

(1) Any Indian who may be admitted to the degree of Doctor of Medicine, or to any other degree by any University of Learning, or who may be admitted in any Province of the Dominion to practice law [...], or who may enter Holy Orders or who may be licensed by any denomination of Christians as a Minister of the Gospel, shall *ipso facto* become and be enfranchised under this Act.

Assented to 12 April 1876

The Indian Act, 1970

Administration

3. (1) This Act shall be administered by the Minister of Indian Affairs and Northern Development, who shall be the superintendent-general of Indian affairs.

[...]

Definition and Registration of Indians

5. An Indian Register shall be maintained in the Department [of Indian Affairs], which shall consist of Band Lists and General Lists and in which shall be recorded the name of every person who is entitled to be registered as an Indian.

[...]

11. Subject to section 12, a person is entitled to be registered if that person

(a) [is] entitled to hold, use or enjoy the lands and other immovable property belonging to the various tribes, bands or bodies of Indians in Canada;

(b) is a member of a band [...]

(c) is a male person who is a direct descendant in the male line of a male person described in paragraph (a) or (b);

(d) is the legitimate child of

(i) a male person described in paragraph (a) or (b), or

(ii) a person described in paragraph (c);

(e) is the illegitimate child of a female person described in paragraph (a), (b) or (d); or

(f) is the wife or widow of a person who is entitled to be registered by virtue of paragraph (a), (b), (c), (d), or (e).

[...]

12. (1) The following persons are not entitled to be registered [...]:

(a) a person who

(i) has received or has been allotted half-breed lands or money scrip,

(ii) is a descendant of a person described in subparagraph (i),

(iii) is enfranchised

[....]

(b) a woman who married a person who is not an Indian, unless that woman is subsequently the wife or widow of a person described in section 11.

[...]

14. A woman who is a member of a band ceases to be a member of that band if she marries a person who is not a member of that band, but if she marries a member of another band, she thereupon becomes a member of the band of which her husband is a member.

Enfranchisement
[Previous Sections pertaining to enfranchisement are replaced by Sections 109 – 112]
109. (1) On the report of the Minister that an Indian has applied for enfranchisement and that in his opinion the Indian

(a) is of the full age of twenty-one years,

(b) is capable of assuming duties and responsibilities of citizenship, and

(c) when enfranchised, will be capable of supporting himself and his dependents, the Governor in Council may by order declare that the Indian and his wife and minor unmarried children are enfranchised.

[...]

(2) On the report of the Minister that an Indian woman married a person who is not an Indian, the Governor in Council may by order declare that the woman is enfranchised as of the date of her marriage and, on the recommendation of the Minister may by order declare that all or any of her children are enfranchised as of the date of the marriage or such other date as the order may specify.

[...]

III. *Bill C-31: An Act to Amend the Indian Act, 1985*
Clause 4: This amendment would substitute for the existing scheme of band membership [...].

It would also eliminate provisions relating to entitlement to registration that discriminate on the basis of sex and would replace them with non-discriminatory rules for determining entitlement. As well, it would eliminate the distinction between "legitimate" and "illegitimate" children and provide for the reinstatement of persons who have lost their entitlement to registration under discriminatory provisions or, in certain cases, through enfranchisement.

The proposed sections 5 to 7 would deal with registration in the Indian Register, sections 6 and 7 replacing the present sections 11 and 12.

[...]

6. (1) Subject to section 7, a person is entitled to be registered if

[...]

(c) the name of that person was omitted or deleted from the Indian Register, or from a band list [...] under subparagraph [...] 12(1)(b), subsection 12(2) or subsection 109(2) [...] or under any former provision of this Act relating to the same subject matter as any of those provisions.

[...]

Clause 12: The amendment to subsection 68(1) and the repeal of subsection 68(2) [based on section 72 in the 1876 Indian Act] would establish the same rule for male and female Indians with respect to support payments in circumstances such as desertion. The repeal of subsection 68(3) would remove a special rule for "illegitimate" children.

[...]

Clause 14: The repeal of sections 109 to 113 would remove the concept of enfranchisement from the Indian Act.

References

Arnot, David M. 2000 [1998]. "The Five Treaties in Saskatchewan: An Historical Overview." In Ron. Laliberte et al. (eds.), *Expressions in Canadian Native Studies*. Saskatoon: University of Saskatchewan Extension Press.

Bartlett, Richard. 1988. *The Indian Act of Canada*, second edition. Saskatoon: University of Saskatchewan Native Law Centre.

Hunter, Anna. 2011. "For and By Men: Colony, gender and Aboriginal Self-Government." In C. Lesley Biggs, Pamela Downe and Susan Gingell (eds.), *Gendered Intersections: An Introduction to Women's and Gender Studies*. Halifax/Winnipeg: Fernwood Publishing.

Indian and Northern Affairs Canada. 2002. "Minister Introduces First Nations Governance Legislation." *News Release Communiqué*, June 14. Ottawa: Government of Canada.

Lawrence, Bonita. 2000. "Mixed-Race Urban Native People: Surviving a Legacy of Policies of Genocide." In Ron. Laliberte et al. (eds.), *Expressions in Canadian Native Studies*. Saskatoon: University of Saskatchewan Extension Press.

RCAP (Royal Commission on Aboriginal Peoples). 1996. *Report of the Royal Commission on Aboriginal Peoples*. Ottawa: Canada Communication Group.

IMMIGRATION

Chapter 18

"MANAGING" CANADIAN IMMIGRATION

Racism, Racialization, and the Law

Lisa Marie Jakubowski and Elizabeth Comack

From: *Locating Law: Race/Class/Gender Connections,* third edition, pp.
88–115 (reprinted with permission).

For centuries Canada has been identified as "a nation of immigrants" (Samuel 1990:
383). A recent National Household Survey showing that one in five Canadians
(20.6 percent of the population) was born outside of the country reinforces this
identifier (Statistics Canada 2013). Given this multicultural population, it is not
surprising that Canadian governments have publicly placed immigration in a positive light. We have been regularly reminded that the history of immigration has
been a positive and unifying force for the country. Immigration helps us to prosper
economically, and through our contact with diverse groups of people we learn to
become more tolerant and respecting of difference.

This vision, however, can be misleading. Immigration has enriched Canadian
society, but Canada has not always embraced the immigrant. Indeed, Canada is
plagued by a history — albeit a lesser-known history — of racist immigration
laws and policies.

For decades Canadian immigration law was influenced by a racist-inspired

"White Canada" policy. It was not until the 1960s, with the implementation of the points system, that a formally colour-blind immigration policy became the defining feature of the Canadian state's response to immigration. While in principle Canadian immigration law moved from being explicitly restrictive to non-discriminatory, a closer examination of contemporary immigration patterns reveals that racism and racialization — "the process through which groups come to be designated as different and on that basis subjected to differential and unequal treatment" (Block and Galabuzi 2011: 19) — have not disappeared. Rather, law, policy, and practice in the area of immigration now reflect a more subtle and systemic form of discrimination. In a "post-9/11" world, in particular, immigration has become a security matter (Chan 2004: 40–41), with immigration officials justifying their actions through the rhetoric of "balance" — specifically the need to balance between facilitating the movement of people and controlling Canada's borders, or the need to balance between "defending [Canada's] security interests without unduly limiting human rights" (Dolin and Young 2004: 5.)

The purpose of this chapter is twofold: 1) to examine the early history of Canadian immigration laws and to contextualize these laws, both economically and politically, with a view to revealing their explicitly racist nature; and 2) to argue that, despite the *appearance* of equity and fairness in contemporary immigration law and policy, there is evidence of more subtle and systemic discrimination at work.

THE ECONOMIC AND POLITICAL CONTEXT

Prior to 1968, Canada's overtly prejudicial immigration law was based on a "nationality preference system" favouring European immigrants (Simmons 1990: 141). Then, with the emergence of the more "liberal," "non-discriminatory" points system in October 1967 the characteristics of the Canadian immigrant began to change. Between 1968 and 1987 about 2.8 million immigrants from new countries of origin in Africa, Asia, and Latin America arrived in Canada (Simmons 1990).[1] This new wave of immigration persisted and came to constitute two-thirds to three-quarters of the inflow to Canada (Simmons 1990; Citizenship and Immigration Canada 1996: 25; Young 1997: 5; Knowles 1997: 195). In 2011, 45.6 percent of the 248,748 permanent residents admitted to Canada originated from just three source countries: the Philippines, China, and India (CIC 2012a).

Clearly the law now enables more racialized people to come to Canada, but discrimination, in less obvious forms, persists. What is the relationship among "race,"[2] class, gender, immigration and the state? Does the presence of "new," visibly different immigrants expedite the persistence and advancement of capitalism in Canada? Obviously, links do exist between immigration and Canadian political economy, and many theorists (for example, Basran 1983; Bolaria and Li 1988; Cappon 1975) have analyzed the relationship between state immigration policies and Canadian capitalist development. The work of Alan Simmons, for example, highlights how Canada's immigration and refugee policies are shaped by the prevailing economic context. As Simmons (1992: 13) points out, "The Canadian state has promoted immigration policies favouring relatively large inflows of immigrant workers during periods of economic expansion and more selective inflows of skilled workers, entrepreneurs and visa workers in periods of economic recession."

Still, the admission of immigrants goes beyond the demands of the labour market. Historically, three, often competing, factors have determined *who* is admitted and *how many* are admitted: the desire to populate Canada with British people (or those whose characteristics most resemble the British); the need to be respecting of, and attentive to, concerns of the international community; and economic conditions (Law Union of Ontario 1981: 17). In other words, a multiplicity of factors, including ideological and political considerations, international obligations, and economic requirements, has shaped the content and objectives of laws and policies (Elliott and Fleras 1996: 290). In law creation, the relationship among these considerations, obligations and requirements has become increasingly more complex as the nation's population has grown more diverse. But, over time, one goal has remained constant — maintaining immigration control.

NATION-BUILDING AND THE "WHITE CANADA" POLICY

Officially abandoned only in 1962, "White Canada" policies were deeply rooted in the mid-nineteenth century. As Freda Hawkins (1989: 8) notes, beginning with these early origins "the whole lengthy episode of 'White Canada' is often downplayed, or clothed in discreet silence or simply not extrapolated from its historical context."

Initially, immigration policies were ethnically selective: "racist in orientation, assimilationist in objective" (Elliott and Fleras 1996: 290). Striving to preserve the British character of Canada, authorities directed their efforts towards excluding certain people from entry, while encouraging others to settle. Potential migrants were ranked into categories, with "preferred" immigrants being drawn from Great Britain, the United States,[3] France, and, to a lesser extent, Northern and Western Europe (Manpower and Immigration 1974: 4). When these recruitment efforts failed to produce the large numbers required to settle Canada's Western prairie lands, the federal government extended its preferential policies to include other white immigrants — for example, Ukrainians, Italians, Poles, and Hutterites — previously classified as "non-preferred" (Henry et al. 2006: 75). The emphasis was placed on white immigrants because they were considered to be of "superior stock," more desirable, and more easily assimilated than immigrants of colour

(Elliott and Fleras 1996: 290). However, even with the expansion of the preferred categories to include more white immigrants, Canadian labour needs could not be met. In the 1880s thus began the recruitment of an "undesirable," visibly different source of cheap labour — the Chinese. It was during this time period that "race" first became an issue of significance in relation to Canadian immigration law and policy formation (Henry et al. 2006: 75).

One of the central events triggering the immigration of the Chinese to Canada was the building of the Canadian Pacific Railway (CPR). During the period of its construction (1881–85) over 15,000 Chinese men were brought to Canada under labour contracts; more than half arrived during 1882–83, when the demand for their labour was at its height (Comack 1991: 68). Chinese immigrants were particularly attractive because of their large supply and cheap cost. While they were nation-building, the Chinese railway workers were tolerated by the white workers, as long as no other source of labour was available. But once the CPR was completed and Canada now had a surplus of labour, sentiments towards the Chinese presence changed. Accordingly, a conflict between business and labour arose.

It was clearly in the interests of Canadian capitalists to have this reserve army of labour. For the capitalist, the appeal of immigrant labour, in this case Chinese labour, resided not only in the apparent willingness of the immigrants to do undesirable work cheaply but also in the opportunity to "weaken the organizational efforts and bargaining position of the dominant workforce" (Bolaria and Li 1988: 34; Portes 1978). The reaction of white Canadian labourers to the Chinese presence was less enthusiastic. The ultimate result was the emergence of a split-labour market.

According to Edna Bonacich (1972: 549), a split-labour market produces a three-way conflict between the dominant class and two groups of labourers. The dominant business class strives to maximize profits by utilizing the cheapest available sources of labour power. Through the process of super-exploitation (Cox 1948), the dominant class replaces higher-paid labour with cheaper labour. Bonacich (1980: 15) argues that because employers prefer to hire the cheaper labourers of colour, white workers fear and become hostile towards the more exploitable racialized minorities. One way in which white workers can respond to this hostility and fear is to put pressure on the state to restrict the capitalists' access to cheaper labour through "exclusion" (Bonacich 1972: 554–57; 1976: 45). Controlling immigration is one strategy of exclusion.

This pattern was clearly visible in the case of the Chinese labourers in Canada. Antagonistic towards, and feeling threatened by, these visibly different newcomers, white labourers began pressing the Canadian government to restrict immigration. Thus, when nation-building projects such as the construction of the CPR were close to completion and the need for the cheap labourers had diminished, the federal government began passing highly discriminatory, exclusionary pieces of immigration legislation (Henry et al. 2006: 74; Elliott and Fleras 1996: 290–91). A statement made by Prime Minister John A. Macdonald in 1883 reflects the particular logic used to justify these legislative changes. A Chinese person "was a sojourner in a strange land … and he has no common interest with us," Macdonald said. He "gives us his labour and is paid for it and is valuable, the same as a threshing machine or any other agricultural implement which we may borrow from the United States, or hire and return to its owner" (quoted in Knowles 1997: 51).

Elements of restriction, first directed towards the Chinese in 1885 and subsequently towards other racialized immigrants, began appearing in immigration legislation from the 1880s onward (Hawkins 1989: 16). While the general term "race" did not emerge as a prohibitive or restrictive legal category until the *Immigration Act* of 1910, the federal government did pass specific regulations and pieces of legislation that were blatantly discriminatory towards certain racialized groups. In particular, Ottawa devised different strategies for "discouraging immigration" from China, Japan and India (Law Union of Ontario 1981: 25). These strategies included the *Chinese Immigration Act* of 1885, the 1907 Gentleman's Agreement with Japan, and the Continuous Journey Stipulation of 1908 — this last one directed especially towards India and the curtailing of East Indian immigration.

The *Chinese Immigration Act* of 1885 imposed a head tax on all Chinese people arriving in Canada — which effectively meant Chinese men, as they were the ones being brought into the country under labour contracts. While the 1885 Act set the tax at $50, it rose to $100 in 1900 and $500 by 1903 (Bolaria and Li 1988: 107). As Nupur Gogia and Bonnie Slade (2011: 20) note, "At the time, $500 represented two years of wages for a Chinese labourer, and today it is equivalent to over $55,000." But even with the burdensome head tax, the flow of Chinese immigrants continued, in large part because Chinese labour was proving profitable in the burgeoning mining, fishing and forestry industries of British Columbia (Phillips 1967). Facing more and more pressure to eradicate this "immigration problem," in 1923 the Canadian government passed the *Chinese Exclusion Act,* which served to prohibit Chinese immigration from 1923 to 1947 (Bolaria and Li 1988: 107).[4]

In the case of Japanese immigration, matters were a little more complicated. The Japanese were allies of the British at the turn of the last century, and any action that Canada might take against Japanese immigration had to be carried out without jeopardizing British-Japanese relations. Japan also had the potential to become a trading partner with Canada, so that some degree of co-operation was considered desirable. Taking these factors into consideration, Rodolphe Lemieux, postmaster general and minister of labour, was sent to Japan to negotiate what came to be known as the Gentleman's Agreement: "Under the terms of this agreement, Canada agreed not to impose discriminatory laws against Japanese immigrants, but the

Japanese government was to voluntarily restrict the number of people permitted to emigrate to Canada" (Law Union of Ontario 1981: 26).

As for India, William Lyon Mackenzie King, the deputy minister of labour, was not as successful in negotiations. India was clearly resistant to such restrictions, leaving the Canadian government with a dilemma. Not wanting to cause rifts within the British Empire, Canada could not take direct, discriminatory action. How then could it more subtly control East Indian immigration? The solution was the Continuous Journey Stipulation of 1908. According to this regulation, immigrants who came to Canada "otherwise than by continuous journey from countries of which they were natives or citizens, and upon through tickets purchased in that country, may be refused entry" (Bolaria and Li 1988: 170). This particular regulation highlights the political nature of law. Because they were citizens of the British Empire, East Indians should have been entitled to immigrate to Canada, but the Continuous Journey Stipulation made this almost impossible. Specifically, at that particular historical moment, the only company that could provide transportation from India to Canada was the CPR. Thus, to achieve its exclusionary objective the government issued the CPR express orders not to sell any "through tickets" to Canada (Law Union of Ontario 1981: 26). From the standpoint of lawmakers and politicians, the stipulation was both functional and politically calculating.

The Act did indeed curtail Indian immigration to Canada after 1908. For example, in 1907 and 1908 a total of 4,757 East Indians immigrated to Canada. After the legislation became effective in 1909, the numbers decreased dramatically. In 1909 Canada admitted only six East Indians, while the total admission of East Indians to Canada from 1909 to 1913 was twenty-nine (Bolaria and Li 1988: 169). In an effort to preserve its positive relations with the rest of the British Empire, the Canadian government ensured that the Stipulation did not *explicitly* bar any particular group of people from entry into Canada. Highlighting its political nature, the Continuous Journey Stipulation "amended the *Immigration Act* to allow the government to control East Indian immigration without having the appearance of doing so" (Henry et al. 2006: 75).

The now famous "*Komagata Maru* Incident" was an attempt by East Indians to challenge this racist policy. On May 23, 1914, the ship *Komagata Maru* arrived in Vancouver carrying 376 mostly Sikh passengers. Because the ship had made numerous stops along the way on its voyage from India, all but twenty of the passengers were denied entry into Canada. Officials cited the Continuous Journey Stipulation. After a two-month standoff between the East Indian passengers and their onshore supporters and the Canadian government, the *Komagata Maru* was escorted out of Vancouver Harbour by a naval ship. Similar to the *Chinese Exclusion Act*, the Continuous Journey Stipulation remained in force until its repeal in 1947 (Elliott and Fleras 1992: 240; Bolaria and Li 1988: 171).

In essence, the *Chinese Exclusion Act,* the Gentleman's Agreement, and the Continuous Journey Stipulation were effective mechanisms for controlling immigration, ensuring that almost no Asian people immigrated to Canada until after World War II (Henry et al. 2006: 75). Such mechanisms were consistent with the racist stance towards immigration that had emerged in the late nineteenth and early twentieth centuries. As a government pamphlet from this period aimed at attracting new immigrants proclaimed: "Canada is situated in the North Temperate Zone ... The climate is particularly suited to the white race. It is the land of homes — the new homeland of the British people ... British people soon find themselves at home in Canada. It is a British country, with British customs and ideals" (from *Canada — The New Homeland,* as cited in Law Union of Ontario 1981: 26).

SECTION 38(C): CANADIAN XENOPHOBIA ENSHRINED IN LAW

The term "race" first emerged as a prohibitive/restrictive legal category in section 38(c) of the Immigration Act of 1910 (Hawkins 1989: 17). This section, amended in 1919 to include "nationality," is most representative of "White Canada's" xenophobia. In essence, section 38(c) created a class of immigrants considered to be "undesirable" for admission to Canada. Included among those who could be denied entry were

> any nationality or race of immigrants ... deemed unsuitable having regard to the climatic, industrial, social, educational, labour [conditions] ... or because such immigrants are deemed undesirable owing to their peculiar customs, habits, modes of life, methods of holding property and because of their probable inability to become readily assimilated or to assume the duties and responsibilities of Canadian citizenship within a reasonable time after their entry.

By including section 38(c) in the *Immigration Act,* the government's discriminatory policies were enshrined in law — differential treatment based on "race" or nationality was firmly established as a government policy.

One form of differential treatment was the creation of a list of "preferred" countries, as Mackenzie King explained in a report:

> The policy of the [Labour] Department at the present time [1910] is to encourage immigration of farmers, farm labourers, and female domestic servants from the United States, the British Isles, and certain Northern European countries, namely, France, Belgium, Holland, Switzerland, Germany, Denmark, Norway, Sweden and Iceland. On the other hand, it is the policy of the Department to do all in its power to keep out of the

country ... those belonging to nationalities unlikely to assimilate and who consequently prevent the building up of a united nation of people of similar customs and ideals. (Quoted in Manpower and Immigration 1974: 9–10)

Most conveniently, the legislation of 1910 did not specify the "undesirable" nations. Instead, it gave immigration officials "wide discretion to exclude almost any prospective immigrant on the basis of race, national or ethnic origin or creed" (Henry et al. 2006: 75).

As Irving Abella and Harold Troper (1983) note, the hierarchy continued to reflect the preferences of earlier decades: 1) British and U.S. immigrants; (2) Northern and Western European immigrants; and — as a last resort — (3) Jews, Blacks, and "Orientals." The third group comprised the least desirable candidates for immigration to Canada. They were acceptable only as long as they "were out of sight, risking life and limb in the mines and smelters of the west and north, holed up in lumber camps deep in the forest, or farming the more marginal areas of the western wheat frontier" (Abella and Troper 1983: 5).

What was particularly problematic for immigration officials was when these "undesirables" left the more rural and isolated areas and drifted towards the city. In this respect, Jews were "the worst culprits." They were "city people" who would not be kept on the farm. This drift towards the city became a rationale for the drastic immigration restrictions that emerged in the mid-1920s. By 1928 the deputy minister of immigration, W.J. Egan, ordered that Eastern European immigration numbers be reduced by two-thirds. With the economy doing well, he used the following reasoning to justify the action: "Non-preferred country immigrants had drifted into non-agricultural work almost immediately upon arrival ... and [were] filling positions that might have been filled by immigrants from the Mother Country" (Egan quoted in Abella and Troper 1983: 5).

From the outbreak of World War I through to the Depression and World War II, Canadian immigration went through a long period of uncertainty (Manpower and Immigration 1974: 10). In response to the need to settle Western Canada, immigration had peaked at 400,870 in 1913. However, the unstable and uncertain conditions generated by the two world wars and the Depression resulted in fewer people coming to Canada, with immigration reaching an all-time low of 7,576 in 1942 (Elliott and Fleras 1996: 291). During these troubled political and economic times, anti-immigrant sentiments came to be embodied in extremely discriminatory and inhumane policies and practices.

The Depression, for instance, gave the government the justification it needed to further strengthen its already restrictive legislation. The new legislation reflected the intensified anti-immigrant sentiments among Canadians, who were generally of the opinion that immigrants were attempting to steal jobs from "more deserving" citizens. Basically, immigration from continental Europe came to a halt in March 1931 with the passage of Order-in-Council P.C. 695. By offering admission only to certain categories of people, the order made its racial and class biases quite transparent: "British subjects and American citizens with sufficient capital to maintain themselves until employment was secured; agriculturalists with sufficient means to farm in Canada, farm labourers with guaranteed employment, any individual engaged in the mining, lumbering or logging with assured employment in one of these industries; and the wives and children of adult males legally resident in Canada" (Knowles 1997: 115). The anti-immigrant sentiment in the country was so strong that Canada was not even prepared to distinguish between the "ordinary immigrant" and the "refugee." As Europeans were desperately fleeing Europe in search of refuge from the growing Nazi movement, Canada refused to open its doors.

During this time, the man responsible for enforcing Canadian immigration policy, Frederick Charles Blair, was particularly determined to keep Jewish refugees out of Canada. For Blair, "the term 'refugee' was a code word for 'Jew.' Unless safeguards were adopted, Canada was in danger of being 'flooded by Jewish people,' and his task was to make sure that the safeguard didn't fail" (Abella and Troper 1983: 8). A case in point is the now infamous "Voyage of the Damned." In 1939 the SS *St. Louis* docked at a Canadian port carrying some 907 Jewish refugees who had already been rejected by Cuba, various Latin and South American countries, and the United States. Canada was their last hope. But here, too, the Jewish refugees were denied entry, and the ship set sail for Europe, where many of its passengers would die in gas chambers and crematoria (Abella and Troper 1983: 63–64).

Beyond closing the door to new immigrants and refugees, the country also used deportation on a much more regular basis. New immigrants who had not yet obtained citizenship, who became unemployed, or "who got into any trouble" could be easily expelled from the country (Knowles 1997: 116). In some cases even those innocent of wrongdoing were "persuaded" to leave. Between 1930 and 1935, some 30,000 people were deported (Gogia and Slade 2011: 26). After the Japanese bombing of Pearl Harbor on December 8, 1941, over 20,000 Japanese-Canadians were evicted from their homes in British Columbia and sent to labour camps or farms in Alberta and Manitoba, or interned in detention camps/centres until the conclusion of the war (Knowles 1997: 124). At the war's end about 4,000 Japanese-Canadians (half of them Canadian-born — of whom two-thirds were Canadian citizens) gave in to the anti-Asiatic sentiments and government pressure, leaving Canada for Japan under the government's "repatriation" scheme (Knowles 1997: 124; Sunahara 1981; Ujimoto 1988).

Following World War II, immigration rates once again skyrocketed in response to a postwar boom in the Canadian economy. But even with an overwhelming need for labour, "discrimination and ethnic selectivity in immigration would remain" (Reimers and Troper 1992: 20). The "peacetime policy" (Manpower and Immigration Canada 1974: 18) was unveiled in Prime Minister Mackenzie King's 1947 "Statement on Immigration":

> With regard to the selection of immigrants ... I wish to make it quite clear that Canada is perfectly within her rights in selecting persons who we regard as desirable future citizens. It is not a "fundamental human right" of any alien to enter Canada. It is a privilege. It is a matter of domestic policy ... the people of Canada do not wish, as a result of mass immigration, to make a fundamental alteration in the character of our population. Large scale immigration from the Orient would change the fundamental character of the Canadian population ... The government therefore ... has no intention of removing existing regulations respecting Asiatic immigration unless and until alternative measures of effective control have been worked out. (King, in Manpower and Immigration Canada 1974: 205)

Essentially, as this excerpt highlights, with the rejuvenation of immigration in 1947 came a return to the "policy, regulations and racial priorities of an earlier era" (Reimers and Troper 1992: 21). Policies were still racist in orientation, assimilationist in objective. Care would still be taken to ensure that those applicants from groups considered to be "most easily assimilated" — that is, "British subjects from the United Kingdom, Ireland, Newfoundland, New Zealand, Australia or the Union of South Africa, and also citizens of the United States" (King, in Manpower and Immigration Canada 1974: 203) — would be given preferential treatment during the admission process.

To reinforce this xenophobic position, the *Immigration Act* of 1952 maintained the explicitly restrictive clause 38(c), although the category "race" was changed to "ethnic group" (Hawkins 1989: 17). Consistent with the exclusions outlined in the 1910 Act, the immigration minister was given wide-sweeping discretion to prohibit or limit the admission of people on the basis of ethnicity, nationality, geographic origin, peculiarity of custom, unsuitability of climate, or inability to become assimilated (Reimers and Troper 1992: 25). Through the use of such discretion, Alan Green (1976: 21) points out, the "national and racial balance of immigration would be regulated so as to not to disturb the existing *character* of the Canadian population."

ABANDONING THE "WHITE CANADA" POLICY?

From the *Immigration Act* of 1910 up to and including the 1952 Act, section 38(c) was the principal instrument through which the implicit "White Canada" policy on immigration was implemented. However, with the passage of new, non-discriminatory regulations in the 1962 *Immigration Act*, the "White Canada" policy was, as Hawkins (1989: 39) states, "virtually dead." These regulations officially ended racial and ethnic discrimination in the processing of independent immigrants, with skills — specifically, skills in relation to Canadian labour market needs — becoming the main selection criterion (Reimers and Troper 1992: 32).

A number of factors contributed to this policy shift. One was that Canadian businesses were having difficulty recruiting skilled workers. "It was estimated that in the mid-1960s only 7 percent of the Canadian workforce had secondary schooling or better and that over 40 percent had not even finished primary school" (Gogia and Slade 2011: 28). Another was that international bodies had been taking action on social inequality, exemplified by the passage of the United Nation's Universal Declaration of Human Rights in 1948. As Hawkins (1989: 39) suggests, senior Canadian officials realized that "Canada could not operate effectively with the United Nations, or in a multiracial Commonwealth, with the millstone of a racially discriminatory immigration policy round her neck." As well, Canada passed its own Bill of Rights in 1960, "making discrimination based on race, colour, national origin, religion or gender illegal" (Gogia and Slade 2011: 28). The introduction of the immigration points system in October 1967 — the first of its kind for determining immigration selection — took this policy shift even further.

The purpose of the points system was to establish an "objective" assessment system for the admission of immigrants. The criteria for admission were education and training, personal assessment (later changed to "personal suitability"), occupational demand, occupational skill, age, arranged employment, knowledge of French or English, relatives in Canada, and employment opportunities in the area of destination (Hawkins 1988: 405). These nine factors had a combined potential value of one hundred. An applicant who received fifty or more points was considered likely to settle successfully. An applicant who received less than fifty points was deemed unlikely to settle successfully (Manpower and Immigration Canada 1974: 42). While the original points system has been revised at least six times since 1967 (Gogia and Slade 2011: 31; Hawkins 1988: 380),[5] its intent has remained the same: immigration policy would be applied on "a universal basis which can be interpreted to mean that everyone seeking admission to Canada is assessed under the same set of standards regardless of race, religion or country of origin" (Green 1976: 42).

Although the establishment of "a formally colour-blind immigration policy"

(Elliott and Fleras 1996: 292) made it appear as though racial discrimination had been eliminated, the evidence indicated the contrary (Henry et al. 2006; Bolaria and Li 1988; Malarek 1987; Green 1976). While the regulations no longer contained blatant discriminatory provisions, subtle discriminatory mechanisms remained.

In the matter of immigration offices outside of Canada, for example, Green (1976: 43) notes, "As the government shifts from a national/ethnic-based policy to a universal admission approach, it would have to expand its overseas offices so that, in theory at least, right of review was equal for prospective immigrants regardless of their country of origin." But Green's (1976: 47–54) analysis of overseas expenditures indicates that from 1951 to 1969 the largest concentration of resources committed to the recruitment of migrants was in "developed," traditional source countries. Specifically, in the period 1951–57, 91 percent of total expenditures for recruitment went to developed countries and only 9 percent to less developed countries. In the years 1962–69, the distribution in resources remained largely unbalanced, with 78 percent of total expenditures for recruitment going to developed countries and 22 percent to less developed countries (Green 1976: 47). The distribution of overseas offices was reflected in the data on the source countries of immigrants: Britain and the United States remained as the primary source countries throughout the 1960s and 1970s (Gogia and Slade 2011: 30). As Anthony Richmond observed, Canada had "evidently no intention of abandoning the traditional preference for British immigrants" (quoted in Green 1976: 51).

The commitment, in theory, to the elimination of racial discrimination was more formally enshrined in the *Immigration Act* of 1976. Consistent with trends of past immigration law and policy formation, an interplay among several factors shaped the decision to include a non-discriminatory clause in the Act. From an economic standpoint, Canada moved from "a dependence on unskilled manual labour toward a more highly educated and skilled workforce" (Henry et al. 2006: 77). Because of a decline in immigration from traditional source countries, Canada began to open its doors to "non-preferred" countries in search of economically suitable immigrants. From a more political and social standpoint, pressure to eradicate overt racism surfaced. Influences ranged from the newly implemented multicultural policy (introduced by the Trudeau Liberal government in 1971), which recognized racial and cultural diversity in Canada, to increasing pressure from well-organized, politically active, and increasingly influential racialized groups, human rights activists and lawyers, and from the international community (Henry et al. 2006). In response to these various influences, section 3(f) of the 1976 Act stated:

> It is hereby declared that Canadian Immigration policy and the rules and regulations made under this Act shall be designed and administered in such a manner as to promote the domestic and international interests

ʹ of Canada recognizing the need to ... *ensure that any person who seeks admission to Canada on either a permanent or temporary basis is subject to standards of admission that do not discriminate on grounds of race, national or ethnic origin, colour, religion or sex.* (Cited in Hawkins 1988: 426; emphasis added)

Under the Act, all immigrants would be assessed according to "universal standards" designed to assess ability to "adapt to Canadian life" and settle successfully.

Some analysts hailed the passage of this act into law in 1978 as an extremely positive and important moment in Canadian history. For instance, in the words of Hawkins (1988: xv), "This marked the beginning of a new, more liberal and more cooperative era in Canadian immigration." But were these legislative changes, in practice, as positive as they appeared to be on paper? Despite the more universal system and the commitment, in theory, to equality, discrimination persisted in less obvious forms.

For instance, even with the 1976 Act the distribution of immigration offices revealed a discriminatory policy. For example, the Law Union of Canada pointed out in 1981 that the United Kingdom had five immigration offices, but South America had only three, and of five offices in the whole of Africa, two were located in South Africa. Moreover, "The United States has ten offices, but India, with twice the population, only has one" (Law Union of Ontario 1981: 46). This distribution of immigration offices clearly indicated the historical preference for white European immigration. Furthermore, the wide use of discretion under the Act and regulations allowed individual officers to make discriminatory decisions.

The issue of "personal suitability" was one key to this discrimination. Under the original points system, this criterion — then known as "personal qualities" — was the only element that involved a subjective judgement on the part of the immigration officer. Within the original points system, this factor was worth fifteen points out of one hundred. On a scale of fifteen, immigration officers were to use their discretion in deciding on "a person's ability to become settled in a new country." This ability was based on the officer's perceptions of the applicant's adaptability, motivation, initiation, and resourcefulness (Manpower and Immigration Canada 1974: 44). Under the various amended forms of the 1976 Act, this criterion persisted within the points system, although its weighting changed to ten points out of one hundred and it was renamed "personal suitability" (Young 1991a: 20).[6]

The reduced weighting of "suitability" criterion might seem to imply a limitation on the immigration officer's use of personal discretion. But another regulation in the 1976 Act provided immigration officers with the discretion to override the points system "in exceptional cases." A statement by Manpower and Immigration

Canada (1974: 50) outlined the department's justification for the inclusion of this regulation:

> Introduction of weighted selection factors in 1967 was a totally new immigration concept. It was hoped that totalling the units of assessment awarded for each of the factors would indicate, within reasonable limits, the likelihood of most applicants' success or failure in becoming established in Canada. It was recognized, however, that it was impossible to cover every eventuality, and that the regulations should contain a mechanism for dealing with the exceptional case. Accordingly, when a selection officer is satisfied that there are significant circumstances affecting an applicant's prospects that have not been reflected in the assessment under the nine selection factors he is authorized, subject to concurrence of a designated senior officer, to accept or reject the applicant irrespective of the number of units of assessment that may have been awarded.

Under the 1976 Act, section 11(3) of the immigration regulations "authorize[d] officers to exercise their discretion in respect of immigrants whose applications are unit-rated under the selection criteria, and to accept, or refuse to accept an applicant, whether the applicant achieves or does not achieve the number of units of assessment." The section specifies that discretion is to be exercised "solely on the basis that the unit-rating does not accurately reflect an immigrant's chances of becoming successfully established in Canada" (Employment and Immigration Canada 1991: 07-90-6).[7]

In principle, then, Canadian immigration law moved from being explicitly restrictive to "non-discriminatory." But although couched in the politically acceptable language of equity and fairness, this claim of being "non-discriminatory" did not automatically mean that the law was being equitably applied to all potential immigrants.

CLASS AND GENDER CONSIDERATIONS

While immigration numbers increased during the 1980s and 1990s, certain types of immigrants had a better likelihood of gaining entrance to Canada, and with fewer restrictions. In the 1980s, Brian Mulroney's Conservative government added a new category of immigrants: investors. These wealthier applicants were "given preferential treatment in that they were not assessed on all criteria of the points system if they met the criteria of the investors program" (Chan 2012: 170). During the years leading up to Hong Kong being returned to China in 1997, class privilege seemed to trump "race" as a factor in terms of "who gets in" to Canada. Hong Kong was the top source country to Canada from 1987 to 1997 (Gogia and

Slade 2011: 30). Many of these immigrants came in under the business category because they had large sums of money to invest. To accommodate the influx of these business immigrants, Canada maintained a Hong Kong office staffed with eighteen officers. By comparison, access to immigration offices in other parts of the world was far more restricted; for instance, there were only four immigration offices to service all of Sub-Saharan Africa (Aiken 2007: 68).

As Wendy Chan (2012: 170) suggests, gender also plays a role in terms of "who gets in": "Typically, men are the primary or main applicant, and women are in the category of dependent spouse. Although many women who come to Canada are skilled, they may not have access to a traditional education, which is recognized through the point system and which in turn makes it difficult for them to succeed as the main applicant." As well, Chan (2012: 170) notes that "patriarchal attitudes continue to cast women into the role of being dependent on men, and Canadian immigration policies and practices rely on these assumptions in the processing of applications." The "net effect," according to Chan (2012: 171), is that "potential female immigrants have the best chances of entering into Canada by assuming the role of dependent spouse regardless of whether they fit that category or not."

One of the ways in which women could enter Canada is by taking up work as domestics. Historically, the demand for domestic labour — deemed to be quintes-sentially "women's work" — was met by importing white, working-class British women. Seen as "ideal future mothers and wives of the nation," they were granted landed immigrant status on arrival to Canada contingent on spending six months as live-in caregivers (Hsiung and Nichol 2010: 767). As the supply of British and subsequently European nannies diminished by the end of the Second World War, more and more women were being recruited from the Caribbean. Under the Caribbean Domestic Scheme "women had to be unmarried, between twenty-one and thirty-five, and willing to do domestic work for at least a year with an assigned employer" (Arat-Koç 1999: 140). No sponsorship of spouses or children was allowed under the scheme, and the women could be deported if deemed to be "unsuitable" once they arrived.

With the implementation of the points system in 1967 the Caribbean Domestic Scheme was disbanded. However, because domestic work was ranked so low on the occupational points scale, few domestic workers could qualify as independent immigrants. As a result, those who did come to Canada to carry out this work were brought in on temporary permits. In 1981, the Foreign Domestic Movement (FDM) program was implemented, which "made it possible for domestic workers who had worked in Canada continuously for two years to apply for landed immigrant status without leaving the country" (Arat-Koç 1999: 145). Workers were required to live with their employers during the two-year period, which meant that "home" and "work" were one and the same place for these women, creating the conditions for exploitation and abuse (see Silvera 1989). In 1992 the FDM program was re-named the Live-In Caregiver Program (LCP). In 2011, 11,247 immigrants, the vast majority of whom are women, were admitted under this program (CIC 2012a).

Critics of the LCP point out that the demand for live-in caregivers has been generated by a childcare crisis (as well as increasing pressures on families to care for aging parents). Traditionally, childcare and domestic labour have been relegated to the private sphere and deemed the primary responsibility of women. With the increasing participation of women in the labour force — 65 percent of children aged twelve or below had a mother in the labour force in 2006 (Friendly and Prentice 2009: 16) — the issue of who is to care for the children has become paramount. With licensed daycare spaces at a premium, many parents who can afford it have turned to the option of hiring a live-in caregiver or nanny. Because domestic labour is so de-valued in our society, it is difficult to attract Canadians to these positions. In response, the Canadian state has been willing to meet this demand of (mostly privileged) parents for domestic labour through exploitative immigration (as opposed to, for example, implementing a national childcare policy; see Friendly and Prentice 2009).

RACIALIZATION AND REFUGEES

The *Immigration Act* of 1976 introduced a more liberal, less discriminatory period in Canadian immigration law and policy, to some extent changing the face of Canadian immigration. From the 1980s onwards, neither Britain nor the United States has been the top source country (Gogia and Slade 2011: 30). But an increase in the number of immigrants from non-traditional source countries (such as India, Hong Kong and the Philippines) has not necessarily resulted in a more tolerant Canada. Anti-immigrant sentiments persisted — particularly towards racialized immigrants and refugees, who have come to be viewed as "threats not only to the social, cultural and linguistic order of the nation, but also to the security of the nation" (Chan 2012: 181). This preoccupation with security and the need to better control our borders made a "marked resurgence" (Chan 2004: 35) in the 1980s and has been intensifying ever since.

The legislative changes that reinforced this security and control mentality coincided with public concern and anxiety around the increasing numbers of refugees and asylum seekers attempting to enter Canada in the effort to escape traumatic circumstances — persecution, war, political oppression and natural disaster (Gogia and Slade 2011: 51) — in their home country. As Benjamin Dolin and Margaret Young (2004: 2) note, when large numbers of people arrive on Canada's doorstep and the public does not recognize these arrivals as legitimate, a backlash invariably results and the immigration system appears to be in crisis. For example, in the 1980s, the "illegal" arrival, in lifeboats, of 150 Tamils on the coast of Newfoundland and 174 Sikhs on the Nova Scotian shore generated public outcry and led to further amendments to Canada's immigration system.

While Canada signed on to the U.N. Convention Relating to the Status of Refugees in 1969, refugees were not formally included in Canada's immigration policy until 1978 (CCR 2005a). In 1985 the Supreme Court ruled in *Singh* that the *Charter of Rights and Freedoms* applies to refugee claimants and that claimants had the right to an oral hearing to address their claim. In response, the government introduced Bill C-55, the *Refugee Reform Act*, in 1987. Bill C-55 created the Immigration and Refugee Board of Canada and restructured the refugee determination process; refugees were now required to undergo a screening hearing to determine the credibility of their claims. As Chan (2012: 172) notes, however, the procedure of screening refugees was removed in 1992 when it was realized that 95 percent of refugee claims were legitimate.

Bill C-84, the *Refugee Deterrents and Detention Act*, was also introduced in 1987 (both bills became law in 1989). Bill C-84 "increased penalties for smuggling refugees, levied heavy fines for transporting undocumented aliens, and extended government powers of search, detention and deportation" (Encyclopedia of Immigration 2011). For instance, the Act authorized the government to turn away ships when there were "reasonable grounds" for believing the vessels were transporting anyone in contravention of the Act. As William Angus and James Hathaway (1987: 8) note, "this provision brings back shameful memories of Canada's decision in 1939 to turn away the ship *St. Louis* with its cargo of around 1,000 Jewish refugees, most of whom were forced back to Europe and Hitler's gas chambers." Bill C-84 also made it an offence to assist anyone to come to Canada who was not in possession of proper travel documents, regardless of whether the person was a bona fide refugee (Aiken 2007: 77). According to Angus and Hathaway (1987: 9),

> The law would criminalize the work of church and other humanitarian agencies which assist undocumented refugees to apply for status under Canadian law. Most genuine refugees — those for whom persecution is imminent — simply cannot wait in their country of origin while a Canadian consulate processes an application for landing. They fear for their freedom and often their lives, and realize that they must escape at any price. True refugees are thus often compelled to escape surreptitiously, using false passports and travelling by unconventional means and routes.

With anti-immigration sentiments persisting into the 1990s the Conservative government introduced yet another change to the *Immigration Act*.

BILL C-86 AND "MANAGING REFUGEES"

Initiated in 1992, Bill C-86 was a complex and lengthy piece of legislation that represented the most extensive amendment to the *Immigration Act* since 1976 (Young 1992: 1). Bill C-86 was purported to be based on principles of non-discrimination, reflective of Canada's humanitarian obligations towards refugees and asylum seekers, and committed to an immigration practice that would be in Canada's best interests economically (see prefacing comments on *Managing Immigration* [Immigration Canada 1992]).

When introducing the Bill, Immigration Canada (1992: 3) argued for the rather pressing need to develop new ways of "managing" Canada's immigration program, largely because "over the past decade, there have been growing large scale movements of people from one country to another." Bernard Valcourt, employment and immigration minister at the time, noted that the number of immigrants and refugees who gained admission to Canada had increased from 88,000 in 1983 to 250,000 in 1992 (Canada 1992a: 12540). Furthermore, the majority were people of colour arriving from non-traditional (and therefore "less desirable") regions of the world. These racialized immigrants and refugees arrived when the climate of acceptance in Canada was chilly. Canadians were feeling vulnerable economically. They were developing a growing sense of mistrust and intolerance towards "outsiders" (particularly visibly different "outsiders") and were increasingly disillusioned and discontented with the government (Gallup Report 1992; *Maclean's* 1993: 42; Harper 1992: A24).

In response to the growing belief among Canadians that our borders were being flooded by "illegal" immigrants rather than legitimate refugees, the government proposed and ultimately passed very restrictive revisions to the refugee determination process — for example, fingerprinting refugee claimants, classifying as inadmissible Convention refugees (individuals who hold a well-founded fear of persecution as defined by the U.N. Convention Relating to the Status of Refugees) who did not have valid travel documentation or identification on landing, and excluding individuals with "criminal" or "terrorist" links (Chan 2004: 36–37). However, a more subtle and long-term strategy for better managing the number and types of refugees seeking safety and protection in Canada came through the Safe Country Provision, which, consistent with the approach as a whole, has been little more than code for "controlling immigration from the developing world."

According to section 46.01(1)(b) of Bill C-86: "A person who claims to be a Convention Refugee is not eligible to have the claim heard by the Refugee division if the person ... came to Canada, directly or indirectly, from a country, other than a country of the person's nationality, or where the person has no country of nationality, the country of the person's habitual residence, that is a prescribed country." Similar to a provision of Bill C-55, this section, in essence, prevents "refugee claimants from entering Canada if they arrived from a 'safe country' which was prepared to grant them refugee status" (Knowles 1997: 198). The justification for introducing the Safe Country Provision was to prevent "asylum shopping" — that is, "coming to Canada from a position of safety as a matter of personal choice" (Young 1991b: 1).

The provision was quickly attacked on two related grounds. First, the number of refugees entitled to come to Canada would be drastically reduced, since at least 40 percent were coming via the United States (Young 1991b). Second, with an estimated 95 percent of the world's refugees originating in developing countries, the Safe Country Provision was seen as discriminating against people of the poor and developing world (Wong in Canada 1992b, no. 5, July 30: 61). In his comments on the racist nature of the provision, the NDP immigration critic of the time, Dan Heap, noted that refugees from many African, Asian, and Central American countries could not come to Canada via direct air routes. They had to come via Europe or the United States, unlike refugee claimants from Eastern Europe or the Soviet Union, who could usually take direct flights (Knowles 1997: 198; see also Canada 1992b, no. 4, July 29 and no. 8, Aug. 12, 1992).

This particular provision of Bill C-86 bears a striking resemblance to the Continuous Journey Stipulation of 1908.[8] During the debates on the Bill in 1992, the Jesuit Centre for Social Faith and Justice in Toronto offered an analysis of how — in tangible terms — the Safe Country Provision would impinge on a refugee's ability to gain access to the Canadian system.

> If these changes had been in effect in … 1991, the following situation could have resulted. In all there were 30,539 claims made in 1991. Of these, 19,111 were made at border points, with the balance being made by people who were already in Canada. Looking then, at the 19,111 claims made at border points, 14,780 were made by people who came through safe third countries, that is, the United States, European countries and Japan. All are countries which would no doubt end up on the list of pre-scribed countries. If all of these 14,780 border claimants had been ruled ineligible, then 48% fewer claimants would have been heard by the CRDD [Convention Refugee Determination Division]. (Canada 1992b, no. 10, Sept. 15: 10A-27)

The ultimate effect of the legislation, then, without ever mentioning the word "race," is to control a particular dimension of the refugee population — "developing world" refugees, the majority of them classified as "visible minorities." As the Inter-Church Committee for Refugees suggested, historians correctly criticized the

Continuous Journey Stipulation because it was used as a means of controlling what groups of people would be permitted to stay in Canada. The organization pointed out that, on reflection, many historians would offer a similar criticism of the Safe Country Provision (Canada 1992b, no. 10, Sept. 15: 4A-58; 65).

Regardless of the controversy surrounding this provision, on December 5, 2002, officials from Canada and the United States signed the Safe Third Country Agreement, which became operational on December 29, 2004 (CIC 2004: 1). This agreement is part of the Smart Border Action Plan and is designed to enhance the ability of both governments to manage refugee claims by people crossing the border points on land between Canada and the United States. The Canada Border Services Agency — and not Citizenship and Immigration Canada — processes claims that fall under the agreement (CIC 2004: 1–2). After reviewing the agreement, the Canadian Council for Refugees (CCR 2005b) argued that it was problematic because the United States was not a safe place for refugees. Those seeking protection in the United States are at greater risk of detention for long periods of time, often in jails alongside convicted criminals. They do not always get the protection they require; because of more restrictive rules in the United States, numerous claims rejected there were actually recognized as legitimate in Canada. As well, people seeking protection in the United States can experience discrimination based on nationality, ethnicity, and religion (two of the most obvious examples being Haitians and Muslims).

No situation more effectively highlights this last point than does the case of Maher Arar, the Syrian-born Canadian citizen who, in 2002 while en route home from a family vacation in Tunis, was detained in New York City while waiting for a connector flight to his home of Montreal. After being unlawfully detained for twelve days, Arar was deported by the United States to Syria because the U.S. government suspected that he had "terrorist" links. He was given no explanation, no right to counsel. He was just deported and jailed for a year in Syria, where he was subject to torture. Thanks to the advocacy and persistence of his wife Monia, he was ultimately released because no evidence supported the U.S. suspicions. The Canadian government subsequently ordered a commission of inquiry into the Arar case, which confirmed that he had no links to terrorism and had been tortured during his detention (Arar 2003; Gogia and Slade 2011: 35).

The bigger issue here is if a Canadian citizen is not safe in the United States, why would refugee claimants — who have no government protection — be safe? The CCR notes that the goal of the Safe Third Country Agreement is to reduce the number of refugees who can claim protection in Canada. Yet, as the council points out, "Canada receives less than one quarter of one percent of the world's refugees.... Why should we reduce our share even further?" (CCR 2005b).

SECURITY AND CONTROL

The Immigration and Refugee Protection Act (IRPA)

The debate over the adequacy of Canada's immigration laws and policies intensified in 1999, when some 600 Chinese migrants arrived (in four boats) off the coast of British Columbia. Most of them were without documents, some were teenagers, and most claimed refugee status (Chan 2004). The negative reaction of the public to their arrival once again brought into question the ability of the government to administer the immigration program effectively. Confidence in that regard was further shaken in 2000 when the auditor general of Canada reported to Parliament that "information needed by visa officers to establish admissibility of immigrants on criminality and security grounds was scant and it appeared the Department was open to fraud and abuse ... Moreover, the safety of Canadians could not be ensured due to insufficient control of our borders" (Dolin and Young 2004: 3). These issues of security and control — combined with the global repercussions of the attacks on the World Trade Center and the Pentagon on September 11, 2001 — set the stage for the emergence of a new and arguably harsher immigration law.

Replacing the *Immigration Act* of 1976, the *Immigration and Refugee Protection Act* (IRPA) received royal assent on November 1, 2001 (Sinha and Young 2002) and came into force with a new set of regulations on June 28, 2002 (Dolin and Young 2004: 3). Citizenship and Immigration Canada describes this new legislation, introduced by the Liberal government, as "modern" and "balanced."

> It recognizes the many contributions of immigrants and refugees make to Canada; it encourages workers with flexible skills to choose Canada; and helps families reunite more quickly. IRPA is also tough on those who pose a threat to Canadian security while continuing Canada's tradition of providing a safe haven to people who need protection. (CIC 2005)

Although the IRPA is described as "balanced," and its application should be consistent with the *Canadian Charter of Rights and Freedoms* — including its principles of equality and freedom from discrimination as outlined in section 3(3)(d) — most organizations that made submissions in relation to the Act (see, for example, the Maytree Foundation 2001; Amnesty International 2001; National Association of Women and the Law 2001; CCR 2001) strongly believed that it would have negative repercussions on racialized individuals and communities. As Chan (2004: 49) notes, "The strong rhetoric of safety, the need for enhanced national security and the threat of terrorism have not been countered in the new Act by any recognition of the need to [prioritize the protection of] vulnerable migrants." Dolin and Young (2004: 13–14) discuss the "irresolvable contradiction" that this omission creates for Canada. We have an obligation to take in people who need protection, but we are simultaneously expected, through various means, to strictly control our borders and deter the annual arrival of claimants. In an attempt to manage the contradiction, the IRPA excludes and criminalizes as a means of deterring arrivals, with officials ultimately justifying these actions as in the interests of the nation — as a way of better securing and controlling our borders. Consider, as examples, the implications of the newly created category "foreign national," the Permanent Resident Card, and the new or revised categories of "inadmissibility" (IRPA 2001 s.33–43).

In the IRPA, the term "foreign national" is used to refer to everyone except Canadian citizens and permanent residents. In fact, throughout the new Act, neither "immigrant" nor "visitor" appears in the text (Sinha and Young 2002: 3). Additionally, according to its section 31(1), all those classified as "permanent residents" will be required to carry a "Permanent Resident Card" as proof of their immigration status.

Critics of the IRPA point out that choice of language and the imposition of a status card reinforce the idea of the immigrant as "Other." The use of such forms of exclusion is described as "patronizing," "stigmatizing," and "controlling" (Coalition for a Just Immigration and Refugee Policy 2001: 11). While Citizenship and Immigration Canada (2003: 1) stresses that identifiers, particularly the Permanent Resident Card, are designed to minimize fraud and abuse of the system and represent a response to the "immediate and long term challenges of national security," there is an alternative interpretation: that is, non-citizens are socially constructed as less than deserving of equal treatment and as "potential security threats that require surveillance" (Chan 2004: 50).

The tone of the new act is more exclusionary than welcoming. When she was introducing it, Minister of Citizenship and Immigration Canada Elinor Caplen described the IRPA as "designed to curb abuse of the immigration system" while striving to attract "the world's best and brightest to Canada" (CIC 2000: 1). She stressed that managing immigration and refugee protection is about balancing diverse needs — "closing the back door to those who would abuse the system allows us to ensure that the front door remains open."

Beyond its exclusionary tone, the IRPA places emphasis on identifying and deterring criminality. Included among the various classes of inadmissible persons (s.33–43) are those who are deemed to be security risks; are connected to human and international rights violations; have been convicted of serious criminality; have been found guilty of misrepresentation; and belong to groups engaged in organized crime. Particularly significant are the issues of misrepresentation and "organized crime" — that is, those who are "engaging, in the context of transnational crime, in activities such as people smuggling, trafficking in persons, or money laundering" (s.37(1)(b)).

In both the cases of misrepresentation and human trafficking or people smuggling, the IRPA falls short of balancing its national security needs with its humanitarian obligations. For example, CIC recognizes human trafficking or people-smuggling as a growing problem and accordingly is managing it through the imposition of severe penalties — up to life imprisonment, or a $1 million fine, or both (s.120). In this process of criminalization, what is not clear is whether a distinction will be made between people motivated by profit and people motivated by humanitarian concerns. Will anyone be protected from prosecution? Will family members be punished if they resort to smuggling as a last resort to save a relative? Will criminalization apply to those who are being smuggled? The IRPA now only protects from prosecution smuggled individuals who are recognized as legitimate refugees. This leaves vulnerable the many migrants who, out of desperation, resort to being smuggled to flee persecution, conflict or human rights abuses, but don't succeed in convincing the CIC that they are legitimate refugees in need of protection. Failing to protect trafficked and smuggled migrants puts Canada in violation of international protocols (Chan 2004: 43; CCR 2001; National Association of Women and the Law 2001).

A similar concern can be raised around misrepresentation and offences related to documents (s.122–123). It is an offence to possess, use, and/or sell false documents "for the purpose of entering or remaining in Canada" (s.122(1)(b)). Possession of such a document is punishable by up to five years in prison (s.123(1)(a)), and the sale or use of such a document is punishable by up to fourteen years in prison (s.123 (1)(b)). Only those refugees who actually make it to Canada are safe from charges of misrepresentation, "pending disposition of their claim for refugee protection, or if refugee protection is conferred" (s.133). What is problematic about this crime is that no distinction is made between refugees and non-refugees. As refugee advocates and human rights groups point out, it is quite probable that travellers with false documents are legitimate refugees seeking any means of escape. Trying to escape via unconventional channels is often the only chance that refugees have to reach safety. If there is greater enforcement of this offence at points overseas, and immigration officials deny travel to someone as a result of false documents, will Canada be in violation of its humanitarian obligations — that is, denying possible refugees access to the refugee determination process and sending them back to persecution?

Given the imbalance between security and control and humanitarian concerns, how does CIC manage the various and dissenting voices? How does CIC deal with the critique that racialized individuals and communities will be most hurt by the legislative changes? Quite simply, by "cleansing" the legislation of racial categories and making it an issue of law, order, and national security, Canada can continue to recruit the preferred, best, and brightest, while simultaneously closing its doors to many of the most vulnerable. As Chan (2004: 53) states:

Only by conflating immigrants of colour with crime is it possible to construct their "master status" as criminals and/or terrorists and therefore to justify the strong initiatives used to counteract their activities. Moreover, if immigrants' activities are regarded as criminal, then their treatment is depoliticized because it is transformed from an issue of race into an issue of law and order. It is much more difficult to oppose punitive strategies made in the name of safety than it is to oppose punitive treatment of a racial group. Thus, any resistance is silenced.

The imbalance between security and control and humanitarian concerns has continued to characterize the government's approach to immigration law and policy, especially with regard to refugees and asylum seekers. In June 2012 the Harper Conservative government implemented a reform to the IRPA. Protecting Canada's Immigration System Act (Bill C-31) gave the immigration minister greater discretion in determining which countries are to be deemed "safe"; eliminated the possibility of appeal for refugee claimants from countries on the safe country list; extended the period to one year for claimants applying for permanent residency on compassionate and humanitarian grounds (during which time they are to be detained and could be deported); and required biometric identification (digital fingerprints) for people applying for visas to visit Canada. While Bill C-31 was promoted as a way of making the asylum system "faster" and "fairer" (CIC 2012b), the Justice for Refugees and Immigrants Coalition (which includes Amnesty International Canada, the Canadian Association of Refugee Lawyers, the Canadian Civil Liberties Association, and the Canadian Council for Refugees) has argued that these new provisions will "detain groups of refugees, keep families apart, undermine the refugee claim and protection process, introduce the use of biometrics, and authorize the stripping of permanent residence from refugees" (CCR 2012).

THE POST-9/11 WORLD: PROTECTING THE NATION

In its earliest forms, Canadian immigration law was overtly prejudicial and based on a "nationality preference system" favouring European immigration. After 1962 came a shift towards universal, non-discriminatory treatment of all applicants applying for admission to Canada. The principle of equality was formalized in section 3(f) of the *Immigration Act* of 1976 and remains a central principle of the IRPA. While we acknowledge these changes as gains, the immigration system is not as just and fair as it appears to be. Legislation, although cleansed of racial identifiers, continues to have a harmful impact on racialized minorities from "less preferred" source areas. While the majority of immigrants and refugees to Canada continue to be visibly different, many Canadians have never adjusted to this changing face of immigration. Xenophobia and intolerance persist. Regardless of their documented contributions to the nation, non-preferred immigrants and refugees continue to be demonized and criminalized, often being blamed for the social, political, moral, and/or economic problems plaguing the nation.

In a "post-9/11" world, the process of state legitimation is complex. In Canada, in particular, reconciling the competing philosophies and goals associated with capitalism, liberal democracy, and multiculturalism has been further complicated by the preoccupation with national security. Protecting the nation has become a priority, and immigration has become a matter of security. While the IRPA has come under criticism for its harsh and exclusionary tone, immigration officials defend the legislation as "balanced" — specifically, a balance between maximizing Canada's benefits from the global movement of people, protecting refugees, and securing our borders by more effectively managing access to Canada. As we consider the implications of recent legislative changes, clearly, immigration is more about exclusion and "closing the backdoor" than it is about welcoming people to the nation.

Notes

1. According to de Silva (1992: 3–4), immigrants are classified as either "traditional" or "new" on the basis of their country of origin and skin colour. Although classification on the basis of these criteria is far from perfect, it appears to be "basically true" that, for the most part, "traditional" immigrants are white, whereas "new" immigrants are visibly different.

2. Throughout this chapter the term "race" is placed in quotation marks in formal acknowledgement of its uselessness as an analytic term (Miles 1989: 72; Guillaumin 1980: 39). As Robert Miles (1984: 232) notes, "race" is an ideological construction that has "profound meanings in the everyday world, but which has no scientific credibility." As such, awarding analytical power to the word "race" or using it uncritically only lends legitimacy to the misconception that "races" are real or correctly apprehensible. For a more detailed discussion of why the concept of "race" has been scientifically discredited, see Rex (1983).

3. In soliciting immigrants from the United States, the country took care to pursue only white immigrants. It made no attempts to recruit Black Americans, for "blacks were widely regarded as being cursed with the burden of their African ancestry" (Knowles 1997: 90). More precisely, it was assumed that slavery had disabled Blacks — rendering them incapable of developing the qualities necessary for citizenship in a democracy.

4. Although the *Chinese Exclusion Act* was repealed in 1947, the only category of immigration open to the Chinese until 1962 was "sponsored relatives" of Chinese-Canadians (Bolaria and Li 1988: 118).

5. The points system has been revised over time, with some criteria being more heavily weighted and others dropped off the assessment entirely. Work experience was added to the criteria in 1992, worth a possible 8 out of 112 points. In 2002 work experience was elevated to the most important criteria, worth 21 out of 100 points. Points for occupation were dropped in 2003, although the regulations allow applications for only

certain occupations (such as health care workers). For a discussion of the points system see Gogia and Slade (2011).

6. The Immigration and Refugee Protection Act (IRPA) replaced "personal suitability" with "adaptability."

7. This discretionary power still exists under the more recent IRPA. Specifically, Regulation 11(3) is replaced by Regulation 76(3), which outlines the "circumstances for officer's substituted evaluation." In essence, the officer's substituted evaluation amounts to discretion. Under 76(3), if an applicant for admission to Canada has obtained the required number of points for entry under the points system, the immigration officer, with support from a senior officer, may use positive or negative discretion to accept or reject the applicant if the officers believe that the points awarded are "not a sufficient indicator of whether the skilled worker may become economically established in Canada."

8. For further discussion of this comparison, see HC no. 4, July 29, 1992: 64–65, 73–76.

References

Abella, Irving, and Harold Troper. 1983. *None Is Too Many: Canada and the Jews of Europe, 1933–1948.* Toronto: Lester and Orpen Dennys.

Aiken, Sharryn J. 2007. "From Slavery to Expulsion: Racism, Canadian Immigration Law, and the Unfulfilled Promise of Modern Constitutionalism." In Vijay Agnew (ed.), *Interrogating Race and Racism.* Toronto: University of Toronto Press.

Amnesty International. 2001. *Brief on Bill C-11.* March. <amnesty.ca/Refugee/Bill_C-11.pdf>.

Angus, William and James Hathaway. 1987. "Deterrents and Detention: An Ill Conceived Afterthought." *Refuge* 7, 1.

Arar, Monia. 2003. *Maher Arar: Chronology of Events September 26th, 2002 to October 5th, 2003* (November). <amnesty.ca/library/canada/Arar_Chronology.pdf>.

Arat-Koç, Sedef. 1999. "'Good Enough to Work but Not Good Enough to Stay': Foreign Domestic Workers and the Law." In Elizabeth Comack (ed.), *Locating Law: Race/Class/Gender Connections.* Halifax: Fernwood Publishing.

Basran, G.S. 1983. "Canadian Immigration Policies and Theories of Racism." In Peter S. Li and B. Singh Bolaria (eds.), *Racial Minorities in Canada.* Toronto: Garamond Press.

Block, Sheila, and Grace-Edward Galabuzi. 2011. *Canada's Colour Coded Labour Market: The Gap for Racialized Workers.* Ottawa and Toronto: Canadian Centre for Policy Alternatives and the Wellsley Institute.

Bolaria, B. Singh, and Peter S. Li (eds.). 1988. *Racial Oppression in Canada,* second edition. Toronto: Garamond Press.

Bonacich, Edna. 1972. "A Theory of Ethnic Antagonism: The Split Labor Market." *American Sociological Review* 37 (October).

____. 1980. "Class Approaches to Ethnicity and Race." *The Insurgent Sociologist* 10, 2.

Canada. 1992a. *House of Commons Debates.* 3rd Session, 34th Parliament, June 22.

____. 1992b. *Minutes of Proceedings and Evidence of the Legislative Committee on Bill C-86.* 4, July 29; 5, July 30; 8, August 12; 10, September 15.

Cappon, P. 1975. "The Green Paper: Immigration a Tool of Profit." *Canadian Ethnic Studies* 7.

CCR (Canadian Council for Refugees). 2005a. "An Overview of Canada's Refugee Policy." <cleonet.ca/resource_files/refpolicy.pdf>.

____. 2005b. "10 Reasons Why Safe Third Country Is a Bad Deal." <ccrweb.ca/10reasons. html>.

____. 2012. "Protect Refugees from Bill C-31: Joint Statement." <ccrweb.ca/en/ print/14390>.

Chan, Wendy. 2004. "Undocumented Migrants and Bill C-11: The Criminalization of Race." In Law Commission of Canada (ed.), *What Is Crime? Defining Criminal Conduct in Contemporary Society.* Vancouver: UBC Press.

____. 2012. "Keeping Canada White: Immigration Enforcement in Canada." In Wayne Antony and Les Samuelson (eds.), *Power and Resistance: Critical Thinking About Canadian Social Issues,* fifth edition. Halifax and Winnipeg: Fernwood Publishing.

CIC (Citizenship and Immigration Canada). 1996. *Annual Report to Parliament.* Ottawa: Citizenship and Immigration.

____. 2000. *News Release: Caplan Tables New Immigration and Refugee Protection Act.*

____. 2003. *Fact Sheet. CIC's Role in Public Safety.* <cic.gc.ca/english/pub/sept11.html>.

____. 2004. *Fact Sheet: The Safe Third Country Agreement.* <cic.gc.ca/english/department/ laws-policy/menu-safethird.asp>.

____. 2005. *Immigration and Refugee Protection Act.* <cic.gc.ca/english/irpa/index.html>.

____. 2012a. *Annual Report to Parliament on Immigration. Section 2: Managing Permanent Immigration and Temporary Migration.* Ottawa. <cic.gc.ca/english/resources/ publications/annual-report-2012/section2.asp>.

____. 2012b. "News Release – Legislation to Protect Canada's Immigration System Receives Royal Assent." <news.gc.ca/web/article-en.do?crtr.sj1D=&crtr. mnthndVl=12&mthd=advSrch&crtr.dpt1D=6664&nid=683929&crtr.lc1D=&crtr. tp1D=1&crtr.yrStrtVl=2002&crtr.kw=&crtr.dyStrtVl=1&crtr.aud1D=&crtr. mnthStrtVl=1&crtr.page=18&crtr.yrndVl=2013&crtr.dyndVl=31>.

Coalition for a Just Immigration and Refugee Policy. 2001. *Position Paper on Bill C-11.* Toronto.

Comack, Elizabeth. 1991. "'We Will Get Some Good Out of This Riot Yet': The Canadian State, Drug Legislation and Class Conflict." In Elizabeth Comack and Stephen Brickey (eds.), *The Social Basis of Law: Critical Readings in the Sociology of Law,* second edition. Toronto: Garamond Press.

Cox, Oliver C. 1948. *Caste, Race and Class.* New York: Modern Reader Paperbacks.

de Silva, Arnold. 1992. *Earnings of Immigrants: A Comparative Analysis.* A study prepared for the Economic Council of Canada. Ottawa: Supply and Services Canada.

Dolin, Benjamin, and Margaret Young. 2004. *Canada's Immigration Program (Background Paper)* (October). Ottawa: Library of Parliament, Parliamentary Information and Research Service.

Elliot, J.E., and A. Fleras. 1996. *Unequal Relations: An Introduction to Race and Ethnic and Aboriginal Dynamics in Canada,* second edition. Toronto: Oxford University Press.

Employment and Immigration Canada. 1991. "Admission to Canada — Immigrants (General)." *Immigration Manual — Selection and Control, Volume 1.* Ottawa: Supply and Services Canada (looseleaf insert).

Friendly, Martha, and Susan Prentice. 2009. *About Canada: Childcare.* Halifax and Winnipeg:

Fernwood Publishing.

Gallup Report. 1992. *Economic Difficulties Preoccupy Canadian Public*. May 7.

Gogia, Nupur, and Bonnie Slade. 2011. *About Canada: Immigration*. Halifax and Winnipeg: Fernwood Publishing.

Green, A. 1976. *Immigration and the Postwar Canadian Economy*. Toronto: Macmillan.

Guillaumin, Colette. 1980. "The Idea of Race and Its Elevation to Autonomous Legal Status." In UNESCO (ed.), *Sociological Theories: Race and Colonialism*. Paris: UNESCO.

Harper, T. 1992. "Immigration Plan: Is Canada Getting Meaner?" *Toronto Star*, September 14: A1 and A24.

Hawkins, Freda. 1989. *Critical Years in Immigration: Canada and Australia Compared*. Montreal: McGill-Queen's University Press.

Henry, Frances, Carol Tator, Winston Mattis, and Tim Rees. 2006. *The Colour of Democracy: Racism in Canadian Society*, third edition. Toronto: Harcourt Brace and Company.

Hsiung, Ping-Chun, and Katherine Nichol. 2010. "Policies on and Experiences of Foreign Domestic Workers in Canada." *Sociology Compass* 4, 9.

Immigration Canada. 1992. *Managing Immigration: A Framework for the 1990s*. Ottawa: Supply and Services Canada.

Knowles, Valerie. 1997. *Strangers at Our Gates: Canadian Immigration and Immigration Policy, 1540–1997*, revised edition. Toronto: Dundurn Press.

Law Union of Ontario. 1981. *The Immigrant's Handbook*. Montreal: Black Rose.

Maclean's. 1993. "Voices of Canada: Maclean's/CTV poll." January 4.

Malarek, Victor. 1987. *Haven's Gate: Canada's Immigration Fiasco*. Toronto: Macmillan.

Manpower and Immigration Canada. 1974. *The Immigration Program*. Ottawa: Information Canada.

Maytree Foundation. 2001. *Brief to the Standing Committee on Citizenship and Immigration regarding Bill C-11, Immigration and Refugee Protection Act*. March. <maytree.com/ PDF_Files/summarybriefc-11immigrationandrefugeeprotectionact2001.pdf>.

Miles, Robert. 1984. "Marxism Versus the Sociology of 'Race Relations'?" *Ethnic and Racial Studies* 7, 2.

____. 1989. *Racism*. London: Routledge.

National Association of Women and the Law. 2001. *Brief on the Proposed Immigration and Refugee Protection Act (Bill C-11)*. <nawl.ca/brief-immig.htm>.

Phillips, Paul. 1967. *No Power Greater: A Century of Labour in British Columbia*. Vancouver: B.C. Federation of Labour.

Portes, A. 1978. "Migration and Underdevelopment." *Politics and Race* 8, 1.

Reimers, David M., and Harold Troper. 1992. "Canadian and American Immigration Policy Since 1945." In Barry R. Chiswick (ed.), *Immigration, Language and Ethnicity*. Washington: AEI Press.

Rex, John. 1983. *Race Relations and Sociological Theory*. London: Routledge and Kegan Paul.

Samuel, T. John. 1990. "Third World Immigration and Multiculturalism." In Shivalingappa S. Halli, Frank Trovato, and Leo Driedger (eds.), *Ethnic Demography: Canadian Immigrant, Racial and Cultural Variations*. Ottawa: Carleton University Press.

Silvera, Makeda, 1989. *Silenced*. Toronto: Sister Vision.

Simmons, Alan. 1990. "'New Wave' Immigrants: Origins and Characteristics." In Shivalingappa S. Halli, Frank Trovato, and Leo Driedger (eds.), *Ethnic Demography:*

Canadian Immigrant, Racial and Cultural Variations. Ottawa: Carleton University Press.

____. 1992. "Canadian Migration in the Western Hemisphere." Paper prepared for the workshop *Canada's Role in the Hemisphere: Setting the Agenda*. University of Miami: North-South Centre, March 27–28.

Sinha, Jay, and Margaret Young. 2002. *Bill C-11: The Immigration and Refugee Protection Act (Legislative Summary)*. Ottawa, Library of Parliament, Parliamentary Research Branch, January.

Statistics Canada. 2013. "2011 National Household Survey: Immigration, Place of Birth, Citizenship, Ethnic Origin, Visible Minorities, Language and Religion." *The Daily* (May 8). <statcan.gc.ca/daily-quotidien/130508/dq130508b-eng.pdf>.

Sunahara, Ann G. 1981. *The Politics of Racism: The Uprooting of Japanese-Canadians During the Second World War*. Toronto: Lorimer.

Ujimoto, Victor K. 1988. "Racism, Discrimination and Internment: Japanese in Canada." In B. Singh Bolaria and Peter S. Li (eds.), *Racial Oppression in Canada*. Toronto: Garamond Press.

Young, M. 1991a. *Canada's Immigration Program (Background Paper)*. Ottawa: Library of Parliament Research Branch—Law and Government Division, February.

____. 1991b. *Canada's Refugee Determination System (Background Paper)*. Ottawa: Library of Parliament Research Branch, February.

____. 1992. *Bill C-86: An Act to Amend the Immigration Act (Legislative Summary)*. Ottawa: Library of Parliament Research Branch.

____. M. 1997. *Canada's Immigration Program (Background Paper)*. Ottawa: Library of Parliament Research Branch.

Legislation Cited

An Act Respecting Chinese Immigration, 1923, SC 13-14, c 38

An Act of Respecting and Regulating Chinese Immigration into Canada, 1885, SC 48-49 Victoria, c 71

An Act Respecting Immigration, 1910, SC 9-10, c27

An Act to Amend the Immigration Act, 1908, SC 7-8, c 33

An Act to Amend the Immigration Act, SC 1992, c 49 (Bill C-86)

Canadian Charter of Rights and Freedoms, Part I of the *Constitution Act*, 1982, being Schedule B to the Canada Act 1982 (UK), 1982, c 11

The Immigration and Refugee Protection Act (IRPA), SC 2001, c 27 (Bill C-11).

Protecting Canada's Immigration System Act, SC 2012, c 17 (Bill C-31)

Chapter 19

COMPLICATING NARRATIVES

Chinese Women and the Head Tax

Sandra Ka Hon Chu

From: *Gendered Intersections: An Introduction to Women's and Gender Studies,*
2nd edition, pp. 70–73 (reprinted with permission).

Seeking to curtail Chinese immigration to Canada, in 1885 the Canadian government passed the *Chinese Immigration Act,* which mandated that all Chinese
immigrants, with the exception of clergymen and merchants, pay a $50 head tax.[1]
Realizing that $50 was an inadequate deterrent, the government increased the head
tax to $100 in 1900 and again in 1903 to $500, an amount that was equivalent to
approximately two years' wages for a Chinese labourer working in Canada at the
time (Chan 1983: 67).

Over a century later, in December 2000, Shang Jack Mack, Quan Ying Lee and
Yew Lee filed a class action law suit with the Ontario Superior Court of Justice
seeking the return of the amounts of the head tax paid by them, their spouses or
their direct descendants to the government of Canada.[2] Of the three plaintiffs,
only Shang Jack Mack had personally paid the head tax. Quan Ying Lee was the
widow of a head-tax payer, and Yew Lee was her third child, both of whom had
immigrated to Canada in 1949.

Despite the focus of the legal arguments on compensation for the head tax, the plaintiffs stressed "the single most devastating consequence of the various forms of the Act was the separation of families and the resulting impediment to the growth of the Chinese Canadian community"[3] — a harm that would have been shared by Chinese men and women alike. Nevertheless, the plaintiffs framed the case primarily in terms of head tax compensation — a harm that most Chinese women could only claim as surviving spouses of head-tax payers. In 2001, the case was dismissed and appeals to the Ontario Court of Appeal and the Supreme Court of Canada were rejected. The redress campaign thus returned to the political arena where lobbying by head-tax claimants culminated in Prime Minister Stephen Harper's 2006 official apology and symbolic redress payments of $20,000 to surviving head-tax payers and persons who had been in conjugal relationships with head-tax payers deceased by 2006.

While Chinese immigrants during the era of the head tax did not conform to Canadian immigration law's model citizens who were "White, particularly British-origin, Protestants" (Abu-Laban and Gabriel 2002: 38), Chinese men have since found it easier to articulate their discrimination in terms of racial subordination. Since redress was largely predicated upon payment of the head tax, the claims of Chinese women, most of whom had not been directly financially harmed by discriminatory legislation, were contingent on the head tax paid by their spouses. Both Chinese women and men experienced emotional injury as a result of discriminatory immigration legislation, but such harms were characterized as subsidiary in relation to monetary loss in the head-tax payers' class action.

In the national dialogue about the head tax, the experiences of Chinese women have been largely conflated with those of Chinese men. In part, the state's inability to recognize the harms done to Chinese women can be attributed to the paucity of narrative tropes available to describe Chinese women's confrontation with discriminatory state policy and the corresponding strength of existing narratives describing Chinese women's rightful place at home in China (Chu 2006). The separation of Chinese women from their spouses in Canada was rendered "natural" by the Canadian state, and, consequently, Chinese women's absence from discourses of Canadian citizenship was only to be expected.

HISTORICAL BACKGROUND

From its beginning in the late 1840s, immigration from China was overwhelmingly a male activity (Sugiman 1992, cited in Women's Book Committee, 17; Con et al. 1982: 17). Until the 1950s, the majority of Chinese women with spouses in Canada remained in China where they cared for children and, often, extended family (Das Gupta 2000: 146 and 159; Li 1998: 46). The few Chinese women who did come to Canada were often labelled as prostitutes (Sugiman 1992, cited in Women's Book Committee: 19). Nevertheless, the larger Canadian population initially welcomed them in limited numbers as an outlet for Chinese men's sexuality.[4] Although the politics of racial purity already made entering into familial relations with white women difficult for Chinese men, Chinese women were seen as lessening the threat of miscegenation that single Chinese men posed to the dominant white society (Das Gupta 2000: 153). At the same time, the concern for "racial purity," a cornerstone of British-Canadian nation-building and key to immigration policy, meant that reproduction by women from the perceived "lower races" was also seen as undesirable (Abu-Laban and Gabriel 2002: 38). As such, Chinese women experienced a paradoxical relationship with white settlers; while their presence mitigated the "vice" of Chinese male sexuality, that presence also enabled Chinese reproductive life.

Upon the completion of the Canadian Pacific Railway, the Canadian government passed successive iterations of the *Chinese Immigration Act* and imposed an increasingly higher head tax on Chinese immigrants. Married Chinese women's migration to Canada depended significantly on their husband's race, financial status and occupational classification. Wealthy merchants, whose businesses were favoured by the Canadian government, were allowed to migrate to Canada with their wives and children; these merchants and their families were all exempt from the head tax, while poor labourers paid a heavy tax that unfairly deprived them of most of their families (Adilman 1984: 56).

According to Tamara Adilman (1984), the head tax was the most important constraint on Chinese women's entry into Canada (55). Effectively, the fee ensured that the majority of the Chinese-Canadian population would continue to be male: women were viewed as expensive economic liabilities and not productive workers who would be able to repay the head tax. Nevertheless, a major anxiety of the white population was that "if Chinese were allowed, without restriction, to bring their wives to Canada, they would reproduce at an alarming rate and [might] eventually outnumber whites" (Adilman 1984: 64). This fear culminated in the passage of a new *Chinese Immigration Act* in 1923. Referred to as the "Exclusion Act" by Chinese Canadians, the new act prohibited the immigration of virtually all Chinese, except for consular officials, children born in Canada, students and merchants.

The effects of the law were dramatic. According to David Lai (1988: 58), between 1923 and 1947, only twelve Chinese were admitted to Canada as immigrants. Peter Li (1998: 72) reports that in 1941, of the 29,033 Chinese men living in Canada, 20,141 had wives outside the country. While their spouses were abroad, women in China struggled to raise their children, often with the assistance of their extended families (Li 1998: 69; Yee 1996: 45; Sugiman 1992: 102, cited in Women's Book Committee). The *Exclusion Act* was not repealed until 1947.

"INSIDE PEOPLE"

One frequently proffered explanation for the apparent reluctance of Chinese women to emigrate with their husbands during the era of the head tax is the prevalence of Confucian values in Chinese culture, values which stress the importance of family (Sugiman 1992, cited in Women's Book Committee: 17; Yung 1986: 10). According to Sucheng Chan (1991: 95), "given the central importance of filial piety in traditional Chinese culture, the moral duty of wives to remain in China to wait on their parents-in-law was greater than their obligation to accompany their husbands abroad." Dutiful wives were thus left home to tend to the family while their husbands went overseas in search of fortune (Yung 1986: 11). Chinese women were stereotypically described by Chinese patriarchal discourse as *Nei-jen,* or "inside people," a notion that emanated from centuries of Confucian prescriptive literature defining women's place in the domestic sphere (Adilman 1984: 54).

The obedience of Chinese wives was summarized by Commissioner John Gray of the Royal Commission on Chinese Immigration (RCCI) when he maintained that "the married woman is subject to the will of her husband, and sometimes to the control of her husband's mother" (RCCI [1985] 1978: 269). In this version of the stereotype, Chinese women are represented as passive figures who exist to serve men. This paradigm suggests that Chinese women who did not migrate to Canada remained in China out of deference to their husbands and not because of the severely racist, sexist and classist immigration legislation directed towards their community.

While there is no question that patriarchal cultural values, a sojourning mentality and differentials in the cost of living all worked in tandem to limit the number of Chinese female immigrants during the early decades of the Chinese influx, the assumption that cultural restraints were solely responsible for the skewed sex ratio of the Chinese immigrant community should be challenged (Zhao 2002: 9). According to Li, "there is a profound difference between the ideals of traditional familism, as incorporated in the ethical precepts of neo-Confucianism, and the form of the Chinese family as an empirical reality ... economic necessity compelled both the husband and the wife to participate actively and jointly in agricultural production" (1998: 62). Given the poor economic conditions at home, where most women, particularly among rural Chinese, needed to work to support the immediate and extended family, George Peffer (1999: 6) suggests that sufficient economic incentives existed for tolerating, and even encouraging, female emigration from China rather than prohibiting it. In Li's view, a more important reason for the gross disproportion between males and females in Chinese immigrant communities was anti-Chinese sentiment among the white public (Li 1998: 61).[5] Coupled with the animosity directed towards Chinese women in particular, the severe marginalization of the Chinese in Canada had an equal, if not more profound, impact on discouraging the migration of women than "family-oriented" Confucian values, Li argues.

Although the influence of Confucianism appears to have been overstated, a conception of Chinese women as "inside people" was compatible with existing Canadian narratives describing women's place within the private sphere. The understanding that Chinese women were *Nei-jen* rendered their absence from Canada "natural." As a result, the impact of discriminatory immigration legislation on Chinese women has been left unexamined and the phenomenon of transnational households in the Chinese-Canadian community could be attributed to Orientalist notions of the solitary Chinese male and the domesticated Chinese female.[6] Given the ideological framework confining maternalized Chinese women to the home, it is hardly surprising that any harm arising from forced separation has yet to be considered by the Canadian state.

CONCLUSION

While Chinese women during the era of the head tax presumably experienced harms just as severe as those experienced by their male partners, reparation law has not, thus far, recognized the particularities of their experience. A narrative trope which seemingly robbed Chinese women of their agency diminished the harm of legislated separation from their spouses. Because Chinese women were characterized as passively subject to law, they were deemed unable to comprehend harm, much less "talk back" to dominant discourses confining them to one-dimensional narratives. Thus, not only have the head tax and twenty-four years of legislated exclusion subjected Chinese women to the emotional injury of forced separation, but they also have reinforced the message that Chinese women are limited to narratives characterized by subordination.

These narratives can be reconstructed. An awareness of their restrictive nature may enable Chinese Canadian women to transcend the arrested development entailed by such scripts. Recent works of literature documenting Chinese women's experiences during the period of the head tax already signal a shift in those narratives (see for example, Chong 1995; Lee 1990, 2007). Correspondingly, Chinese Canadian women's participation in a reparation movement may enable the reclamation of their rights through their own narratives which reject stereotypes of docility and portray Chinese women as more than passive objects of oppression. A reparation movement predicated upon the emotional injury associated with separation may also underscore the particular conditions of Chinese women's historical struggles and, in turn, affirm this experience of harm for the larger community.

Then, the current notion of harm would be recoded, or at least destabilized. For Chinese Canadian women, complicating the traditional legal paradigm may be a critical way to prevent their being disappeared.

Notes

1. The term "Chinese" is used in this article to describe a socially constructed race of people, since discrimination against the Chinese was based on purely physical racial grounds. As such, naturalized Chinese Canadians were subjected to the same anti-Chinese legislative bills as "alien" Chinese.
2. Statement of Claim of Shang Jack Mack, Quan Ying Lee and Yew Lew at para. 1.
3. Memorandum of Argument of the Applicant for Leave to Appeal, *Shang Jack Mack et al. v. Attorney General of Canada*, Court of Appeal File No. C36799 at para. 7.
4. According to J. Brian Dawson, Alberta Supreme Court Justice Nicholas Beck stated in 1913 that if some Chinese led immoral lives in Canada, "the Dominion Parliament [was] to be held responsible [as it had imposed] the poll tax on Chinese women of $500" so that few Chinese could "afford to pay this sum for a prospective wife or go home to get married." *Calgary Albertan* November 27, 1913 (cited in Dawson 1991: 123).
5. In Canada, the hostile treatment of Chinese migrants is evidenced in the 1902 *Royal Commission Report on Chinese and Japanese Immigration* (1902: 263) in which a Chinese merchant from Vancouver testified that "a large proportion of [Chinese men in Canada] would bring their families here, were it not for the unfriendly reception they got here during recent years."
6. According to Said (2003: 3), "Orientalism" is the process by which Western states have, for at least the past five centuries, defined themselves in opposition to "Oriental" others. The construction of the Oriental male as perpetually isolated reinforces the assumption that the legislated separation of Chinese families was voluntary and natural to Oriental others.

References

Abu-Laban, Yasmeen, and Christina Gabriel. 2002. *Selling Diversity: Immigration, Multiculturalism, Employment Equity, and Globalization.* Peterborough: Broadview Press.

Adilman, Tamara. 1984. "A Preliminary Sketch of Chinese Women and Work in British Columbia 1858–1942." In B. Latham and R. Pazdro (eds.), *Not Just Pin Money: Selected Essays on the History of Women's Work in British Columbia.* Victoria: Camosun College Press.

Chan, Anthony. 1983. *Gold Mountain: The Chinese in the New World.* Vancouver: New Star Books.

Chan, Sucheng. 1991. "The Exclusion of Chinese Women, 1870–1943." In S. Chan (ed.), *Entry Denied: Exclusion and the Chinese Community in America, 1882–1943.* Philadelphia: Temple University Press.

Chong, Denise. 1995. *The Concubine's Children.* Toronto: Penguin Canada.

Chu, Sandra Ka Hon. 2006. "Reparation as Narrative Resistance: Displacing Orientalism and Recoding Harm for Chinese Women of the Exclusion Era." *Canadian Journal of*

Women and the Law 18, 2.

Con, Harry, Ronald Con, Graham Johnson, Edgar Wickberg and William Willmott. 1982. *From China to Canada: A History of the Chinese Communities in Canada*. Toronto: McClelland and Stewart.

Das Gupta, Tania. 2000. "Families of Native People, Immigrants, and People of Colour." In N. Mandell and A. Duffy (eds.), *Canadian Families: Diversity, Conflict and Change*. Toronto: Harcourt Canada.

Dawson, J. Brian. 1991. *Moon Cakes in Gold Mountain: From China to the Canadian Plains*. Calgary: Detselig Enterprises.

Lai, David Chuenyan. 1988. *Chinatowns: Towns Within Cities in Canada*. Vancouver: UBC Press.

Lee, Jen Sookfong. 2007. *The End of East*. Toronto: Knopf Canada.

Lee, Sky. 1990. *Disappearing Moon Café*. Vancouver: Douglas and McIntyre.

Li, Peter. 1998. *The Chinese in Canada*, second edition. Toronto: Oxford University Press.

Peffer, George. 1999. *If They Don't Bring Their Women Here: Chinese Female Immigration Before Exclusion*. Urbana: University of Illinois Press.

Royal Commission on Chinese and Japanese Immigration. 1902. *Report*. Ottawa: King's Printer.

Royal Commission on Chinese Immigration. 1978 [1885]. *Report*. New York: Arno Press.

Said, Edward. 2003. *Orientalism*. London: Penguin.

Women's Book Committee. 1992. *Jin Guo: Voices of Chinese Canadian Women*. M. Sugiman (editor). Toronto: Chinese Canadian National Council and Women's Press.

Yee, Paul. 1996. *Struggle and Hope: The Story of Chinese Canadians*. Toronto: Umbrella Press.

Yung, Judy. 1986. *Chinese Women of America: A Pictorial History*. Seattle: University of Washington Press.

Zhao, Xiaojian. 2002. *Remaking Chinese America: Immigration, Family, and Community, 1940–1965*. New Brunswick, NJ: Rutgers University Press.

MULTICULTURALISM

Chapter 20

THE BILINGUAL LIMITS OF CANADIAN MULTICULTURALISM

The Politics of Language and Race

Eve Haque

From: *Critical Inquiries: A Reader in Studies of Canada*, pp. 18–32 (reprinted with permission).

On October 8, 1971, Prime Minister Pierre Elliott Trudeau stood up in the House of Commons and declared Canada to be "multicultural within a bilingual framework," ushering in Canada's first policy on multiculturalism. Since that moment, multiculturalism has become a term with great elasticity, which has allowed it to be taken up across the political spectrum even as its demise has been heralded time and time again. As the resilience and polyvalence of multiculturalism as a signifier of various national ideals has become apparent, its connection to bilingualism has been overtly severed to the point that on the one hand multiculturalism has come to indicate a preoccupation with racialized others in the nation, and on the other, bilingualism has become the given white settler foundation of the nation. The normalization of this national framework can be traced in a genealogy of its emergence through the Royal Commission on Bilingualism and Biculturalism (RCBB) (1963–1970). In fact, Trudeau's declaration that Canada was to be multicultural within a bilingual framework is part of his response to the tabled *Book IV: The Cultural Contribution of Other Ethnic Groups* of the RCBB's final report.

In this chapter, I trace a genealogy of the emergence of multiculturalism within a bilingual framework and its eventual sedimentation as a racialized hierarchy of national belonging. Specifically, I show that the culturalization of difference — particularly racialized difference — through the RCBB in the post–World War II era has meant that bilingualism continues to limit any attempt to revision or revalorize multiculturalism's inclusive and emancipatory potential by foregrounding the collective claims of the two "founding" nations — the English and the French — over all others. It is through a genealogy of the RCBB that the culturalization and reinscription of this racially hierarchized national narrative can be traced, as it is the RCBB that gave rise to the *Official Languages Act* in 1969 and Trudeau's multiculturalism policy in 1971.

A GENEALOGY OF ROYAL COMMISSIONS

Foucault states that genealogy "operates on a field of entangled and confused parchments, on documents that have been scratched over and recopied many times" (1977: 139). This documentary basis of the genealogical approach means that a broad and heterogeneous array of documents can be drawn upon, including, in the case of this chapter, transcripts of royal commission hearings, related research reports, memos, associated conference proceedings, commission briefs, parliamentary debates, newspaper articles and two of the five volumes of the RCBB's final report. The genealogical method eschews the search for origins or beginnings and is instead oriented towards discontinuities even in present social formations. Genealogy is a "history of the present" which evaluates the present by reflecting upon the ways the discursive and institutional practices of the past impinge on the constitution of the present (Tamboukou 1999: 205). Foucault outlines the three main elements of the genealogical method as eventalization, descent and emergence. For Foucault, eventalization seeks to record the singularity of events in the most unpromising places and define even those instances when "they are absent, the moment in which they remain unrealized" (1977: 139). This forces the event under scrutiny to be analyzed within the matrix of discursive and non-discursive practices that have given rise to its existence and forces a rethinking of "power relations that at a certain historical moment decisively influenced the way things were socially and historically established" (Tamboukou 1999: 207). Descent disrupts the notion of any uninterrupted continuity by maintaining the passing of events in their proper dispersion. That is, through the identification of accidents, minute deviations or reversals, errors and faulty calculations, the birth of those things "that continue to exist and have value" shows that "truth or being does not lie at the root of what we know and what we are, but the exteriority of accidents" (Foucault 1977: 144). Finally, emergence is the moment of arising that Foucault locates in the interstices of the "endless repeated play of domina- tions" between distant adversaries that "established marks of power and engrave memories on things and even within bodies" (1977: 144). In this way, genealogy is situated within the articulation of the body and history, and its task is to expose a "body totally imprinted by history and the process of history's total destruction of the body" (Foucault 1977: 146). Thus, eventalization, descent and emergence can operate to disrupt the continuity and historical development of the national narrative, revealing discontinuities and forcing a multiplication of causes to be considered in this historical imprinting of different bodies in the nation.

There have been several hundred royal commissions in Canada since Confederation, and as Jenson (1994: 40) states, royal commissions are institu- tions that go beyond mere policy-making and serve as a platform through which Canadians debate the representation of themselves in order to "set out the terms of who we are, where we have been and what we might become." Corrigan and Sayer (1985) add that commissions also serve to increase the density of state regulation through the centralization of knowledge, that is, the legitimization of some forms of knowledge in order to justify features and forms of particular state policies. Ashforth (1990: 6) describes commissions of inquiry as schemes of legitimiza- tion whereby some principles underlying policy are systematized and explained in the language of "objective" knowledge of facts. He outlines three phases of the inquiry. The first of these is the investigative phase, where the official representa- tives chosen by the state — the commissioners — engage with representatives of selected social interests within the parameters of the inquiry. These engagements are not merely modes of investigation but are in fact performances which serve ultimately to authorize a form of social discourse. In the persuasive phase, the publication of the final reports of the commission as the authoritative statement also symbolizes an invitation for dialogue between a purportedly neutral state and civil society (Ashforth 1990: 7). In the archival phase, the reports become part of the nation's interpretative framework and history — in the case of the RCBB, the founding of Canada as a bilingual nation with a policy of multiculturalism. Central to the commission's work is the investigation of the "problem," which can be tackled rationally and singularly as an object of inquiry. Ultimately, in the case of the RCBB, it was the terms of reference[1] that served to delineate the singularity of the problem to be investigated.

HISTORICAL CONTEXT FOR THE RCBB

The federal government established the RCBB at a particular historical juncture when challenges to Anglo-Celtic dominance by others within the nation posed a threat to national social cohesion. These challenges were being posed not only by Francophones, but also by Indigenous peoples and what at the time were lumped together by the royal commission as "other ethnic groups." Although the federal government eventually created the RCBB to tackle the task of crafting a new articulation of national community, concurrent changes to immigration policy, proposed changes to the *Indian Act* and the transformations ushered by the Quiet Revolution in Québec also framed the formation of the RCBB.

The 1960s were a time of great changes in Canadian society, and one area of critical change was in relation to immigration policy. A paradigmatic shift in immigration regulations was presented by the immigration minister, Ellen Fairclough, to the House of Commons in early 1962. These new regulations foregrounded education, training and skills as the main criteria for admission regardless of the country of origin of the applicant over the previous admission criteria, which openly discriminated on the basis of racial and geographical exclusions. This was the first set of proposed immigration regulations in the history of Canada which were not explicitly racist in wording and intent, that is, discouraging of non-white and non-European immigration (Hawkins 1988: 91). These changes in immigration policy were developed in conjunction with the decline in numbers of immigrants from Europe, a strong demand for labour and a growing belief — at least in government — of the benefits of immigration. This is not to say all discriminatory elements of immigration were eliminated, since restrictive sponsorship criteria and uneven distribution of Canadian immigration offices around the world still maintained a level of less overt racialized discrimination in immigration policy. However, these changes resulted in an overall shift in source countries for immigration, and by the 1970s, it was clear that the new immigrants arriving in Canada were an increasingly racialized group. If multiculturalism emerged as policy out of the RCBB, it was as a result of pressures mainly from those whose ancestry was European in origin and for whom language was the most salient marker of identity and difference. However, as multiculturalism became policy and immigrants became an increasingly racialized category, multiculturalism increasingly came to be associated with racialized communities as the European "other ethnic groups" slowly assimilated into the white settler category (Burnet 1978; Lupul 1983).

In the 1960s, another paradigmatic change that the federal government attempted to institutionalize was the forced assimilation of the Indigenous peoples of Canada through the abolition of the *Indian Act*. In 1969, the minister of Indian affairs and northern development, Jean Chrétien, proposed the *Statement of the Government of Canada on Indian Policy* (Government of Canada 1969a), better known as the White Paper. The White Paper was based on the idea that any disadvantages that Indigenous peoples suffered in Canadian society were based on their different legal status from non-Indigenous Canadian citizens; thus, assimilation as regular Canadian citizens could be justified — within a rapid five-year transitional period — even if this meant the continued and, in some cases, accelerated abrogation of treaties and land claims. The White Paper was based on an individual notion of equality and pointedly ignored input from Indigenous leaders, which had been sought during consultations in the previous summer of 1968 and also ignored a previous report, *The Hawthorn Report* (1967), commissioned by the Department of Citizenship and Immigration, which had rejected assimilation and also recommended a "citizens plus" status for Indigenous groups. Indigenous communities also reacted to the White Paper, and in 1970 drafted a brief called *Citizens Plus* (see Indians Chiefs of Alberta 2011 for a reprinted version), also known as the Red Paper, and presented it to the federal cabinet. The Red Paper called for the maintenance of the special status of Indigenous groups and reaffirmed the importance of treaties, rejecting the White Paper outright. Shortly thereafter, the White Paper was withdrawn. The federal government's plans for assimilating Indigenous groups during this period meant that there was no mention of them in the terms of reference for the RCBB; a plan which fit well with the assertion in the terms of reference that Canada had only two founding nations, the English and the French, a strategy to reinscribe the white settler logic of the nation. However, Indigenous groups did mount a challenge to this foundational bicultural logic, even if the outcome of a policy on multiculturalism was not necessarily what they had envisioned.

In the wake of the Quiet Revolution,[2] the 1960s ushered in an era in which French Canadian demands for equality — particularly those in Québec — could no longer be ignored by the federal government. Although at Confederation language rights for both English and French were enshrined in section 133 of the *British North America Act*, increasing immigration and industrialization meant the Anglicization of the economy as the English language moved more rapidly than the French out of farming into manufacturing. This meant that immigrant assimilation was oriented more towards English-speaking communities, which exacerbated the marginalization of French in the economy and the federal civil service. Thus, by the 1950s, most of the major economic institutions and industries in Québec were controlled by Anglophones, making English the language of work at higher levels of management. This in turn relegated Francophones to smaller and more peripheral levels of economic activity, all of which translated into significant economic disparities between the two groups, particularly in Montréal (Levine 1990). These economic disparities, alongside the growing urban Francophone middle class in the aftermath of the Quiet Revolution, all worked to mobilize Québec's nationalist movement, with language rights at its centre.

In the post–World War II period, immigrants began to arrive in increasing numbers to Montréal so that by 1970, they accounted for 23 percent of Montréal's population (Levine 1990: 55). As well, the majority of these immigrants chose to send their children to schools with English as the medium of instruction in order to ensure some sort of future economic mobility for their children, but also because of the poor schooling offered to their children at French-language schools — a problem compounded by the fact that the French Catholic school board would not admit non-Catholic children. With the publication of sensationalist demographic projections about the declining Francophone birthrate and increase in immigration rates (Levine 1990), the schooling choices of immigrant children ignited nationalist sentiments and became the site for nationalist action including agitation for unilingual French schooling. These increasing pressures led to riots in Montréal's Saint Leonard neighbourhood — a neighbourhood with a growing Italian immigrant population — on September 10, 1969, in which a hundred people were injured and fifty were arrested and the *Riot Act* was imposed to set curfews and restore order (Levine 1990: 78; Mills 2010: 142–43). In the aftermath of the riots, the provincial government issued Bill-63, which guaranteed parents a choice in language schooling. Ensuing activism on the part of Francophones would see this bill replaced with future legislation that would guarantee much stronger protections for the French language and the eventual loss of any choice in language of public schooling for immigrant parents. In this era, nationalist sentiment was growing throughout many segments of Francophone society; however, it was the extreme fringes of this movement which garnered the most publicity and ultimately influenced political will. This was emblematized in the example of the Front de libération du Québec (FLQ) which was responsible for over 160 violent incidents between 1960 and 1970, including bombings, kidnapping and deaths, all culminating in the October Crisis of 1970[3] (Levine 1990: 90).

The 1960s were a period of great social upheaval in Canadian society, which included the questioning of existing national narratives; hence the adoption of the Canadian flag (1965), the extensive centennial celebrations (1967) and the Royal Commission on the Status of Women (1968). Although the RCBB was a way for the federal government to respond to the perceived challenges to national unity triggered by French Canadian demands, the increasingly visible Indigenous activism and the sea changes in immigration policy and immigrant demographics made the 1960s a time when established modes of organizing national belonging were being called into question and the reworking and rearticulation of a new basis of Canadian national identity had to be considered. It was in the midst of these pressures for social and political changes in Canadian society that calls for a royal commission on bilingualism and biculturalism were made, foremost in a seminal editorial by André Laurendeau in *Le Devoir*, on January 1962. This editorial triggered other calls for an inquiry, and when the federal Liberals were elected with a minority government in 1963, Prime Minister Lester B. Pearson immediately established the RCBB, foregrounding his primary concern with the French Canadian challenges to national unity: "The greater Canada that is in our power to make will be built not on uniformity but on continuing diversity, and particularly on the basic partnership of English speaking and French speaking people" (Government of Canada 1963a: 6). The commission's terms of reference were finalized as an order-in-council on July 19, 1963:

> To inquire into and report upon the existing state of bilingualism and biculturalism in Canada and to recommend what steps should be taken to develop the Canadian confederation on the basis of an equal partnership between the two founding races, taking into account the contribution made by the other ethnic groups to the cultural enrichment of Canada and the measures that should be taken to safeguard that contribution.[4]
> (Government of Canada 1965a: 151–52)

In response to a letter from Prime Minister Pearson to the provincial premiers that asked whether they would "favour" an inquiry, the majority of the provinces expressed support for the RCBB terms of reference, and shortly thereafter ten commissioners were appointed, including co-chairs André Laurendeau and Davidson Dunton.

THE PRELIMINARY PHASE

The RCBB entered the investigative phase of the inquiry with preliminary hearings held November 7 and 8, 1963, in Ottawa. The key task of these preliminary hearings — which would be extended as regional hearings across the country the following year — and the ensuing preliminary report was to confirm the "problem" as set out in the terms of reference: that is, that the greatest crisis facing Canada was relations between the English and French. However, the framing of the French-English crisis as the singular "problem" for the RCBB to tackle was contested vigorously by members of other ethnic groups throughout the hearings.

Members of other ethnic groups contested the RCBB's singular framing through a variety of strategies; however, two main ones were contesting the hierarchy implied amongst groups in the terms of reference and questioning the historical claims upon which the category founding races was restricted to only the English and French. At the hearing, a representative from the Canadian Polish Congress began by questioning the hierarchy suggested in the very name of the commission:

"Although it is stated that the Commission is to study other ethnic groups and cultures, the very name of the Commission suggests that Canadian culture is or should be bicultural" (Government of Canada 1963b: 183–84). He went on to caution that "we cannot limit a culture in a mechanical way to one or two or three or four elements ... multiculture is a necessity" (Government of Canada 1963b: 183–84). This suggestion of the necessity for "multiculture" foreshadowed the ensuing hearing discussions, which would also advocate multiculturalism as a way to break out of the bicultural binary being foregrounded by the commission.

This query over the name of the commission gave rise to a concern with the terms of reference and the hierarchy among groups it implied. Thus, a representative from the Ukrainian Canadian Congress argued that the terms of reference implied a division of Canadian citizens into "first- and second-class citizens" and that the hierarchization of one group of Canadians over another on the basis of a "so-called prior historic right" would ultimately mean a "return to colonial status" (Government of Canada 1963b: 83). These concerns gave way to contentions around particular terms such as "new Canadians," which was used with great frequency throughout the hearings to refer to all groups other than the English, French and Indigenous communities. For example, the president of the National Council of Women of Canada (NCWC) argued that the term "new Canadian" had shifted from describing those who had come after 1947, to meaning "all those who are in Canada after 1759 who are not of French or Anglo-Saxon origin," which would mean that, "if a person came from England in 1960, he is Canadian, but if a Pole or a Ukrainian or a Jew traces his origin in Canada to his great grandfather in 1799, he is a 'new Canadian'" (Government of Canada 1963b: 488). This example was given to show the contradictions embedded within the hierarchy between "Canadian" and "new Canadian," which was paralleled in the terms of reference by the labels "other ethnic groups" and "founding races." As the president of the NCWC continued, the use of these terms suggested "a kind of a priori conclusion — that, whatever the findings of the Commissioners should be, this is a conclusion that they must, by the very terms of reference, arrive at" (Government of Canada 1963b: 452).

Although many spoke out at the hearings about the hierarchization of communities in the terms of reference, another strategy also extensively used at the hearings was not to necessarily challenge the distinctions between groups but to widen their inclusion. Specifically, the idea of a "prior historic right" was an ongoing point of contention and one that various groups representing the Ukrainian community in particular used to make their claims for also fitting into the founding race category. For example, a representative from the Ukrainian Professional and Businessmen's Club spoke about how "Canadian Ukrainian citizens felt that they too are a founding race since to a large extent it was the Ukrainians that did the work of building the railways, and ... opened up the backwoods ... and transformed

[Canada] into the Canadian breadbasket of the world" (Government of Canada 1963b: 220). It was on the basis of these prior historical claims that a territorial argument for language rights was made by the same presenter:

> When you consider the fact that now we have third generation Canadians and now my children are fourth generation and speak Ukrainian, having learned it in Canada, these people find themselves in a milieu which enables them to speak that language and be understood ... in Winnipeg or in many Manitoba and Saskatchewan towns, one can shop during a complete day and do business during that day using only this language which has been learned in Canada ... this is a Canadian language. (Government of Canada 1963b: 231)

Not only did members of other ethnic groups come to the preliminary hearings, but a member of the National Indian Council of Canada also made a bid for Indigenous peoples to be considered as a founding race and therefore to have their language rights also acknowledged: "We respectfully submit that Canada is a tri-lingual country. Our imprint is indelibly on this land ... Indians possess a culture quite distinct from biculturalism" (Government of Canada 1963b: 144). Although Indigenous groups were explicitly excluded from the terms of reference, they did come to hearings and participated in the public portion of the commission in order to make clear that they also had a stake in the deliberations of the RCBB.

The preliminary hearings were a forum for groups other than the English and French to contest the hegemony of the idea of two founding races. However, it was clear that for the commissioners, the primary task was to generate agreement on the singularity of the "problem" facing the RCBB as defined through the terms of reference. Published on February 1, 1965, the preliminary report was a surprise best-seller, indicating the depth of national interest in the initial findings of the commission. The publication of the report inaugurated the persuasive phase of the commission as the "truth" (Ashforth 1990: 9) of the hearings. The report opened with the statement that the commissioners "have been driven to the conclusion that Canada, without being fully conscious of the fact, is passing through the greatest crisis in its history" (Government of Canada 1965a: 13). At the end of the report, in a postscript from the commissioners, the exact nature of the crisis is reiterated: "The present crisis is reminiscent of the situation described by Lord Durham in 1838: 'I found two nations warring in the bosom of a single state'" (Government of Canada 1965a: 144). Thus, the extensive deputations from the other ethnic groups challenging the fundamentally binaristic framing of the terms of reference were minimized in favour of reasserting the central crisis as one between the English and French, that is, a primary concern with the "totality of the two societies in

Canada" (Government of Canada 1965a: 144). Challenges from groups other than the English and French were set aside using a number of discursive strategies, but primarily the report relied on presenting the opinions of other ethnic groups as fragmented and atomized, as exemplified in this passage from the report: "An attempt was made at some regional meetings to discover what unifying values are held in common by Canadians of German, Italian, Chinese, Ukrainian and other ethnic extraction, but a full discussion didn't seem to follow, and this variant on the multicultural theme tended to blend with the mosaic idea" (Government of Canada 1965a: 51). Although here in the preliminary phase of the RCBB, the term multicultural emerged as a way to define other ethnic groups, its primacy over other terms such as "mosaic" and "new Canadians" had not yet been established; this would only happen during the course of the public hearings.

THE PUBLIC HEARINGS

Even as the publication of the preliminary report ushered in the persuasive phase of the RCBB, the investigative phase continued concurrently as the much more extensive cross-country public hearings began in March 1965. The key difference between the preliminary and public hearings was that groups/people had to submit briefs — which had specific guidelines for discussion points — to the commission. The ensuing discussions at the hearings were then specific to the issues raised in the briefs. The constraints imposed by having to first submit a brief before being able to participate in the public hearings did limit the involvement of many racialized communities, although there were a few submissions from the Japanese community. Ultimately, it was the longer-established Ukrainian community who made the largest number of submissions at the public hearings.

If the call for multiculturalism was only one of many ways in which other ethnic groups tried to petition for inclusion at the preliminary hearings, at the public hearings multiculturalism became a prominent term around which the inclusion, and limits thereof, of Aboriginal and other ethnic groups began to coalesce. For example, the Social Study Club of Edmonton established their historical claims as "homesteaders" who had come in the early days of Alberta and managed to work and mingle with each other "without bothering about bilingualism, or giving too much thought to the fact that we were helping to form a basic Canadian culture" (Government of Canada 1964: 4). As the brief clarified, they were against the idea of compensating "economic injustices with an artificial form of bi-culturalism which will try, through an artificial bi-lingualism, to overcome an economic problem with a cultural remedy ... rather than recognizing the actual fact that multi-culturalism has already been adopted spontaneously by the people themselves" (Government of Canada 1964: 4). This brief exemplified the emerging consensus among many other ethnic groups that multiculturalism was already an everyday fact of Canadian life and that official recognition of only two languages in Canada would in fact be counter to this grounded spirit of multiculturalism.

Citing data from the 1961 census, the Mutual Co-operation League of Toronto argued that there was "neither one race nor language in this country forming a clear majority"; therefore, "the advancement of bilingualism was insufficient in scope, and that of biculturalism was limited in vision" (Government of Canada 1964: 1). The Canadian Mennonite Association also agreed that biculturalism/bilingualism was limited, arguing that it was a useful idea only insofar as "it moves society from a monocultural status to multilingualism and multiculturalism," and hoped that for the RCBB, "the larger frame of reference will be multilingualism and multiculturalism" (Government of Canada 1965: 3). This was echoed by the International Institute of Metropolitan Toronto, a community-wide voluntary settlement organization, which argued that the increasingly diverse range of immigrants settling in Toronto meant that "the City is moving from a largely monocultural society to a multicultural world now"; thus, "a new idea of citizenship is developing which transcends culture and language," giving Canada an "opportunity to demonstrate to the world the idea of a multicultural country" (Government of Canada 1964: 1). In these and other briefs, both the contemporary shifts in immigration demographics as well as the historical diversity of immigration to Canada were mobilized as arguments against a limited bicultural and bilingual conceptualization of the nation, instead, biculturalism/bilingualism were seen at best as stepping stones to the official recognition of a de facto multicultural nation. In this way, multiculturalism was naturalized as an already existing Canadian reality, both in the past and into an increasingly cosmopolitan future.

The RCBB garnered extensive press coverage during the hearings, not only in the mainstream press but also in the ethnic press. The ethnic press, 80 percent of which was published in languages other than English and French, played an important role in keeping various communities updated on developments throughout the inquiry, and royal commission researchers also collected related press clippings from the various ethnic media in order to remain informed throughout the inquiry. Given the extensive coverage and analysis generated in the ethnic media, the Canada Ethnic Press Federation also submitted a substantive brief on behalf of the other ethnic groups. An overarching theme in the brief was that of "unity in diversity" as a basic Canadian principle (Government of Canada 1964: 15). Similar to many other ethnic groups, for the Canada Ethnic Press Federation (1964: 15), the substantive element of "unity in diversity" or multiculturalism was multilingualism:

> The language of origin is the most powerful instrument in the hands of an
> ethnic group for retaining its cultural heritage ... the selection of English

or French (or both) does not mean that the ethnic groups will or should discard their languages — the best media available to them for the preservation of their cultures and integration into Canadian cultural streams.

During the course of the public hearings, the linking of language preservation to cultural retention became a central argument for many other ethnic groups for moving beyond biculturalism and bilingualism to multiculturalism materialized as multilingual rights. However, not all briefs from other ethnic groups embraced multiculturalism and multilingualism.

Members of both the Polish and German communities made strong demands in community newspapers for multiculturalism even as they did not make any substantive demands for community language support. For example, a German community newspaper article stated: "Canada is not expected to become a Tower of Babel ... but to lay down the rule that Canada should have two cultures is illogical and outright wrong" ("Once Again: Two Languages" 1964); furthermore, the article went on to argue that Canada was built on the roots of many cultures, all of which should be officially recognized. In a brief from the National Japanese Canadian Citizens Association, members of the Japanese community made no demands for any community language preservation support or multiculturalism, arguing that this would promote a "hyphenated Canadian" identity; rather, they argued for "'Canadianism' — one and indivisible," based on their "bitter experiences during the war years," which they attributed in part to "hyphenated Canadianism" (1965: 3). The Toronto-based Italian Aid Society, which was essentially a settlement organization for newly arriving Italian immigrants, echoed the Japanese brief in that they fully endorsed the terms of reference of the commission, arguing that "there should be no special treatment afforded any other ethnic groups towards the perpetuation of the cultures, languages, customs ... of these groups" (Bagnato 1963: 1). The only request for language learning support was for multilingual staff at the various levels of government in order to "expedite the handling of the problems of those who have not, as yet, mastered the English language" (Bagnato 1963: 2). However, the more established Italian community in Montréal, represented in a brief from the Canadian-Italian Business and Professional Men's Association, did argue for support for community language preservation since there was a concern that without the maintenance of Italian, "it is definite that in 30 to 50 years we will not have a medium of communication between us" (Government of Canada 1965b: 4273). Finally, the Ukrainian community, which submitted over half of all the briefs from the other ethnic groups, came out strongly in favour of both multiculturalism and a territorial multilingualism as proposed during the preliminary hearings, exemplified in a community paper: "Since Canadian is not merely bi-lingual and bi-cultural but multilingual and multicultural, our principle is an absolute equality of all Canadians" ("Canada is Ours" 1965: n.p.).

Although not mentioned in the terms of reference, pressure from Indigenous communities and coverage of Indigenous issues in the mainstream media meant that Indigenous groups were able to participate in the public hearings. The briefs from Indigenous groups focused on their extensive socio-economic marginalization from mainstream Canadian society and emphasized their unique identity as a way to challenge their original erasure from the RCBB. As well, the briefs challenged the limited notion of founding races in the terms of reference and emphasized their status as the "first citizens," which made them "more Canadian than any other groups that have arrived since European settlement" (Indian-Eskimo Association of Canada 1965: 2). The threat of assimilation to cultural survival was concretized extensively as the urgent need for Indigenous language preservation and revitalization over English and French bilingualism: "As to two languages, it has long been accepted that Red Men are entitled to their own original ancient language which precedes that of the languages of the Western world by thousands of years" (Caughnawaga Defence Committee 1965: 3). Ultimately, even Indigenous groups gave little support to the commission's notion of biculturalism, arguing instead that "'equality' of groups ... should also include Indians and bring into it 'multi' instead of 'bi'" (Caughnawaga Defence Committee 1965: 4). The public hearings were the central element of the investigative phase in the RCBB, and many other ethnic groups as well as Indigenous groups used this as an opportunity to make clear the exact nature of their opposition to the commission's terms of reference. As well, they used these hearings as a venue to articulate their vision for inclusion and belonging in this moment when the national narrative was being rearticulated, with multiculturalism — substantiated through support for community languages — emerging as a contested idea for other ethnic and Indigenous groups to challenge the commission's limited framework of biculturalism.

BOOK I TO THE OFFICIAL LANGUAGES ACT

The end of the public hearings indicated the close of the investigative phase of the RCBB, and the first volume of the final report, *Book I: The Official Languages*, was tabled in the House of Commons on December 5, 1967, ushering in a new persuasive phase of the commission and entering the archival phase by providing the foundation for the *Official Languages Act*. This report began with a general introduction, which examined the key terms from the commission's terms of reference. One of the most contentious terms discussed in this introduction was "race." The authors of the report admitted that this term had been a source of great "misunderstanding" throughout the hearings and that in fact, "the word 'race' is used in an older meaning as referring to a national group, and carries no biological significance" (Government of Canada 1967: xxii). Given the necessity of divorcing any biological connotations from the word race, the authors were quick to de-emphasize race in favour of language and culture: "We feel that language and culture are truly central concepts in the terms of reference … we shall give them more emphasis than the notions 'race,' 'people,' or even 'ethnic groups'" (Government of Canada 1967: xxii). The authors foregrounded language and culture over race and ethnicity as a response to the critiques made during the hearings that there was an implied hierarchy of founding races over other ethnic groups.

However, even as the report disavowed this hierarchy by citing the openness of language ("membership in a linguistic group is a matter of personal choice"), they brought it back in by demarcating "two classes of citizens, one consisting of Anglophones of British origin and Francophones of French origin, and the other of Anglophones and Francophones of other origins" (Government of Canada 1967: xxiv). Thus, the original distinctions between founding races and other ethnic groups were transposed onto linguistic divisions. These distinctions were concretized as the report stated that for the two founding races "the life of the two cultures implies in principle the life of the two languages" (Government of Canada 1967: xxxviii), which was the rationale for proposing an official languages act that would declare English and French to be the official languages of Canada. However, with respect to the other ethnic groups, the report argued that "much of the culture of one's forbears could be preserved even when one no longer spoke their language" (Government of Canada 1967: xxiii). This was the critical difference then between founding races and other ethnic groups; the former needed language to retain their culture and the latter could manage their culture without language. This disparity in the right to language would set the mode for differential inclusion between these two groups and reinstall the hierarchy of difference of the original terms of reference, but this time on the terrain of language and culture.

Despite the original omission from the terms of reference, Indigenous groups had made great efforts to participate in the hearings, and, in turn, the commission spent resources researching issues related to Indigenous communities. Reports were commissioned, memos were written, experts were consulted and meetings were arranged.

At the end of these efforts, the conclusions drawn by the commission were clear: "The Canadian Indian problem is so complex that an inquiry into the existing situation of this large and important group should be handled by a special Royal Commission" (Varjassy 1964: 5). The pathologization of Indigenous issues by the RCBB served to set them outside of the ambit of the inquiry and also exempted the commission from having to consider the cultural and linguistic claims of the Indigenous founding peoples: "The social and economic problems of the Indians are so great, deep and bitter, that the cultural and language problems must wait until they realize them" (Varjassy 1964: 3). All this culminated in the clear statement in *Book I* of the report, which handily discounted the one undeniable challenge to a bicultural notion of founding races: "We should point out here that the Commission will not examine the question of the Indians and Eskimos ... since it is obvious that these two groups do not form part of the 'founding races' as the phrase is used in the terms of reference" (Government of Canada 1967: xxvi).

With challenges from other ethnic and Indigenous groups set aside in this report, the proposal to declare English and French the official languages of Canada could go ahead, and in the final chapter of the report, "The Necessary Legislation," the proposed principles for an official language policy were spelled out in detail. As Bill C-120 regarding the Official Languages of Canada was presented in the House on October 17, 1968, Trudeau echoed the terms of reference and gave a glimpse at his future formulation of official multiculturalism: "We believe in two official languages and in a pluralist society, not merely as a political necessity but as an enrichment" (Government of Canada 1968: 1509).

BOOK IV TO MULTICULTURALISM
WITHIN A BILINGUAL FRAMEWORK

Book IV: The Cultural Contribution of Other Ethnic Groups was published in October 1969. Even before the publication of this volume of the final report, the commissioners were grappling with the impact of the other ethnic groups, particularly their desire for multiculturalism over biculturalism. One internal working paper concluded: "In summary we can say that the mainspring (*l'idée force*) of the terms of reference is the question of bilingualism and biculturalism (i.e., English and French) adding immediately that this mainspring is working in a situation where there is a fact of multiculturalism" (Study Group D 1963: 1). This multicultural fact was not one to necessarily be celebrated, but rather one to watch out for as another internal commission memorandum warned that "the most striking characteristic of Other Ethnic Group immigration is its increased strength at the expense of the British element," and, therefore, "the imposing growth of the number of the Other Ethnic Groups has disturbed the balance of the core societies' strength" (Wyczynski 1966: 4). Given these concerns, it is not surprising that when the report was finally published, it repudiated multiculturalism altogether and began the introduction from the position that, "while the terms of reference deal with the question of those of ethnic origin other than British or French, they do so in relation to the basic problem of bilingualism and biculturalism from which they are inseparable" (Government of Canada 1969b: 3).

In *Book I*, the commission made the shift from race and ethnicity to language and culture for identifying and delineating groups within the nation. Here in *Book IV*, the shift away from race and ethnicity was emphasized right from the introduction as contact between groups and the contribution of other ethnic groups was couched in terms of language and culture: "We will look at the contribution to Canadian life, and especially to the enrichment that results from the meeting of a number of languages and cultures" (Government of Canada 1969b: 3). As well, if in *Book I* this shift meant that founding races had now putatively become Anglophones and Francophones, here in the *Book IV*, the shift was completed as "we would rather regard the 'other ethnic groups' as cultural groups" (Government of Canada 1969b: 11). The crucial difference was that, in the case of other ethnic groups, culture was foregrounded and language was not. The hierarchy between founding races and other ethnic groups that was transposed onto language and culture was clearly reiterated throughout the report: "It is thus clear that we must not overlook Canada's culture diversity, keeping in mind that there are two dominant cultures, the French and the English" (Government of Canada 1969b: 13). Although *Book I* set the foundations for the *Official Languages Act*, in *Book IV* commensurate support for the languages of cultural groups was clearly lacking and language preservation for these groups was essentially to be privatized:

> The presence of other cultural groups in Canada is something for which all Canadians should be thankful. The members must always enjoy the right — a basic one — to safeguard their languages and cultures. The exercise of this right requires an extra effort on their part, for which their fellow Canadians owe them a debt of gratitude. (Government of Canada 1969b: 14)

The extra effort would clearly stem from the limited enforceable legislation and lack of constitutional protections for languages other than English and French, as well as the limited funding that would be allocated for this purpose. On these matters, the report was clear: "The learning of third languages [languages other than the two official languages] should not be carried on at the expense of public support for learning the second official language" (Government of Canada 1969b: 138). Ultimately, the authors of *Book IV* remained unequivocal in their support for biculturalism; however, cultural groups across Canada did not let the matter rest, and several conferences on the report were organized. Among these was the Canadian Cultural Rights Concern conference held in Toronto in December 1968, which ended with six resolutions specific to the demands of cultural groups, stating "the Conference unequivocally rejects the concept of biculturalism and seeks official recognition of the multicultural character of Canada" (Canadian Cultural Rights Committee 1968: iii). These resolutions were sent out to the provincial ministers as well as the Prime Minister's Office and garnered mainstream media coverage, generating headlines such as "Ethnics Attack Biculturalism" in the *Toronto Telegram*.

Book IV was published in 1969, but it wasn't until October of 1971 that Prime Minister Trudeau made his now famous speech announcing the implementation of a policy of multiculturalism within a bilingual framework, "For although there are two official languages, there is no official culture, nor does any ethnic group take precedence over any other ... a policy of multiculturalism within a bilingual framework commends itself to the government as the most suitable means of assuring the cultural freedom of Canadians" (Government of Canada 1971: 8545). Even as Trudeau repealed the report's support for biculturalism, he reprised the hierarchy by maintaining that there were two official languages even if there was no official culture. Trudeau concluded his speech by emphasizing "the view of the government that a policy of multiculturalism within a bilingual framework is basically the conscious support of individual freedom of choice" (Government of Canada 1971: 8546). Therefore, as Trudeau cast his new formulation for national belonging as individual rights, he also maintained the collective rights to language of the English and French over other cultural groups. This entrenched a critical difference between the rights of cultural groups and those accorded to the English and French, even as it was stated that there was no official culture and that henceforth Canada was to be multicultural. Ultimately, although Trudeau had ushered in a policy of multiculturalism, this was a very different idea from the substantive and grounded notion of multiculturalism that had been advanced by other ethnic groups at the hearings.

Materially nothing much had changed in this formulation of multiculturalism as Trudeau based most of the actual details of his multiculturalism policy on the recommendations of *Book IV*; originally recommendations for a bicultural Canada. As well, the clear funding imbalance also concretized this hierarchy, as was pointed out by members of other ethnic groups: "This year, the Federal government has allocated fifty million dollars for French language and culture development outside the province of Québec. For all other minorities combined in all of Canada, the budget is forty thousand" (Multiculturalism for Canada Conference 1970: 30). This disparity was also noted by politicians such as leader of the opposition Robert Stanfield, who in response to Trudeau's announcement of a policy of multiculturalism within a bilingual framework stated: "I do not think that members of other cultural groups with other cultural traditions are at all happy with the relatively pitiful amounts that have been allocated to this other aspect of the diversity about which the Prime Minister spoke this morning, multiculturalism" (Government of Canada 1971: 8547). In short, Trudeau's announcement of a policy of multiculturalism within a bilingual framework as a response to the recommendation of biculturalism in *Book IV* grew out his need to balance the interests of national unity from competing claims put forward by Francophones, Québec and other ethnic groups, among others. However, adopting the recommendations of *Book IV* almost wholesale ensured collective rights to language only for the English and French and essentially relegated community language rights to the private sphere, through a paucity of legislation and underfunding. Thus, the multiculturalism policy did little to disrupt the original white settler formulation of bilingualism and biculturalism put forward in the original terms of reference for the RCBB.

CONCLUSION

The RCBB was established at a particular historical moment when demands from various communities within the nation meant that the federal government had to rearticulate its formulation for nation building. A genealogy of the RCBB shows that in the present, multiculturalism as a narrative of Canadian national identity cannot be considered outside the constraints of bilingualism. The need to always consider the dual poles of this formulation in tandem is critical if we are to understand the limits of multiculturalism in Canada. Even with the shift from race and ethnicity onto the terrain of language and culture, the original racialized hierarchy of difference and belonging remains; however, they are now articulated through a differential set of linguistic rights. These differential rights are now entrenched in the *Canadian Charter of Rights and Freedoms*, where, as Meyerhoff (1994: 918) argued, the collective rights of linguistic dualism in sections 16–23 in comparison to those for multicultural rights in section 27 result in a significant disparity between ethnic minorities and official language minorities with respect to the rights and status each enjoy.[5] Specifically, Meyerhoff showed that section 27 has never been interpreted as a collective right and therefore is no way a substantive provision of rights (Meyerhoff 1994: 935), unlike sections 16–23, which guarantee substantive collective official language rights. Thus, the hegemony of linguistic dualism has not only limited the current conception of multiculturalism but also concretized a racially ordered disparity of rights. The cultural equality and substantive pluralism that other ethnic groups originally sought in their vision of multiculturalism is now entrenched as a single limited interpretative section in the Charter. Ultimately, any future attempt to re-envision, rehabilitate or revalorize multiculturalism's inclusive and emancipatory potential must first address the limitation that official bilingualism presents. This is essential if the goal to move beyond a white settler national narrative in Canada is to be realized.

Notes
1. Their terms of reference were "to inquire into and report upon the existing state of bilingualism and biculturalism in Canada and to recommend what steps should be taken to develop the Canadian confederation on the basis of an equal partnership between

the two founding races, taking into account the contribution made by the other ethnic groups to the cultural enrichment of Canada and the measures that should be taken to safeguard that contribution" (Government of Canada 1965a: 151–52).

2. After the death of Duplessis in 1959 and the subsequent death of his successor, Paul Sauvé, Jean Lesage led his Liberal Party to victory over the Union Nationale in 1960, propelling Québec into an era now commonly known as the "Quiet Revolution" — a time of accelerated social, political and economic reforms spanning the early to late 1960s.

3. During the October Crisis of 1970, British Trade Commissioner James Cross was kidnapped and Québec Labour Minister Pierre Laporte was murdered. This crisis led to Prime Minister Trudeau's implementation of the *War Measures Act*, the arrest of almost 500 people and the deployment of federal troops in Montréal.

4. For the full text of the terms of reference, see Government of Canada 1965a: 151–52.

5. Section 27 of the *Charter of Rights and Freedoms* states: "This Charter shall be interpreted in a manner consistent with the preservation and enhancement of the multicultural heritage of Canadians" (Government of Canada 1982a).

References

Ashforth, A. 1990. "Reckoning Schemes of Legitimation: On Commissions of Inquiry as Power/Knowledge Forms." *Journal of Historical Sociology* 3, 1: 1–22.

Bagnato, V.E. 1963. Library and Archives Canada, Italian Immigrant Aid Society. November 19.

Burnet, J. 1978. "The Policy of Multiculturalism within a Bilingual Framework: A Stock-Taking." *Canadian Ethnic Studies* 10, 2: 107–113.

Canada Ethnic Press Federation. 1964. "Brief Presented to the Royal Commission on Bilingualism and Biculturalism."

"Canada Is Ours." 1965. June. *Zhinochyi Svit*. Department of Citizenship and Immigration, Canadian Citizenship Branch, Foreign Language Press Review Service. Library and Archives Canada.

Canadian Cultural Rights Committee. 1968. December 13–15. "Canadian Cultural Rights Concern: A Conference to Study Canada's Multicultural Patterns in the Sixties." Toronto.

Canadian Mennonite Association. 1965. "Brief to the Royal Commission on Bilingualism and Biculturalism." Winnipeg.

Caughnawaga Defence Committee. 1965. "Brief to the Royal Commission on Bilingualism and Biculturalism." Caughnawaga.

Corrigan, P., and D. Sayer. 1985. *The Great Arch: English State Formation as Cultural Revolution*. New York: Blackwell.

Foucault, M. 1977. "Nietzsche, Genealogy, History." In D.F. Bouchard (ed.), *Language, Counter-Memory, Practice*. Ithaca, NY: Cornell University Press.

Government of Canada. 1963a. House of Commons Debates. May 16. Vol. 1, 1st Session, 26th Parliament. Ottawa: Queen's Printer.

_____. 1963b. Royal Commission on Bilingualism and Biculturalism. Transcript of "Preliminary Hearing." Ottawa.

_____. 1965a. *A Preliminary Report of the Royal Commission on Bilingualism and Biculturalism*.

Ottawa: Queen's Printer.

____. 1965b. "Transcripts of Public Hearings." Ottawa. Microfilm.

____. 1967. *Book I: The Official Languages*. Ottawa: Queen's Printer.

____. 1968. House of Commons Debates. October 17. Vol. II, 1st Session, 28th Parliament. Ottawa: Queen's Printer.

____. 1969a. *Statement of the Government of Canada on Indian Policy*. Presented to the First Session of the 28th Parliament by the Honourable Jean Chretien, Minister of Indian Affairs and Northern Development. Department of Indian Affairs and Northern Development. Ottawa: Queen's Printer.

____. 1969b. *Book IV: The Cultural Contribution of the Other Ethnic Groups*. Ottawa: Queen's Printer.

____. 1971. House of Commons Debates. October 8. Vol. 8, 3rd Session, 28th Parliament. Ottawa: Queen's Printer.

____. 1982a. "Charter of Rights and Freedoms." <laws-lois.justice.gc.ca/eng/charter/>.

Hawkins, F. 1988. *Canada and Immigration: Public Policy and Public Concern*, second edition. Montreal: McGill-Queen's University Press.

Hawthorn, H.B. (ed.). 1967. *A Survey of the Contemporary Indians of Canada: Economic, Political, Educational Needs and Policies*. Ottawa: Queen's Printer.

Indian Chiefs of Alberta. 2011. "Citizens Plus." *Aboriginal Policy Studies* 1, 2: 188–281.

Indian-Eskimo Association of Canada. 1965. "A Brief to the Royal Commission on Bilingualism and Biculturalism." Toronto.

International Institute Canada. 1964. "Brief to the Royal Commission on Bilingualism and Biculturalism." Ottawa.

Jenson, J. 1994. "Commissioning Ideas: Representation and Royal Commissions." In S.D. Phillips (ed.), *How Ottawa Spends, 1994–95*. Ottawa: Carleton University Press.

Laurendeau, A. 1962. "Pour une enquête sur le bilinguisme." *Le Devoir*, January 20.

Levine, M.V. 1990. *The Re-conquest of Montreal: Language Policy and Social Change in a Bilingual City*. Philadelphia, PA: Temple University Press.

Lupul, M.R. 1983. "Multiculturalism and Canada's White Ethnics." *Canadian Ethnic Studies* 15, 1: 99–107.

Meyerhoff, T. 1994. "Multiculturalism and Language Rights in Canada: Problems and Prospects for Equality and Unity." *American University Journal of International Law and Policy* 9: 913–1013.

Mills, S. 2010. *The Empire Within: Postcolonial Thought and Political Activism in Sixties Montreal*. Montreal: McGill-Queen's University Press.

Multiculturalism for Canada Conference. 1970. *Report of the Conference*. University of Alberta. August 28–9.

Mutual Co-Operation League of Canada. 1964. "Brief to the Royal Commission on Bilingualism and Biculturalism." Toronto.

National Japanese Canadian Citizens Association. 1965. "Brief to the Royal Commission on Bilingualism and Biculturalism." Toronto.

"Once Again: Two Languages — Yes! Only Two Cultures." 1964. September 12. Department of Citizenship and Immigration, Canadian Citizenship Branch, Foreign Language Press Review Service. Library and Archives Canada.

Social Study Club of Edmonton. 1964. "Brief to the Royal Commission on Bilingualism and Biculturalism." Edmonton.

Study Group D. 1963. "Working Paper." Library and Archives Canada.

Tamboukou, M. 1999. "Writing Genealogies: An Exploration of Foucault's Strategies for Doing Research." *Discourse: Studies in the Cultural Politics of Education* 20, 2: 201–217.

Varjassy, I.M. 1964. "Confidential Distribution: The Ontario Conference of the Indian Eskimo Association." November 20–22. London, ON: Library and Archives Canada.

Wyczynski, P. 1966. May 28. "Les autres groupes ethniques — Rapport Préliminaire." Library and Archives Canada.

VIOLENCE

Chapter 21

INVISIBILIZING VIOLENCE AGAINST WOMEN

Ruth M. Mann

From: *Power and Resistance: Critical Thinking About Canadian Social Issues,* fifth edition, pp. 48–71 (reprinted with permission).

Intimate violence against women continues to be a serious problem in Canada. Yet the public policy discourse has shifted away from violence against women and gender inequality towards one that nominally prioritizes family, children and, most recently, elders. As part of this shift, women's issues are being displaced, or as Jane Jenson describes it, "folded in" (2008b: 139), with other policy concerns, resulting in an "invisibilization" (Dobrowolsky 2008) of women's systemically structured vulnerability to abuse and the problem of gender inequality that is at the root of this problem. Or, as Janine Brodie and Isabella Bakker (2008) phrase it, women's issues are being delegitimized, dismantled and disappeared from Canadian public policy. This is particularly apparent in the federal Family Violence Initiative (FVI), a multi-agency co-ordinating and funding authority established in 1988 to reduce and eliminate violence against women and other aspects of abuse in relationships of intimacy and trust. Since 2006, the FVI has reoriented its sponsored funding and Internet-disseminated resources away from a focus on women's victimization towards a broad degendered concern with violence against intimates. At the same time, it has significantly restricted the resources and the mandate of what has been a key FVI partner, Status of Women Canada (DeKeseredy and Dragiewicz 2007).

This chapter situates recent changes in the focus of FVI activities in relation to the problem of violence against women and in relation to broader changes in Canadian society and Canadian public policy. Drawing on Jane Jenson (2008a: 235–36), it situates the diminishing visibility of violence against women in relation to a broad and fundamental shift in Canada's "citizenship regime," a construct that captures ways the Canadian state allocates responsibilities among state, market and community sectors, defines rights and duties, affords citizens access to policy arenas and selects voices for inclusion and exclusion in policy considerations.

THE FAMILY VIOLENCE INITIATIVE

The FVI was launched by the Progressive Conservative government of Brian Mulroney in 1988 with an initial $40 million time-limited investment directed towards the establishment of two hundred shelters for abused women and the development of a long-term prevention strategy. From 1997 forward, the Government of Canada has provided an annual budget of $7 million, which is currently distributed among eight of fifteen partnering agencies. These eight agencies channel project funding to an array of governmental and civil society partners that participate in efforts to advance FVI aims at provincial-territorial and local levels. In addition, all fifteen agencies are expected to direct funds from their general operating budgets to FVI activities, and all serve on the FVI steering committee, which "monitors and co-ordinates networking and information sharing" across the fifteen agencies along with a representative of the Privy Council (which serves the prime minister and Cabinet) (Government of Canada 2010: 5).

The mandate of the FVI is to promote public awareness of the risk factors of family violence and the need for public involvement, to strengthen the ability of the criminal justice, health and housing systems to respond and support data collection, and to research and evaluate efforts to identify effective interventions (Government of Canada 2002, 2004, 2010). Table 3-1 summarizes the FVI activities that are relevant to this mandate. As this table indicates, Public Health Agency of Canada is currently the lead and most heavily funded partner agency, having replaced Health Canada as the lead agency in 2005. As the lead agency, Public Health Agency of Canada hosts the National Clearinghouse on Family Violence (NCFV), which currently operates as a set of webpages that post selected resources on various aspects of the family violence problem. In addition, the Department of Justice hosts a dedicated FVI webpage with links to research reports and other resources. Of the remaining thirteen partner departments, two provide links to one or both of these FVI-identified resource lists and nine post their own family violence–relevant publications or provide links to other FVI partner department resources (see Table 21-1).

FVI Partner Departments (Funding as per 2010 Performance Report, April 2004 to March 2008)

	FVI funded $	FVI cited	Link to FVI and/or partner depart.	Posts/links FVI resources	Search FVI	Search FV	Search VAW	Search gender equality
Canada Mortgage and Housing Corporation (CMHC)	1,900,000	—	INAC	—	9	143	6	—
Citizenship and Immigration Canada (CIC)	new 2010	6 links buried	DJC-FVI	links to resources	—	29	8	8
Correctional Services of Canada (CSC)	—	2 links logical	DJC-FVI PHAC-NCFV HC RCMP	posts/links to resources	29	271	47	8
Department of Canadian Heritage (DCH)	460,000	3 links buried	SWC INAC	links to resources	16	117	62	24
Department of Justice Canada (DJC)	1,450,000	FVI host	FVI homepage	posts/links to resources	344	2,474	252	78
Department of National Defence (ND)	—	—	—	—	—	—	—	—
Health Canada (HC) (lead role 1988-2004)	—	3 links logical	PHAC-NCFV	posts/links to resources	11	48	24	7

	FVI funded $	FVI cited	Link to FVI and/or partner depart.	Posts/links FVI resources	Search FVI	Search FV	Search VAW	Search gender equality
Human Resources and Skills Development Canada (HR)	—	—	—	—	3	95	10	134 (not FV relevant)
Indian and Northern Affairs Canada (INAC)	—	3 links buried	CMHC	—	12	148	11	24
Public Health Agency of Canada (PHAC)	2,140,000	NCFV host.	FVI homepage	posts resources	76	312	143	32
Public Safety Canada (PSC)	—	—	—	posts/links to resources	3	74	8	—
Royal Canadian Mounted Police (RCMP)	450,000	3 links buried	FVI homepage DJC-FVI	posts/links to resources	1	28	10	5
Service Canada (SC)	—	—	—	—	5	4	5	2
Statistics Canada (StatsCan)	350,000	—	—	posts resources	8	103	45	24
Status of Women Canada (SWC)	250,000	3 links buried	PHAC-NCFV StatsCan	links to resources	5	84	443	88

OFFICIAL EVIDENCE ON VIOLENCE AGAINST WOMEN IN CANADA

FVI partner Statistics Canada has played a key role in developing and analyzing knowledge on the prevalence and nature of violence against women and other aspects of family violence in Canada. The most recent ten of Statistics Canada's heretofore annual *Profile on Family Violence in Canada* reports (hereafter Profile or Profiles) are among the twenty-seven resources posted on the NCFV webpage (Resources > Family Violence [general]). Holly Johnson's (2006) assessment of statistical trends on violence against women, published by Statistics Canada and commissioned by Status of Women, is located under "Additional resources > Women > Reports and Articles." All thirteen Profiles (1998–2009, 2011) and Johnson's (2006) violence against women report are also posted on the Statistics Canada website itself, as are past and current *Juristat* reports relevant to family or intimate violence. Finally, Edward's (forthcoming) assessment of gender and elder abuse, using Statistics Canada data, is listed on the NCFV "What's New" webpage, and is provided on request by NCFV personnel.

CRIMINALIZED VIOLENCE

As in other national jurisdictions, Canadian crime reports identify men as both the primary perpetrators and the primary victims of assaults and homicides (Kong and AuCoin 2008). Focusing on perpetration, from 1997 to 2007, men represented approximately 80 percent of all persons accused of violent offences and women represented a very small, indeed "negligible" (Kong and AuCoin 2008: 4), proportion of persons accused of the most serious violent offences, namely homicide, attempted murder and sexual assault.

In the case of intimate partner violence, a subcategory of police-reported violence, women and girls are the primary victims while men and boys remain the primary perpetrators. From 1998 to 2008, more than eight out of ten police-reported victims of physical assault perpetrated by an intimate partner were female, as were 98 percent of intimate partner victims of forcible confinement and sexual assault, 79 percent of victims of spousal homicide, and comparable proportions of victims of attempted homicide at the hands of a spouse or dating partner (83 percent and 71 percent respectively) (Dauvergne 2009; Mahony 2010; Taylor-Butts and Porter, 2011; see also Kong, Johnson, Beattie and Cardillo 2003). In the case of criminal harassment or stalking, 90 percent of spousal-related perpetrators were male (Bressan 2008: 13). Even in same-sex relationships, violence that comes to the attention of the police is overwhelmingly more likely to be male-perpetrated. In 2008, 10 percent of male intimate partner victims compared to 1 percent of female intimate partner victims were victims of a same-sex spouse or dating partner (Mahony 2010: 12).

The 2011 Profile does not provide a breakdown of perpetrators by gender for family related violence and homicide against children — a probable consequence of decreased funding for analysis allocated to Statistics Canada (Ditchburn 2010). Instead, much like the updated NCFV and Department of Justice factsheets and overviews, the latest Profile contrasts perpetration by "parents," "siblings" and "extended family" with perpetration by non-family members, and ignores in particular how perpetration varies by gender (Sinha 2011a; Taylor-Butts and Porter 2011). This is a notable change from the 2009 Profile, which documents that in 2007 men accounted for 96 percent of all police-reported family related sexual assaults against children and 71 percent of all family related physical assaults against children (Nemr 2009; Ogrodnik 2009). The 2009 Profile also reports that from 1997 to 2007, fathers accounted for 54 percent and mothers 32 percent of all family members accused of murdering an infant or child, and men represented an overwhelming majority of other family related homicide perpetrators (Ogrodnik 2009: 51).

Family related violence against seniors, the rarest variety of intimate violence (Ogrodnik 2009), is likewise overwhelmingly male perpetrated at nearly 80 percent (Edwards, 2012: 17). Unfortunately, as in the case of family related violence against children, the most recent Profile neglects to provide a gender breakdown of perpetration of physical or sexual violence or harassment against seniors (Sinha 2011b). Focusing therefore on homicides, between 1999 and 2009, more than three of every four (77 percent) of female seniors killed by a family member were killed by either a husband or an adult son, while 72 percent of male seniors were killed by an adult son. In the extremely rare phenomenon of spousal homicides involving seniors, female seniors were eight times more likely to be killed by a spouse than were male seniors (41 percent of family related homicides against female seniors versus 5 percent of family related homicides against male seniors) (Taylor-Butts and Porter 2011: 37), a gender ratio that is twice as large as for spousal homicides overall (Dauvergne and Turner 2010).

SELF-REPORTED VIOLENCE — THE GENERAL SOCIAL SURVEY

Every five years Statistics Canada measures self-reported experiences of victimization through the General Social Survey (GSS), which, since 1999, has included victimization at the hands of a current or previous married or common-law spouse (Brennan 2011). Findings on spousal violence are generated through a special module that uses a modified version of Murray Straus's Conflict Tactics Scale (CTS) in conjunction with other measures that were developed for the groundbreaking Violence Against Women (VAW) survey in 1993 (Johnson and Sacco 1995). In addition to CTS measures of physical violence, which range from pushes and shoves to assaults with knives and guns and sexual assaults, the spousal victimization module assesses what previous Profiles termed "controlling and emotionally abusive" behaviours (Bunge and Levette 1998; Bunge 2000) or alternately tactics of "power and control" (Mihorean 2005). These range from verbal putdowns, name calling, and jealous efforts to limit contacts with friends and family, to threats to harm someone close to the victim, destructions of property and financial abuse — acts identified as "emotional and financial abuse" in the latest Profile (Brennan 2011). Finally, the spousal victimization module assesses consequences that range from injuries and fear to seeking help from friends, family, medical services, community services and police authorities.

Three GSS findings are important in highlighting the invisibilization process. First, in both victimization data and crime reports, women are overwhelmingly the victims of intimate or family related criminal harassment and stalking (AuCoin 2005; Bressan 2008). Notably, while analysis of intimate partner stalking perpetration by gender is not yet available from the 2009 GSS, a majority of women who reported intimate stalking or other criminal harassment in the 2004 GSS also reported having experienced physical violence at the hands of a current spouse or ex-spouse over the previous five years (Ogrodnik 2006: 22).

Second, in all three cycles, women and men have reported roughly equivalent prevalence rates for experiencing at least one CTS-measured act of spousal violence over the previous five years. In 2009, this was reported by 6.4 percent of female and 6 percent of male GSS respondents respectively. As in previous cycles, however, the most chronic and severe patterns of spousal violence, the most physically and emotionally injurious spousal violence, and spousal violence most associated with fear and efforts to involve police and other formal helping agents was much more likely to be reported by women. As noted above, the most recent Profile does not address how "power and control" is evidenced in GSS findings. Nevertheless, as in previous cycles, forms of emotional abuse that result in the denigration and terrorizing of a current or previous spouse are overwhelmingly male-perpetrated (Brennan 2011, see Chart 1.5: 14). Moreover, as in previous cycles, female victims report dramatically higher rates of injury, fear and help seeking — at ratios ranging from three women to one man to six women to one man, depending on the measure (Brennan 2011: 10–12). Finally, as in previous cycles, respondents who describe spousal violence as having "little effect" remain overwhelmingly male.

Third, while female-versus-male distributions in victimization and offending have remained more or less stable, the overall prevalence of spousal violence victimization has declined significantly since the 1993 VAW survey, in which 12 percent of female spouses reported one or more acts of violence at the hands of a current or ex-spouse over the previous five years (Brennan 2011; Holly Johnson 2006).

By 1999, and in each of the two subsequent GSS cycles, women were reporting progressively lower victimization rates, as have men since 1999. This decline in self-reported victimization is consistent with declines in intimate partner homicides and family related violence generally — spousal homicides are at a thirty-year low (Ogrodnik 2009). This in turn is consistent with declines in the prevalence and severity of crime and homicide generally (Dauvergne and Turner 2010).

INTERSECTING VULNERABILITIES

Police reports and victimization data confirm that both female gender and same-sex orientation are risk markers for victimization. Sex and gender are not, however, the sole indicators of risk or vulnerability. Police and self-report data show that young people, Aboriginal people and disabled people, including in particular people struggling with drug and alcohol abuse, are also consistently overrepresented as victims of physical and sexual violence, stalking and other criminal harassment at the hands of an intimate partner (AuCoin 2005; Brennan 2011; Bressan 2008; Perreault and Brennan 2010). Importantly, youth, Aboriginal status and substance abuse problems also characterize offender populations — both intimate violence offender populations and offender populations overall (Brzozowski, Taylor-Butts, and Johnson 2006; Mahony 2010). That is, while there are multiple dimensions of vulnerability in intimate partner violence, gender intersects with other risks to produce heightened vulnerabilities for females (H. Johnson 2006). Put simply, while young, Aboriginal, and disabled people in general are more often the victims of violence, it is young, Aboriginal, and disabled women who are most likely to be the victims of intimate partner violence. Only in the case of same-sex intimate partner violence are males more likely than females to be victims, and, with the exception of the statistically very rare case of infanticide, perpetrated almost equally by mothers and fathers (51 percent and 47 percent respectively), in no facet or variety of the larger family violence problem are females equally or more likely to be perpetrators (Ogrodnik 2009: 51).

STATUS OF WOMEN AND THE EVIDENCE

Canada's successes in reducing the prevalence of intimate homicide and the severity of intimate violence is in part attributable to the influence of Status of Women within the FVI prior to 2006. Though never officially feminist, this 1976-founded "women's policy machinery" (Weldon 2002: 149) enabled feminist and feminist-sympathetic individuals and groups across the country to network and strategize to enhance supports for women, conduct research, inform the public, and pressure federal and provincial governments on violence against women and other issues relevant to women's struggle for social, economic and political equality (see also

Mann 2008; Morrow, Hankivsky, and Varcoe 2004; Rankin and Vickers 2001; Shaw and Andrew 2005; Teghtsoonian and Chappell 2008; Walker 1990).

In 2005, the year after FVI leadership was transferred from Health Canada to Public Health Agency of Canada (Government of Canada 2010), Status of Women's extensive collection of research and analysis was folded into Library and Archives Canada, which posts some publications but increasingly refers clients to institutional libraries that house listed but no longer archived texts on a host of policy concerns. However, during the first phase of this research many Status of Women publications were posted on the NCFV Library References Collection. Included were a number of frequently cited and also frequently critiqued reports that unapologetically focus on violence against women and link physical and sexual battering of women to historically constituted structures of gender inequality (for example, Canadian Panel on Violence Against Women 1993).

Recent reports produced and commissioned by Status of Women note that abuse takes multiple forms and that multiple risks intersect to foster victimization and offending (for example, F-P-T Ministries Responsible for the Status of Women 2002). This observation draws upon an emergent feminist intersectionality perspective that is displacing earlier versions of violence-against-women analyses in the work of many scholars (see M. Johnson 1995; Mann 2003, 2007; Tutty 1999). Similar to the feminist multifactor ecological model described by Dragiewicz (2011: 83), feminist intersectionality is shaped by theoretical developments and, importantly, by the voices of Aboriginal and other racialized women who testify to the multiple injustices that fuel violence both against women and by women in marginalized communities (for example, Burgess-Proctor 2006; DeKeseredy and Dragiewicz 2007; Jenson 2008b; MacQuarrie 2005; Nixon and Humphreys 2010; Mann 2007, 2008; Perilla, Frndak and Lillard 2003; Rankin and Vickers 2001; Swan and Snow 2006; Tutty 2006; Weldon 2002).

Intersectionality makes an important contribution to discourse and theory on violence against women and family violence generally. It fosters awareness of the heightened vulnerability of racially and economically marginalized women and men to abuse, including the abuse inherent in a predominantly criminal justice–focused response to family violence (Minaker and Snider 2006). Unfortunately, the intersectionality construct has been co-opted in recent FVI discourse. This is evidenced in the endorsement of intersectionality on the Status of Women website, which focuses on "issues" and "factors" rather than the systemically anchored structures of inequality which feminist discourse identifies as key to the struggle to eliminate violence against women, on the one hand, and promote equality for women, on the other. The Status of Women website continues to espouse these two goals (SWC homepage, as modified March 4, 2011). However, consistent with the Harper government's imposed "no advocacy" mandate, Status of Women's endorsement of intersectionality directs attention not to impediments to equality but rather to a need to address "issues" and "factors," not "in isolation," but rather in how these come together in the lives of "diverse" categories of women:

> The issues that affect women are as diverse as the circumstances in which they live and can seldom be viewed in isolation. For this reason, Status of Women Canada promotes an awareness of the combined impact, or intersectionality, of a variety of factors in women's lives such as age, place of residence, economic status, level of education, immigration status, and whether they are Aboriginal, among other factors. (swc "Who We Are" webpage, as modified March 4, 2011)

ANTI-FEMINIST BACKLASH
— THE ASCENDANCE OF GENDER SYMMETRY

In October 2006, the Harper government officially removed research and advocacy from the Status of Women mandate and closed twelve of the sixteen federal-provincial-territorial offices — offices through which a host of civil society groups had networked to build supports and knowledge on women's issues since the establishment of Status of Women more than three decades ago (Ditchburn 2006; see also DeKeseredy and Dragiewicz 2007). Canadian Heritage Minister Bev Oda, under whose authority Status of Women then operated, justified this effective dismantling and silencing of Status of Women as an end to the practice of separating women from men:

> We don't need to separate the men from the women in this country ... This government as a whole is responsible to develop policies and programs that address the needs of both men and women. (cited in Canadian Press 2006)

Minister Oda's justification for the Harper government's effective dismantling of Status of Women reflects the ascendant influence of anti-feminist "men's rights" lobbying. This lobbying is documented in press reports on the Harper government's decision to change the funding and mandate of Status of Women, and in scholarship on challenges to feminist-influenced domestic violence policy on both sides of the Canadian and U.S. border (DeKeseredy 1999, 2009; DeKeseredy and Dragiewicz 2007; Dragiewicz 2008, 2010; Girard 2009; Mann 2003, 2005, 2007, 2008; Minaker and Snider 2006). This backlash draws upon a "gender symmetry" analysis and argument that is based almost exclusively on survey evidence generated through various versions of the cts. In what Straus (2010) estimates are now over two hundred studies, cts-based research indicates that women and men are roughly equally likely to perpetrate one or more act of violence against an intimate partner over a twelve month, five year or lifetime reporting period. As in Canada's GSS, CTS-measured violence ranges from throwing things, shoves, pushes and slaps, to kicking, choking and beating up, to assaults with knives and guns and sexual assaults. As feminist critics have long observed (see review in Mann 2007), CTS-based findings are generated by practices which include, for example, coding a single punch or kick by a female as "severe" violence, and a push that results in a woman falling down the stairs as "minor," while sexual abuse, social isolation, stalking, financial control and other features of battering lay outside the analysis. While women and men both clearly express or perpetrate acts of violence against intimate partners, these cannot, especially from the perspective of social policy, be conflated. The truly terrorizing battering by males, captured in studies of women's shelter clients and other clinical populations is qualitatively different from the characteristically minor physical explosions of male and female partners captured in social surveys.

However, with increasing insistence, gender symmetry advocates contend that, regardless of the greater rates of physical and emotional injury sustained by women compared to men, CTS-based evidence "proves" that in intimate contexts men are equally or "more" victimized than women. Some gender symmetry advocates even argue that men and women are equally "battered," or in contemporary language "terrorized" and "controlled" (Dutton 2006; Dutton and Nicholls 2005; Dutton and Corvo 2006; Laroche 2005, 2008; Lupri 2004; Straus 2006, 2007, 2009, 2010). Gender symmetry advocates contend, moreover, that feminist-inspired claims that women are the primary victims of abuse are founded in an ideologically rooted denial and suppression of evidence, particularly evidence that psychopathological issues are the principal cause of intimate violence for women and men alike. They further contend that feminism is responsible for a pervasive anti-male bias that allegedly pervades social and criminal justice policy and front-line intervention. Finally, they contend that research confirming gender symmetry is concealed, distorted and suppressed as a consequence of the influence of feminism — a claim that coincides with the assertion that more than two hundred publications "prove" gender symmetry (Straus 2009: 552, 2010: 332).

The invisibilization of violence against women in FVI discourse and action that is the primary focus of this chapter must be situated in relation to the increasing vehemence and prominence of this gender symmetry perspective. As documented in the work of Ruth Mann (2005, 2008), April Girard (2009) and others, this perspective has made its way into Canadian policy deliberations at provincial and federal levels, as has also occurred in the United States and other jurisdictions (see for example, Dragiewicz 2008, 2010, 2011). Across these policy forums progressive politicians and representatives of civil society groups concerned with women's equality and freedom from violence have lobbied to maintain a central focus on the problem of violence against women, while conservative politicians and anti-feminist advocates for men have advanced claims that this focus constitutes bias against men. Increasingly, this "men are equally victims" stance is supplanting a focus on women's victimization, as is demonstrated in the resources on intimate violence featured on the websites of partnering agencies within the FVI.

NATIONAL CLEARINGHOUSE ON FAMILY VIOLENCE — DISSEMINATING KNOWLEDGE

Public Health Agency of Canada (PHA) hosts the National Clearinghouse on Family Violence (NCFV), as noted earlier in this chapter. As described on its home webpage, the NCFV is a "one-stop source for information on violence and abuse within the family" that operates on behalf of the fifteen partner departments within the FVI. Its mandate is to collect, develop and disseminate resources on prevention, protection and treatment with the aim of "encouraging Canadian communities to become involved in reducing the occurrence of family violence" (NCFV, About Us). Prior to March 2011 the NCFV housed an online Library Reference Collection of almost 12,000 family violence resources published or commissioned by the NCFV itself, or deemed worthy of inclusion in the NCFV collection (Government of Canada 2010: 24). In March 2011, the NCFV dismantled this collection. Curiously, while some previously housed resources are available through the Library and Archives Canada collection, to which Status of Women Canada refers web visitors, the NCFV website does not inform the public of this resource. Rather, it provides links to webpages that provided a small number of selected resources.[1]

FVI factsheets and overviews of various aspects of family violence produced and commissioned by the Department of Justice, the Royal Canadian Mounted Police (RCMP), and the NCFV itself reflect a reframing of the intimate violence problem that draws on both a co-opted intersectionality perspective and gender symmetry arguments. The result is a discourse that effectively writes women out by folding gender in with other aspects of vulnerability and inequality (Brodie and Bakker 2008; Dobrowolsky 2008; Jenson 2008b).

This writing-out and folding-in of women and gender is explicit in an overview of family violence posted both on the Department of Justice FVI website and on the PHA-NCFV website. As Jenson (2008b) would predict, this text does not exclude women or gender; rather it situates gendered vulnerability to victimization in the context of what is "clear" when analysis moves beyond competing arguments on the salience of social structures and individual pathologies. This is that "regardless of gender" a number of identifiable categories of individuals may be vulnerable to being abused, while "webs of intersecting inequalities" may foster vulnerability. In the list of "people" who may be vulnerable, women come third, or fourth, depending on whether children and youth are counted as one or two categories of people:

> Some experts believe that family violence is linked to power imbalances in relationships and inequities in our society ... Other experts focus on the socio-psychological characteristics of the individuals involved ... Regardless of the diversity in perspective, it is clear that ... people from every walk of life — regardless of gender ... may be vulnerable to being abused.
>
> The most vulnerable groups in our society are Aboriginal people, children and youth, women, individuals with low socio-economic status, people with disabilities, visible minorities, immigrants and refugees, gays and lesbians and individuals living in rural and remote communities. For people in these vulnerable groups, being victimized and abused are linked to the web of intersecting inequalities ... that may contribute to abuse. (DJC 2009: 12)

NCFV "RESOURCES" — WOMEN AND MEN

The NCFV disseminates selected materials on six key aspects of intimate abuse. These six "Resources" webpages contain seemingly unorganized lists of articles, reports, analyses, overviews, factsheets, pamphlets and posters on "Abuse of Older Adults" (12 resources), "Abuse and Neglect of Children" (28 resources), "Child Sexual abuse" (15 resources), "Intimate Partner Abuse Against Women" (20 resources), "Intimate Partner Abuse Against Men" (3 resources), and "Family Violence (generally)" (27 resources). During the first phase of the research for this chapter, three reports were posted under each heading, "Intimate Partner Abuse Against Women" and "Intimate Partner Abuse Against Men" — a rhetorical strategy that indicates an NCFV commitment to frame violence against women and men as equal concerns. When the webpage was updated in March 2011, however, seventeen additional resources were added to the "Intimate Partner Abuse Against Women" set, while the other five resource sets remained unchanged.

The three reports under "Intimate Partner Abuse Against Women" posted in 2009 and remaining at the top of the 2011 update do not engage with the gender symmetry debate. Nor do these three reports explicitly cite intersectionality. Rather, each addresses a specific vulnerable population, namely Aboriginal women (NCFV 2008), lesbian women (Chesley, MacAulay and Ristock 1998), and immigrant women (DJC 2006). This focus on special populations is also evident in the seventeen resources added in the March 2011 update. What is noteworthy, however, is that the 2011 update includes a number of texts produced by FVI partner departments or commissioned by the NCFV that ignore women's heightened vulnerability to victimization and/or cite research that challenges or purports to refute it. These texts include pamphlets on dating violence, stalking and spousal abuse produced by the RCMP (RCMP 2007a, 2007b, 2007c). All of these use gender-neutral terms when referring to perpetrators, such as "a partner," "an individual," and "his/her" or "him/her." While the spousal abuse pamphlet acknowledges women's heightened vulnerability to severe violence, it emphasizes that "men are also victims." The pamphlets on dating violence and stalking, in contrast, neglect entirely to address how victimization or perpetration vary by gender.

A NCFV commissioned report on dating violence (Kelly 2006) goes even further in erasing women's disproportionate vulnerability to intimate violence. In addition to citing Straus (2004) and other research that purports to "prove" gender symmetry, it addresses "tests" of Michael Johnson's argument that there are multiple types of intimate partner violence and that the prevalence and consequences of female-versus-male victimization and perpetration vary according to type, by framing Johnson's argument as empirically challenged and as salient to only the rarest variety or type of intimate violence, so-called "intimate terrorism" (Kelly 2006: 2–3, see also footnote 10). Prominent in their absence are Statistics Canada's reports on dating violence (Mahony 2010), forcible confinement (Dauvergne 2009), and stalking (Perreault and Brennan 2010) — to access these one must go to the Statistics Canada website. Also prominent for their absence are the Profiles, where these and other facets of intimate partner abuse are addressed. For the Profiles, one must go to either Statistics Canada or to the NCFV webpage "Resources > "Family Violence (general)."

This elision of women is equally evident in the three "Resources" posted on the "Intimate Partner Abuse Against Men" webpage in 2009, which remain unchanged after the 2011 update. These resources consist of a *Directory of Services for Abused Men in Canada* (Government of Canada 2008), a NCFV commissioned report on abuse in gay male relationships (Kirkland 2004), and, most significantly, a NCFV commissioned report on *Intimate Partner Abuse Against Men* (Lupri and Grandin 2004) that uses 1999 GSS findings and other CTS-based research to advance a strong, yet muted, gender symmetry argument (see discussion on an alleged Health Canada enforced muting of this argument in Lupri 2004). Prominent for its absence is Leslie Tutty's (1999) earlier report on *Husband Abuse*, the first NCFV commissioned publication to address intimate abuse against men, denounced by Lupri (2004) and other anti-feminists as biased (see Mann 2008). Tutty reviews findings and arguments advanced in research and lobbying that challenge the prioritization of violence against women in policy initiatives, and concludes that while clearly men may also be abused, assertions by "some Canadian scholars that research is proving men are equally victims" is unsupported, but that more research is needed (1999: 23). Currently, this pre-2009 posted text is only available through institutional libraries — listed by Library and Archives Canada. It has, therefore, effectively disappeared from the FVI landscape.

NCFV "ADDITIONAL RESOURCES"

Focusing on intimate partner abuse against women and men, the "Additional Resources"> "Women" webpage posts thirty-eight documents identified as "Research and Reports." Among these documents is Holly Johnson's (2006) analysis of violence against women as evidenced in GSS data. In contrast, the "Additional Resources" > "Men" webpage posts two research reports in English, plus a French version of one of these, authored by Denis Laroche (2005, 2008). The Laroche reports use the same GSS data to document the extent and nature of male victimization.

Holly Johnson's (2006) report frames inequality as a root or principal source of women's vulnerability to spousal and other forms of intimate abuse, but she does not frame this as a polemic. She does, however, preface her analysis of GSS and other indicators of the prevalence and nature of intimate partner abuse with a justification for the gender-specific focus on violence against women. This justification speaks to an emergent de-legitimation of gender in research and policy on intimate abuse in Canada:

> Generic programs meant to address violence against all Canadians risk failing to adequately address women's experiences of violence. Gender-specific data can pinpoint those areas where the need for support services is different for women and men ... Data that are made available by gender demonstrate the specific risk areas for men and women and highlight the need for targeted programs to address violence for each gender ... To achieve true equality, actions must be taken that adjust for the differences in experiences and situations between women and men, and among women, and that correct the systemic nature of inequality. (Johnson 2006: 8)

Holly Johnson's (2006) analysis does not address whether and how intimate violence is or is not symmetrical. Nor does she address debates on whether and how motivations differ by gender. Rather, she reports on the ways GSS measures of serious violence, stalking and control fit with other measures, particularly measures of fear, cited forty-nine times (for example, pp. 13, 27, 30, 32–34). More importantly, in an implicit nod to a feminist version of the intersectionality perspective, Holly Johnson links violence against women to other dimensions of diversity that she argues foster heightened vulnerability for women and men who are "outside the dominant culture" — and calls for action to "correct the systemic nature of inequality":

Barriers to equality are rooted in long-standing attitudes and traditions not only about women, but also about race, age, sexual orientation, disability, colour, etc. In particular, the life situations of women outside the dominant culture ... are quite different from the mainstream. For them, the path to equality has been, and continues to be, even more difficult ... To achieve true equality, actions must be taken that adjust for the differences in experiences and situations between women and men, and among women, and that correct the systemic nature of inequality. (Johnson 2006: 8)

Holly Johnson's (2006: 13) main conclusion is that while both the prevalence and severity of intimate violence against women has declined significantly since the 1993 VAW survey, women continue to be the principal victims of the most severe forms of spousal assault, spousal homicide, sexual assault and stalking, and that the concentration of these most serious forms of intimate violence among marginalized women must be addressed.

In contrast, Denis Laroche (2008) uses GSS data to "reveal" the context and consequences of intimate abuse against men. Using variations of the word "reveal" over sixty times, his major goal is not to document prevalence, consequences or correlates, but rather to refute the argument that self-report data confirm women are the predominant victims of intimate terrorism and that control is the key motivation for and dynamic of this predominantly male-driven variety of intimate violence. Specifically, Laroche challenges Michael Johnson and Janel Leone's (2005: 334) "very conservative test" of what they clearly frame as "hypotheses" on how four theoretically distinct varieties of intimate violence vary by gender and how these fit with tactics of power and control assessed in the 2004 GSS:

1) common couple or situational violence: intimate partner violence marked by a single or occasional — rarely physically consequential — push, shove, slap or other act of violence perpetrated in the context of anger and frustration, hypothesised to be more or less equally male- or female-perpetrated;

2) intimate terrorism: intimate partner violence marked by the systemic and instrumental use of violence and associated threats and abuse aimed at or resulting in denigration, control and fear, hypothesised to be primarily male-perpetrated;

3) resistance violence: intimate partner violence marked by violence perpetrated in defence of self or a child in the face of intimate terrorism, hypothesised to be primarily female-perpetrated; and

4) mutual violent control: intimate partner violence marked by violent and controlling acts perpetrated by both partners in a struggle for dominance.

Consistent with other critiques of Michael Johnson's work (for example, Dutton 2006; Dutton and Corvo 2006; Dutton and Nicholls 2005; Fergusson, Horwood and Ridder 2005a, 2005b; Kelly 2006; Straus 2006), Laroche (2008: 66) contrasts Johnson and Leone's "argument" that intimate terrorism is driven by male control with what he frames as the methodologically and conceptually more validated body of evidence on psychopathology and intimate violence. He concludes that while "gender asymmetry" (Laroche 2008: 102) is unquestionably in evidence for the most severe patterns of intimate violence, especially with respect to consequences, policy needs to attend to "diverse types of psychopathology and personality disorder" rather than gender (Laroche 2008: 103). This is to say, rather than research on "control" and the "patriarchal ideology" (Laroche 2008: 73) alleged to be at its root, policy needs to address the mental health issues that fuel intimate violence regardless of the gender of perpetrators.

> These observations [on psychopathology and personality disorder] empirically contradict Johnson's assertion … that domestic violence is not the result of individual pathology or a mental health problem. (Laroche 2008: 103)

It is important to note that Michael Johnson does not advance the "assertion" that mental health problems are irrelevant to intimate abuse. To the contrary, he directs considerable attention to mental health outcomes of intimate partner victimization. Moreover, from 1995 forward, Michael Johnson has acknowledged that the causes of intimate abuse are multiple, as have other feminist researchers from the mid-1990s forward. What he does emphatically argue, based on Canada's GSS and other feminist-influenced research, is that the most serious variety of intimate partner violence is gender-specific, that gendered power and control tactics are at the heart of this truly terrorizing variety of intimate violence, and that social and criminal justice policies need to continue to prioritize reducing the prevalence of violence against women and providing victimized women and their children with protection and support (M. Johnson 2005, 2006; Johnson and Ferraro 2000; Johnson and Leone 2005).

POLICY AND GOVERNANCE

The analysis of the FVI advanced in this chapter draws upon theorizing on governance and citizenship as outlined in the works of Mitchell Dean and Jane Jenson. Mitchel Dean (2007) focuses on the importance of politics and therefore the state in late modern democracies. He posits a new authoritarian brand of politics that can be and is mobilized to undo progressive achievements. This is accomplished, Dean argues, through the folding of neo-conservative mentalities and values into state agendas — a process that proponents legitimize as essential to safeguard economic, security and cultural interests. The result is enhanced exclusion and punishment of an expanding contingent of individuals and groups identified as outside the confines of what the state is willing to recognize as responsible, self-supporting and self-regulating citizenship. Jane Jenson (1997, 2008a, 2008b) outlines mechanisms at play in this process — in particular mechanisms involved in shifts in how responsibilities are allocated and how evidence and the voices making claims on evidence are heard in the development and reform of policy.

Changes in the governance of the FVI described in the three performance reports are consistent with Dean's and Jenson's analyses. Each of the three reports describes the FVI as a collaborative horizontal management strategy aimed at reducing the prevalence of violence and abuse in "relationships of kinship, intimacy, dependency and trust" (Government of Canada 2002, 2004, 2010). Formally instituted in 1997, the original intent of horizontal management was "to ensure a shared federal perspective, foster collaboration, create partnerships and provide opportunities for joint action" (Government of Canada 2002: ii). By 2004 horizontal management had become an "evolving management approach" that aimed to "ensure a shared federal perspective," "prevent duplication" and "offer opportunities for joint action and partnership" (2004: 2), a rhetorical shift that reflects the ascendant influence of neo-liberal or market mentalities under the Liberal governments of Jean Chrétien and Paul Martin. Under the Harper Conservatives, horizontal management was again reconstituted. As described in the 2010 report, horizontal management had become a strategy to "ensure a strategic focus and guard against overlap and duplication of effort," ensure "partners continue to focus on addressing the issues and often unique circumstances of specific sub-populations affected by violence," and, as "a key focus," refine "initiative-level performance measurement, reporting and evaluation activity" (Government of Canada 2010: 32). Facilitated by the introduction of the Privy Council as a member on the FVI steering committee in 2007 (Government of Canada 2010: 5), horizontal management was reconfigured to situate politics at the head of FVI action. Rhetorically and practically, collaboration between state and civil society actors disappears, except in the delivery of services deemed by the government to not involve advocacy (Canadian Press 2006; DeKeseredy and Dragiewicz 2007; Ditchburn 2006, 2010).

One effect of these changes has been the elision of violence against women from FVI discourse. This action was well underway in 2009, evidenced in the texts selected by the PHA for posting on NCFV "Resources" and "Additional Resources" webpages. The 2011 updates took this elision of violence against women further. In addition to adding texts to the webpages dedicated to the intimate abuse of women that explicitly challenge arguments that women are the principal victims of intimate partner abuse, the NCFV dismantled their archive that documents this.

Importantly, the 2010 performance report boasts that between 2004 and 2008 the NCFV distributed "over 475,000 publications across the country and abroad" (Government of Canada 2010: 24). Rather than formally fold this "immediate expected result" (Government of Canada 2010: 24) of FVI activities into the Library and Archives Canada collection, the Public Health Agency of Canada is opting to treat this rich body of research and analysis as though it never existed. The message seems clear: prior to the election that resulted in Prime Minister Harper winning a "stable, secure Conservative majority" (2011 campaign rhetoric), the government had decided that this "Canadiana collection" (NCFV email to author March 28, 2011) is no longer useful to the purpose of governing family violence, in Canada or internationally.

Prior to the coming into power of the Harper government, gender symmetry arguments had already entered into FVI discourse (for example, Lupri and Grandin 2004; Tutty 1999). This accelerated subsequent to changes to the mandate and funding of Status of Women in 2006, which was followed by the addition of the Privy Council to the FVI steering committee. Under the surveillance of the prime minister and Cabinet, partner departments began updating factsheets and overviews to reflect a degendered discourse that ignores or challenges research produced and analyzed by key FVI expert Statistics Canada. At the same time, Statistics Canada began removing gender from among the factors routinely addressed in analyses of child and elder abuse (Sinha 2011a, 2011b; Taylor-Butts and Porter 2011), reducing the extent and depth of gendered analyses of GSS data on spousal violence, and in particular muting discussions on the salience of controlling behaviours as evidenced in measures of emotional and financial abuse (Brennan 2011). Gender analysis is left, therefore, to special reports such as Holly Johnson's soon outdated (2006) analyses of trends in violence against women since 1993, the NCFV-ignored report on dating violence (Mahony 2010), and a 2010 NCFV "What's New" report, produced but still forthcoming, on gender and elder abuse (Edwards 2012).

The major voice lost in these developments is that of Status of Women. For decades Status of Women provided moral leadership in a citizenship regime committed to advancing equality and justice for women, and for all oppressed people. However, the feminist intersectionality perspective that Status of Women reports and website commentary endorse has been co-opted, as Jenson (2008b) notes this is occurring across jurisdictions. Under the Harper Conservatives, however, women's heightened vulnerability to intimate abuse is not simply folded in with other concerns, it is effectively invisibilized (Dobrowolsky 2008). This erasure of violence against women draws on a self-proclaimed "scientific" body of research and analyses that refuses to consider evidence on the salience of gender to abuse (for example, Dutton and Corvo 2006; Straus 2006). Misrepresenting and denigrating research that focuses on how motivations and consequences of intimate violence vary by sex, gender symmetry analysts increasingly choose to prioritize psychopathological responses to situations and experiences identified as too "rare" (Kelly 2006) to serve as a primary focus for family violence policy. They interpret these rare psychopathological responses, moreover, as a refutation of research and policy associated with the "ideology" (for example, Dutton and Corvo 2006; Laroche 2008; Straus 2006) or indeed the "groupthink" (Dutton and Nicholls 2005) that purportedly underpins research into the salience of gender and other systemically anchored inequalities.

POLITICS TRUMPS EVIDENCE

Over the past several decades, feminists have endeavoured to "marshal the evidence" (Nixon and Humphries, 2010) to better account for the ways multiple and intersecting structures, processes and factors foster women's heightened vulnerability to intimate violence. Status of Women and Statistics Canada have been co-participants in these efforts, exemplified in Holly Johnson's (2006) analysis of GSS data on violence against women. As Jenson (2008a) emphasizes, however, and as recent shifts in FVI discourse demonstrate, it is politics that mediates both what counts as evidence and whether evidence is considered in policy processes (see also Dobrowolsky 2008; Brodie and Bakker 2008). As a Statistics Canada spokesperson stated to the press in relation to the recent elimination of Canada's long-form census and other socially significant surveys, evidence and its analysis are being removed from the domain of state action in the Harper government's "new world order" (Ditchburn 2010). Violence against women is one casualty among many in this development.

Those of us who recognize gender and other inequalities as important evidence-based policy concerns will seek to retain and reinstate not only research and analysis but also supports aimed at what remains the principal family violence problem — male-perpetrated violence against women. Those who see this evidence, analysis, and associated supports as divisive, ideological and biased will instead welcome the changes to the FVI. Those who see truth in both perspectives will look for something more, or something else. In a democracy, it is a responsibility of citizenship to evaluate policy and the interests that shape what counts as evidence in various policy domains — in the media, in scholarly articles and, not least, in policy arenas where individuals and groups give testimony on pending legislation and policy, as described in various publications cited in this chapter (for example, Dragiewicz 2011; Mann 2005, 2008; Girard 2009). Looking to the future, it is incumbent upon us to choose, in Jenson's (1997: 644) words, "what kind of citizens we wish to be" in the "interesting times" that lie ahead for Canada and the world.

Changes in the way the FVI is led, implemented and monitored, a concurrent delegitimizing and curtailment of research and advocacy, and a resulting invisibilization of violence against women participate in shifts in governance that are determining the kind of society that Canada is and will be. These developments participate in and signal a fundamental shift in how responsibilities among state, market and community domains are allocated, in how rights and duties are defined, in how citizens are afforded access to legislative and policy arenas, and in how voices are selected for inclusion and exclusion (Jenson, 2008a). In this "new world order," major exclusions are violence against women, gender equality, power and control, feminism, Status of Women, Canada's national storehouse of information on family violence — the NCFV — and predictably, sooner rather than later, the Family Violence Initiative itself.

Note

1. The NCFV archive was "taken down" in late March 2011 (NCFV email to author, 25 March 2011).

References

AuCoin, K. 2005. "Stalking — Criminal Harassment." In K. AuCoin (ed.), *Family Violence in Canada: A Statistical Profile 2005*. Ottawa: Canadian Centre for Justice Statistics.

Brennan, S. 2011. "Self-Reported Spousal Violence, 2009." *Family Violence in Canada: A Statistical Profile*. Ottawa: Statistics Canada.

Bressan, A. 2008. "Spousal Violence in Canada's Provinces and Territories." *Family Violence in Canada: A Statistical Profile 2008*. Ottawa: Statistics Canada.

Brodie J., and I. Bakker. 2008. *Where Are the Women? Gender Equity, Budgets and Canadian Public Policy*. Ottawa: Canadian Centre for Policy Alternatives.

Brzozowski, J.A., A. Taylor-Butts, and S. Johnson. 2006. "Victimization and Offending among the Aboriginal Population in Canada." *Juristat* 26, 3.

Bunge, V.P. 2000. "Spousal Violence." In V.P. Bunge and D. Locke (eds.), *Family Violence in Canada: A Statistical Profile 2000*. Ottawa: Statistics Canada.

Bunge, V.P., and A. Levett. 1998. "Spousal Violence." In *Family Violence in Canada: A Statistical Profile 1998*. Ottawa: Statistics Canada.

Burgess-Proctor, A. 2006. "Intersections of Race, Class, Gender, and Crime: Future Directions for Feminist Criminology." *Feminist Criminology* 1.

Canadian Panel on Violence Against Women. 1993. *Changing the Landscape: Ending the Violence-Achieving Equality,* first edition. Ottawa: Minister of Supply and Services Canada.

Canadian Press. 2006. "Tories Shutting Status of Women Offices." CBC *News Online,* November 30.

Chesley, L., D. MacAulay, and J. Ristock, J. 1998. *Abuse in Lesbian Relationships: Information and Resources*. Public Health Agency of Canada, Catalogue Cat. H72-21/153-1998. <phac-aspc.gc.ca/ncfv-cnivf/pdfs/fem-lesbianabuse.pdf>.

Dauvergne, M. 2009. "Trends in Police-Reported Serious Assault." *Jurista* 29, 4.

Dauvergne, M., and J. Turner. 2010. "Police-Reported Crime Statistics in Canada, 2009." *Juristat* 30, 2.

Dean, M. 2007. *Governing Societies: Political Perspectives on Domestic and International Rule.* New York: McGraw Hill.

DeKeseredy, W.S. 1999. "Tactics of the Antifeminist Backlash against Canadian National Woman Abuse Surveys." *Violence Against Women* 5.

____. 2009. "Canadian Crime Control in the New Millennium: The Influence of Neo-Conservative US Policies and Practices." *Police Practice and Research* 10.

DeKeseredy, W.S., and M. Dragiewicz. 2007. "Understanding the Complexities of Feminist Perspectives on Woman Abuse: A Commentary on Donald G. Dutton's *Rethinking Domestic Violence.*" *Violence Against Women* 13: 874–84.

Department of Justice Canada. 2006. *Abuse Is Wrong in Any Language.* Ottawa: Department of Justice Canada. <justice.gc.ca/eng/pi/fv-vf/pub/abus/abus_lang/fe-fa/eng-ang.pdf>.

____. 2009. *Family Violence: Department of Justice Canada Overview Paper.* <justice.gc.ca/eng/pi/fv-vf/facts-info/fv-vf/fv-vf.pdf>.

Ditchburn, J. 2006. "Social Conservatives Press Harper Government to Axe Status of Women Canada." *Canadian Press,* August 25. Online.

____. 2010. "Tories Scrap Mandatory Long-Form Census." *Globe and Mail,* June 19. Online.

Dobrowolsky, A. 2008. "Interrogating 'Invisibilization' and 'Instrumentalization': Women and Current Citizenship Trends in Canada." *Citizenship Studies* 12.

Dragiewicz, M. 2008. "Patriarchy Reasserted: Fathers' Rights and Anti-VAWA Activism." *Feminist Criminology* 3.

____. 2010. "A Left Realist Approach to Antifeminist Fathers' Rights Groups." *Crime, Law and Social Change* 54.

____. 2011. *Equality With a Vengeance: Men's Rights Groups, Battered Women, and Antifeminist Backlash.* Boston: Northeastern University Press

Dutton, D.G. 2006. "A Briefer Reply to Johnson: Re-Affirming the Necessity of a Gender-Neutral Approach to Custody Evaluations." *Journal of Child Custody: Research, Issues and Practices* 3.

Dutton, D.G., and K. Corvo. 2006. "Transforming a Flawed Policy: A Call to Revive Psychology and Science in Domestic Violence Research and Practice." *Aggression and Violent Behavior* 11.

Dutton, D.G., and T.L. Nicholls. 2005. "The Gender Paradigm in Domestic Violence Research and Theory: Part 1 — The Conflict of Theory and Data." *Aggression and Violent Behavior* 10.

Edwards, P. 2012. *Elder Abuse in Canada: A Gender-Based Analysis.* Ottawa, ON: Public Health Agency of Canada. <publications.gc.ca/collections/collection_2012/aspc-phac/HP10-21-2012-eng.pdf>.

Federal/Provincial/Territorial Ministries Responsible for the Status of Women. 2002. *Assessing Violence Against Women: A Statistical Profile.* Status of Women Canada. At 'orphaned' SWC website <swc-cfc.gc.ca/pubs/0662331664/200212_0662331664_e.pdf>.

Fergusson, D.M., L.J. Horwood, and E.M. Ridder. 2005. "Rejoinder." *Journal of Marriage and Family* 67.

_____. 2005. "Partner Violence and Mental Health Outcomes in a New Zealand Birth Cohort." *Journal of Marriage and the Family* 67.

Girard, A.L. 2009. "Backlash or Equality? The Influence of Men's and Women's Rights Discourses on Domestic Violence Legislation in Ontario." *Violence Against Women* 15.

Government of Canada. 2002. *The Family Violence Initiative: Year Five Report 2002.* <phac-aspc.gc.ca/ncfv-cnivf/pdfs/fv-fiveyear-report_e.pdf>.

_____. 2004. *The Family Violence Initiative Performance Report 2002–2003 and 2003–2004.* <phac-aspc.gc.ca/ncfv-cnivf/pdfs/fv-2004-FVI-eng.pdf>.

_____. 2008. *Directory of Services for Abused Men in Canada.* National Clearinghouse on Family Violence, Catalogue # HP20-8/2008. <phac-aspc.gc.ca/ncfv-cnivf/pdfs/male-dir-services-progs_e.pdf>.

_____. 2010. *Family Violence Initiative Performance Report for April 2004 to March 2008.* <phac-aspc.gc.ca/ncfv-cnivf/pdfs/fvi-perf-rprt-eng.pdf>.

Jenson, J. 1997. "Fated to Live in Interesting Times: Canada's Changing Citizenship Regimes." *Canadian Journal of Political Science* 30: 627.

_____. 2008a. "Getting to Sewers and Sanitation: Doing Public Health within Nineteenth-Century Britain's Citizenship Regimes." *Politics and Society* 36.

_____. 2008b. "Writing Women Out, Folding Gender In: The European Union 'Modernises' Social Policy." *Social Politics* 15.

Johnson, H. 2006. *Measuring Violence Against Women: Statistical Trends 2006.* Statistics Canada. <dsp-psd.pwgsc.gc.ca/Collection/Statcan/85-570-X/85-570-XIE2006001.pdf>.

Johnson, H., and V.F. Sacco. 1995. "Researching Violence Against Women: Statistics Canada's National Survey." *Canadian Journal of Criminology. Special Issue: Focus on the Violence Against Women Survey* 37.

Johnson, M.P. 1995. "Patriarchal Terrorism and Common Couple Violence: Two Forms of Violence Against Women." *Journal of Marriage and the Family* 57.

_____. 2005. "Domestic Violence: It's Not About Gender. Or Is It?" *Journal of Marriage and the Family* 67.

_____. 2006. "Conflict and Control: Gender Symmetry and Asymmetry in Domestic Violence." *Violence Against Women* 12.

Johnson, M.P., and K.J. Ferraro. 2000. "Research on Domestic Violence in the 1990s: Making Distinctions." *Journal of Marriage and the Family* 62.

Johnson, M.P., and J.M. Leone. 2005. "The Differential Effects of Intimate Terrorism and Situational Couple Violence: Findings From the National Violence Against Women Survey." *Journal of Family Issues* 26.

Kelly, K.D. 2006. *Violence in Dating Relationships.* National Clearinghouse on Family Violence. <phac-aspc.gc.ca/ncfv-cnivf/pdfs/fem-2006-dat_e.pdf>.

Kirkland, K. 2004. "Abuse in Gay Male Relationships: A Discussion Paper." National Clearinghouse on Family Violence. <vawnet.org/advanced-search/summary.php?doc_id=938&find_type=web_desc_GC>.

Kong, R., and K. AuCoin. 2008. "Female Offenders in Canada." *Juristat* 28, 1.

Kong, R., H. Johnson, S. Beattie, and A. Cardillo. 2003. "Sexual Offences in Canada." *Juristat* 23.

Laroche, D. 2005. "Aspects of the Context and Consequences of Domestic Violence-Situational Couple Violence and Intimate Terrorism in Canada in 1999." Institut de la statistique du Québec. <stat.gouv.qc.ca/publications/conditions/pdf/AspectViolen_an.pdf>.

____. 2008. "Context and Consequences of Domestic Violence Against Men and Women in Canada in 2004." Institut de la statistique du Québec. <stat.gouv.qc.ca/publications/conditions/pdf2008/ViolenceH_F2004_an.pdf>.

Lupri, E. 2004. "Institutional Resistance to Acknowledging Intimate Male Abuse, Revised." Counter-Roundtable Conference on Domestic Violence Calgary, Alberta, Canada, May 7. <fact.on.ca/Info/dom/lupri05.htm>.

Lupri, E., and E. Grandin. 2004. *Intimate Partner Abuse Against Men*. National Clearinghouse on Family Violence, Catalogue # H72-21/190-2004E. <phac-aspc.gc.ca/ncfv-cnivf/pdfs/fv-intime_e.pdf>.

MacQuarrie, B. 2005. *Voices from the Front Lines*. The Middlesex County Coordinating Committee to End Woman Abuse and the London Coordinating Committee to End Woman Abuse. <crvawc.ca/documents/VoicesfromfrontlinesFinalReport.pdf>.

Mahony, T.H. 2010. "Police-Reported Dating Violence in Canada, 2008." *Juristat* 30, 2.

Mann, R.M. 2003. "Violence Against Women or Family Violence: The 'Problem' of Female Perpetration in Domestic Violence." In L. Samuelson and W. Antony (eds.), *Power and Resistance: Critical Thinking About Canadian Social Issues*, third edition. Halifax, NS: Fernwood.

____. 2005. "Fathers' Rights, Feminism, and Canadian Divorce Law Reform, 1998–2003." *Studies in Law Politics and Society* 35.

____. 2007. "Intimate Violence in Canada: Policy, Politics, and Research on Gender and Perpetration/Victimization." In W. Antony and L. Samuelson (eds.), *Power and Resistance*, fourth edition. Halifax: Fernwood Publishing.

____. 2008. "Men's Rights and Feminist Advocacy in Canadian Domestic Violence Policy Arenas: Contexts, Dynamics and Outcomes of Anti-Feminist Backlash." *Feminist Criminology* 3.

Mihorean, K. 2005. "Trends in Self-Reported Spousal Violence." *Family Violence in Canada: A Statistical Profile 2005*. Statistics Canada.

Minaker, J.C., and L. Snider. 2006. "Husband Abuse: Equality with a Vengeance." *Canadian Journal of Criminology and Criminal Justice* 48.

Morrow, M., O. Hankivsky, and C. Varcoe. 2004. "Women and Violence: The Effects of Dismantling the Welfare State." *Critical Social Policy* 24.

National Clearinghouse on Family Violence. 2008. "Aboriginal Women and Family Violence." Public Health Agency of Canada. <phac-aspc.gc.ca/ncfv-cnivf/pdfs/fem-abor_e.pdf>.

Nemr, R. 2009. "Fact Sheet — Police-Reported Family Violence Against Children and Youth." *Family Violence in Canada: A Statistical Profile*. Ottawa: Statistics Canada.

Nixon, J., and C. Humphreys. 2010. "Marshalling the Evidence: Using Intersectionality in the Domestic Violence Frame." *Social Politics* 17.

Ogrodnik, L. 2006. "Spousal Violence and Repeat Police Contact." In L. Ogrodnik (ed.), *Family Violence in Canada: A Statistical Profile 2006*. Statistics Canada.

____. 2009. "Fact Sheet — Family Homicides." In *Family Violence in Canada: A Statistical*

Profile. Statistics Canada.

Perilla, J.L., K. Frndak, and D. Lillard. 2003. "A Working Analysis of Women's Use of Violence in the Context of Learning, Opportunity and Choice." *Violence Against Women* 9.

Perreault, S., and S. Brennan. 2010. "Criminal Victimization in Canada, 2009." *Juristat* 30, 2.

Rankin, L.P., and J. Vickers. 2001. *Women's Movements and State Feminism: Integrating Diversity into Public Policy*. Ottawa: Status of Women Canada. <rwmc.uoguelph.ca/cms/documents/88/Rankin_1-68.pdf>.

Royal Canadian Mounted Police. 2007a. "Dating Violence — Say No." National Clearinghouse on Family Violence. <phac-aspc.gc.ca/ncfv-cnivf/publications/rcmp-grc/fem-crimedatvio-eng.php>.

____. 2007b. "Criminal Harassment: Stalking — It's NOT Love." National Clearinghouse on Family Violence. <phac-aspc.gc.ca/ncfv-cnivf/publications/rcmp-grc/fem-crimeharas-eng.php>.

____. 2007c. "Spousal and Partner Abuse — It Can Be Stopped." National Clearinghouse on Family Violence. <rcmp-grc.gc.ca/cp-pc/spouse-epouse-abu-eng.htm>.

Shaw, M., and C. Andrew. 2005. "Engendering Crime Prevention: International Developments and the Canadian Experience." *Canadian Journal of Criminology and Criminal Justice* 47.

Sinha, M. 2011. "Police-Reported Family Violence Against Seniors, 2009." *Family Violence in Canada: A Statistical Profile*. Statistics Canada.

____. 2011. "Police-Reported Family Violence Against Children and Youth, 2009." *Family Violence in Canada: A Statistical Profile*. Statistics Canada.

Straus, M.A. 1999. "The Controversy Over Domestic Violence by Women: A Methodological, Theoretical, and Sociology of Science Analysis." In X.B. Arriaga and S. Oskamp (eds.), *Violence in Intimate Relationships*. Thousand Oaks, CA: Sage.

____. 2004. "Prevalence of Violence against Dating Partners by Male and Female University Students Worldwide." *Violence Against Women* 10.

____. 2006. "Future Research on Gender Symmetry in Physical Assaults on Partners." *Violence Against Women* 12.

____. 2007. "Processes Explaining the Concealment and Distortion of Evidence on Gender Symmetry in Partner Violence." *European Journal on Criminal Policy and Research* 13.

____. 2009. "Why the Overwhelming Evidence on Partner Physical Violence by Women Has Not Been Perceived and Is Often Denied." *Journal of Aggression* 18.

____. 2010. "Thirty Years of Denying the Evidence on Gender Symmetry in Partner Violence: Implications for Prevention and Treatment." *Partner Abuse* 1.

Swan, S.C., and D.L. Snow. 2006. "The Development of a Theory of Women's Use of Violence in Intimate Relationships." *Violence Against Women* 12.

Taylor-Butts, A., and L. Porter. 2011. "Family-Related Homicides, 2000 to 2009." *Family Violence in Canada: A Statistical Profile*. Ottawa: Statistics Canada.

Teghtsoonian, K., and L. Chappell. 2008. "The Rise and Decline of Women's Policy Machinery in British Columbia and New South Wales: A Cautionary Tale." *International Political Science Review* 29.

Tutty, L. 1999. "Husband Abuse: An Overview of Research and Perspectives." National Clearinghouse on Family Violence. <phac-aspc.gc.ca/ncfv-cnivf/familyviolence/pdfs/husbandenglish.pdf>.

____. 2006. "Effective Practices in Sheltering Women: Leaving Violence in Intimate Relationships, Phase II Report 2006." Toronto: YWCA Canada. <ywca.ca/public_eng/advocacy/Shelter/YWCA_ShelterReport_EN.pdf>.

Walker, G.A. 1990. *Family Violence and the Women's Movement*, first edition. Toronto: University of Toronto Press.

Weldon, S.L. 2002. *Protest, Policy, and the Problem of Violence Against Women: A Cross-National Comparison*. Pittsburgh: University of Pittsburgh Press.

Custom Textbooks from Fernwood Publishing

Custom textbooks are for instructors and professors who want to hand-select material for their students from every Fernwood Publishing title. Teaching a course on Indigenous social work? Labour unions in Canada? Racism and the law? We have content on a huge range of topics in the social sciences and humanities that can be combined to fit your course.

HOW IT WORKS

We will compile individual chapters from any title we've previously published and deliver a professionally printed and bound book to be used in your course. No photocopies, and no coiled binding. You need only provide us with the titles of the chapters from our books that you want to use. Because the material is already published by us, we can create these custom texts quickly and cost effectively.

You can browse our full title list on our website (www.fernwoodpublishing.ca) for more detailed information as well as the tables of contents, and we're happy to provide examination copies if you need a closer look.

If you have a course but you need some help with choosing material, please contact us at marketing@fernpub.ca.

THE FINE PRINT

We need at least six months notice prior to the course start date to create your custom textbook. The minimum number of students enrolled is 40. Retail price is based on the number of students enrolled in the course and length of the book.

For more information, please contact marketing@fernpub.ca.